# Discover Peru

Throughout this book, we use these icons to highlight special recommendations:

**The Best...**
Lists for everything from bars to wildlife – to make sure you don't miss out

**Don't Miss**
A must-see – don't go home until you've been there

Local experts reveal their top picks and secret highlights

**Detour**
Special places a little off the beaten track

**If you like...**
Lesser-known alternatives to world-famous attractions

These icons help you quickly identify reviews in the text and on the map:

**Sights**

**Eating**

**Drinking**

**Sleeping**

**Information**


**This edition written and researched by**

Carolina A Miranda, Carolyn McCarthy, Kevin Raub, Brendan Sainsbury, Luke Waterson

## Lake Titicaca



- Around Lake Titicaca
- Gaze Upon Elaborate Costumes
- Visit Awe-Inspiring Funerary Towers
- Hike to a Peaceful Ruin
- Set Foot on a Floating Island
- Shack Up with a Local Family

## Cuzco & Machu Picchu



- Cuzco
- Machu Picchu
- Enjoy Tranquility in Urubamba
- See the 'Sistine Chapel of Latin America'
- Dig into the Rich Cuisine
- Shop 'til You Drop in Pisac
- Trek the Inca Trail

## Lima



- Lima's Culinary Scene
- Museo Larco
- Bar-Hop Through Barranco
- Behold the Skulls of Saints
- Admire the Best Peruvian Art
- Walk the Sandy Ruins of Ancient Civilizations
- Leap off the Miraflores Clifftops

## Nazca, Arequipa & the South



- Nazca Lines
- Cañón del Colca
- Admire Squawking Sea Life
- Gaze Upon a Sacrificial Maiden
- Sail Down Sand Dunes
- Explore an Unusual Colonial Monastery
- Take a Tour of Vineyards

## Huaraz, Trujillo & the North



- The Cordilleras
- Kuélap
- Hang 10 in Máncora
- Gaze Upon the Vast Wealth of a Moche Burial Site
- Dip into Seafood in Trujillo
- Visit a 2000-Year-Old Mountain Temple
- Vist Ancient Chan Chan

## Iquitos & the Amazon



# Contents

## Plan Your Trip



## On the Road

# Contents

## On the Road

## In Focus



## Survival Guide

# This Is Peru

Luminous archaeological sites? Check. Lush rainforest? Check. An arid coast lapped by a highly surfable Pacific swell? Check. Peru, it seems, has it all.

**Every cranny of the Andes offers a unique glimpse into singular cultures.** Not to mention incredible foods and enough natural wonders to keep a *National Geographic* photographer employed for decades. On the coast, adobe pyramids and ancient temples sit quietly amid shifting desert sands and bulging seaside cities. Here, the culture is boisterous – infused with African soulfulness, indigenous know-how and the feistiness of the Spanish. The people are effusive and the music is bound to get your hips shaking.

**To the east lie the Andes.** This mountain range has served as the heart of countless empires. Its sights are staggering: mountains that seem to erupt from the earth into the heavens, plunging gorges, icy pinnacles and steamy cloud forest. Plus, of course, the masterful ruins of a civilization that could be put on par with ancient Rome in terms of size and infrastructure: the Incas. This is a place of chilly windswept plains and coffee-colored soil, where Catholic ritual veils indigenous belief, where the culture is stoic and the music is laced with pre-Columbian instrumentation. In comparison to the coast, it might as well be another planet.

**Lastly, there is the Amazon – the earth's most fabled rainforest.** It is in this tangled jungle that Peru fuses with the lowland cultures of so many other South American countries. This sprawling lowland area is home to companies of cackling macaws and playful pink river dolphins, as well as remote ethnicities that maintain a deep knowledge of the forest. Scattered about are old rubber boomtowns, where a previous century's entrepreneurs left behind town squares dotted with tropical architecture.

**All of this, combined, comes together to make up Peru.** It is a wondrous, surreal mix of peoples, cultures, geographies, languages and food. Enjoy the trip. It's going to be an adventure.

> “plunging gorges, icy pinnacles and steamy cloud forest”

Playing a traditional bamboo flute

# Peru

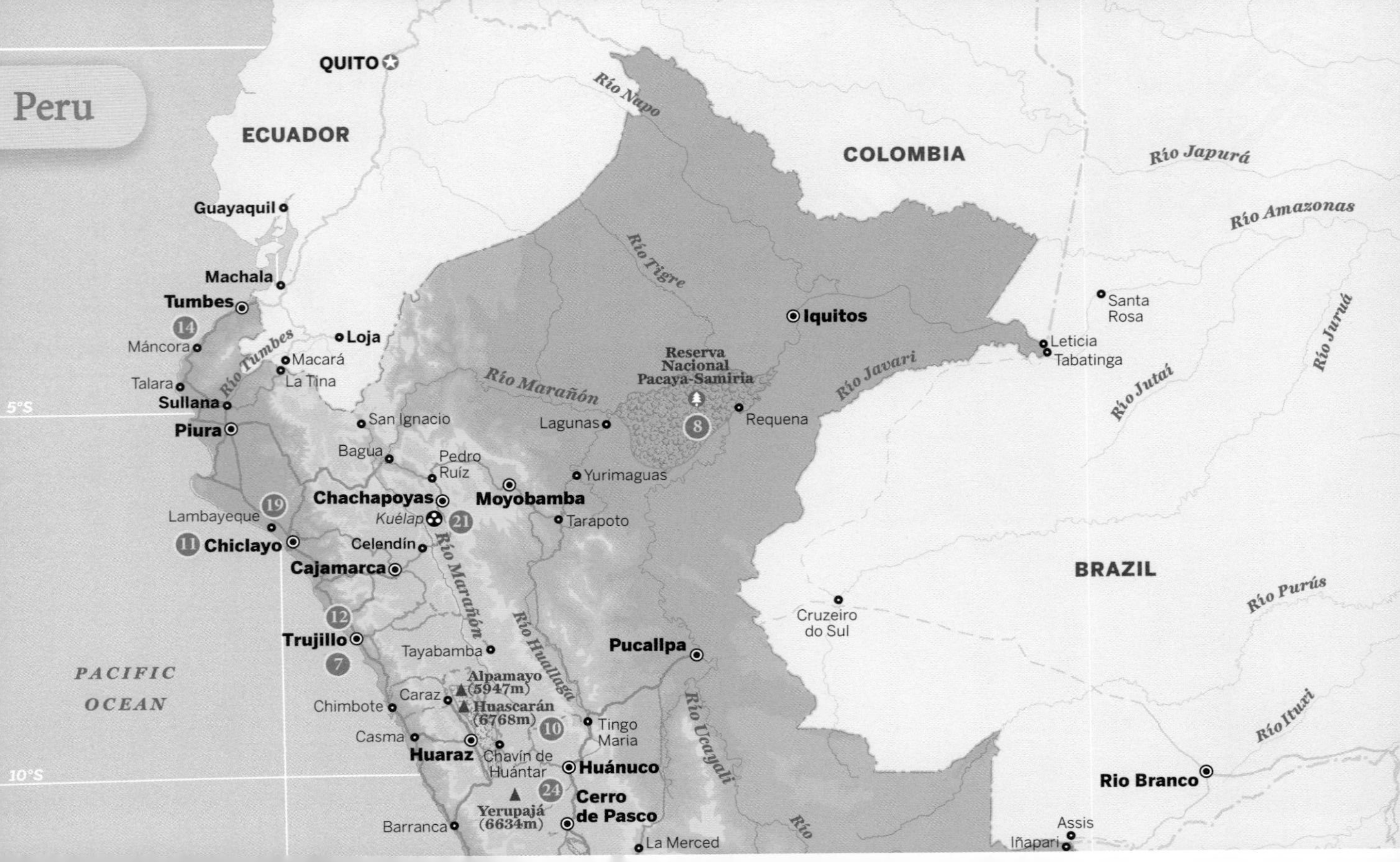

QUITO
ECUADOR
COLOMBIA
BRAZIL
PACIFIC OCEAN
Guayaquil
Machala
Tumbes
Máncora
Talara
Sullana
Piura
Loja
Macará
La Tina
Río Tumbes
San Ignacio
Bagua
Pedro Ruíz
Chachapoyas
Kuélap
Moyobamba
Lambayeque
Chiclayo
Celendín
Cajamarca
Trujillo
Tayabamba
Alpamayo (5947m)
Huascarán (6768m)
Caraz
Chimbote
Casma
Huaraz
Chavín de Huántar
Yerupajá (6634m)
Barranca
Huánuco
Cerro de Pasco
Tingo Maria
La Merced
Pucallpa
Lagunas
Yurimaguas
Tarapoto
Reserva Nacional Pacaya-Samiria
Requena
Iquitos
Leticia
Tabatinga
Santa Rosa
Cruzeiro do Sul
Rio Branco
Assis
Iñapari
Río Napo
Río Tigre
Río Marañón
Río Huallaga
Río Ucayali
Río Javari
Río Japurá
Río Amazonas
Río Jutaí
Río Juruá
Río Purús
Río Ituxi
Río
5°S
10°S
14
19
11
21
12
7
10
24
8

# 25 Top Experiences

1. Machu Picchu
2. Nazca Lines
3. Floating Islands, Lake Titicaca
4. Cuisine, Lima
5. Cañón del Colca
6. Islas Ballestas
7. Trujillo
8. Reserva Nacional Pacaya-Samiria
9. Cuzco
10. Cordillera Blanca
11. Inca Kola, Chiclayo
12. Chan Chan
13. Museums, Lima
14. Máncora
15. Inca Trail
16. Huacachina
17. Parque Nacional Manu
18. Textiles, Cuzco
19. Sipán
20. Colonial Arequipa
21. Kuélap
22. Sillustani
23. Baroque Churches, Lima
24. Chavín de Huántar
25. Sacred Valley

# 25 Peru's Top Experiences

## Machu Picchu

A fantastic Inca citadel lost to the world until its rediscovery in the early 20th century, Machu Picchu (p217) stands as a ruin among ruins. With its emerald terraces backed by steep peaks, and Andean ridges echoing on the horizon, the sight simply surpasses the imagination. This wondrous marvel of engineering has withstood six centuries of earthquakes, foreign invasion and howling weather (not to mention millions of foreign travelers). Discover it for yourself: wander through the stone temples and scale the dizzying heights. You'll be glad you did.

1

2

## Islas Ballestas

A barren collection of guano-covered rocks that protrude out of the Pacific Ocean, the Islas Ballestas (p106) support an extraordinary ecosystem of birds, sea mammals and fish. They also represent one of Peru's most successful conservation projects. Boat trips around the island's cliffs and arches allow close encounters with barking sea lions, huddled Humboldt penguins and tens of thousands of birds.

## Nazca Lines

Made by aliens? Laid out by prehistoric balloonists? Conceived as a giant astronomical chart? No two evaluations of Peru's giant geoglyphs – known as the Nazca Lines (p110) – are the same. The mysteries have attracted outsiders since the 1940s, when German archaeologist María Reiche would devote half her life to studying them. No one, however, has been able to fully crack the code. The lines remain unfathomed, enigmatic and loaded with historic intrigue.

## The Best... Experiences for Kids

**STAY WITH A FAMILY ON A LAKE TITICACA ISLAND**

A unique experience your children will never forget. (p156)

**MAKE CHOCOLATE IN CUZCO**

The Choco Museo is sure to grab every tyke's attention. (p182)

**VISIT THE CIRCUITO MÁGICO DEL AGUA IN LIMA**

Dart about the fountains at a popular family park. (p69)

**LOOK FOR MONKEYS IN THE AMAZON**

Clamber onto a 30m-high canopy walkway at Río Madre de Dios. (p303)

# The Best... Cities for Food

**LIMA**
The crème de la crème of the country's fusion cuisine. (p80)

**AREQUIPA**
The locals like their dishes spicy, including the stuffed peppers known as *rocoto relleno*. (p121)

**CHICLAYO**
Stews simmered for hours in beer and cilantro. (p269)

**CUZCO**
Hearty soups and crackling pork – not to mention plenty of guinea pig. (p194)

**TRUJILLO**
This coastal city is tops for seafood, including the marinated seafood dish ceviche. (p259)

FRANK GAGLIONE COLLECTION: STONE/GETTY IMAGES ©

## 4 Cañón del Colca

First colonized by pre-Inca civilizations, the cultural history of the Colca Canyon (p125) is as alluring as the endless trekking possibilities. Stretching 100km from end to end and plunging over 3400m at its deepest, the canyon has been embellished with terraced agricultural fields, pastoral villages, colonial churches, and ruins that date back to pre-Inca times. Hike it, bike it, raft it or zip-line it, just keep your eyes peeled for its emblematic condors.

KELLY CHENG TRAVEL PHOTOGRAPHY/GETTY IMAGES ©

## 5 Floating Islands of Lake Titicaca

Less a lake than a highland ocean, Titicaca is home to fantastical sights – none more surreal than the floating islands crafted entirely of tightly woven *totora* reeds. Centuries ago, the Uros people constructed the Islas Uros (p156) to escape more aggressive mainland peoples. Requiring near-constant renovation, the reeds are also used to build thatched homes and elegant boats.

## Chavín de Huántar

6

The Unesco-recognized ruins of Chavín de Huántar (p253) were once a ceremonial center. Today this feat of engineering, built between 1200 BC and 800 BC, has striking templelike structures above ground and a labyrinthine complex of corridors, ducts and chambers below ground. Nearby, the outstanding Museo Nacional de Chavín is home to intricate, horrifying carved heads that once embellished Chavín's walls.

7

## Trujillo

Rising from the sand-strewn desert like a kaleidoscopic mirage of colonial color, old Trujillo (p255) boasts a dazzling display of preserved splendor. The city's historic center is chockfull of elegant churches, mansions and otherwise unspoiled colonial constructions, which are steeped today in a modern motif that lends the city a lovely, livable feel. Add the close proximity of impressive Chimú ruins such as Chan Chan, and the Moche pyramids at Las Huacas del Sol y de la Luna, and Trujillo easily trumps its northern rivals in style and grace.

Colonial building on the Plaza de Armas

## Reserva Nacional Pacaya-Samiria

Located in the northern Amazon, Peru's biggest national park (p297) is home to weird and wonderful creatures rarely glimpsed elsewhere: manatees, pink river dolphins, 6m caimans and giant river turtles. Just getting here is an adventure: the park is a day's journey by boat from the Iquitos. And unlike a lot of Peruvian reserves, it's a walk on the wild side. Transport is by boat or dugout canoe and there are no fancy lodges. Welcome to pure, unadulterated tropical nature.

Pink river dolphin

8

## The Best... Andean Vistas

**MACHU PICCHU**
Soaring peaks coated by steamy cloud forest. (p217)

**HUARAZ**
The Cordillera Negra on one side, the Cordillera Blanca on the other. (p242)

**PUNO**
Rugged Andean plains surround the shimmering Lake Titicaca. (p146)

**AREQUIPA**
The conical El Misti volcano always looms in the distance. (p114)

**THE SACRED VALLEY**
An undulating mountainscape hugs a string of local villages. (p205)

**KUÉLAP**
Extravagant valley views atop a cloud forest peak. (p272)

## Máncora

Sometimes a vacation is just that – a break from everything real life throws your way. In Máncora (p274) expect your diet of activities to be of the leisurely sort: lounging on the beach, watching the sun set, enjoying fine seafood at breezy patio restaurants, and sipping ice-cold cocktails at one of the town's hopping drinking establishments. If it all sounds too relaxed, fear not. This trendy little beach town sits amid a series of excellent surf breaks.

9

## The Best... Adventures

**EXPLORE PARQUE NACIONAL MANU**
One of the Amazon's most remote corners. (p307)

**SANDBOARD HUACACHINA**
Fly down a sand dune as tall as a building. (p108)

**TREK THE CAÑÓN DEL COTAHUASI**
One of Peru's lesser visited, but truly magnificent canyons. (p132)

**SURF IN HUANCHACO**
A renowned spot for the wave-riding set. (p263)

## 10 Chan Chan

The extraordinary Chimú capital of Chan Chan (p261) is the largest pre-Columbian city in the Americas, and the largest adobe city in the world. Once home to some 60,000 inhabitants and a trove of treasures, Chan Chan today is a work in progress, with the Tschudi complex being the only one of the 10 walled citadels within restored to its near former glory. Despite numerous weather beatings courtesy of El Niño over the years, Chan Chan's ceremonial courtyards, decorative walls and labyrinthine audience rooms nonetheless resonate with resilience.

14th-century Chimú relief

## 11 Inca Kola

It's not a grandiose ruin or a majestic church or a jaw-dropping peak, but you haven't experienced Peru until you've sampled this nuclear-colored soda. It tastes faintly of bubble gum (though it's allegedly flavored with lemon verbena). Most significantly, it's yellow, a color that is widely believed to bring good luck. You can find it anywhere, but we recommend ordering it with a hearty lunch in Chiclayo (p269). Ask for it *bien fría* (very cold) – a sweet balm for the heat of the northern desert.

## 12 Parque Nacional Manu

Peru's best-protected wilderness, Parque Nacional Manu (p307), is brimming with opportunities to see fabled jungle creatures such as the anaconda, the tapir, the jaguar and the thousands of feasting macaws that festoon clay licks with their bright plumage. In this deep forest, tribespeople live as they have for centuries, with barely any contact with the outside world. Toucan

CAROLINA MIRANDA ©

## 13 Cuisine in Lima

Lima (p80) is a city where life is often planned around the next meal. Consider it an experience worth savoring: the coastal capital is replete with options ranging from street carts to haute cuisine eateries offering exquisite interpretations of Peru's unique fusion cuisine. Dishes are a complex blend of Spanish, indigenous, African and Asian (both Chinese and Japanese) influences. There's a reason that magazines such as *Bon Appétit* have feted Lima as the 'next great food city.' Ceviche

## Cuzco

With ancient cobblestone streets, grandiose baroque churches and the remnants of masterful Inca temples, no city looms larger in Andean history than Cuzco (p174), which has been inhabited continuously since precolonial times. Once the capital of the Inca empire, Cuzco also serves as the gateway to Machu Picchu. Mystic, commercial and chaotic, this unique city is still a stunner. Where else would you find ornately dressed women walking llamas on leashes, a museum for magical plants, and the wildest nightlife in the high Andes?

14

## The Best... Hiking

**THE INCA TRAIL**
The most fabled ancient roadway in the Americas can be walked on a four-day trek. (p224)

**CAÑÓN DEL COLCA**
One of the world's deepest canyons promises pastoral sights galore. (p125)

**CORDILLERA BLANCA**
A graceful mountain range that can be trekked in two days or two weeks. (p251)

**LAKE TITICACA ISLANDS**
Sparkling water views with Andes Mountains in the distance. (p156)

**MACHU PICCHU**
The famous mountaintop citadel offers excellent walks. (p217)

# The Best... Markets

**MERCADO SAN PEDRO, CUZCO**
Everything from pig heads to fresh juice – along with plenty of local color. (p200)

**MERCADO MODELO, CHICLAYO**
A bustling market that has an expansive witch doctors' section peddling charms and potions. (p266)

**MERCADO INDIO, LIMA**
Get your souvenir shopping on. (p87)

**MERCADO DE ARTESANÍA, PISAC**
Fresh vegetables, bounteous souvenirs and infinite photo ops. (p205)

**BELÉN MERCADO**
Tropical fruits and deep-fried ants. (p291)

LEFT: PICTUREGARDEN/GETTY IMAGES © RIGHT: TRISTAN BROWN/GETTY IMAGES ©

## Inca Trail

The continent's most famous pedestrian roadway, the Inca Trail (p224) snakes 43km up stone steps and through thick cloud-forest mists. A true pilgrimage, the four- to five-day trek ends at the famous Intipunku (Sun Gate), where trekkers get their first glimpse of the extravagant ruins at Machu Picchu. While there are countless ancient roads all over Peru, the Inca Trail, with its mix of majestic views, staggering mountain passes and clusters of ruins, remains the favorite of travelers. **Left:** Trekking the Inca Trail; **Above:** Llamas

# Extraordinary Textiles

16

If there's one thing that united the myriad ancient cultures that settled the Andes over the centuries, it's a textile tradition that is beyond accomplished. Skilled weavers have long produced elaborate pieces out of wool, cotton and even feathers – some with record-setting thread counts and mind-boggling designs. Today, the practice continues all over the country, but one of the best places to acquire a singular piece is at a textile shop in Cuzco (p199), where various fair-trade organizations are keeping traditional weaving alive.

STEPHEN COLLECTOR/GETTY IMAGES ©

# Lima Museums

17

Want to understand Peru's ancient civilizations? Begin your trip here. Lima's museums hold millennia worth of treasures, from ceramics and carved rock stelae to breathtaking textiles. You could make a dozen visits without seeing it all. Some of the best collections are at Museo Larco (p69), Museo Andrés del Castillo (p69) and the Museo Nacional de Antropología e Historia del Perú (p69). Extended evening hours at Museo Larco offer an alternative to conventional nightlife.

Chimú idol, Museo Larco

## Huacachina

For the adventurous set, this tiny south coast oasis offers one of Peru's more unusual adrenaline rushes: the opportunity to motor to the top of a dune the size of a small building, strap on a board and then fly down the face of a towering wall of sand. Apart from making you pick the gritty stuff out of your every nook and cranny, Huacachina (p108) is home to another highly popular activity – namely whooping it up come nightfall at one of the various local drinking establishments. Sand dunes at Huacachina

18

## The Best... Hotels

**MIRAFLORES PARK HOTEL, LIMA**
Sumptuous ocean views and a bath butler. (p77)

**HOSTAL COLONIAL, TRUJILLO**
A rose-colored mansion with lovely courtyards. (p258)

**PALACIO NAZARENAS, CUZCO**
This former convent is home to the city's most luxe accommodations. (p189)

**HOSTAL CASONA SOLAR, AREQUIPA**
Live like a colonial *caballero* (gentleman). (p120)

**TITILAKA, LAKE TITICACA**
A luxurious lodge offering splendid lake views. (p149)

**SUNSET HOTEL, MÁNCORA**
Boutique fabulousness right in front of the Pacific. (p276)

## The Best... Fiestas

**INTI RAYMI**
Cuzco's 'Festival of the Sun' is a tradition with Inca roots. (p43)

**LA VIRGEN DE LA CANDELARIA**
Puno's multiday tribute to the Virgin offers plenty of highland music and dance. (p42)

**Q'OYORITI**
A Christian pilgrimage with animist overtones is held on a chilly mountain in the Cuzco region. (p43)

**EL SEÑOR DE LOS MILAGROS**
Lima's biggest religious procession brings out masses dressed in purple. (p44)

## Sillustani

On the windswept Andean plain northwest of Puno is one of Peru's more unusual burial sites. Dotting a chain of rolling hills that comprise the Lago Umayo peninsula are a series of *chullpas* (funerary towers) that once held the remains of entire clans. The Sillustani *chullpas* (p154) have long since been pillaged for their artifacts, but the towers remain – some of them up to 12m tall – guarding the plain like monumental silent sentinels from the past. A Sillustani *chullpa*

19

SIMON MONTGOMERY/GETTY IMAGES ©

## 20 Colonial Arequipa

Peru's second-largest metropolis bridges the historical gap between the Inca glories of Cuzco and the clamorous modernity of Lima. Crowned by some dazzling baroque-*mestizo* architecture hewn out of the local white *sillar* rock, Arequipa (p114) is primarily a Spanish colonial city that hasn't strayed far from its conception. Its ethereal natural setting amid snoozing volcanoes and oxygen-lite high pampa is complemented by a 400-year-old monastery, a humungous cathedral and interesting Peruvian fusion cuisine showcased in traditional *picanterías* (country restaurants). La Catedral (p114).

# The Treasures of Sipán

21

Dedicated archaeologists have spent decades piecing together the history of Peru's ancient civilizations. Unfortunately, what the Spanish didn't ransack, generations of looters have. In the 1980s, however, a rare discovery was made outside Chiclayo: an almost-intact Moche tomb. Its treasures are now on display at the Museo Tumbas Reales de Sipán (p273), providing visitors with a rare opportunity to admire priceless objects in their historical context. El Señor de Sipán (p271)

22

# Lima's Baroque Churches

Though Lima is today a noisy, modern metropolis of almost nine million people, its colonial heart – an area of narrow streets on the southern banks of the Río Rímac – contains a veritable treasure of colonial churches. Among the finest: the Iglesia de Santo Domingo (p68), which contains the skull of Santa Rosa; the Monasterio de San Francisco (p66), home to underground catacombs; and the astonishing Iglesia de la Merced (p66), which boasts a hyperornate facade and enough towering baroque altars to turn anyone into a believer. Iglesia de la Merced

## The Sacred Valley

Ragtag Andean villages, crumbling Inca military outposts and agricultural terraces used since time immemorial are linked by the Río Urubamba as it curves through the Sacred Valley (p205). Located between Cuzco and Machu Picchu, this picturesque destination is an ideal base for exploring the area's famed markets and historic structures. Accommodations range from inviting inns to top resorts, and adventure options include horseback riding, rafting and treks that take you through remote agricultural villages where life has changed little over the centuries. The Sacred Valley stretching in front of Nevado Salkantay

23

## The Best... Off-the-Beaten-Path Spots

**CHICLAYO**
A bustling coastal city which has excellent food and a rollicking music scene. (p266)

**PARQUE NACIONAL BAHUAJA-SONENE**
One of the southern Amazon's most remote wilderness areas is a good place to see spider monkeys. (p303)

**CHUCUITO**
Just 19km south of Puno, this charming colonial village houses a highly unusual pre-Columbian site. (p155)

**ICA**
A southern coastal city renowned for its wineries and pisco distilleries. (p108)

## Kuélap

Although lacking a Unesco listing, the extraordinary stone fortress at Kuélap (p272) is second to Machu Picchu in little else. Standing 3100m above the Río Utcubamba, this remarkably preserved citadel was built by the enigmatic and strong-willed 'People of the Clouds.' Some 400 circular dwellings and at least one gravity-defying structure are surrounded by an impregnable rock wall that is a testament to one of the few cultures to successfully resist the all-consuming Incas.

24

## The Best... Surreal Sights

**SKULLS OF SAINTS**
Tidily displayed in glass cases at a Lima church. (p68)

**EDIBLE CLAY**
Dirt you can eat, found near the funerary towers of Sillustani. (p154)

**FROZEN INCA MAIDEN**
In a glass-walled freezer at the Museo Santuarios Andinos in Arequipa. Haunting. (p114)

**GOLF AMID PIRANHAS**
Only in the Amazon. (p293)

**GAS STATION MUSEUM**
A Repsol basement in Trujillo contains priceless pre-Columbian relics. (p257)

25

## Cordillera Blanca

The white mountaintops of Cordillera Blanca (p251) stand sentinel over Huaraz and the surrounding region like an outrageously imposing granite Republican Guard. The highest mountain range in the world outside of the Himalayas, 18 of the Andes' ostentatious summits breech 6000m, making it the continent's most challenging collection of summits-in-waiting. Glacial lakes, massive *Puya raimondii* plants and shards of sky-pointed rock all culminate in Parque Nacional Huascarán, where the Santa Cruz trek rewards the ambitious with a living museum of painted-perfect peaks.

# Peru's Top Itineraries

# Around the Capital Days & Nights in Lima

*Five days will provide you with an opportunity to truly enjoy Lima's excellent fine dining and see a bevy of incredible pre-Columbian and fine-art museums. Better yet: you'll have time for a day trip (or two) to fabled ruins along the desert coast.*

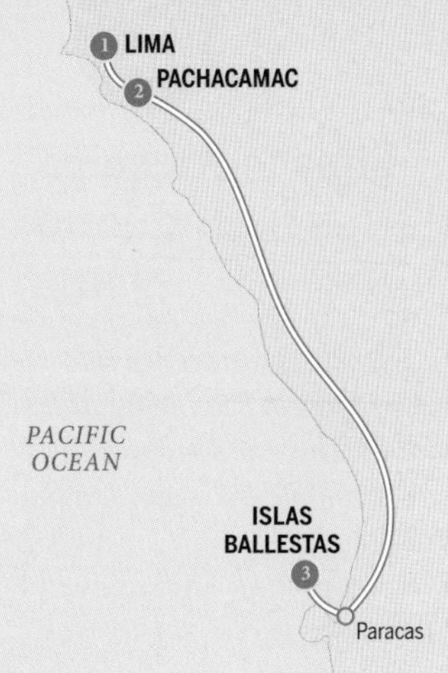


## 1 Lima (p64)

For the Peru first-timer, Lima's chaotic, bustling downtown is a must. Begin at the **Plaza de Armas**, where you can ogle the **Palacio de Gobierno** (presidential palace), then pay a visit to the stately **Catedral de Lima**. Nearby, you'll find the **Monasterio de San Francisco**, with its bone-lined catacombs, and the **Iglesia de Santo Domingo**, which displays the skull of Santa Rosa. End up at the **Plaza San Martín** for a different type of religious experience: here, **El Bolivarcito** serves up renowned pisco sours (grape brandy cocktails).

On day two, hit the renovated **Museo de Arte de Lima (MALI)**, which contains an inspiring collection of Peruvian art. For dinner, go *novoandina* (Peruvian nouvelle cuisine) at one of the renowned haute cuisine restaurants in **Miraflores**.

A third day in Lima will allow you to pay a leisurely visit to the exquisite **Museo Larco**, to see fine pre-Columbian artifacts and dine at its bougainvillea-draped restaurant. Afterwards, walk off the meal in Miraflores, where you can shop for souvenirs at the sprawling **Mercado Indio**.

LIMA ➔ PACHACAMAC

**One hour** Taxis and tour agencies both make the trip.

## 2 Pachacamac (p79)

A perfect half-day trip is a visit to this **archaeological complex** just 31km south of the city. Dating back to AD 100, its temple sites have been used by every culture from the Wari to the Incas. On your return to Lima, have the driver drop you off in **Barranco**, where you'll find the city's most hopping bars and lounges.

LIMA ➔ ISLAS BALLESTAS

**Four hours** Private taxis and tour agencies make the trip to Paracas. **One hour** From Paracas, catch a morning tour boat to the islands.

## 3 Islas Ballestas (p106)

A wilder, full-day excursion is a trip to visit the rocky outcrops known as the 'poor man's Galápagos' – islands inhabited by honking sea lions and colonies of birdlife. Tours generally include a visit to the nearby **Paracas reserve**. Just plan on waking up *early:* boat tours depart around 8am.

Monasterio de San Francisco (p66), Lima

# Lima to Arequipa
## Southern Highland Jaunt

*This brisk itinerary allows two days to see the capital's main sights (and make a tasty gastronomic pit stop). On the third day, head south for a visit to the charming highland city of Arequipa, known for its rich history and spicy cuisine.*

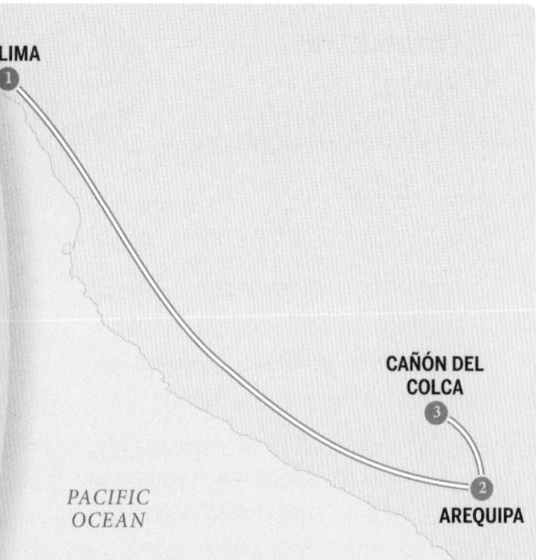

## 1 Lima (p64)

Start in downtown, Lima's historic, colonial heart. At the **Plaza de Armas**, you can tour **La Catedral de Lima**. From here, numerous colonial churches radiate outwards. Among the best: the **Iglesia de Santo Domingo**, with its saints' reliquaries, and the **Monasterio de San Francisco**, which contains creepy catacombs. At the **Plaza San Martín**, pop into **El Bolivarcito** – a streetside watering hole that helped make the pisco sour famous.

On the second day see spectacular pre-Columbian artifacts at the **Museo Larco**, which is now open late into the evenings. Afterward, shop 'til you drop in the seaside neighborhood of **Miraflores**. Once you've built up an appetite, hit one of the area's internationally acclaimed eateries.

**LIMA ➜ AREQUIPA**

✈ **90 minutes** Multiple daily departures from Aeropuerto Internacional Jorge Chávez.

## 2 Arequipa (p114)

Begin your visit by wandering around the city's handsome **Plaza de Armas**, where the key historic structures are crafted from *sillar*, a luminous white volcanic stone. From the plaza, you'll see the massive **Catedral** and the extravagant **Iglesia de la Compañía**, known for its Spanish-baroque altar smothered in gold leaf. Just off a side street is the **Museo Santuarios Andinos**, which houses 'Juanita, the ice princess,' a frozen Inca maiden sacrificed on the summit of a nearby peak many centuries ago.

Devote the second day to exploring the renowned **Monasterio de Santa Catalina**, a citadel-sized convent – also crafted from *sillar* – stuffed with period furnishing and religious art. This is a behemoth sight, so take your time. Afterwards, grab a table at one of Arequipa's renowned **picanterías**, informal country restaurants where the cooking is homespun, the portions are generous and the *chicha* (corn beer) is sweet and fresh.

**AREQUIPA ➜ CAÑON DEL COLCA**

🚗 **Four hours** Tour agencies in Arequipa can arrange private and group tours.

## 3 Cañón del Colca (p125)

On the last day, get an early start (as in 4am early) for a day trip to see one of Peru's most famous natural sights. Cañon del Colca, covered in agricultural terraces and dotted with minuscule villages and historic churches, is a world unto itself. It's also a place where it's still possible to see condors in flight. At **Cruz del Condor**, the high altitude lookout, you'll get to stand a dizzying 1200m over the valley floor as these magnificent birds cruise the currents before you. Totally unforgettable.

Cañón del Colca (p125)

10 DAYS

# Lima to Cuzco & Machu Picchu

## A Tour of Inca Country

*Ten days allows you ample time to soak up the wonders of the ancient Inca capital and the Sacred Valley. Starting with a couple of days in Lima ensures that you won't head to the highlands without a few exquisite meals in your belly.*

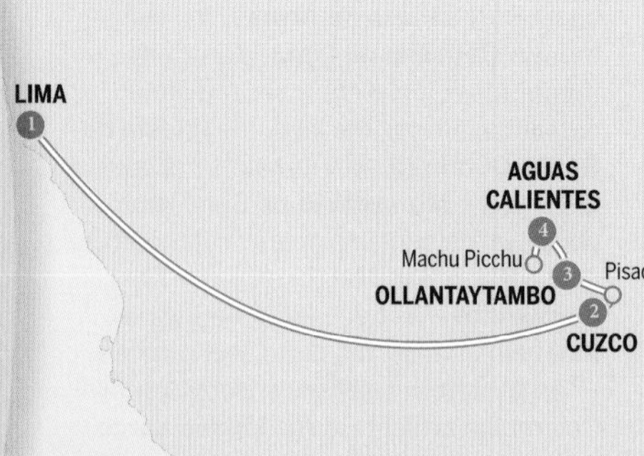

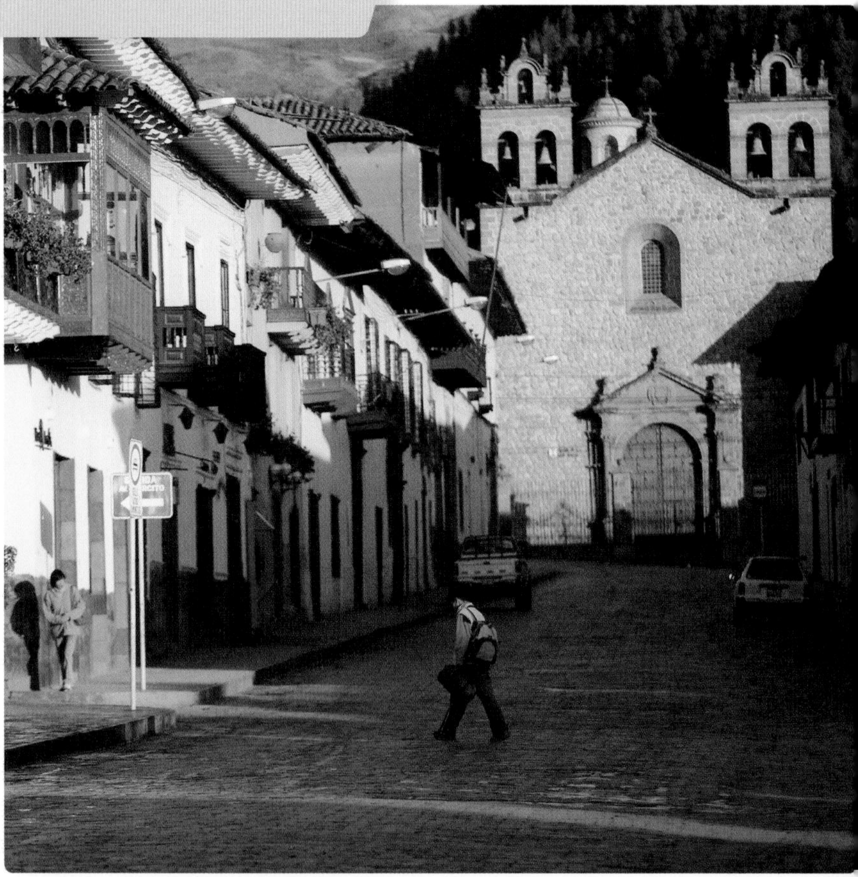

## 1 Lima (p64)

A couple of days in Lima is a great start to your Peruvian adventure, and will ground you in the country's history. The city's **colonial churches**, along with the **Museo Larco**, which is stocked with sublime pre-Columbian pottery, are great places to learn about all the cultures that have come together to create Peru.

On your second day, keep it simple: amble around the galleries at the **Museo de Arte de Lima**, then eat a delectable seafood dinner at a restaurant in **Miraflores**.

**LIMA ➜ CUZCO**

✈ **One hour, 15 minutes** Multiple daily departures from Aeropuerto Internacional Jorge Chávez.

## 2 Cuzco (p174)

Fly to Cuzco – and then *chill out* (you're at 3326m above sea level). Once you've gotten your high-altitude legs, amble about the **Plaza de Armas**, pay a visit to the **Catedral** or the ornate Jesuit church, the **Iglesia de la Compañía de Jesús**, to see the baroque art.

From here, spend a couple of days grounding yourself in the area's Inca history: see some of the culture's most exquisite textiles and pottery at the **Museo Inka**. Not to be missed: the **Qorikancha**, once the Incas' most important temple, and **Sacsaywamán**, a jaw-dropping fortress.

**CUZCO ➜ OLLANTAYTAMBO**

**40 minutes** The best option is to hire a private taxi for the day. **One hour** Multiple departures daily.

## 3 Ollantaytambo (p210)

In the morning, drive out into the **Sacred Valley**. The first stop is the charming village of **Pisac**, renowned for its sprawling artisan's market. The hills above town are home to an **Inca fortification** that offers wondrous views of the valley.

Afterwards, continue the journey to Ollantaytambo (about an hour away), a charismatic indigenous village that retains its inherently Inca form. Bed down here for the night. Then wake up early to see its **Inca ruins** – an important spot where the Incas once fended off the Spanish in a historic battle.

**OLLANTAYTAMBO ➜ AGUAS CALIENTES & MACHU PICCHU**

**Two hours**

## 4 Aguas Calientes & Machu Picchu (p214)

A scenic train ride takes you to Aguas Calientes, the bustling transit point that serves as a base for exploring the fabled Machu Picchu. Our recommendation: arrange to spend two to three nights here. The ruins are sprawling, the scenery is spectacular and there are amazing opportunities for day hikes to the peaks of **Huayna Picchu** and Machu Picchu as well as the **Intipunku**, the point known as the Sun Gate.

Cuzco (p174)

10 DAYS

# Trujillo to Máncora
## Rambling on the North Coast

*The remnants of adobe pyramids and walled cities, a witch doctors' market and some of Peru's best beaches: 10 days along the north coast, from Trujillo through Chiclayo and on to Máncora, will satisfy cravings for history – as well as surf and sand.*

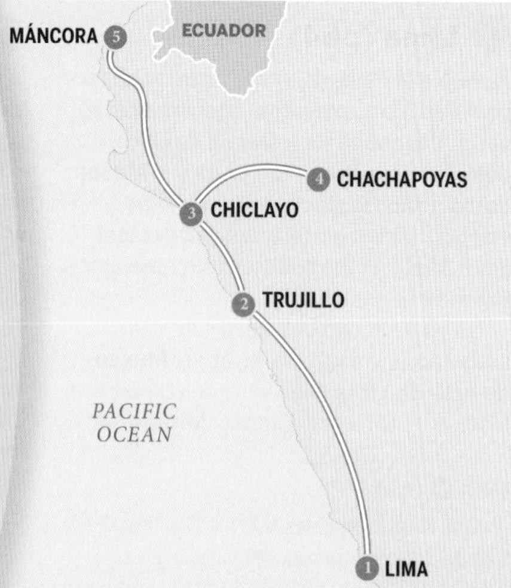

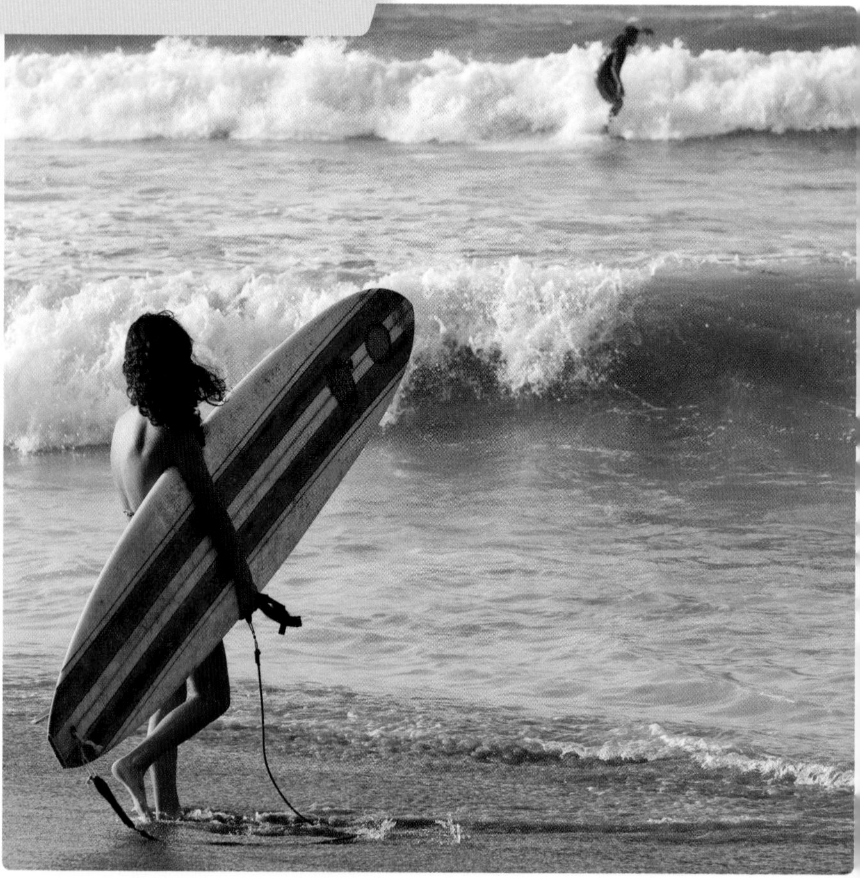

## 1 Lima (p64)

As with all journeys in Peru, the trip begins in Lima. For something out of the ordinary, hit Barranco's **Museo Pedro de Osma**, a vintage mansion stocked with a stellar collection of colonial religious art and sparkling silver. Spend your second day taking in the treasures at the **Museo Larco**, before sampling the city's fine food.

**LIMA ➲ TRUJILLO**

**70 minutes** Multiple daily departures from Aeropuerto Internacional Jorge Chávez.

## 2 Trujillo (p255)

Trujillo is a chaotic coastal city that is home to some of the country's best-kept colonial structures. One not to miss: **Casa de Urquiaga**, which has been spectacularly restored – and has a desk that once belonged to Peruvian liberator Simón Bolívar. Spend the following two days exploring the area's pre-Columbian ruins. To the west is **Chan Chan**, a sprawling adobe city constructed by the Chimú (don't miss the friezes!) To the southeast are the **Huacas del Sol y de la Luna**, two mud-brick pyramids built by the Moche culture.

**TRUJILLO ➲ CHICLAYO**

**Three hours** Myriad services have multiple daily departures.

## 3 Chiclayo (p266)

From Trujillo, catch a deluxe bus service north to Chiclayo. The city is no thing of beauty, but the regional cuisine is divine and the nearby pre-Columbian museums are jaw-dropping. At the top of the list: the **Museo Tumbas Reales de Sipán**, in nearby Lambayeque, which contains the sparkling grave goods of a Moche lord.

Surfing in Máncora (p274)



Also worthwhile is a visit to the **Mercado Modelo**, renowned for its cluttered witch doctors' market.

**CHICLAYO ➲ CHACHAPOYAS**

**Nine hours** **Seven hours** Several long-haul bus companies make the trip, but it's faster to go by car; tour agencies can make the arrangements.

## 4 Chachapoyas (p272)

Now that you've had a good dose of coast, make for the highland. A day's journey into the Andes is the charming settlement of Chachapoyas, the ideal base for spending two or three days exploring some highly unusual pre-Columbian sites. This includes **Kuélap**, a thousand-year-old mountaintop citadel, and **Karajía**, a burial site – in which towering sarcophagi were buried in niches on the sides of mountains.

**CHACHAPOYAS ➲ MÁNCORA**

**Seven hours** Ride back to Chiclayo, then transfer for passage to Máncora. **Five hours** Many travelers hire private drivers for a faster trip.

## 5 Máncora (p274)

A journey through various desert oases brings you to the north coast resort town of Máncora. Here, the trip becomes all about hanging out. Spend the remaining days of your journey reading books, chilling out on the palm-lined beaches and eating some of the finest seafood around. You've earned it!

# Lake Titicaca, Cuzco & the Amazon

## Highland/Jungle Combo

*On this two-week trip through the Andes and then down into the Amazon, you'll see a little bit of everything Peru has to offer: Inca ruins, pastoral highland settings, steamy lowland jungle and more wildlife than you ever dreamed of.*

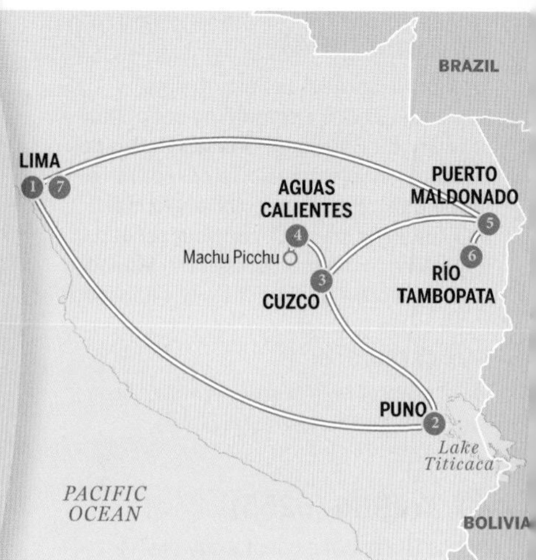


### 1 Lima (p64)

Ease into the journey with a relaxed day in Lima. The ideal plan: pay a visit to the **Museo Larco**, where you can admire artfully presented ancient treasures and dip into a tasty lunch on the patio restaurant.

**LIMA ➔ PUNO**

**About two hours** Multiple daily departures from Aeropuerto Internacional Jorge Chávez to Juliaca.

**One hour** Airport taxis are available for the ride from Juliaca to Puno.

### 2 Puno (p146)

Catch a flight to Puno and then lay low (you are now at 3830m above sea level). Some chilled-out activities include visiting the **Catedral** and strolling around the **Coca Museum**. The next day, make a day trip to one of the fabled islands of **Lake Titicaca**. If you like your islands to float, hit the **Islas Uros**, which are built out of reeds. Spend an evening enjoying Puno's colorful nightlife.

**PUNO ➔ CUZCO**

**55 minutes** Multiple daily departures from Aeropuerto Inca Manco Cápac in Juliaca.

### 3 Cuzco (p174)

Cuzco, the ancient capital of the Inca empire, is all it's cracked up to be. Most flights will get you into town in the morning, leaving you plenty of time to explore the heart of the city, including the **Catedral** (where you can see a painting of Christ eating a guinea pig), as well as the over-the-top ornamentation of the **Iglesia de la Compañía de Jesús**. Then take a couple of days to explore the city's must-see Inca sights, including the **Qorikancha**, which once harbored the most important Inca temple, and **Sacsaywamán**, the photogenic fortress just above town.

**CUZCO ➔ AGUAS CALIENTES & MACHU PICCHU**

**Three hours** Departures from Estación Poroy, east of town.

Isla Amantaní (p158), Lake Titicaca
PHOTOGRAPHER: SEAN CAFFREY/GETTY IMAGES ©

## 4 Aguas Calientes & Machu Picchu (p214)

The picturesque train line winds through the **Sacred Valley**, depositing travelers in the teeming town of Aguas Calientes – base camp for Machu Picchu. Most folks come in for the day; we recommend sticking around for at least two. For one, Machu Picchu is huge – and exploring it takes time. Two, being there overnight means you can get in early before the crowds arrive. Be sure to book your train ride back to Cuzco, as these fill up early.

**CUZCO ➔ PUERTO MALDONADO**

✈ **One hour** Multiple daily flights from Aeropuerto Internacional Alejandro Velasco Astete.

## 5 Puerto Maldonado (p300)

A quick flight plunges straight from the Andean highlands into lowland Amazon jungle. Here, the raffish town of Puerto Maldonado serves as a gateway to this storied rainforest's most remote jungle lodges. Take a day to acquaint yourself with the area – a good way to orient yourself is to clamber to the top of the **Obelisco**, a 30m tower that offers a good overview of the town.

**PUERTO MALDONADO ➔ RÍO TAMBOPATA**

**Two hours** There are taxi boats at the Tambopata dock, but your lodge can arrange private transfer.

## 6 Río Tambopata (p305)

A tributary of the **Río Madre de Dios**, the Río Tambopata leads into the **Reserva Nacional Tambopata**, an important protected area. Here, a string of riverside lodges offer various levels of accommodations (from jungle rustic to downright luxe) within reach of countless day hikes and one of the largest macaw clay licks in the country. Expect to see innumerable birds, frogs, alligators, giant river otters and the unusual spike-haired avian species known as the jungle chicken (its official name: *hoatzin*). For the best exploring, plan on spending at least three nights in the area. A lovely riverboat ride will take you back to Puerto Maldonado.

**PUERTO MALDONADO ➔ LIMA**

✈ **Three hours** Several daily departures from Aeropuerto Padre José Aldámiz during high season.

## 7 Lima (p64)

Spend your last day in the capital enjoying some excellent shopping and Peru's finest cuisine at the top-flight eateries of **Miraflores**.

# Peru Month by Month

## Top Events

**Carnaval,** before the start of Lent (February/March)

**Inti Raymi,** June

**Fiestas Patrias,** July

**Feast of Santa Rosa de Lima,** August

**El Señor de los Milagros,** October

## January

January through March is the busiest (and most expensive) season on the coast, and the best time to find beach facilities open and festivals rocking. In the mountains and canyons it's rainy season and best avoided by trekkers and mountaineers.

**Año Nuevo (New Year's Day)**

Partygoers wear lucky yellow (including underwear) to ring in the New Year.

**Fiesta de la Marinera**

A national dance festival held during the last week of January is especially popular in Trujillo. The *marinera* (sailor dance) is a synchronized dance between a man and a woman. They seductively step around each other without ever touching.

## February

The Inca Trail is closed all month. Many Peruvian festivals echo the Roman Catholic calendar and are celebrated with great pageantry, especially in indigenous highland villages.

**La Virgen de la Candelaria**

Held on February 2, this highland fiesta also known as Candlemas is particularly colorful around Puno, where folk music and dance celebrations last for two weeks.

**Carnaval**

Carnaval is held on the last few days before Lent (February/March), and is often celebrated with weeks of water fights, singing, dancing, parades and lots of rowdy mayhem. It's especially popular in highland towns, such as Huaraz.

**April** Semana Santa (Holy Week), Cuzco

## March

Beach resort prices go down and crowds disperse, though the coast remains sunny. The Inca Trail is open once again.

**Fiesta de la Vendimia**

Now is the perfect time to sample local piscos and wines in Ica (p108). The festival is held in the second week of March, when you are likely to see fairs, floats, musicians, and beauty queens stomping grapes.

## April

Holy Week is a major event, so book a hotel and transportation well in advance.

**Semana Santa (Holy Week)**

While Easter itself is a solemn event, the week prior to it is celebrated with spectacular religious processions almost daily all over Peru. The biggest of these are in the highlands, in cities such as Cuzco, Arequipa and Huaraz.

## May

Drier weather sees the start of trekking season in Huaraz and around Cuzco.

**Noche en Blanco**

Inspired by Europe's White Nights, the streets of Miraflores in Lima are closed to cars and arts, music and dance take over. Held in early May.

**Q'oyoriti**

A fascinating indigenous pilgrimage to the holy mountain of Ausangate, outside of Cuzco, in May/June. Though it has Catholic overtones, it is full of elements of animist indigenous faith.

**Festival of the Crosses**

This festival, held on May 3, is at its most intense in Lima, Ica and Cuzco. During the festivities, folks carry crosses of various sizes in a procession that leads to church.

## June

High season for international tourism starts. Reserve Machu Picchu train tickets and admission in advance. It's also the busiest time for festivals in and around Cuzco.

**Corpus Christi**

This celebration commemorates the Holy Eucharist as the body of Christ, held on the ninth Thursday after Easter. Processions in Cuzco are especially dramatic.

**Inti Raymi (Festival of the Sun)**

Also the Feast of St John the Baptist and Peasant's Day, it's the greatest of Inca festivals, celebrating the winter solstice on June 24. It's certainly the spectacle of the year in Cuzco, attracting thousands of Peruvian and foreign visitors.

**San Juan**

The feast of San Juan is all debauchery in Iquitos, where dancing, feasting and cockfights go until the wee hours of June 23 to the actual holiday of June 24.

**San Pedro y San Pablo (Feasts of SS Peter & Paul)**

Peter and Paul are the patron saints of fishers and farmers and are honored with processions. An image of St Peter is taken by a decorated boat to bless the waters for the fishing season, usually near Lima and Chiclayo on June 29.

# July

High season continues. *Garúa,* a thick, grey sea mist, settles over Lima for several months and brings a chill.

**La Virgen del Carmen**

This holiday (July 16) is mainly celebrated in the southern Andes, and is particularly important in Pisac and Cuzco. The Virgin is the patron of *mestizos* (people of mixed indigenous and Spanish decent).

**Fiestas Patrias (National Independence Days)**

Independence from Spain is celebrated nationwide on July 28 and 29, with festivities in the southern Andes beginning with the Feast of St James (Santiago) on July 25. Good luck trying to find a seat on a bus or a plane during this time.

# August

The last month of high visitation and the most crowded at Machu Picchu.

**Feast of Santa Rosa de Lima**

Major processions are held on August 30 around the country, with some of the biggest in Lima, Cuzco and Arequipa, to commemorate the New World's first saint.

# September

Low season everywhere, September can still offer good weather to highland trekkers without the crowds. Migrating birds become another attraction.

**El Festival Internacional de la Primavera (International Spring Festival)**

Expect horse parades, dancing and cultural celebrations in Trujillo during the last week of September.

**Mistura**

This weeklong foodie fest in Lima gathers Peru's top chefs, along with invited gastronomes from all over the world, for cooking demonstrations, talks and lots of sampling. For dates and locations, log on to www.mistura.pe.

# October

The best time to hit the Amazon is between September and November when drier weather means better wildlife watching.

**Great Amazon River Raft Race**

The longest raft race in the world flows between Nauta and Iquitos in September or early October.

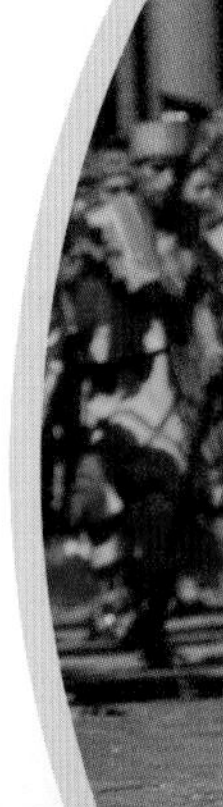

### La Virgen del Rosario

On October 4, this saint's celebration comes to Lima, Arequipa and Cuzco.

### El Señor de los Milagros

Celebrated with processions all over Peru, the biggest Lord of the Miracles celebration is held in Lima. Expect to see a lot of Peruvians decked out in purple.

## November

A good month for festivals, it's worth checking out the wild celebrations in Puno.

### Todos Santos (All Saints' Day)

All Saints' Day is November 1, and many Peruvians head to mass.

### Día de los Muertos (Day of the Dead)

On November 2 food, drink and flowers are taken to family graves. It's especially colorful in the Andes.

### Puno Week

Starting November 5, this weeklong festival in Puno involves several days of spectacular costumes and street dancing to celebrate the legendary emergence of the first Inca, Manco Cápac from Lake Titicaca.

## December

Beach season returns with warmer Pacific temperatures. The Amazon experiences heavy rains from the end of the month through early April.

### Fiesta de la Purísima Concepción

The Feast of the Immaculate Conception is a national holiday celebrated with religious processions in honor of the Virgin Mary. It's held on December 8.

### Christmas Day

Held on December 25, Christmas is less secular and more religious.

**Far left: July** Traditional bamboo flute playing, Puno **Left: June** Inti Raymi (Festival of the Sun), Cuzco

PHOTOGRAPHERS: (FAR LEFT) ERIC L. WHEATER/GETTY IMAGES ©; (LEFT) HUGHES HERVÉ / HEMIS.FR/GETTY IMAGES ©

# What's New

*For this new edition of Discover Peru, our authors have hunted down the fresh, the transformed, the hot and the happening. These are some of our favorites. For up-to-the-minute recommendations, see lonelyplanet.com/peru.*

1 **NOCHE EN BLANCO, LIMA**
Lima's take on White Nights, this night-time art and music festival takes over entire parks and venues throughout the Miraflores in early May. (p43)

2 **CENTRAL, LIMA**
Sustainable fish, a rooftop herb garden and one dazzling suckling pig – Chef Virgilio Martínez is currently commanding Lima's hottest eatery. (p81)

3 **3B BARRANCO B&B, LIMA**
An intimate Barranco inn has design-conscious boutique touches: minimalist rooms with polished-concrete vanities. (p79)

4 **MUSEO JULIO C TELLO, RESERVA NACIONAL DE PARACAS**
Opened in 2012, this refurbished museum contains artifacts found at an adjacent archaeological site. (p104)

5 **LOS TAMBOS HOSTAL, AREQUIPA**
A fine new boutique hotel with gourmet breakfasts and thoughtful touches – such as chocolates on the pillow – sits just off Arequipa's main square. (p121)

6 **ZINGARO, AREQUIPA**
Arequipa's latest addition to the *novandina* scene (Peruvian nouvelle cuisine) is a good spot for alpaca ribs and fresh ceviche. (p121)

7 **TITILAKA, LAKE TITICACA**
South of Puno, on the shores of Lake Titicaca, this sparkling boutique option is both whimsical and wondrous. (p149)

8 **CASA ANDINA ISLA SUASI, LAKE TITICACA**
A private island on the remote northern end of Lake Titicaca offers full nature immersion – and a pampering spa. (p159)

9 **PALACIO NAZARENAS, CUZCO**
A sprawling colonial convent has been transformed into Cuzco's most luxurious hotel – complete with a full spa, a fantastic restaurant (Senzo run by Virgilio Martínez), and the city's only outdoor pool – heated, of course! (p189)

10 **CASA ANDINA, CHACHAPOYAS**
An idyllic location by the Río Utcubamba provides an ideal base for exploring the nearby ruins of Kuélap. (p274)

11 **LA SIRENA D' JUAN, MÁNCORA**
Serving yellow curry *tiradito* (sashimi) and grilled fish with mango-pepper chutney, this new coastal spot is a delicious addition to Máncora. (p277)

12 **FRÍO Y FUEGO, IQUITOS**
Succulent river-fish dishes and the best night-time views of Iquitos can be found at this top-of-the-line Amazon eatery, located at the mouth of the Río Itaya. (p295)

# Get Inspired

##  Books

- **Turn Right at Machu Picchu** (2012) Mark Adams retraces explorer Hiram Bingham's early journeys to Machu Picchu.
- **Cradle of Gold: the Story of Hiram Bingham, a Real-Life Indiana Jones, and the Search for Machu Picchu** (2010) A highly readable bio by Christopher Heaney.
- **Aunt Julia & the Scriptwriter** (1977) Nobel laureate Mario Vargas Llosa's comic novel about a radio scriptwriter in love with his much older divorced sister-in-law.
- **The Conquest of the Incas** (1970) A gripping historical classic by John Hemming.
- **At Play in the Fields of the Lord** (1965) Peter Matthiessen's true-to-life novel about conflicts in the Amazon.

##  Films

- **Madeinusa** (2006) An Andean girl's tragic coming-of-age drama by director Claudia Llosa.
- **Undertow** (2009) A fictional tale about a married fisherman coming to terms with his dead boyfriend's ghost.
- **La muralla verde** (1970) Armando Robles Godoy's classic feature film about an idealistic city couple who move to the Amazon.

## Music

- **Arturo 'Zambo' Cavero** (1993) The eponymous album of the crooner best known for his soulful Peruvian waltzes.
- **Chabuca Granda: Grandes Éxitos** (2004) Breathy lyrics full of longing and nostalgia by the legendary singer and composer.
- **Eva! Leyenda Peruana** (2004) Bluesy *landós* performed by premiere Afro-Peruvian songstress Eva Ayllón.
- **The Roots of Chicha** (2007) Retro-psychedelic Amazon-meets-the-Andes-meets-Colombian-*cumbias* dance music.

## Websites

- **iPerú** (www.peru.info) The official government tourism agency.
- **Peru Links** (www.perulinks.com) A portal to helpful sites in Spanish and English.
- **Peruvian Times** (www.peruviantimes.com) The latest news, in English.
- **Peru Guide** (www.theperuguide.com) A broad travel overview.

### Short on time?

This list will give you an instant insight into the country.

**Read** *The Last Days of the Incas* (2007) is Kim MacQuarrie's page-turner about the history-making clash between two civilizations.

**Watch** *La teta asustada* (The Milk of Sorrow; 2009) is Claudia Llosa's film about a girl suffering from a trauma-related affliction.

**Listen** *Coba Coba* (2009) is a groovy fusion of Peruvian classics and chilled-out electronica.

**Log on** *Living in Peru* (www.livinginperu.com) is an expat guide and calendar and an excellent source of news.

Wearing masks in the highlands
PHOTOGRAPHER: BERNARD GRILLY/GETTY IMAGES ©

# Need to Know

### Currency
Nuevo sol (S)

### Languages
Spanish, Quechua and Aymara

### ATMs
Widely available in larger cities and towns

### Credit Cards
Visa and MasterCard widely accepted

### Visas
Generally not required for stays of up to 90 days

### Cell Phones
Local SIM cards (and top-up credits) are cheap and widely available; can be used on unlocked triband GSM 1900 world phones

### Wi-Fi
Common in midrange and top-end hotels

### Internet Access
Widely available; access is generally S2 to S3 per hour.

### Driving
On the right side of the road

### Tipping
Tip 10% for good service. Taxi drivers don't expect tips for short trips (unless they've assisted with heavy luggage); porters and tour guides do.

## When to Go



### High Season (Jun–Aug)
- Dry season in the Andean highlands and in the Amazon rainforest
- Best time for hiking and trekking in the highlands
- Busiest time due to North American and European holidays

### Shoulder (Sep–Nov & Mar–May)
- Occasional rainstorms in the highlands
- Ideal for less-crowded visits
- September to November are good rainforest-visit times

### Low Season (Dec–Feb)
- Rainy season in the highlands; very wet in the Amazon
- The Inca trail closed February for clean up
- Summer on the coast makes it high season for beach activities

## Advance Planning

- **Three to six months before** Make a reservation for trekking the Inca Trail (p188). Start shopping for your flight and check your passport expiration date.
- **One month before** Reserve accommodations and see a doctor for any vaccines or medications you may need (especially if you are traveling to the Amazon). Reserve in-country flights.
- **One week before** Confirm your hotel reservation. Book any tours you might wish to take.

## Your Daily Budget

Although the official currency is the nuevo sol, the prices of many hotels and tours in Peru may be quoted in US dollars.

### Budget less than S130

- Inexpensive hotel room or dorm bed S25–S85
- Set lunches under S10
- Entry fee to historic sights: average S10

### Midrange S130–S390

- Double room in midrange hotel S130
- Multicourse lunch at midrange restaurant S30
- Group tours from S104

### Top End more than S390

- Double room in top-end hotel S250
- Private city tour from S150 per person
- Fine restaurant dinner from S70

### Exchange Rates

| | | |
|---|---|---|
| **Australia** | A$1 | S2.72 |
| **Canada** | C$1 | S2.67 |
| **Europe** | €1 | S3.40 |
| **Japan** | ¥100 | S3.28 |
| **New Zealand** | NZ$1 | S2.15 |
| **UK** | UK£1 | S4.22 |
| **USA** | US$1 | S2.60 |

For current exchange rates, see www.xe.com

## What to Bring

- **Passport** You'll need one that's valid for six months beyond your entry date into the country.
- **Money belt** It can be handy in avoiding pickpockets.
- **Travel insurance** Carry a copy of your policy.
- **Spanish phrasebook** It'll make ordering food and talking to locals much easier.
- **Windbreaker** It gets cold in the Andes; pack a sturdy, lined windbreaker or raincoat and a warm wool cap.
- **An adventurous appetite** Peru has the best gastronomic scene in South America – try something new and delicious!

## Arriving in Peru

- **Aeropuerto Internacional Jorge Chávez**

Taxis S50; from 30 minutes to one hour (at rush hour) for San Isidro, Miraflores and Barranco; less for downtown Lima.

## Getting Around

- **Air** Numerous domestic flights; most require a change in Lima.
- **Bus** Private companies cover the whole country; go with recommended operators.
- **Car** You can rent one but it is not recommended.
- **Train** Small, privatized rail system has daily service from Cuzco to Aguas Calientes and Puno.

## Accommodations

- **Hostales and hospedajes** These are generally budget accommodations (though they do reach boutique levels of niceness); some may have shared bathrooms.
- **Homestays** In tiny villages these may be the only option.
- **B&Bs** Popular in tourist areas.
- **Apartments** A great choice if you are staying with a group.
- **Hotels** A wide selection at every budget level.

## Be Forewarned

- **Inca Trail** During the months of July and August, passes to hike the trail should be reserved up to six months in advance. (We're not kidding!)
- **Business hours** Some businesses shut down during the height of summer (December and January). In smaller towns, many shops and sights close for two hours during lunch.
- **Health** Water is unsafe to drink; boil it first or drink bottled water.
- **Crime** Robberies (pickpocketing and muggings) can be a problem at some tourist sites. Do not keep your wallet in your back pocket. Make back-up photocopies of your passport.
- **Service** Meals are a leisurely affair, so relax. If you're in a rush, go to the register to ask for your bill.

# Lima

**A perpetual fog envelops concrete facades.** Broad thoroughfares are stuffed full of horn-tooting vans and hollering street vendors. It can take imagination to get beyond the grit of Lima's first impression. Rising above a long coastline of crumbling cliffs, this sprawling metropolis is the second-driest world capital after Cairo. The best way to enjoy it? Embrace the chaos. Lima has high-rise condos, pre-Columbian temples, high-end malls and religious processions that date back to the 18th century. Think one part southern California doused with a heavy dose of *América Latina*.

But the city's a sophisticate, too. Stately museums display sublime pottery, galleries debut edgy art, and crowded restaurants serve up the latest in Andean fusion – part of a gastronomic revolution more than 400 years in the making.

Lima is a city shrouded in history, gloriously messy and full of aesthetic delights. Don't even think of missing it.

Lima coastline
AMANDA RICHTER/GETTY IMAGES ©

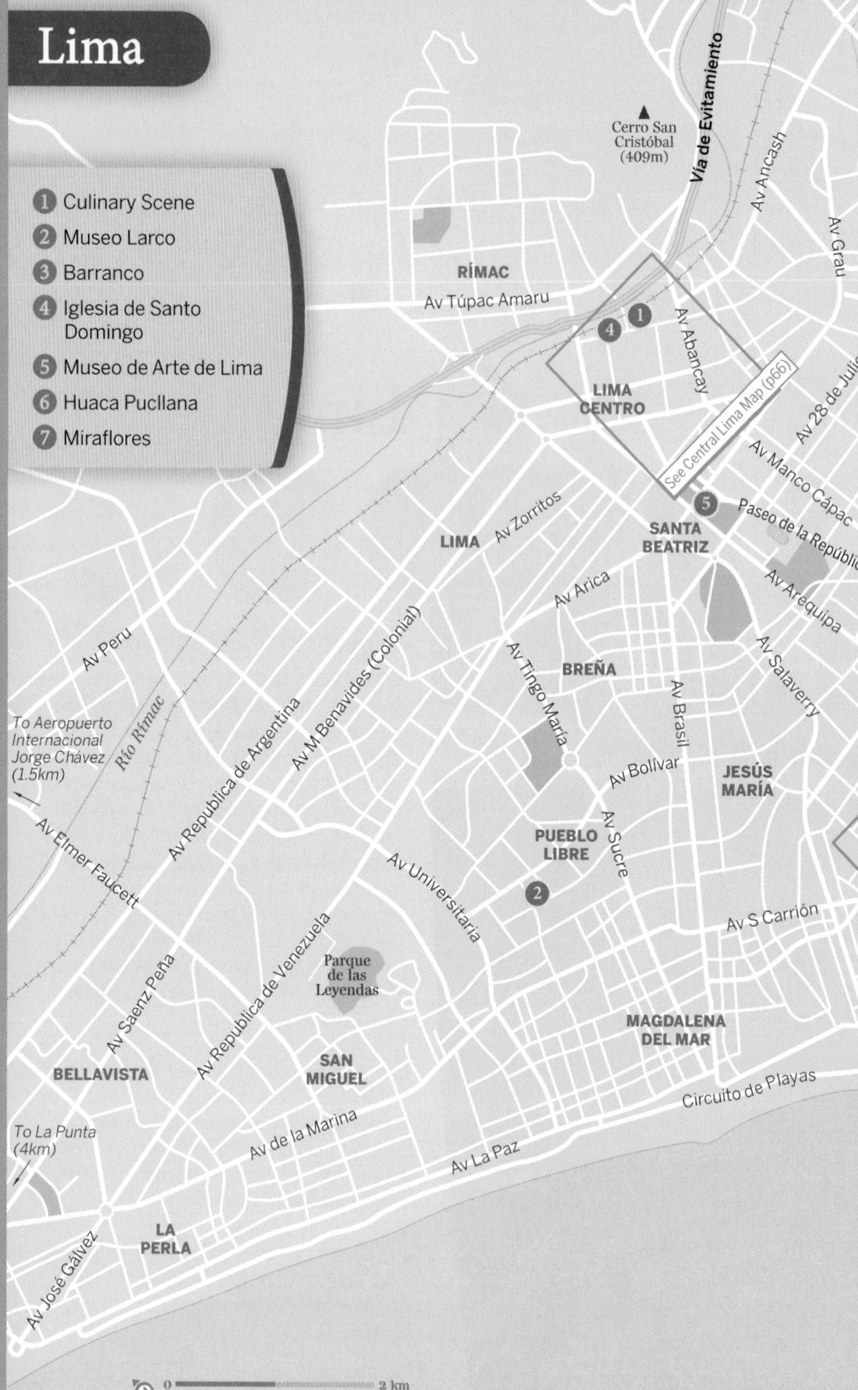
Lima
1 Culinary Scene
2 Museo Larco
3 Barranco
4 Iglesia de Santo Domingo
5 Museo de Arte de Lima
6 Huaca Pucllana
7 Miraflores
Cerro San Cristóbal (409m)
Vía de Evitamiento
Av Ancash
Av Grau
RÍMAC
Av Túpac Amaru
Av Abancay
LIMA CENTRO
See Central Lima Map (p66)
Av 28 de Julio
Av Manco Cápac
Paseo de la República
Av Arequipa
SANTA BEATRIZ
LIMA
Av Zorritos
Av Arica
Av Peru
BREÑA
Av Tingo María
Av Brasil
Av Salaverry
To Aeropuerto Internacional Jorge Chávez (1.5km)
Río Rímac
Av Republica de Argentina
Av M Benavides (Colonial)
Av Bolívar
JESÚS MARÍA
Av Sucre
Av Elmer Faucett
PUEBLO LIBRE
Av Universitaria
Av S Carrión
Av Saenz Peña
Av Republica de Venezuela
Parque de las Leyendas
MAGDALENA DEL MAR
BELLAVISTA
SAN MIGUEL
Circuito de Playas
To La Punta (4km)
Av de la Marina
Av La Paz
LA PERLA
Av José Gálvez
0 2 km
0 1 miles

Cerro El Agustino (482m)
Vía de Evitamiento
Av R Ferrero
Club Golf Los Incas
Av N Ayllon
Av El Polo
EL AGUSTINO
MONTERRICO
Hipódromo de Monterrico
SAN LUIS
Av Nicolas Arriola
Av Panamericana Sur
Av de Molina
LA VICTORIA
Parque Zonal Túpac Amaru
Av México
SAN BORJA
Av Javier Prado Este
Av Canada
Av Primavera
(Vía Expresa)
Av Aviación
Río Surco
Av A Benavides
LINCE
Paseo de la República
SURQUILLO
To Pachacamac (30km)
See San Isidro Map (p70)
Av República de Panamá
Av Santiago de Surco
SAN ISIDRO
(Vía Expresa)
Av Benavides
SANTIAGO DE SURCO
Lima Golf Club
Av Santa Cruz
Av Jose Pardo
MIRAFLORES
Av Jorge Chávez
BARRANCO
Playa Costa Verde
See Miraflores Map (p72)
Av Aguilar Pastor
See Barranco Map (p76)
Playa Agua Dulce
Av Huaylas
PACIFIC OCEAN

# Lima Highlights

1

## Lima's Culinary Scene

It's no secret that some of the most succulent dishes on the continent can be found in the Peruvian capital. Here, a mind-boggling number of eateries serve sophisticated renditions of the country's fusion cuisine: nutty stews, colorful potato terrines and of course, the renowned marinated seafood dish known as ceviche.

**Above:** El Cordano (p80)

### Need to Know

**HOT SPOTS** Miraflores is the city's dining hub. **AT THE BAR** Pisco sours are the classic cocktail. **TIP** Portions tend to be extravagant; order accordingly. **For further coverage, see p335.**

# The Capital's Must-Eat List

BY ARTURO ROJAS, LIMA NATIVE, DEVOUT EATER AND FOUNDER OF THE FOODIE TOUR COMPANY LIMA TASTY TOURS

## 1 EL CORDANO

Located in downtown Lima, this old-world cafe (p80) is in the middle of some of the city's most important historic sights. Order the *sandwich de jamón serrano* (Peruvian ham sandwich) with marinated onions and accompany it with a tall glass of *chicha morada* (a sweet, purple corn punch). Want something stronger? The bar is renowned for a cocktail known as the 'Capitán' – pisco with red vermouth and Cinzano.

## 2 RESTAURANT HUACA PUCLLANA

This high-end Miraflores restaurant (p82) has incredible views of the Huaca Pucllana pre-Columbian site and some award-winning dishes – including a renowned *lomo saltado* (stir-fry of beef with potatoes and onions). Vegetarians will enjoy the quinoa dishes, including a salad of fava beans, corn and peppers.

## 3 CENTRAL

This fashionable restaurant (p81) is run by the chef of the moment, Virgilio Martínez. He is known for his global fusion cooking – all very dramatically presented – and his roast suckling pig is terrific. Order the *menú degustación* if you can't make up your mind which dish to pick.

## 4 PESCADOS CAPITALES

This modern *cevichería* (p82) in the Miraflores warehouse district consistently prepares some of the freshest and tastiest ceviches in the city. Its perfectly grilled swordfish will totally blow your mind. If you are into seafood, it's practically a requirement to eat here.

## 5 RAFAEL

Rafael (p83) is one of those places that is consistently good. It is known for its high-end Peruvian classics, but I like it because it has a great bar scene. It's a great place to pop in and have some cocktails and eat Peruvian-Mediterranean tapas. The mini toasts with foie gras are truly excellent.

## Museo Larco

One of the country's most pleasant museums also happens to be one of its best. What should visitors expect? A scholarly and visually stunning series of exhibits detailing the triumphs of Andean civilizations over more than 5000 years. To understand Peruvian history, the journey begins here. **Below:** Café del Museo

### Need to Know

**GO LATE** The museum is open until 10pm every night. **DINING TIP** The restaurant gets busy; reserve a table upon arrival for a tasty post-art meal. **For further coverage, see p69.**

2

Local Knowledge

# Museo Larco Don't Miss List

BY ANDRÉS ÁLVAREZ CALDERÓN, DIRECTOR OF THE MUSEO LARCO SINCE 2003

## 1 SACRIFICE VESSELS

Pre-Columbian cultures were agricultural societies that worshipped the forces of nature. Human sacrifice, therefore, was considered integral to maintaining the natural order. In the Sacrifice Ceremony Gallery you will find elaborate depictions of this ritual – the most important liturgy within the Moche culture of the north coast.

## 2 LORD OF CHAN CHAN

Imagine a time when the only gleaming things were the sun, the moon, the stars – and all-powerful lords dressed entirely in silver and gold. They shone like heavenly beings and were considered, by their people, divine creatures. In this context, this gold ceremonial suit from Chan Chan, near Trujillo, will take your breath away.

## 3 THE PARACAS MANTLE

This incredible textile from the Paracas region was woven in 200 BC and is considered a treasure. It originally wrapped the body of a dead ruler – an assurance of successful passage to the afterlife. If you look closely at its borders, you'll recognize stylized representations of three animals sacred to ancient societies: the feline (representing the human world), the serpent (underworld) and birds (heaven).

## 4 THE EROTIC GALLERY

Indigenous cultures throughout Peru graphically depicted sexual acts in their art. While our present-day culture might look upon these as pieces of pornography, they are in fact representations of rituals associated with fertility and agriculture. This gallery showcases dozens of erotic ceramics, all in an incredible state of conservation.

## 5 CAFÉ DEL MUSEO

Last but not least, I like to recommend that visitors unwind on the restaurant's terrace. Not only will you sample some extraordinary local cuisine, but you can admire the museum's breathtaking grounds, which won first prize for Best Gardens in Peru in 2009. Thanks to Lima's mild climate, the colorful orchids and blooming bougainvilleas thrive all year.

## Bar-Hop Through Barranco

During the 19th century, Barranco's baronial mansions were the place to see and be seen. They still are. This oceanside neighborhood, chock-full of vintage structures, is filled with watering holes galore (p85). As they say in Peru – *¡Salud!* (Cheers!) Ayahuasca (p85)

3

4

## Behold the Skulls of Saints

The city is saturated with the history of the colony and the religious transformation it wrought. There's no better place to soak it up than the Iglesia de Santo Domingo (p68), where venerated saints such as Santa Rosa and San Martín de Porres have their craniums on display in glass cases.

THE ART ARCHIVE / ALAMY ©

## Admire the Best Peruvian Art 5

The remodeled Museo de Arte de Lima (p68) – otherwise known as MALI – is home to the country's finest collections of art through every significant historical period. Expect to see centuries-old textiles, groundbreaking early-20th-century paintings, and contemporary art installations. Overall, a fine opportunity to investigate Peru's present as much as its past. 11th-century wooden idols

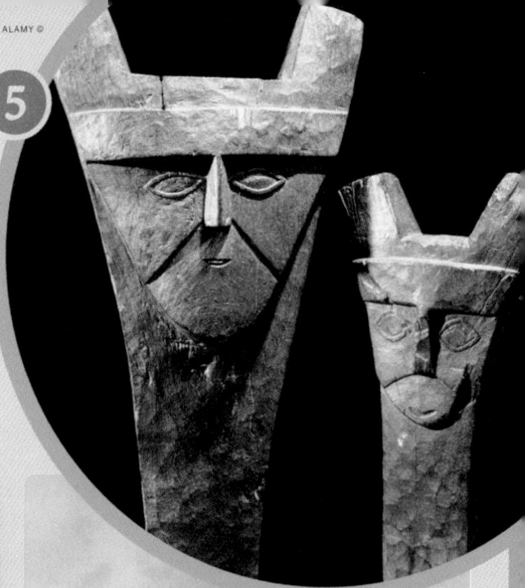

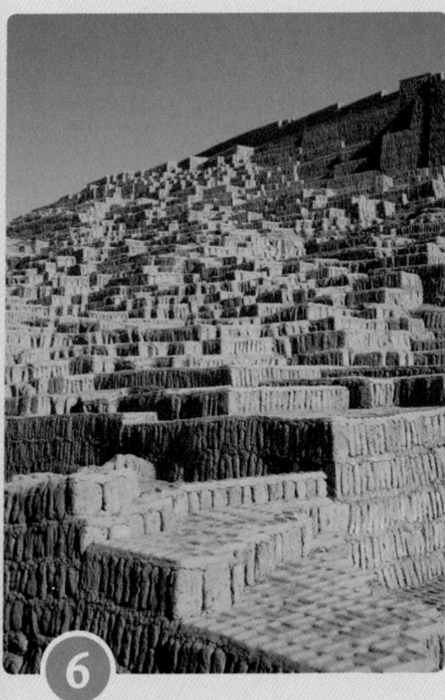

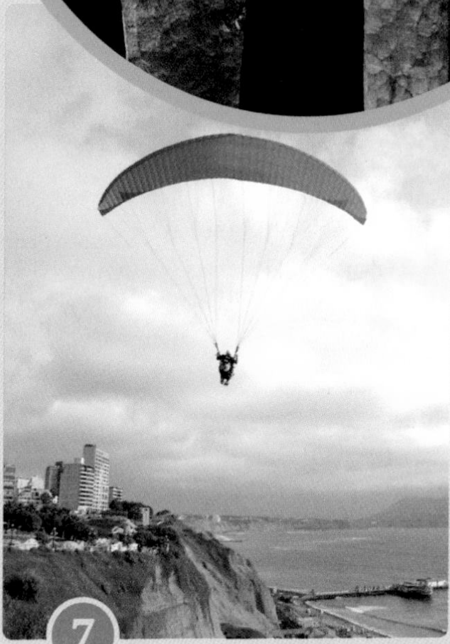

PAUL KENNEDY/GETTY IMAGES ©

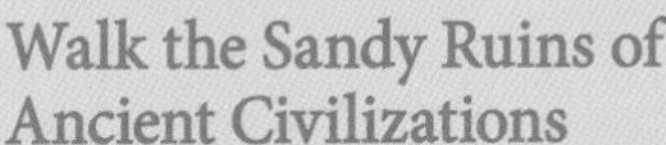

## 6 Walk the Sandy Ruins of Ancient Civilizations

Tucked in between Lima's condo towers are the remains of settlements that go back thousands of years. If you have a couple of hours, visit the adobe complex at Huaca Pucllana (p71), in the heart of Miraflores. Got an afternoon? Head south to Pachacamac (p79), a much bigger site.

Ruins at Huaca Pucllana

## 7 Leap off the Miraflores Clifftops

If you thought Lima was all shopping and eating and drinking – well, you're right. But there are sporty activities, too. Namely: paragliding along the Miraflores clifftops (p74), past all the shoppers and diners sipping cappuccinos at the trendy LarcoMar shopping mall. A total adrenaline rush!

# Lima's Best...

## Restaurants

- **Central** (p81) Lima's new hot spot – overseen by celebrity chef Virgilio Martínez –serves up one fine suckling pig

- **Astrid y Gastón** (p80) The Miraflores restaurant that helped launch Peru's gastronomic renaissance

- **El Verídico de Fidel** (p81) This ramshackle spot in Central Lima attracts everyone from lawyers to laborers with the most aphrodisiacal ceviches ever

- **El Enano** (p82) Towering sandwiches made with the freshest roasted meats

## Museums

- **Museo Larco** (p69) Naughty erotic pots and nighttime hours make this pre-Columbian collection a must-see

- **Museo de Arte de Lima** (p68) A renovation has infused this grande dame with new energy

- **Fundación Museo Amano** (p71) An appointment-only collection offers an intimate glimpse of ancient textiles and ceramics

- **Museo Pedro de Osma** (p74) Full of exquisite Cuzco School canvases and relics

## Churches

- **La Catedral de Lima** (p65) Contains the remains of conquistador Francisco Pizarro

- **Iglesia de la Merced** (p66) An unbelievably ornate facade and baroque altars galore

- **Monasterio de San Francisco** (p66) Bone-filled catacombs and a stunning library

- **Iglesia de Santo Domingo** (p68) The final resting place of Peru's most venerated saints

## Hotels

- **3B Barranco B&B** (p79) Hopping Barranco is home to this sleek new boutique spot
- **DUO Hotel Boutique** (p77) A stylish, family-run inn on a quiet residential side street
- **Miraflores Park Hotel** (p77) Sumptuous is the word to describe this ocean-view property by Orient-Express
- **Country Club Lima Hotel** (p77) A charming, historic hotel that dates back to the 1920s

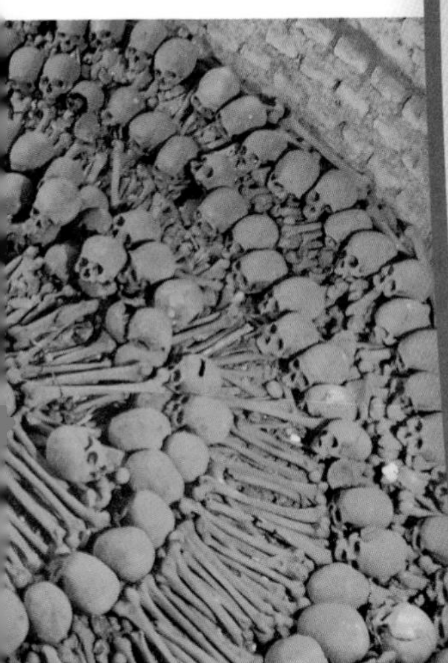

**Left:** La Catedral de Lima (p65); **Above:** Human bones in the Monasterio de San Francisco (p66)



# Need to Know

### ADVANCE PLANNING

- **Three weeks before** Make hotel reservations
- **Three days before** Arrange private day trips
- **One day before** Reserve a table at popular, high-end eateries

### RESOURCES

- **El Comercio** (www.elcomercio.pe) The daily newspaper is the best place to keep up on the city's cultural events
- **Living in Peru** (www.livinginperu.com) Keeps a helpful up-to-date calendar of major happenings
- **Oveja Negra** (www.ovejanegra.com.pe/) This directory of nightlife goings-on has a handy web edition
- **Lima: A Cultural History** A good read on the city's history by James Higgins
- **Lima la horrible** For Spanish-speakers, a collection of essays from the '60s by Sebastián Salazar Bondy incisively deconstructs the city's culture

### GETTING AROUND

- **Air** Major airlines fly to/from Aeropuerto Internacional Jorge Chávez, 12km west of Central Lima
- **Bus** Minivans and buses ply all the major avenues, such as Avs Arequipa and Prado
- **Electric bus** A limited line that connects Central Lima with Miraflores on the Vía Expresa
- **Taxis** Found just about everywhere, 24 hours a day
- **Walk** The best way of exploring tight neighborhoods like Central Lima, Miraflores and Barranco

### BE FOREWARNED

- **Chilly weather** Lima bathes in a damp fog from April to November; pack sweaters
- **Museums** Generally closed on Mondays
- **Noise** The city is noisy; streetside hotel rooms can interfere with beauty rest
- **Watch your pockets** Theft is an issue; dress down and carry only the cash you'll need

# Lima Walking Tour

*Get to know the city's colonial heart – a network of labyrinthine streets lined with baroque churches, historic parks, eccentric museums and one very grandiose presidential palace.*

**WALK FACTS**

- **Start** Plaza San Martín
- **Finish** Barrio Chino
- **Distance** 3km
- **Duration** two hours

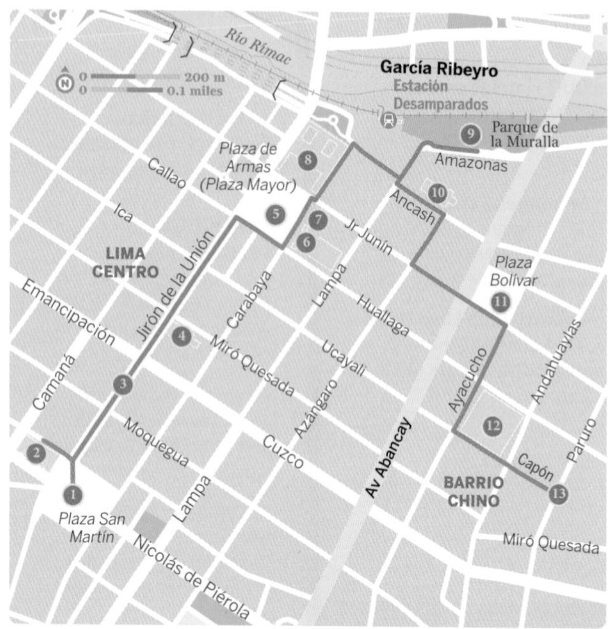


## 1 Plaza San Martín

Start by imbibing the city's faded grandeur at this bustling square, featuring a bronze statue of 19th-century revolutionary hero José de San Martín. Below him is a rendering of Madre Patria, Peru's symbolic mother.

## 2 Gran Hotel Bolívar

On the west side of the plaza is this stately hotel from 1924, renowned for its pisco cocktails.

## 3 Jirón de la Unión

This humble pedestrian passageway, now lined with cinemas and shoe stores, was once the heart of aristocratic life in the city.

## 4 Iglesia de la Merced

First constructed in 1541, this ornate baroque church stands on the site of the first Mass in Lima. Peek inside for a glimpse at the impressive mahogany altars and a venerated silver crucifix.

## 5 Plaza de Armas

Jirón de la Unión ends at the square where the city was founded. In the era of the viceroys it served as market, bullpen and even execution site for the condemned.

## 6 La Catedral de Lima

On the eastern side of the plaza is the restored cathedral. By the main door, look for the once-misplaced remains of conquistador Francisco Pizarro.

### 7 Palacio Arzobispal

On the adjacent corner, the Archbishop's Palace boasts some of the city's best-preserved Moorish balconies – perfectly designed for retiring people-watchers.

### 8 Palacio del Gobierno

To the northeast, a grandiose structure occupies an entire city block. This is Peru's presidential palace. Time your visit to pass at noon to see the changing of the guard, executed to the sounds of a brass band tapping out 'El Condor Pasa.'

### 9 Parque de la Muralla

On the southern banks of the Río Rímac is this pleasant city park, installed along the remains of the colonial *muralla* (city wall).

### 10 Monasterio de San Francisco

Afterwards, walk along Amazonas to Lampa to this fabled church containing a stunning colonial-era library, as well as underground catacombs full of skulls and bones.

### 11 Plaza Bolívar

Cross Av Abancay to this small colonial plaza, strolling past the old Congress, a neoclassical building constructed over the site of the Inquisition Tribunals.

### 12 Mercado Central

Follow Ayacucho two blocks south, to the Central Market, where stalls of goods feature everything from cuts of beef to soccer jerseys to mountains of Andean fruit.

### 13 El Barrio Chino

Calle Capón is a short pedestrian passageway that serves as the heart of Lima's miniscule Chinatown. It's an excellent spot for tea and an end-of-walk Cantonese meal.

## Lima in...

### TWO DAYS

After a walking tour of the city's colonial heart, view the Chancay pottery at the pristine **Museo Andrés del Castillo**. End the day with a pisco sour at **El Bolivarcito**, the renowned bar inside the Gran Hotel Bolívar.

The next day, go pre-Columbian or contemporary. See breathtaking artifacts at the **Museo Larco** or a gripping exhibit on the Internal Conflict at the **Museo de la Nación**. In the afternoon stroll through **Barranco**, full of 19th-century mansions, or visit **Huaca Pucllana**, the pre-Columbian temple site in Miraflores.

Spend the evening sampling *novoandina* (Peruvian nouvelle cuisine) at one of the city's many fine restaurants.

### THREE DAYS

In the morning visit the **Museo Pedro de Osma** in Barranco to ogle intriguing Cuzco School canvases and an abundance of relics from the viceroyalty. Otherwise, make the day trip to **Pachacamac** to stand amid arid ruins dating back two millennia.

Spend the afternoon haggling for crafts at the **Mercado Indio** in Miraflores.

Templo del Sol, Pachacamac (p79)

# Discover Lima

## At a Glance

- **Central Lima** (p65) The city's colonial heart.
- **San Isidro** (p69) Swanky area with sumptuous hotels.
- **Miraflores** (p71) Bustling oceanside district bursting with excellent eateries.
- **Barranco** (p74) Lima's nightlife hub, full of thumping clubs and bars.
- **Pachacamac** (p79) Ancient ceremonial center that dates back almost 2000 years.

## LIMA

☎01 / POP 8.5 MILLION / ELEV 108M

### History

In pre-Hispanic times, the area now occupied by this expansive metropolis had been an important coastal settlement to various cultures, including the Lima, the Wari and the Ichsma. In fact, when Francisco Pizarro sketched out the boundaries of his 'City of Kings' in 1535, there were roughly 200,000 indigenous people living in the area. But by the 18th century, the Spaniards had turned Lima into the capital of a continent-wide viceroyalty, where fleets of ships arrived to transport the conquest's spoils back to Europe.

In the late 19th century, the city found itself under siege when it was occupied by the Chilean military during the war of the Pacific (1879–83). A period of expansion followed in the early 20th century, during which time a network of broad boulevards (inspired by Parisian urban design) were constructed to crisscross the city.

Since then, it has endured earthquakes, population growth and, in the '80s, bouts of guerrilla warfare due to the Internal Conflict. But the last decade has seen an unparalleled rebirth. A robust economy and a vast array of municipal improvement efforts have led to repaved streets, refurbished parks, and safer public areas – not to mention a thriving cultural and culinary life.

Miraflores

TODD LAWSON/GETTY IMAGES ©

La Catedral de Lima

ROBERT HARDING WORLD IMAGERY/GETTY IMAGES ©

## Sights

The city's colonial heart, Lima Centro (Central Lima), lies at a bend on the Río Rímac. From here, Av Arequipa, one of Lima's principal thoroughfares, plunges southeast, through San Isidro, into Miraflores. Immediately to the south lies Barranco.

### Central Lima

**PLAZA DE ARMAS** Historic Plaza

(Map p66) The 140-sq-meter **main plaza**, also called the Plaza Mayor, was the heart of the 16th-century settlement established by Francisco Pizarro. To the east is the **Palacio Arzobispal** (Archbishop's Palace), boasting some of the most exquisite Moorish-style balconies in the city.

To the north is the block-long **Palacio de Gobierno**, a grandiose baroque-style building serving as the presidential palace. Out front stands a handsomely uniformed guard that conducts a changing-of-the-guard ceremony every day at noon. It's a pomp-filled affair that involves slow-motion goose-stepping to a brass band playing 'El Cóndor Pasa' as a military march.

The palace is not open to visitors.

**LA CATEDRAL DE LIMA** Cathedral

(Map p66; 427-9647; admission S10; 9am-5pm Mon-Fri, 10am-1pm Sat) Next to the Archbishop's palace resides the cathedral, on the same plot of land that Pizarro designated for the city's first church in 1535. Though it has a baroque facade, the interior was redone in a simple neoclassical style in the 19th century. Even so, baroque pieces remain scattered throughout, such as the ornate wood **choir** from the early 17th century, a masterpiece of rococo sculpture. A worthwhile **religious museum**, in the rear, features paintings, vestments and an intricate sacristy.

By the cathedral's main door is a **mosaic-covered chapel** where the battered remains of Pizarro have long lain. The authenticity of these came into question in 1977, after workers cleaning out a crypt discovered a sealed lead box, containing a skull, that bore the inscription, 'Here is the head of the gentleman Marquis Don Francisco Pizarro, who found and conquered the kingdom of Peru...' After a battery of tests in the 1980s, a US forensic scientist concluded that the body previously on display was of an unknown official and

## Central Lima

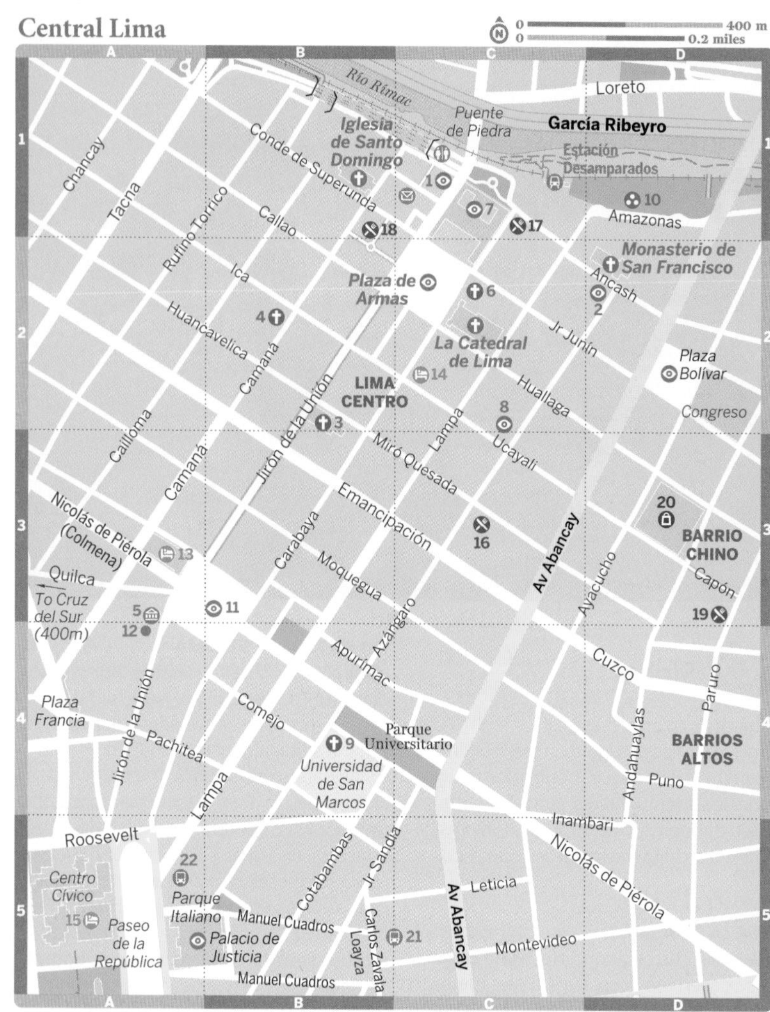


that the brutally stabbed and headless body from the crypt was Pizarro's. Head and body were reunited and transferred to the chapel, where you can also see the inscribed lead box.

**MONASTERIO DE SAN FRANCISCO** Church

**(Map p66; ☎426-7377; www.museocatacumbas.com; cnr Lampa & Ancash; adult/child under 15 S7/1; ⏰9:30am-5:30pm)** This bright-yellow Franciscan monastery and church is most famous for its bone-lined catacombs and remarkable library, where you can take in the sight of 25,000 antique texts, some of them predating the conquest. There are many other things worth seeing, too, including a Moorish-style cupola, over the main staircase, which was carved in 1625 (restored 1969) out of Nicaraguan cedar. Admission includes guided tours in English or Spanish.

**IGLESIA DE LA MERCED** Church

**(Map p66; ☎427-8199; cnr Jirón de la Unión & Miró Quesada; ⏰10am-noon & 5-7pm)** The first

## Central Lima

**Top Sights**

Iglesia de Santo Domingo .................... B1
La Catedral de Lima .................... C2
Monasterio de San Francisco .................... D2
Plaza de Armas .................... C2

**Sights**

1 Casa Aliaga .................... C1
2 Casa de Pilatos .................... D2
3 Iglesia de la Merced .................... B2
4 Iglesia de San Agustín .................... B2
5 Museo Andrés del Castillo .................... A3
6 Palacio Arzobispal .................... C2
7 Palacio de Gobierno .................... C1
8 Palacio Torre Tagle .................... C2
9 Panteón de los Próceres .................... B4
10 Parque de la Muralla .................... D1
11 Plaza San Martín .................... B3

**Activities, Courses & Tours**

12 Lima Tours .................... A4

**Sleeping**

13 Gran Hotel Bolívar .................... A3
14 Hotel Maury .................... C2
15 Lima Sheraton .................... A5

**Eating**

16 Domus .................... C3
17 El Cordano .................... C1
18 Tanta .................... B1
19 Wa Lok .................... D3

**Drinking**

El Bolivarcito .................... (see 13)

**Shopping**

20 Mercado Central .................... D3

**Transport**

21 Ormeño .................... C5
22 Tepsa .................... A5

Latin Mass in Lima was held in 1534, on a small patch of land now marked by this incredible church, most of which dates to the 18th century. Its most striking feature is the imposing granite facade, which is carved in the *churrigueresque* manner (a highly ornate late-baroque style). Inside, the nave is lined by more than two-dozen magnificent baroque and Renaissance-style altars, some of which are carved entirely out of mahogany.

To the right as you enter is a large silver cross that once belonged to Father Pedro Urraca (1583–1657), a priest renowned for having had a vision of the Virgin. Peruvians often come and place a hand on the cross and pray for miracles.

**PARQUE DE LA MURALLA** Park

**(Map p66; ☎427-4125; Amazonas, btwn Lampa & Av Abancay; 9am-9pm)** During the 17th century, the heart of Lima was ringed by a *muralla* (city wall), much of which was torn down in the 1870s as the city expanded. This park contains remains of the wall, as well as a famous bronze of Francisco Pizarro, created by American sculptor Ramsey MacDonald in the early 20th century.

The figure once commanded center stage in the Plaza, but over the years has been displaced as attitudes toward Pizarro have grown critical. The best part: the statue isn't really Pizarro. It's an anonymous conquistador of the sculptor's invention. MacDonald made three copies of the statue. One was erected in the US; the other, Spain. The third was donated to the city of Lima (after Mexico rejected it). Now Pizarro's proxy sits at the edge of the park, a silent witness to a daily parade of flirty Peruvian teens.

### Colonial Mansions

**PALACIO TORRE TAGLE** Historic Building

**(Map p66; Ucayali 363)** There are few remaining colonial mansions in Lima since many of them have been lost to expansion and earthquakes. Many now operate as private offices, which can make seeing interiors difficult. The most immaculate of these *casonas* (mansions) is this famous structure, completed in 1735, with its ornate baroque portico (the best in Lima) and striking Moorish balconies. It is home to Peru's Foreign Ministry, so visitors are

HEMIS / ALAMY ©

## Don't Miss Iglesia de Santo Domingo

One of Lima's most storied religious sites, the **Iglesia de Santo Domingo** and its graceful **priory** are built on land granted to the Dominican friar Vicente de Valverde, who accompanied Pizarro throughout the conquest. The nave is lined with intricate chapels, but Santo Domingo is most renowned for being the final resting place of the three most important Peruvian saints: San Juan Macías, Santa Rosa de Lima (the first saint of the Americas) and San Martín de Porres (the continent's first black saint).

The priory – a sprawling courtyard-studded complex lined with baroque paintings and Spanish tile – contains the saints' tombs. The impressive pink church, however, has the most interesting relics: namely, the skulls of San Martín and Santa Rosa, encased in glass, in a shrine to the right of the main altar.

### NEED TO KNOW

**Map p66; ☎427-6793; cnr Camaná & Conde de Superunda; admission church/convent free/S5; ⏰9am-1pm & 5-7:30pm Mon-Sat)**

only allowed a gander at the exterior. Even so, it's worth it.

**CASA ALIAGA** Historic Building

**(Map p66; ☎427-7736; www.casadealiaga.com; Jirón de la Unión 224)** Innocuously tucked on a side street by the post office stands this mansion, on land given to Jerónimo de Aliaga, one of Pizarro's followers, in 1535. Since then, it has been occupied by 16 generations of his descendants. Its interiors are lovely, with vintage furnishings and tile-work. It can be visited via organized excursions with Lima Tours (p75).

### Other Sights

**MUSEO DE ARTE DE LIMA** Museum

**(☎423-6332; www.mali.pe; Paseo Colón 125; suggested donation S6-12; ⏰10am-7pm Tue-Sun)** Known locally as MALI, Lima's principal fine-arts museum is housed in a striking beaux-arts building with an excellent permanent collection. This includes pre-Columbian artifacts, colonial furniture and cutting-edge pieces by contemporary artists. Of particular interest is a strong collection of early-20th-century *indigenista* painting, which celebrated indigenous aspects of Peruvian society. A recent remodel has left the galleries wonderfully refreshed.

**PLAZA SAN MARTÍN** Historic Plaza

**(Map p66)** This attractive plaza is named for the liberator of Peru, José de San Martín, who sits astride a horse at its center. At the base, don't miss the bronze rendering of Madre Patria, the symbolic mother of Peru. Commissioned in Spain under instruction to give the good lady a crown of flames, nobody thought to iron out the double meaning of the word flame in Spanish (*llama*), so the hapless craftsmen duly placed a delightful little llama on her head.

**MUSEO ANDRÉS DEL CASTILLO** Museum

**(Map p66; ☎433-2831; www.madc.com.pe; Jirón de la Unión 1030; admission S10; ⏲9am-6pm, closed Tue)** Housed in a pristine 19th-century mansion with Spanish-tile floors, this worthwhile private museum showcases a vast collection of minerals, as well as breathtakingly displayed Nazca textiles and Chancay pottery.

**EL CIRCUITO MÁGICO DEL AGUA** Park

**(Parque de la Reserva, Av Petit Thouars, cuadra 5; admission S4; ⏲4-10pm)** An indulgent series of fountains so over-the-top it can't help but induce stupefaction even among the most hardened traveling cynic. A dozen different fountains – all splendiferously illuminated – are capped, at the end, by a laser light show at the 120m-long Fuente de la Fantasía (Fantasy Fountain). The whole display is set to a medley of Peruvian folk music.

## San Isidro & Around

**MUSEO LARCO** Museum

**(☎461-1825; http://museolarco.org; Bolívar 1515, Pueblo Libre; adult/child under 15 S30/15; ⏲9am-10pm)** An 18th-century viceroy's mansion houses this museum, which has one of the best-presented displays of ceramics in Lima. Founded by Rafael Larco Hoyle in 1926, the collection showcases ceramic works from the Cupisnique, Chimú, Chancay, Nazca and Inca cultures, but the highlight is the sublime Moche portrait vessels, presented in simple, dramatically lit cases. Equally astonishing: a Wari weaving in one of the rear galleries that contains a record 398 threads to the linear inch. What lures many visitors here, however, is a separately housed collection of pre-Columbian erotic pots that illustrate, with comical explicitness, all manner of sexual activity.

On-site, the highly recommended **Café del Museo (mains S28-40)** faces a garden draped in bougainvillea – a perfect spot for ceviche and a pisco sour (grape brandy cocktail).

**MUSEO NACIONAL DE ANTROPOLOGÍA, ARQUEOLOGÍA E HISTORIA DEL PERÚ** Museum

**(National Museum of Anthropology, Archaeology & History; ☎463-5070; http://museonacional.perucultural.org.pe; Plaza Bolívar, cnr San Martín & Vivanco, Pueblo Libre; adult/child S10/1; ⏲9am-5pm Tue-Sat, to 4pm Sun)** This rambling museum traces the history of Peru from the Preceramic Period to the early republic. Displays include the famous Raimondi Stela, a 2.1m rock carving from the Chavín era that is at least 2000 years old. Also on view are numerous late-colonial and early republic paintings, including an 18th-century rendering of the *Last Supper* in which Christ and his disciples feast on *cuy* (guinea pig).

Notably, the building was once the home of revolutionary heroes José de San Martín (from 1821 to 1822) and Simón Bolívar (from 1823 to 1826).

**HUACA HUALLAMARCA** Pre-Columbian Site

**(Map p70; ☎222-4124; Nicolás de Rivera 201, San Isidro; adult/child S6/1; ⏲9am-5pm Tue-Sun)** Nestled among condominium towers and ritzy modernist homes, this restored adobe pyramid was produced by the Lima culture, which dates back to AD 200 to 500. A small museum, complete with a mummy, details its excavation.

## San Isidro

See Miraflores Map (p72)

### San Isidro

**Top Sights**

Huaca Huallamarca .......... C2

**Sights**

1 Bosque El Olivar .......... D4

**Sleeping**

2 Casa Bella Perú .......... A2
3 Country Club Lima Hotel .......... A2
4 Hotel Basadre Suites .......... A2

**Eating**

5 Antica .......... C1
6 Malabar .......... D2
7 Matsuei .......... D2
8 Segundo Muelle .......... C3

**Drinking**

9 Bravo Restobar .......... C4

**Information**

10 iPerú .......... C2

**MUSEO DE LA NACIÓN** Museum

**(Museum of the Nation; ☎476-9878; Av Javier Prado Este 2466, San Borja; admission S7; 🕒9am-6pm Tue-Sun)** A brutalist concrete tower houses this catch-all museum that provides a cursory overview of Peru's civilizations, from Chavín stone carvings and the knotted rope *quipus* of the Incas to artifacts from the colony. Large traveling exhibits are also shown here (for an extra fee), but if there is a single reason to visit, it's to view a permanent installation on the 6th floor called 'Yuyanapaq'. Named for the Quechua word meaning 'to remember,' it was created by Peru's Truth & Reconciliation Commission in 2003 and is a moving photographic tribute to those who died during the Internal Conflict.

**BOSQUE EL OLIVAR** Park

**(Map p70)** This tranquil park consists of the remnants of an old olive grove, part of which was planted by the venerated San Martín de Porres in the 17th century. Perfect for an afternoon stroll.

## Miraflores

**FUNDACIÓN MUSEO AMANO** Museum

**(Map p72; ☎441-2909; www.fundacionmuseoamano.org.pe; Retiro 160; 🕒3-5pm Mon-Fri, by appointment only)** A well-designed museum containing a fine private collection of ceramics, with a strong representation of wares from the Chimú and Nazca cultures. It also has a remarkable assortment of textiles produced by the coastal Chancay culture. Museum visits are allowed by one-hour guided tour only, in Spanish or Japanese.

**CHOCO MUSEO** Museum

**(Map p72; ☎445-9708; www.chocomuseo.com; Berlin 375; admission S2; 🕒10:30am-8:30pm)** On-site chocolate production is the seducing factor of this new 'museum' selling fondue and fair-trade hot cocoa. French-owned (with an outlet in Cuzco), it is already well known for organic chocolate-making workshops (S70 per person).

**HUACA PUCLLANA** Ruin

**(Map p72; ☎617-7138; cnr Borgoño & Tarapacá; admission S7; 🕒9am-4:30pm Wed-Mon)** Located near the Óvalo Gutiérrez, this *huaca* (tomb) is a restored adobe ceremonial center from the Lima culture that dates back to AD 400. In 2010 an important discovery of four Wari mummies – untouched by looting – was made here. The site is accessible by guided tours in Spanish (for a tip). In addition to a tiny on-site museum, there's a fantastic restaurant (p82) that offers incredible views of the illuminated ruins at night.

Palacio Torre Tagle (p67)

# Miraflores

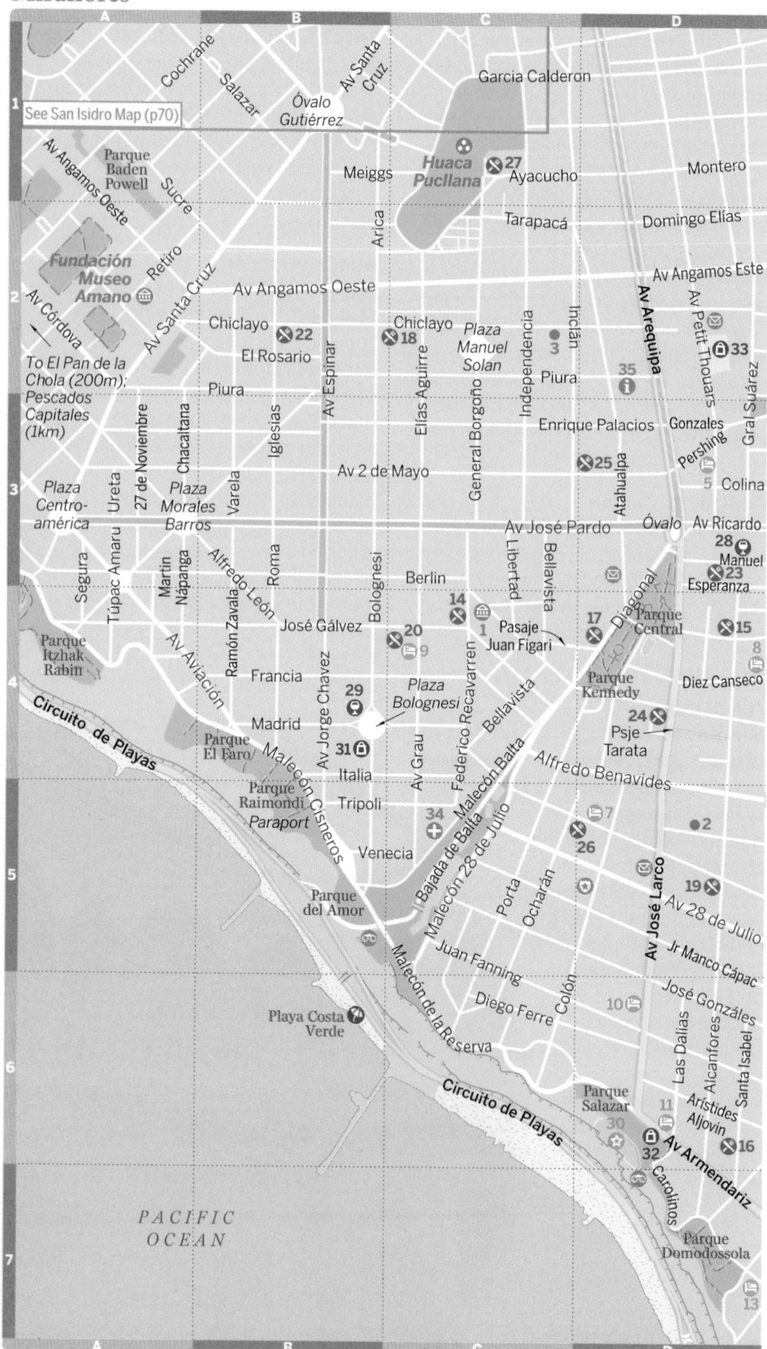
A
B
C
D
1
2
3
4
5
6
7
See San Isidro Map (p70)
Cochrane
Salazar
Óvalo Gutiérrez
Av Santa Cruz
Garcia Calderon
Huaca Pucllana
27
Ayacucho
Montero
Meiggs
Parque Baden Powell
Av Angamos Oeste
Sucre
Tarapacá
Domingo Elías
Arica
Fundación Museo Amano
Retiro
Av Santa Cruz
Av Angamos Oeste
Av Angamos Este
Av Córdova
To El Pan de la Chola (200m); Pescados Capitales (1km)
Chiclayo
22
Chiclayo
18
Plaza Manuel Solan
Independencia
3
Inclán
Av Arequipa
Av Petit Thouars
33
El Rosario
Piura
Piura
35
Av Espinar
Elías Aguirre
General Borgoño
Iglesias
Enrique Palacios
Gonzales
Gral Suárez
Pershing
5
Colina
27 de Noviembre
Chacaltana
Av 2 de Mayo
25
Atahualpa
Plaza Centro-américa
Ureta
Plaza Morales Barros
Varela
Av José Pardo
Óvalo
Av Ricardo
28
Manuel
23
Esperanza
Túpac Amaru
Segura
Martin Nápanga
Alfredo León
Roma
Bolognesi
Berlin
Libertad
Bellavista
Diagonal
Parque Central
15
8
14
1
Pasaje Juan Figari
17
Parque Itzhak Rabin
José Gálvez
20
9
Av Aviación
Ramón Zavala
Francia
Av Jorge Chavez
Plaza Bolognesi
Federico Recavarren
Bellavista
Parque Kennedy
Diez Canseco
29
24
Psje Tarata
Circuito de Playas
Madrid
Parque El Faro
Malecón Cisneros
31
Av Grau
Malecón Balta
Alfredo Benavides
Italia
Parque Raimondi
Paraport
Tripoli
34
Bajada de Balta
Malecón 28 de Julio
7
2
26
Venecia
Porta
Ocharán
Av José Larco
19
Av 28 de Julio
Parque del Amor
Jr Manco Cápac
Malecón de la Reserva
Juan Fanning
Diego Ferre
Colón
10
José Gonzáles
Playa Costa Verde
Las Dalias
Alcanfores
Santa Isabel
Circuito de Playas
Parque Salazar
11
Arístides Aljovin
30
32
16
Av Armendariz
Carolinos
PACIFIC OCEAN
Parque Domodossola
13

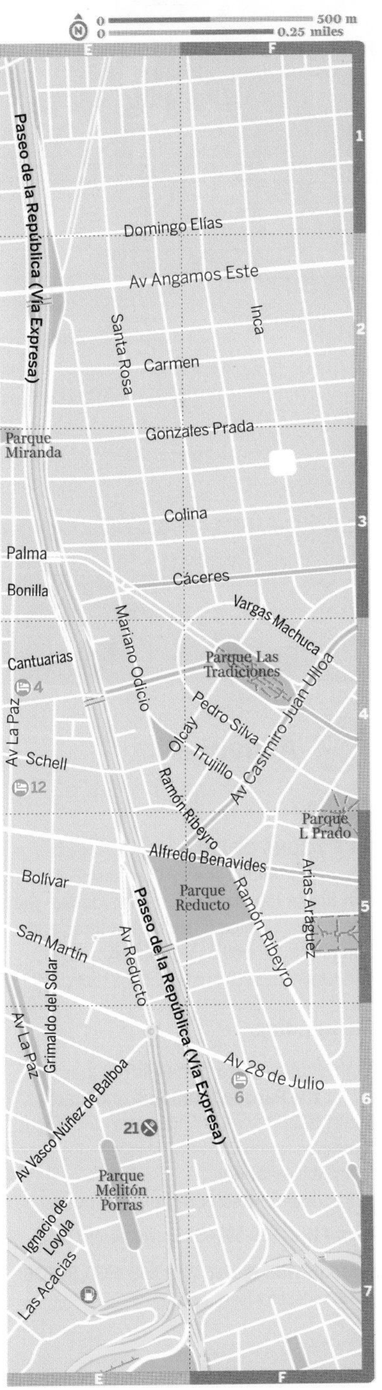


## Miraflores

### Top Sights
Fundación Museo Amano ................. A2
Huaca Pucllana ................................C1

### Sights
1 Choco Museo ................................ C4

### Activities, Courses & Tours
2 Bike Tours of Lima ........................ D5
3 Lima Vision..................................... C2

### Sleeping
4 Casa Andina Colección Privada......... E4
5 Casa Andina Miraflores Centro ......... D3
6 Casa Andina San Antonio ..................F6
7 Casa San Martín................................ D5
8 Hostal El Patio .................................. D4
9 Hotel Antigua Miraflores................... C4
10 Hotel Ibis ......................................... D6
11 JW Marriott Hotel Lima..................... D6
12 La Paz Apart Hotel ........................... E4
13 Miraflores Park Hotel........................ D7

### Eating
14 AlmaZen ........................................... C4
15 Astrid y Gastón.................................. D4
16 Central............................................... D6
17 Dédalo Arte y Cafe ........................... D4
18 El Enano............................................. C2
19 El Punto Azul .................................... D5
20 El Rincón del Bigote ......................... C4
21 Fiesta ................................................. E6
22 Helena Chocolatier............................ B2
23 La Trattoria di Mambrino................... D3
24 Manolo............................................... D4
25 Panchita ............................................ D3
26 Rafael................................................. D5
27 Restaurant Huaca Pucllana ................C1

### Drinking
28 Café Bar Habana ............................... D3
29 Huaringas .......................................... B4

### Entertainment
30 Gótica ................................................ D6

### Shopping
31 El Virrey ............................................. B4
32 LarcoMar ............................................ D6
33 Mercado Indio .................................... D2

### Information
34 Clínica Good Hope ............................ C5
iPerú ............................................ (see 32)
35 South American Explorers Club............................................... D2

## Barranco

An upper-class resort community during the turn of the 20th century, Barranco is lined with grand old *casonas*, many of which have been turned into eateries and bars. A block west of the main plaza, look for the **Puente de los Suspiros** (Bridge of Sighs; Map p76), a narrow wooden bridge over an old stone stairway that leads to the beach. This is a prime spot for Peruvians on first dates.

**MUSEO PEDRO DE OSMA** Museum
(Map p76; ☎467-0141; www.museopedrodeosma.org; Av Pedro de Osma 423; admission S10; ⏰10am-6pm Tue-Sun) Housed in a lovely beaux-arts mansion surrounded by gardens, this colonial museum has an exquisite collection of art and furnishings, some of which date back to the early 16th century. Standouts include a 2m-wide canvas that depicts a Corpus Christi procession in turn-of-the-17th-century Cuzco.

# Activities

### Cycling

**BIKE TOURS OF LIMA** Cycling Tours
(Map p72; ☎445-3172; www.biketoursoflima.com; Bolívar 150, Miraflores; ⏰9am-7pm Mon-Sat) Great for day trips around Miraflores and San Isidro, as well as Sunday excursions into downtown (from S30 for a half day).

### Paragliding

Flights take off from the clifftop 'paraport' at the **Parque Raimondi** and start at about S150 for a 15-minute tandem flight. Agencies do not have offices on-site; reserve in advance.

Recommended companies include:

**Peru Fly** (☎99-591-9928; www.perufly.com)

**Andean Trail Peru** (☎99-836-4930, 99-836-3436; andeantrailperu.com)

**Left:** Barranco;
**Below:** Colorful housing in residential Lima
(LEFT) AARON MCCOY/GETTY IMAGES ©; (BELOW) IMÁGENES DEL PERÚ/GETTY IMAGES ©

## Tours

**LIMA VISION** Tours
**(Map p72; ☎447-7710; www.limavision.com; Chiclayo 444, Miraflores)** A good agency for four-hour city tours (S70) and day-long trips to the pre-Columbian ruins at Pachacamac.

**LIMA TOURS** Tours
**(Map p66; ☎619-6901; www.limatours.com.pe; Jirón Belén 1040, Central Lima; ⏰9:30am-6pm Mon-Fri, to 1pm Sat)** Another reputable, well-known outfit that offers all manner of tours around Lima, including gay-friendly and gastronomic outings.

**LIMA TASTY TOURS** Tours
**(☎99-738-9276; www.limatastytours.com)** Led by the English-speaking Arturo Rojas, this small outfit has preprogrammed and custom itineraries that cover the cuisine scene along with important Lima sights. Reserve in advance.

## Sleeping

The seaside neighborhood of Miraflores tends to be where most travelers congregate. That doesn't mean there aren't excellent places to lay your head in other parts of the city. Credit cards accepted at all of the hotels listed below.

### Central Lima

**GRAN HOTEL BOLÍVAR** Historic Hotel $$
**(Map p66; ☎619-7171; Jirón de la Unión 958; s/d/tr S169/195/234; @)** This venerable 1924 hotel located on the Plaza San Martín was, in its day, one of the most luxurious accommodations in Latin America, where figures like Clark Gable, Mick Jagger and Robert Kennedy laid their heads. Today, it is frayed at the edges, but, like any grand dame, still possesses a rare finesse.

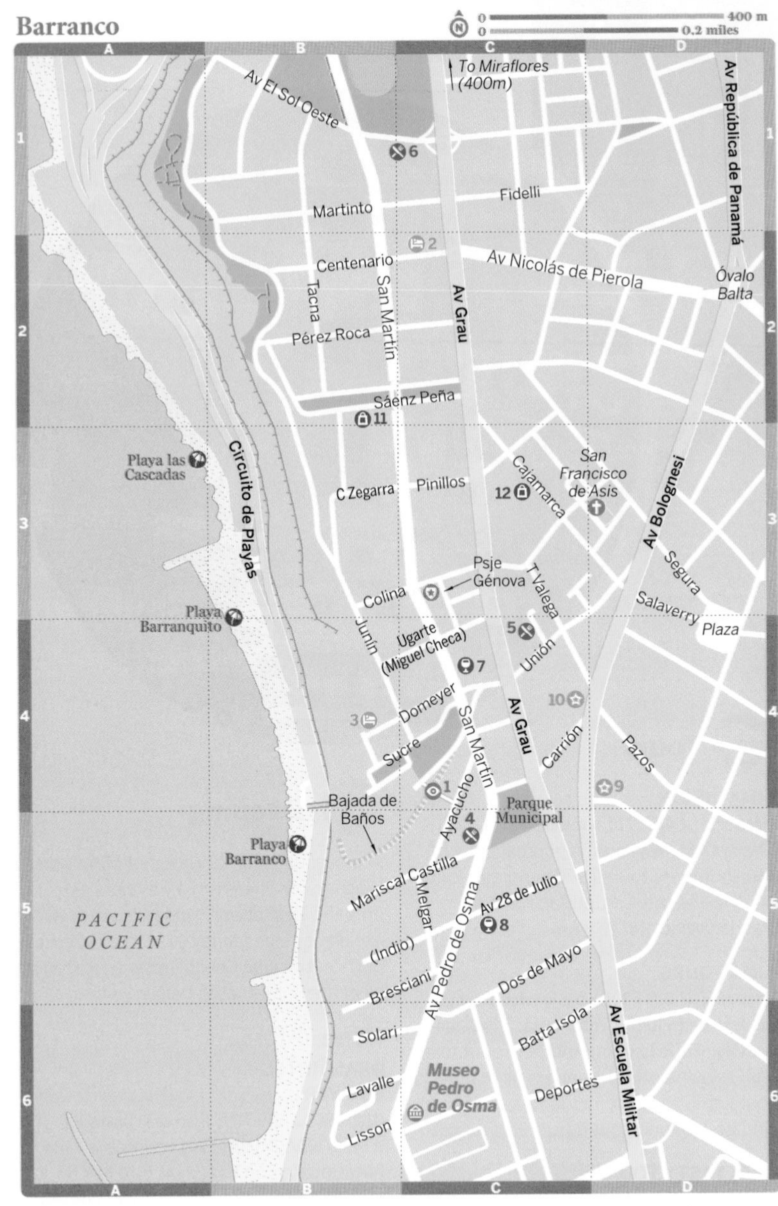


**HOTEL MAURY** Historic Hotel $$

**(Map p66; ☎428-8188; hotmaury@amauta.rep.net.pe; Ucayali 201; s/tw/d incl breakfast S150/190/240; ❄@🛜)** Although the public areas at the Maury retain old-world flourishes (such as gilded mirrors, Victorian-style furniture), the 76 modern rooms are up-to-date: simple, clean and equipped with Jacuzzi tubs. The hotel is renowned for having been one of the first spots to cultivate the pisco sour back in the '30s.

## Barranco

**Top Sights**



**Sights**



**Sleeping**



**Eating**



**Drinking**



**Entertainment**



**Shopping**



**LIMA SHERATON** Hotel $$$

**(Map p66; ☎619-3300; www.sheraton.com.pe; Paseo de la República 170; d S1039; ❄@📶🏊)** Housed in a brutalist high-rise that overlooks the dour Palacio de Justicia (Supreme Court), downtown's top option has more than 400 rooms and suites decorated in an array of desert tones. Units are equipped with wi-fi and cable TV and there is 24-hour room service. In addition, there are two restaurants, a bar, a gym and a swimming pool.

## San Isidro

**DUO HOTEL BOUTIQUE** Boutique Hotel $$$

**(off Map p70; ☎628-3245; www.duohotelperu.com; Valle Riesta 576; s/d/ste incl breakfast S305/398/437; ❄@📶🏊)** With minimalist chic, this intimate hotel features 20 monochromatic rooms outfitted with fresh flowers, soft sheets, slippers and marble baths. Service is excellent and the on-site restaurant offers meals that marry the best of Peruvian and Italian flavors. It's on a serene residential street, two blocks west of the Lima Golf Club.

**COUNTRY CLUB LIMA HOTEL** Historic Hotel $$$

**(Map p70; ☎611-9000; www.hotelcountry.com; Los Eucaliptos 590; d from S1678; ❄@📶🏊)** Set on a sprawling lawn dotted with palms, this regal hotel occupies one of Lima's finest buildings, a 1927 structure built in the Spanish colonial tradition. Clad in colorful tiles, wood-beam ceilings and replica Cuzco School paintings, its signature feature is a stained-glass atrium where breakfast is served. The 83 rooms are replete with amenities.

**CASA BELLA PERÚ** Guesthouse $$

**(Map p70; ☎421-7354; www.casabellaperu.net; Las Flores 459; s/d/tr incl breakfast S183/199/262; @📶)** A great midrange option in an expensive area, this former 1950s home has 14 contemporary rooms stocked with comfy beds, firm pillows, plasma TVs, remodeled bathrooms and Andean textiles. There is a kitchen, an ample garden and a lounge.

**HOTEL BASADRE SUITES** Hotel $$

**(Map p70; ☎442-2423; www.hotelbasadre.com; Jorge Basadre 1310; s/d/ste incl breakfast S154/164/197; ❄@🏊)** Built around a former private home, this attentive inn has 20 attractive modern rooms, each with a minibar, hair dryer, cable TV and lockbox. Breakfast, served in a small room by the garden, is abundant. Check the website for special offers.

## Miraflores

**MIRAFLORES PARK HOTEL** Luxury Hotel $$$

**(Map p72; ☎242-3000; www.mirafloresspark.com; Malecón de la Reserva 1035; d from US$921; ❄@📶🏊)** The best of Lima's small luxury hotels, this Orient-Express property boasts a glorious oceanside setting and every frill imaginable, including a gorgeous library and an infinity pool. Want to truly indulge? For US$55, a bath butler will run a petal-strewn, candlelit bath with champagne and fresh strawberries. Mesa 18, the on-site restaurant, has good Japanese-Peruvian fusion cuisine.

## If You Like… Colonial Architecture

If you like the resplendent baroque lines of the Palacio Torre Tagle (p67), the city contains myriad other colonial treasures worth exploring. A guide to some of the finest:

1 **PANTEÓN DE LOS PRÓCERES** (Map p66; 427-8157; Parque Universitario, Central Lima; 10am-5pm) This little-visited 18th-century Jesuit church is filled with tributes to Peruvian battle heroes and a 16th-century baroque altar that dates back to the 1500s.

2 **CONVENTO DE LOS DESCALZOS** (481-0441; Alameda de los Descalzos s/n, Rímac; admission S6; 10am-1pm & 3-6pm, closed Tue) In the north Lima neighborhood of Rímac lies this somewhat forgotten 16th-century convent and museum run by the Franciscans. In addition to elaborately decorated cloisters and the original monastic cells, it contains some 300 colonial paintings, including canvases by renowned Cuzco School artist Diego Quispe Tito. Taxis from the Plaza de Armas start at S10.

3 **IGLESIA DE SAN AGUSTÍN** (Map p66; 427-7548; cnr Ica & Camaná; 8-9am & 4:30-7:30pm Mon-Fri) The interiors are rather drab, but this church has an elaborate *churrigueresque* facade (completed in 1720), replete with stone carvings of angels, flowers, fruit and, of course, St Augustine.

4 **CASA DE PILATOS** (Map p66; 427-5814; Ancash 390, Central Lima; 8am-1pm & 2-5pm Mon-Fri) The lovely red Casa de Pilatos is home to the offices of the Tribunal Constitucional (Supreme Court). Access is limited; visitors are only allowed into the courtyard if there are no official meetings, so you may have to settle for views of the exteriors only. Enter via Azángaro.

**CASA SAN MARTÍN** Inn $$
**(Map p72; 241-4434, 243-3900; www.casasanmartinperu.com; San Martín 339; s/d/tr incl breakfast S156/218/273; @)** This Spanish Revival building is modern and uncluttered, with 20 pleasant, high-ceiling rooms with terra-cotta tiles and Andean textiles. Breakfast is served in a bright downstairs café.

**HOTEL ANTIGUA MIRAFLORES** Inn $$$
**(Map p72; 241-6116; www.peru-hotels-inns.com; Av Grau 350; s/d/tr incl breakfast S216/257/351; @)** In a converted early-20th-century mansion, this quiet, atmospheric hotel channels colonial charm. Rooms are equipped with the expected modern amenities, but the furnishings display baroque touches. Units vary in size and style; the more expensive ones have Jacuzzi tubs and kitchenettes.

**CASA ANDINA** Hotel $$$
**(213-9739; www.casa-andina.com)** San Antonio **(Map p72; 241-4050; Av 28 de Julio 1088; d incl breakfast S289; @)**; Miraflores Centro **(Map p72; 447-0263; Av Petit Thouars 5444; d incl breakfast S397; @)**; Colección Privada **(Map p72; 213-4300; Av La Paz 463; d/ste incl breakfast from S982/1291; @)** This upmarket Peruvian chain has three hotels at various price points. The San Antonio and Miraflores Centro lean towards the midrange, with 50-plus rooms decorated in contemporary Andean color schemes. Colección Privada is the luxury outpost, situated in a tower that once served as the home of the Hotel César (where Frank Sinatra once stayed). Its elegant lobby lounge maintains the grand piano from the storied César. The hotel's 148 chic, earth-palette rooms are spacious and feature organic bath products and turn-down service.

**HOTEL IBIS** Hotel $$
**(Map p72; 634-8888; www.ibishotel.com; Av José Larco 1140; d incl breakfast S183; @)** New to Lima, this French hotel chain is a good option with a great location. Small-

## Detour: Pachacamac

If you've been to Machu Picchu, the archeological complex of **Pachacamac** (☎430-0168; http://pachacamac.perucultural.org.pe; admission S6; ⏰9am-5pm Mon-Fri), 31km south of Lima, may not seem like much. But these dusty piles of adobe and stone couldn't be more important.

Pachacamac began life as a ceremonial center for the Lima culture beginning at about AD 100 and was later expanded by the Wari, as well as the Incas. When the Spanish arrived it was a bustling coastal city. The name Pachacamac, which can be roughly translated as 'He who Animated the World,' comes from a Wari god, whose wooden, two-faced image can be seen at the on-site museum. Centuries later, archaeologists are still unraveling the citadel's history: in 2012 an untouched burial chamber with 80 bodies was uncovered.

Visitors can climb various temple mounds, including the **Templo del Sol** (Temple of the Sun), which has nice views of the ocean. But the most remarkable structure is the **Palacio de las Mamacuna** (House of the Chosen Women), lined with a series of trapezoidal doorways. (Due to earthquake damage, it can only be admired from a distance.)

A simple map can be obtained at the ticket office. Those on foot should allow several hours to explore. (Take water and a hat – there is no shade to speak of.) Those with a vehicle can drive from structure to structure.

Agencies in Lima (see p75) offer guided tours (about S115 per person). You can also hire a taxi (from S25 per hour) from Lima.

ish rooms have a chic Ikea look, blackout curtains and soundproof windows. The hotel is divided into smoking and non-smoking floors and has biodegradable toiletries.

**HOSTAL EL PATIO** Guesthouse **$$**
**(Map p72; ☎444-2107; www.hostalelpatio.net; Diez Canseco 341A; s/d incl breakfast S126/156, s/d superior S156/186; @ 📶)** On a side street, just steps from the Parque Kennedy, this gem of a guesthouse has a cheery English- and French-speaking owner. Small, spotless rooms with cast-iron beds surround a courtyard with a trickling fountain. A few have small kitchenettes and minifridges.

**LA PAZ APART HOTEL** Apartment **$$$**
**(Map p72; ☎242-9350; www.lapazaparthotel.com; Av La Paz 679; s/d ste incl breakfast S336/420, 2-bedroom ste S700; ❄ @ 📶)** This modern high-rise may have a business-like demeanor, but the 25 suites here are clean and roomy – all equipped with tasteful decor, kitchenettes, minifridges and separate sitting areas. The most spacious sleeps up to five. There is a mini-gym.

**JW MARRIOTT HOTEL LIMA** Hotel **$$$**
**(Map p72; ☎217-7000; www.marriott.com; Malecón de la Reserva 615; d from US$320; ❄ @ 📶 🏊)** The five-star Marriott has a superb seafront location by the LarcoMar shopping mall, as well as rooms that sport a wide range of amenities and a casino and open-air tennis court (though wi-fi costs extra). If you're nervous about your next flight, check the departures board in the lobby.

### Barranco

**3B BARRANCO B&B** B&B **$$**
**(Map p76; ☎247-6915; www.3bhostal.com; Centenario 130; s/d incl breakfast S146/175; @ 📶)** Cool, clean and modern, this new boutique hotel has 16 minimalist rooms with plush burlap-colored bed covers,

CAROLINA MIRANDA ©

## Don't Miss Astrid y Gastón

This is the restaurant that started Peru's current food revolution. Now one of the older outposts of *novoandina* (Peruvian nouvelle cuisine) cooking in Lima, Gastón Acurio's French-influenced standard-bearer nonetheless remains a culinary force to be reckoned with. His seasonal menu is equipped with traditional Peruvian fare, but it's the exquisite fusion specialties – such as the seared fillets of *cuy* (guinea pig), served Peking-style, with fluffy purple-corn crêpes – that make this such a sublime fine-dining experience. The restaurant has a first-rate international wine list.

**NEED TO KNOW**

**Map p72; 444-1496, 242-5387; www.astridygaston.com; Cantuarias 175; mains S39-69; 12:30-3:30pm & 6:30pm-midnight Mon-Sat**

polished-concrete vanities and windows opening onto light boxes of tended greenery. Great value for the price.

**SECOND HOME PERÚ** B&B **$$$**
**(Map p76; 247-5522; www.secondhomeperu.com; Domeyer 366; d/ste incl breakfast S286/325;** @ **)** Run by the children of artist Victor Delfín, this lovely five-room Bavarian-style *casona* has claw-foot tubs, sculpted ironworks, a swimming pool and breathtaking views of the ocean.

## Eating

The gastronomic capital of the continent, Lima offers some of the country's most sublime culinary creations – from simple *cevicherías* (informal ceviche counters) to decorous fusion spots where the cuisine is bathed in foam.

### Central Lima

**EL CORDANO** Peruvian **$**
**(Map p66; 427-0181; Ancash 202; mains S8-26; 8am-9pm)** A Lima institution

since 1905, this old-world dining hall has served practically every Peruvian president for the last century (the presidential palace is across the street). It is known for its skillfully rendered *tacu tacu* (pan-fried rice and beans) and *butifarra* (French bread stuffed with country ham).

**TANTA** Cafe **$$**
**(Map p66; ☎428-3115; Psje de los Escribanos 142; mains S21-46; ⏰9am-10pm Mon-Sat, to 6pm Sun)** One of several informal bistros in the Gastón Acurio brand, Tanta serves Peruvian dishes, fusion pastas and sandwiches. The food is good, but desserts are better – try the heavenly passion-fruit cheesecake mousse.

**EL VERÍDICO DE FIDEL** Ceviche **$$**
**(www.elveridicodefidel.com; Abtao 935, La Victoria; ceviches S20-40; ⏰noon-5pm)** A place of pilgrimage, this hole-in-the-wall across from the Alianza Lima stadium is renowned for its *leche de tigre* (ceviche broth), served not in the typical shot glass but in a soup bowl, and piled high with fresh seafood. The neighborhood is rough; take a taxi.

**DOMUS** Peruvian **$**
**(Map p66; ☎427-0525; Miró Quesada 410; 3-course menús S16; ⏰9am-4:30pm Mon-Fri)** A restored 19th-century mansion houses this modern, yet intimate, two-room restaurant. There is no à la carte dining, just a rotating daily list of well-executed Peruvian-Italian specialties that always includes a vegetarian option. Freshly squeezed juice accompanies this well-tended feast.

**WA LOK** Chinese **$$**
**(Map p66; ☎447-1329, 427-2750; Paruro 878; mains S10-80; ⏰9am-11pm Mon-Sat, to 10pm Sun)** Serving seafood, fried rice and sizzling meats, Wa Lok is among the best *chifas* (Chinese restaurants) in Chinatown. The 16-page menu also offers a good selection of vegetarian options (try the braised tofu casserole). Portions are enormous; don't overorder.

## San Isidro

**MALABAR** Fusion **$$$**
**(Map p70; ☎440-5200; www.malabar.com.pe; Av Camino Real 101; mains S52-68; ⏰12:30-4pm & 7:30-11pm Mon-Sat)** Culinary star Pedro Miguel Schiaffino is the chef at this hot destination restaurant at the heart of San Isidro. Influenced by Amazonian produce, Schiaffino's seasonal menu features deftly prepared delicacies such as river snails bathed in a sauce made with spicy chorizo. Do not forego the cocktails (the chef's father, a pisco expert, consulted on the menu).

**MATSUEI** Japanese **$$**
**(Map p70; ☎422-4323; Manuel Bañon 260; maki S30-49; ⏰12:30-3:30pm & 7:30-11pm Mon-Sat)** Venerated Japanese superchef Nobu Matsuhisa once co-owned this diminutive sushi bar, now situated on a San Isidro side street. It's low-key, but it serves up spectacular sushi. A must-have: the 'acevichado' roll, which is stuffed with shrimp and avocado, and then doused in a house-made mayo infused with ceviche broth.

**SEGUNDO MUELLE** Ceviche **$$$**
**(Map p70; ☎421-1206; www.segundomuelle.com; Conquistadores 490; mains S23-69; ⏰noon-5pm)** A mainstay of impeccable service, this longtime *cevichería* is known for its innovative twists – such as *ceviche de mariscos a los tres ajíes,* a stack of succulent seafood bathed in a three-chili sauce.

**ANTICA** Pizzeria **$$**
**(Map p70; ☎222-9488; Av 2 de Mayo 732; mains S24-42; ⏰noon-midnight)** On a street littered with European restaurants, this is one of the most reasonable: a woody, candle-bedecked spot serving house-made pastas, gnocchis and pizzas from a wood-fired oven. Popular with families.

## Miraflores

**CENTRAL** Novo Andino **$$$**
**(Map p72; ☎242-8515; www.centralrestaurante.com.pe; Santa Isabel 376; mains S52-88; ⏰1-3pm & 8-11:30pm Mon-Fri, 8pm-midnight Sat)** Currently the toast of Lima, Central's chef, Virgilio Martínez, spent a decade in the

top kitchens of Europe and Asia before coming home to Lima. His charred octopus starter is a star and Peruvian classics like suckling pig dazzle, reinvented with pears, mustard and *tomate de arbol* (tree tomato). Sustainable fish and a rooftop herb garden enhance the ultrafresh appeal. Reservations highly recommended.

**EL ENANO** Sandwiches **$**

**(Map p72; Chiclayo 699; sandwiches S7-10; ⏲6am-3am)** Grab a stool at the open-air counter and watch masters making fresh-roasted chicken, ham, turkey and *chicharrón* (pork crackling) sandwiches on French bread dressed with marinated onions and chilis. If you've had one too many piscos, these will cure what ails you.

**PESCADOS CAPITALES** Seafood **$$$**

**(off Map p72; ☎421-8808; www.pescadoscapitales.com; Av La Mar 1337; mains S35-50; ⏲12:30-5pm daily, 7-11pm Mon-Sat)** On the northern edge of Miraflores, this contemporary destination serves some of the finest ceviche around. Try the 'Ceviche Capital,' a mix of flounder, salmon and tuna marinated with red, white and green onions and bathed in a three-chili crème.

**FIESTA** Peruvian **$$$**

**(Map p72; ☎242-9009; www.restaurantfiestagourmet.com; Av Reducto 1278; mains S40-50; ⏲lunch & dinner)** The finest northern Peruvian cuisine in Lima is served at this busy establishment (make a reservation). Not only do staff cook up an *arroz con pato a la chiclayana* (duck and rice Chiclayo-style) that is achingly tender, they also serve *ceviche a la brasa,* traditional ceviche that is given a quick sear, resulting in a fish that is lightly smoky, yet tender. Has to be eaten to be believed.

**RESTAURANT HUACA PUCLLANA** Peruvian **$$**

**(Map p72; ☎445-4042; www.resthuacapucllana.com; Gral Borgoño, cuadra 8; mains S18-60; ⏲12:30pm-midnight Mon-Sat, to 4pm Sun)** A sophisticated establishment overlooking the illuminated ruins at Huaca Pucllana, the menu here features an array of beautifully presented Peruvian dishes, from grilled *cuy* to seafood chowders. Portions are large. Save room for the pisco and lemon parfait come dessert.

**EL PUNTO AZUL** Seafood **$$**

**(Map p72; ☎445-8078; San Martín 595; mains S22-30; ⏲noon-5pm)** Awash in Caribbean

Lima market stall

## Detour: La Punta

A narrow peninsula that extends west into the Pacific Ocean, about 12km west of downtown Lima, La Punta was once a fishing hamlet and, later, in the 19th century, an upscale summer beach resort. Today this pleasant upper-middle-class neighborhood, graced with neocolonial and art-deco homes, is a good spot to stroll by the ocean and enjoy a leisurely seafood lunch.

At the humble fish house **Manolo** (Map p72; ☎429-8453; Malecón Pardo s/n, cuadra 1; ⏲lunch only) seafood diehards line up for fresh ceviche, grilled fish and hearty soups. Or step it up a notch at the waterfront **La Rana Verde** (☎429-5279; Parque Gálvez s/n; mains S29-55; ⏲lunch only), ideal for Sunday lunch within view of craggy Isla San Lorenzo, just off the coast. Dishes are all deftly prepared and the restaurant's *pulpo al olivo* (grilled octopus in a smashed olive sauce) is one of the best in town. It's located on the pier inside the Club Universitario de Regatas.

A taxi ride from Miraflores costs about S30.



blues, this pleasant family eatery dishes up superfresh ceviches and *tiraditos* (Japanese-influenced version of ceviche, served in thin slices and without onion), as well as big-enough-to-share rice dishes. Try the risotto with parmesan, shrimp and *ají amarillo* (yellow chili). It gets packed on weekends; show up before 1pm if you want a table.

**RAFAEL** Novo Andino $$$
(Map p72; ☎242-4149; rafaelosterling.com; San Martín 300; mains S35-68; ⏲1-3:30pm & 8pm-midnight) Don't let this restaurant's demure exterior fool you: this is *the* place in Lima to see and be seen. Here, Chef Rafael Osterling produces a panoply of fusion dishes, such as *tiradito* bathed in Japanese citrus or suckling goat stewed in Madeira wine. The restaurant's bar is an excellent spot for cocktails and Peruvian tapas.

**EL RINCÓN DEL BIGOTE** Ceviche $$
(Map p72; José Galvez 529; S21-28; ⏲noon-4pm Tue-Sun) On weekends, locals line up for seating in this bare-bones ceviche house. The specialty is *almejas en su concha* – marinated clams served in their shell. Pair these with a side of crisp *yuca* fries and a bottle of cold pilsner and you're in heaven.

**PANCHITA** Peruvian $$
(Map p72; ☎242-5957; Av 2 de Mayo 298; mains S33-56; ⏲12:30-9pm Mon-Sat, to 5pm Sun) This Gastón Acurio restaurant pays homage to Peruvian street food in a contemporary setting. *Anticuchos* (beef skewers) are grilled over an open flame to melt-in-your-mouth perfection. Also worth the cholesterol: the crisp suckling pig with *tacu tacu*. Arrive early – especially on weekends – it's first come first serve.

**EL PAN DE LA CHOLA** Cafe $
(off Map p72; Av La Mar 918; mains S8-15; ⏲8am-8pm Tue-Sat, 9am-1pm Sun) In South America, finding real, crusty whole-grain bread is rarer than striking gold. Enter this brick café baking four scrumptious varieties. There's European-style seating at big wooden tables; grab a sandwich or share the tasting plate with bread, olives, hummus and fresh cheese (S9).

**DÉDALO ARTE Y CAFE** Cafe $
(Map p72; Benavides 378; snacks S3-9; ⏲8am-10pm Mon-Fri, 10am-11pm Sat; 📶) Caffeine fiends find their way to this discreet café on the Parque Kennedy where coffee is as serious as a sacrament. Don't miss its moist cakes or the home-decor and accessories shop upstairs.

**Right:** Palacio Arzobispal, Plaza de Armas (p65);
**Below:** Water features at El Circuito Mágico del Agua (p69)

**LA TRATTORIA DI MAMBRINO** Italian $$
**(Map p72; ☎446-7002; Manuel Bonilla 106; mains S30-50; ⏲1-3pm & 8-11pm Mon-Sat, 12:30-4pm Sun)** Overseen by Ugo Plevisani and his wife, Sandra, this is one of the top Italian spots in town, serving traditional house-made pastas (think ravioli stuffed with veal and porcini) as well as delectable gnocchi.

**ALMAZEN** Vegetarian $$
**(Map p72; ☎243-0474; Federico Recavarren 298; mains S30; ⏲11am-11pm Mon-Fri, 5-11pm Sat)** A soothing spot featuring a rotating selection of organic dishes such as sweet-potato and ginger soup, as well as tarts and risottos. Wheat-free and vegan items are available.

**HELENA CHOCOLATIER** Sweets $
**(Map p72; ☎242-8899; http://helenachocolatier.com; Iglesias 498; chocolates from S3; ⏲10:30am-7:30pm Mon-Fri)** A longtime artisanal chocolate shop that crafts scrumptious 'Chocolates D'Gala,' each stuffed with fillings made from pecans, marzipan or raspberries and individually wrapped.

## Barranco

**LA 73** International $$
**(Map p76; ☎247-0780; Av El Sol Oeste 175; mains S34-39; ⏲noon-midnight)** Named for an iconic local bus, this contemporary bistro has an uncomplicated Peruvian-Mediterranean menu. It's not long but it has several standouts, including homemade artichoke ravioli stuffed with goat cheese, and a lovely duck risotto. To end on a sweet note, split the crisp, warm churros for dessert.

**CANTA RANITA** Ceviche $
**(Map p76; Unión s/n; mains S16-20; ⏲12:30-4pm Wed-Mon)** Getting here is a treasure hunt: look for Mercado Capullo in front of the Chung Yion and follow the stalls of

trinkets to the rear. The open-air grill is no-fuss wonderment, with locals drinking jars of *chicha* (corn beer) while biding the time until the divine *ceviche apaltado* (ceviche with avocado) or blackened octopus appears.

**CAFÉ BISETTI** Cafe $

**(Map p76; ☎713-9565; Av Pedro de Osma 116; coffee S8-16; ⏲8am-9pm Mon-Fri, 10am-11pm Sat, 3-9pm Sun)** Locals park their designer dogs out front of this roasting house with the finest lattes in town, well matched with fresh pastries or bitter chocolate pie.

## Drinking

**EL BOLIVARCITO** Bar

**(Map p66; ☎427-2114; Jirón de la Unión 958, Central Lima)** Facing the Plaza San Martín from the Gran Hotel Bolívar, this frayed-yet-bustling spot is known as 'La Catedral del Pisco' for purveying some of the first pisco sours in Peru.

**BAR PISELLI** Bar

**(Map p76; ☎252-6750; Av 28 de Julio 297, Barranco; ⏲10am-11pm Mon-Thu, to 3am Fri & Sat)** This Barranco bar – reminiscent of old Buenos Aires – beats all for ambience. There's live music on Thursdays provoking boisterous sing-alongs.

**CAFÉ BAR HABANA** Bar

**(Map p72; ☎446-3511; www.cafebarhabana.com; Manuel Bonilla 107, Miraflores; ⏲6pm-late Mon-Sat)** Run by a Cuban-Peruvian couple, this homey drinking establishment whips up delicious mojitos.

**AYAHUASCA** Cocktail Bar

**(Map p76; ☎247-6751; www.ayahuascabar.com; San Martín 130, Barranco; ⏲8pm-late)** A trendy lounge resides in a stunning restored *casona* full of Moorish architectural flourishes. There's a long list of contemporary cocktails, including the tasty Ayahuasca sour made with Amazonian *tambo* and coca leaves.

## South American Explorers

Now more than three decades old, the venerable **South American Explorers Club** (SAE; Map p72; ☎445-3306; www.saexplorers.org; Piura 135, Miraflores; 9:30am-5pm Mon-Fri, to 8pm Wed, to 1pm Sat) has long been an indispensable resource for travelers. It has an extensive library as well as a vast array of guides and maps for sale, from topographic plans to trail maps for the Inca Trail and Mt Ausangate near Cuzco, and the Cordillera Blanca and Cordillera Huayhuash near Huaraz.

The club is a member-supported, nonprofit organization (it helped launch the first cleanup of the Inca Trail). Annual dues are US$60 per person (US$90 per couple) and there are additional clubhouses in Cuzco, Quito and Buenos Aires. You can sign up in person at one of the offices or via the website.

Nonmembers are welcome to browse some of the information and purchase guidebooks and maps.

**BRAVO RESTOBAR** Cocktail Bar
(Map p70; ☎221-5700; www.bravorestobar.com; Conquistadores 1005, San Isidro) This mellow San Isidro lounge has able bartenders whipping up an encyclopedic cocktail menu. Try the silky-smooth *aguaymanto sour,* made with pisco and gooseberries.

**HUARINGAS** Lounge
(Map p72; ☎447-1883; Bolognesi 460, Miraflores; 9pm-late Tue-Sat) A popular watering hole located inside the Las Brujas de Cachiche restaurant, Huaringas serves a vast array of cocktails, including a well-recommended passion-fruit sour.

## Entertainment

Peruvian folk music and dance is performed on weekends at *peñas*. There are two main types of Peruvian music performed at these venues: *folklórica* and *criollo*. The first is more typical of the Andean highlands; the other, a coastal music driven by African-influenced beats. Admission varies; dinner is sometimes included in the price.

For tickets, **Teleticket** (☎613-8888; www.teleticket.com.pe) is a handy one-stop shop that sells admission to sporting events, concerts, theater and some *peñas*. See the website for locations.

**LAS BRISAS DEL TITICACA** Peña
(☎715-6960; www.brisasdeltiticaca.com; Wakuski 168, Central Lima; admission from S25) The best *folklórica* show in Lima is at this *peña* near Plaza Bolognesi in downtown.

**LA CANDELARIA** Peña
(Map p76; ☎247-1314; www.lacandelariaperu.com; Av Bolognesi 292, Barranco; admission from S31) In Barranco, a show that incorporates both *folklórica* and *criollo* music and dancing.

**GÓTICA** Club
(Map p72; ☎628-3033; www.gotica.com.pe; LarcoMar, Malecón de la Reserva 610, Miraflores; admission S40) A fashionable, high-energy dance spot in Miraflores comes with a churchy interior and a mix of DJs playing electronica, hip-hop and pop. It sometimes serves as a venue for live Latin dance bands.

**LA NOCHE** Live Music
(Map p76; ☎247-1012; www.lanoche.com.pe; Av Bolognesi 307, Barranco) Get ready to groove! This well-known tri-level bar in Barranco is the spot to see rock, punk and Latin music acts in Lima.

## Shopping

Small shops selling crafts dot the major tourist areas around Pasaje de los Escribanos in Central Lima and near the intersection of Diez Canseco and La Paz in Miraflores.

**LAS PALLAS** Handicrafts
**(Map p76; ☎477-4629; www.laspallasperu.com; Cajamarca 212, Barranco; ⏰10am-7pm Mon-Sat)** A wonderful handicrafts shop featuring a selection of the highest quality products from all over Peru. (It's on the radar of Sotheby's.) Ring the bell if the gate is closed during opening hours.

**DÉDALO** Handicrafts
**(Map p76; ☎477-0562; Sáenz Peña 295, Barranco; ⏰10am-7pm Mon-Sat)** A vintage *casona* housing a contemporary crafts store with a lovely courtyard café.

**MERCADO INDIO** Market
**(Map p72; Av Petit Thouars 5245, Miraflores)** The best place to find everything from T-shirts to pre-Columbian-style clay pottery to alpaca rugs to knockoffs of Cuzco School canvases.

**LARCOMAR** Mall
**(Map p72; Malecón de la Reserva 610, Miraflores)** A well-to-do outdoor mall with high-end alpaca shops and a wide range of eateries.

**EL VIRREY** Books
**(Map p72; ☎444-4141; www.elvirrey.com; Bolognesi 510, Miraflores; ⏰10am-7pm)** Lima's best bookshop has English tomes, as well as a vintage book room stocked with thousands of rare editions.

## Information

### Dangers & Annoyances

While the crime situation in Lima has improved immeasurably since the 1980s, this is still a big city, where a third of the population lives in poverty. Naturally, some crime is to be expected. The most common offense is theft and readers have reported regular muggings. You are unlikely to be physically hurt, but it is nonetheless best to keep a streetwise attitude.

Don't wear flashy jewelry or clothes and keep your camera in your bag when you're not using

Larcomar

it. It is best to keep your cash in your pocket and take only as much as you'll need for the day. Late at night, take taxis, especially in downtown, or if you're partying until late in Barranco.

### Emergency

**Clínica Good Hope** (Map p72; ☎610-7300; www.goodhope.org.pe; Malecón Balta 956) Quality care and there is a dental unit.

**Policía Nacional** (National Police; ☎460-0921; Moore 268, Magdalena del Mar; ⏰24hr)

**Tourism Police** (Policía de Turismo, Poltur; Map p72; ☎460-0844; Colón 246; ⏰24hr) A division of the Policía Nacional that usually has English-speaking officers who can provide theft reports for insurance claims or traveler's check refunds.

### Money

Banks are abundant, as are 24-hour ATMs, many of which dispense soles and US dollars. Use caution when making withdrawals late at night.

### Tourist Information

**iPerú** (www.peru.info) Aeropuerto Internacional Jorge Chávez (☎574-8000; Main Hall; ⏰24hr); Miraflores LarcoMar (Map p72; ☎445-9400; Module 14, on the lower level, LarcoMar, Malecón de la Reserva 610; ⏰noon-8pm); San Isidro (Map p70; ☎421-1627; Jorge Basadre 610; ⏰9am-6pm Mon-Fri) The government's reputable tourist bureau dispenses maps, offers good advice and can help handle complaints.

## Getting There & Away

### Air

Lima's **Aeropuerto Internacional Jorge Chávez** (code LIM; ☎517-3100; www.lap.com.pe; Callao) is stocked with the usual facilities, plus a pisco boutique. For international flights, it is advisable to arrive three hours prior to check-in.

Flights are subject to a departure tax (international/domestic US$31/6). These are generally included in the ticket.

### Bus

There is no central bus terminal; each company operates its ticketing and departure points independently. Some companies have several terminals, so always clarify from which point a bus leaves when buying tickets. In addition, companies have various classes of service. For long trips, look

Miraflores (p77)

for buses with *bus cama* service – large reclining seats. It is best to buy tickets in advance for popular destinations such as Cuzco.

The following companies are recommended:

**Cruz del Sur** (☎311-5050; www.cruzdelsur.com.pe) Central Lima (Off Map p66; ☎431-5125; Quilca 531); La Victoria (☎225-5748, 903-4149; Av Javier Prado Este 1109)

**Oltursa** (☎708-5000, 225-4495; www.oltursa.com.pe; Av Aramburu 1160, Limatambo)

**Ormeño** (☎472-1710; www.grupo-ormeno.com.pe) Central Lima (Map p66; Carlos Zavala Loayza 177); La Victoria (Av Javier Prado Este 1059)

**Tepsa** (☎202-3535; www.tepsa.com.pe) Central Lima (Map p66; ☎427-5642, 428-4635; Paseo de la República 151-A, Central Lima); Javier Prado (☎202-3535; Av Javier Prado Este 1091)

### Car

Lima has major intersections without stoplights, kamikaze bus drivers, spectacular traffic jams and little to no parking. If you still dare to get behind the wheel, there are several US companies that have 24-hour desks at the airport. Prices range from about S130-338 per day, not including surcharges, insurance and taxes (of about 19%). Hiring a taxi is your best option.

## Getting Around

### To/From the Airport

The airport is in the port of Callao, 12km west of downtown or 20km northwest of Miraflores. As you come out of customs, inside the airport to the right is the official taxi service, **Taxi Green** (☎484-4001; taxigreen.com.pe; Aeropuerto Internacional Jorge Chávez; 1-3 people to Central Lima, San Isidro, Miraflores & Barranco S50)

Allow at least an hour to the airport from San Isidro, Miraflores or Barranco. Traffic is lightest before 6:30am.

### Bus

**El Metropolitano** (www.metropolitano.com.pe), a new trans-Lima electric express bus system, is the fastest and most efficient way to get into the city center. Routes are few, though there are intentions to expand coverage. Ruta Troncal (S1.50) goes through Barranco, Miraflores and San Isidro to Plaza Grau in the center of Lima. Users must purchase a *tarjeta inteligente* (card S4.50) that can be credited for use.

Otherwise, caravans of *combis* (minivans) hurtle down the avenues with a *cobrador* (ticket taker) hanging out the door and shouting out the stops. Or you can go by the destination placards taped to the windshield. Your best bet is to know the nearest major intersection or landmark closest to your stop (eg Parque Kennedy) and tell that to the *cobrador* – they'll let you know whether you've got the right bus. *Combis* are generally slow and crowded, but startlingly cheap: fares run from S1 to S3.

The most useful routes link Central Lima with Miraflores along Av Arequipa or Paseo de la República. Minibuses along Garcilaso de la Vega (also called Av Wilson) and Av Arequipa are labeled 'Todo Arequipa.' To get to Barranco, look for buses along Av Arequipa labeled 'Chorrillos/Huaylas/Metro' (some will have signs that say 'Barranco'). You can also find these on the Diagonal, just west of the Parque Kennedy, in Miraflores.

### Taxi

Lima's taxis don't have meters, so negotiate a price with the driver before getting in. Fares will vary depending on the length of the journey, traffic conditions and time of day. Plan for paying extra for registered taxis and any taxi you hail outside a tourist attraction. As a (very) rough guide, a trip within Miraflores will cost S5–S8, while the journey from Central Lima to Miraflores will run S10–S15. If there are two or more of you, be clear on whether the fare is per person or for the car.

The majority of taxis in Lima are unregistered (unofficial). During the day, this is generally not a problem. However, at night it is usually safer to use registered taxis. Look for green or yellow taxis with numbered dome lights and a SETAME sticker on the windshield.

**Taxi Real** (☎470-6263; www.taxireal.com) accepts advance reservations and is recommended.

# Nazca, Arequipa & the South

## A thin ribbon of highway spans Peru's southern coastal desert.

The terrain is arid, punctuated by the presence of palm-fringed oases. Deep in the south, a mountain road turns east and climbs all the way to Arequipa (and beyond that, Lake Titicaca and Cuzco). Welcome to Peru's well-traveled Gringo Trail.

Despite the touristy nickname, it's an area that holds more depth and diversity than you might suspect. In Nazca, mysterious pre-Columbian glyphs cross vast expanses of desert. Off the coast of Paracas, penguins and sea lions come together on rocky outcroppings. And, in Arequipa, you'll find stately religious citadels that date back to the colony – along with some of the world's deepest canyons. It is an area that takes you through coast and mountain, through desert and gorge, along the rim of volcanoes where Incas once made human sacrifices.

What more could anybody possibly ask for?

La Catedral (p114), Arequipa

Sea lions, Islas Ballestas (p106)

# Nazca, Arequipa & the South

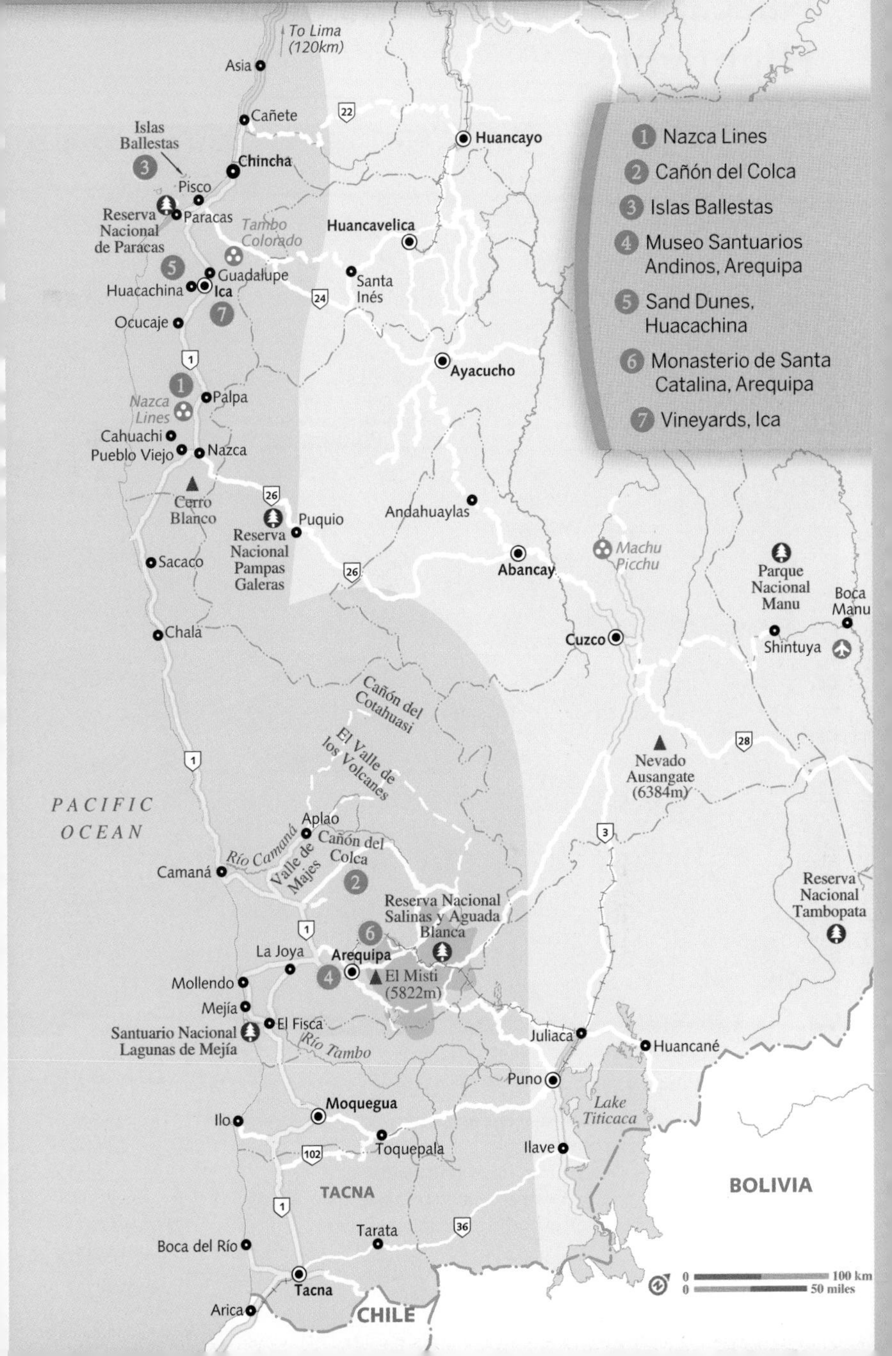

1 Nazca Lines
2 Cañón del Colca
3 Islas Ballestas
4 Museo Santuarios Andinos, Arequipa
5 Sand Dunes, Huacachina
6 Monasterio de Santa Catalina, Arequipa
7 Vineyards, Ica

# Nazca, Arequipa & the South Highlights

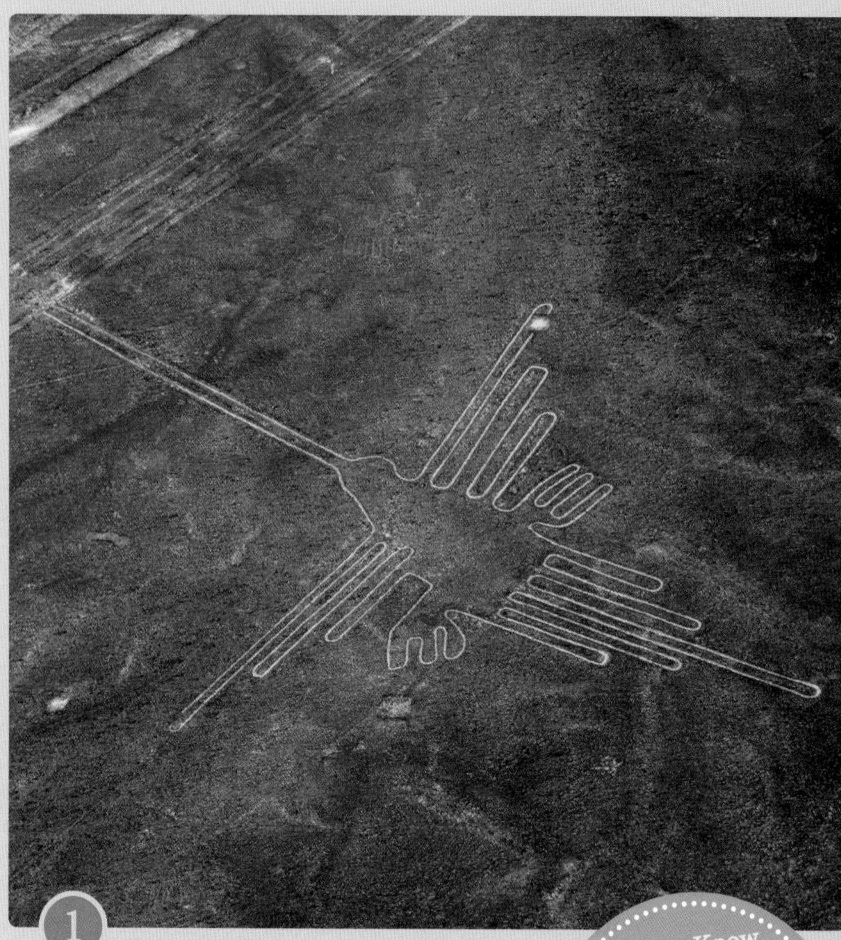

1

## Nazca Lines

The barren desert harbors mysterious ancient ruins: a set of carved glyphs so massive they can only be seen from the air. The Nazca Lines have long captured travelers' imaginations with their precision and scale. But stick around – the region is home to countless other pre-Columbian treasures, too.

**Need to Know**

**BEST TIME TO GO** December through March. **WEATHER** Temperatures are extreme. Take water, a jacket and a hat. **TIP** Book guides with a reputable agency. **For further coverage, see p109.**

# Nazca Lines Don't Miss List

BY ALBERTO URBANO JACINTO, ARCHAEOLOGIST OVERSEEING THE MINISTRY OF CULTURE'S OPERATIONS IN NAZCA

## 1 MUSEO MARIA REICHE

No trip to the Nazca area is complete without a visit to this wonderful little museum (p111) in honor of the archaeologist who dedicated more than 50 years of her life to excavating and documenting the Nazca lines. The region is a destination because of her.

## 2 MIRADOR

Right on the Pan-American Hwy at Km 424 is this 12m-tall viewing tower (p111), which offers unimpeded 360-degree views of the area. From here, you can see the glyphs known as the Tree, the Hand and the Lizard – as well as lots of trapezoidal shapes. It's great for snapping pictures.

## 3 MUSEO DIDÁCTICO ANTONINI

This is an excellent museum (p111) that provides a well-presented historical overview of the region. It also contains numerous finds that have turned up at the nearby tombs of Cahuachi – including lots of mummies.

## 4 REGIONAL COOKING

Nazca is an excellent spot to sample ceviche. We are on the coast so our seafood goes straight from ocean to plate – the freshest! To accompany that, I recommend any dish made with *pallares* (lima beans or butter beans). It's a native legume, grown in the region, and it dates back to pre-Inca times.

## 5 EXPLORE!

Many folks fly over the Nazca Lines and then leave. But this region has lots of amazing sites that don't always get into the guidebooks. In the nearby village of Palpa, there are ancient petroglyphs. To the west, in El Ingenio, you'll find old baroque churches. In San Fernando, about an hour south, there are wild beaches full of sea lions and penguins.

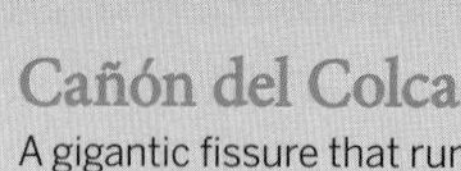

# Cañón del Colca

A gigantic fissure that runs for 100km across the High Andes, the Cañón del Colca (Colca Canyon) is rugged, deep and visually spectacular. Inhabited since pre-Inca times and later colonized by the Spanish, the region is characterized by its steeply terraced fields and fiercely traditional villages.

### Need to Know

**BEST TIME** The clearest months are April to June. **TICKETS** Foreigners need a S70 tourist ticket in Chivay. **AVOID** The rainy season, December to March. **For further coverage, see p125.**

2

Local Knowledge

# Cañón del Colca Don't Miss List

BY CARLOS MISTI ZÁRATE FLORES, NATIVE AREQUIPEÑO AND PROPRIETOR OF CARLOS ZÁRATE AVENTURAS, A RENOWNED TREKKING OUTFIT

## 1 CRUZ DE CONDOR

Despite the crowds, the Cruz del Cóndor (p129) is an essential Colca stop-off where you can view huge Andean condors as they glide above the steep canyon walls, especially between May and September. Arrive early: condors are generally more active between 8am and 10am, before they fly off to feed nearer the coast.

## 2 EL CLÁSICO TREK

The canyon's most popular trekking circuit is not just a hike, it's a revolving slice of Colca culture where you get to stay in houses owned by local people, and walk in the footsteps of their Inca ancestors. The trek, usually known as 'El Clásico,' can be done as a two- or three-day excursion starting and finishing in the village of Cabanaconde.

## 3 ESPINAR DE TUTI

Several kilometres above the village of Tuti in the upper canyon, reached via a footpath, are the remnants of a village abandoned by the Spanish in the early 1600s. It's an eerie place, where the stone walls of roofless houses and the ruins of a colonial church have withstood the ravages of time.

## 4 GEYSER DE PINCHOLLO

Pinchollo, on the south side of the Río Colca is one of the canyon's poorer villages with few tourist facilities. People in the know come here to trek three hours uphill to a geothermal area where a geyser spurts out of the mountainside.

## 5 CHURCHES

Unlike the Cañón del Cotahuasi, the Colca was colonized by the Spanish who brought their religion and ecclesial architecture with them. As a result, each of the dozen or so villages in the canyon has its own church and all of them are a different. Lari's is the largest, Coporaque's is the oldest, Yanque's has the most decorative exterior and Maca's, with a huge gilded altarpiece, is the most impressive inside.

## 3 Admire Rocking, Squawking Sea Life

Honking Humboldt penguins. Barking sea lions. Clacking Peruvian boobies. A boat tour to the Islas Ballestas (p106) – known as the 'poor man's Galapagos' – will offer you prime photo ops of the Pacific Ocean's most astonishing fauna. A plus: the journey will allow you enough distance to admire a candelabra-shaped glyph carved into a faraway mountainside.

Peruvian pelicans

## 4 Gaze Upon a Sacrificial Maiden

The Museo Santuarios Andinos (p114) in Arequipa contains the remains of 'Juanita, the Ice Princess,' a 12-year-old Inca girl who was sacrificed to the gods on a nearby mountain. Discovered in the 1990s, frozen, and almost entirely intact, the wondrous maiden now inhabits a special icy chamber within this small but well-kept university museum. It doesn't get more surreal – or moving – than this.

ANDREW WATSON/GETTY IMAGES ©

## Sail Down Sand Dunes

5

Surfing isn't just about catching waves. In the diminutive desert oasis (and party town) of Huacachina (p108), you can catch a ride on a dune. The area's undulating topography offers thrillseekers an opportunity to tool around in roaring dune buggies and sail down towering walls of sand on nothing but a board. Get ready to shred – and eat a lot of sand.

BILL BOCH/GETTY IMAGES ©

6

## Explore an Unusual Colonial Monastery

A city within a city is how Arequipa's rambling – and architecturally striking – Monasterio de Santa Catalina (p115) is often described. This expansive Catholic citadel, once a well-to-do nunnery, is a labyrinth of cloisters and courtyards. Among the many intriguing sights: a room that once served as a mortuary, where portraits of deceased nuns cover the stone walls.

7

## Take a Tour of Vineyards

Pisco sours. *Chilcano de pisco*. Pisco punch. At some point during your trip to Peru, you will likely sip the many cocktails crafted with Peru's renowned grape brandy. So why not go to the source? The pleasant community of Ica (p108) is home to bodegas (wineries) from the industrial to the artisanal – a perfect place to sip! Pisco sour cocktail

# Nazca, Arequipa & the South's Best...

## Restaurants

- **Zingaro** (p121) Nouveau renditions of Peruvian standards, such as alpaca ribs in red wine sauce
- **As de Oro's** (p107) Delectably fresh seafood served poolside in Pisco
- **Tradición Arequipeño** (p122) Traditional country cooking in Arequipa includes melt-in-your mouth slow-cooked pork
- **Zig Zag** (p121) In Arequipa, Peruvian fusion and hearty meat grills served on volcanic stone

## Museums

- **Museo Didáctico Antonini** (p111) An excellent overview of Nazca culture
- **Museo Regional de Ica** (p108) Trepanned skulls, mummified animals and superb Paracas weavings
- **Museo Santuarios Andinos** (p114) The body of a sacrificial Inca maiden...in a freezer
- **Museo de Arte Virreinal de Santa Teresa** (p117) A Carmelite convent boasting lavish colonial religious treasures

## Wildlife Encounters

- **Condors** (p129) Find them soaring over the Cañón del Colca
- **Humboldt penguins** (p106) These charismatic birds like to nest on the Islas Ballestas
- **Vizcachas** (p126) Fuzzy, superadorable bunnylike rodents that inhabit the flanks of El Misti
- **Flamingos** (p133) Flocks of three different species descend on the Laguna de Salinas during rainy season

## Adventures

- **Nazca Lines** (p110) Giant glyphs in the desert
- **Islas Ballestas** (p106) Protected islands with wildlife galore
- **Reserva Nacional de Paracas** (p104) A vast desert reserve
- **Cañón del Colca** (p125) One of the world's deepest canyons
- **El Misti** (p119) A pointy volcano that was the site of pre-Columbian human sacrifice

**Left:** Flamingos near Cañón del Colca (p125); **Above:** El Misti



# Need to Know

### ADVANCE PLANNING

- **Three months before** Make arrangements to trek the canyons around Arequipa
- **One month before** Reserve an overflight to see the Nazca Lines
- **One day before** Book a table at one of Arequipa's hopping high-end eateries

### GETTING AROUND

- **Air** The only commercial airport is in the city of Arequipa (p124), and offers regular service to Lima and Cuzco; small-craft flights to see the Nazca Lines take off from the aerodrome in Nazca
- **Bus** Frequent and comfortable long-haul buses travel to and from Lima on the coast, as well as Cuzco and Puno in the highlands
- **Boat** Employed only for visits of the Islas Ballestas (p106), the island nature reserve off the coast of Pisco
- **Walk** Perfect for the tight grid of streets in Arequipa (p114) – not to mention the multiday trekking trips in nearby canyons (p124)
- **Bike** Local mountain-biking tours are offered around Arequipa (p119)

### BE FOREWARNED

- **Museums** Most are closed on Mondays
- **Weather** Bad weather may hamper activities such as hiking, boating and trekking; ask about cancellation policies and keep tabs on the forecast
- **Sun** It's relentless on the desert coast. Pack a hat and good sunscreen
- **Unlicensed touts** There's a relentless crew of them in Nazca; stick to recommended agencies and registered guides
- **Robberies** Be careful at isolated beaches and off-the-beaten-path urban areas; it's best to walk in a group or ask locally before setting out

# Nazca, Arequipa & the South Itineraries

*The haul down the coast is long and dusty. If you're short on time, you can do the most significant coastal sites, such as the Nazca Lines, as a day tour from Lima, allowing more time later to explore the southern Andes.*

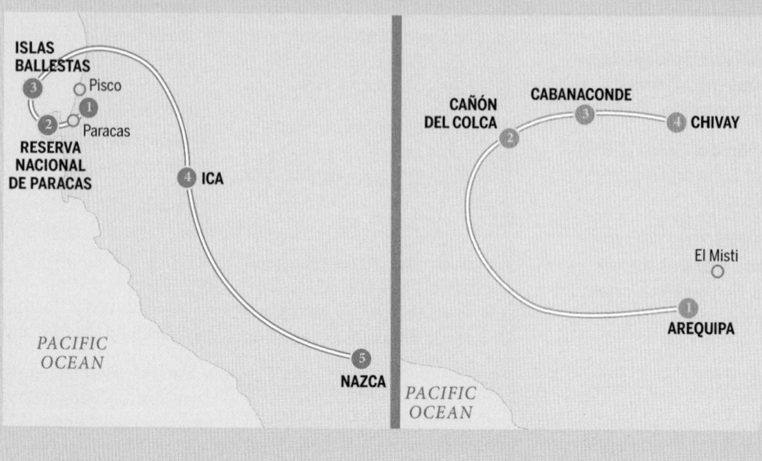

LIMA TO NAZCA

## Desert Caravan

This excursion takes you to the key sites of the southern Peruvian coast. The trip begins in Lima and makes its first stop at **(1) Pisco and Paracas**. The former is the port from which the liquor gets its name; the latter, a small town abutting a wilderness reserve. From here, you can ride through the **(2) Reserva Nacional de Paracas**, home to ancient cemeteries, then go for a boat tour around the **(3) Islas Ballestas**, which offers vistas of dramatic desert arches and colonies of honking birdlife. Afterwards, overnight in Paracas.

The next day, continue the journey down the coast. If you get an early start, pay a visit to the pisco-producing vineyards at **(4) Ica**. Otherwise, head to **(5) Nazca** for a flight over the mysterious pre-Columbian glyphs etched in to the desert. While you're in town, pay a visit to the Chauchilla Cemetery, a pre-Columbian tomb site that is bursting with mummies.

You'll spend the night here (in Nazca – not the cemetery!), and the next morning, return to Lima. If you want to extend the trip, continue on to the highland city of Arequipa.

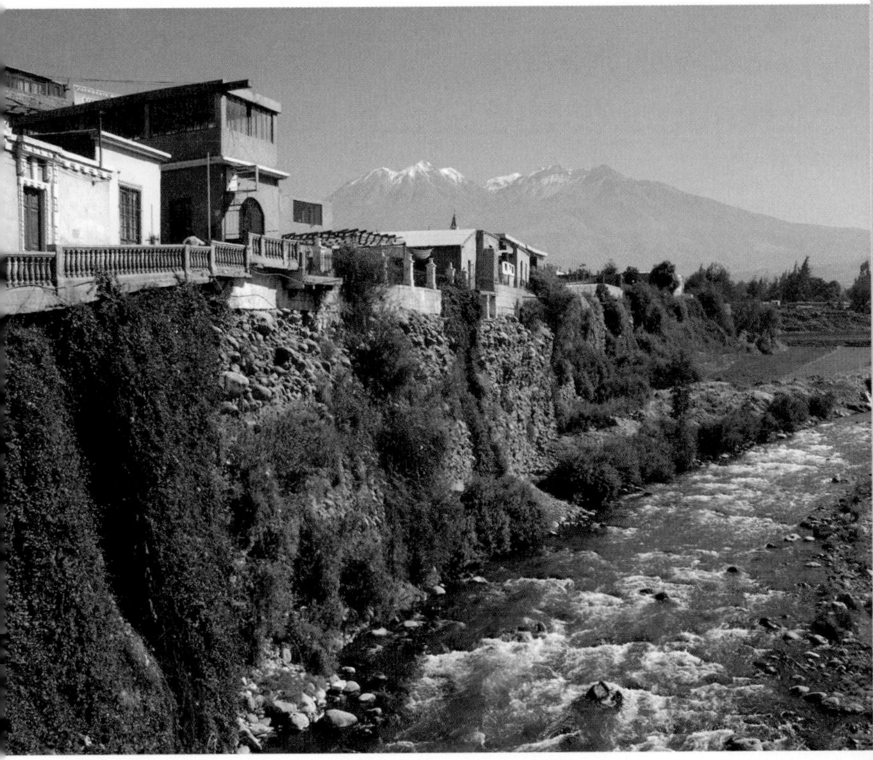

Río Chili (p118), Arequipa
LINDA WHITWAM/GETTY IMAGES ©

5 DAYS

AREQUIPA & THE CANYONS

## A Little Bit City, A Little Bit Country

A dash of colonial splendor. A dollop of rural idyll. And a heaping dose of wilderness. That's what you'll get on this combination trip around Peru's fabled 'White City.'

Start by flying into **(1) Arequipa**, or coming overland from Nazca. (Note: you can also fly from Cuzco.) Spend a day relaxing in the city's rambling colonial center while you acclimatize to the altitude. On your second day, pay a visit to the citadel-sized Monasterio de Santa Catalina and the frozen ice princess at the Museo Santuarios Andinos.

From here, choose between a two- or three-day guided excursion into the **(2) Cañón del Colca**. The first option is an overnight visit, done largely by car, with spurts of hiking and a stop at a lookout that allows for great views of the El Misti volcano. The second option is for the trekking set, and involves walking from **(3) Cabanaconde** to **(4) Chivay** (or vice versa), staying at simple village guesthouses along the way.

Afterwards, return to a day (or two) of rest in Arequipa, an opportunity to enjoy the spicy cuisine, teeming cultural scene and excellent nightlife.

# Discover Nazca, Arequipa & the South

## At a Glance

- **Pisco & Paracas** Side-by-side desert settlements abut coastal wildlife reserves.
- **Nazca** (p109) Home to some massive, mysterious desert glyphs.
- **Huacachina** (p108) A diminutive oasis, popular with sandboarders.
- **Arequipa** (p114) Graceful colonial architecture in a picturesque highland city.
- **Cañón del Colca** (p125) One of the world's deepest canyons.

Sand dune, Huacachina (p108)
ANDREW WATSON/GETTY IMAGES ©

## Pisco & Paracas

☎056 / POP 58,200

An important port situated 235km south of Lima, Pisco and the nearby town of Paracas are generally used as bases to see the abundant wildlife of the Islas Ballestas. Pisco also shares its name with the national beverage, a brandy that is made throughout the region. The area is of historical and archaeological interest, having hosted one of the most highly developed pre-Inca civilizations – the Paracas culture – from 700 BC until AD 400.

Though Pisco was crushed by a powerful 2007 earthquake, its spirit was not – and the city has begun to rebound. Paracas village lies 17km to the south. Its real name is El Chaco, but most people refer to it simply as 'Paracas.' It stands at the entrance to the Reserva Nacional Paracas, an important wildlife reserve, and has a motley resort strip that attracts everyone from youthful backpackers to moneyed *limeños* (inhabitants of Lima).

The area is spread out, but it's easy to get around.

### Sights

**RESERVA NACIONAL DE PARACAS** Nature Reserve

**(admission S5; ⏲7am-6pm)** This vast desert reserve occupies most of the Península de Paracas. About 2km beyond the entrance is the **Centro de Interpretación (⏲7am-6pm)**, which has a twee video devoted to local ecology. A better bet: the new **Museo Julio C Tello** next door, which was opened in 2012, and has a good display of ancient artifacts. The bay in front of the complex is the best

## Reserva Nacional de Paracas

spot to see Chilean flamingos, and there's a walkway down to a **mirador** (lookout), where these can best be spotted (June through August).

A few hundred meters behind the visitor complex are the 5000-year-old remains of the **Paracas Necropolis**, a prominent pre-Inca culture known for its lavish textiles. A stash of more than 400 funerary bundles was found here, each wrapped in many layers of colorful woven shrouds for which the Paracas culture is famous.

Beyond this, 6km away on the southern tip of the peninsula, lies the miniscule (and largely forgettable) fishing outpost of **Lagunillas**. From here, the road continues on a few more kilometers to **Punta Arquillo**, where a clifftop lookout has grand views of the ocean and a sea-lion colony. Other seashore life around the reserve includes flotillas of jellyfish, some of which reach 70cm in diameter, with trailing stinging tentacles of 1m. Swimmers beware!

### Reserva Nacional de Paracas

**Top Sights**

Museo Julio C Tello ........ C3

**Sights**

1 Candelabra Geoglyph ........ B2
2 Centro de Interpretación ........ C3
3 Mirador ........ C3
4 Paracas Necropolis ........ B3
5 Punta Arquillo ........ B3

**Sleeping**

6 Hotel Paracas ........ C3
7 La Hacienda Bahia Paracas ........ C3

**Transport**

8 Boats to Islas Ballestas ........ C2

**TAMBO COLORADO** Ruins
**(off Map p104; admission S9; dawn-dusk)** This early Inca outpost, 45km northeast of Pisco, was named for the red paint that once completely covered its adobe walls. It's one of the best-preserved sites on the south coast and is thought to have served as an administrative base and control point for passing traffic. From Pisco, it takes about an hour to get here by car. Hire a taxi for half a day (S50) or take a tour from Pisco (S60, two-person minimum).

JEFFREY BECOM/GETTY IMAGES ©

## Don't Miss Islas Ballestas

Grandiosely nicknamed the 'poor man's Galápagos,' the Islas Ballestas nonetheless make for a memorable excursion. The only way to see them is on a boat tour – and while the tours do not disembark onto the islands (they are protected), they do get you startlingly close to the wildlife. In general, an hour is spent cruising around the islands' arches and caves and watching herds of noisy sea lions sprawl on the rocks. The most common guano-producing birds in this area are the guanay cormorant, the Peruvian booby and the Peruvian pelican, seen in boisterous colonies several thousand strong. You'll also see cormorants, Humboldt penguins and, if you're lucky, dolphins.

On the outward boat journey, which takes about 90 minutes, you can't miss the famous three-pronged **Candelabra geoglyph** (Map p105), a giant figure etched into the sandy hills in the distance, more than 150m high and 50m wide. No one knows exactly who made the glyph, or when, or what it signifies, but theories abound.

Boats don't come equipped with cabins, so wear a hat, and dress to protect against the wind, spray and sun.

### Tours

Prices and services for tours of Islas Ballestas and Reserva Nacional de Paracas are usually very similar. The better tours are escorted by a qualified naturalist who speaks Spanish and English. Most island boat tours leave daily around 8am and cost around S35 per person, but do not include S6 in dock fees. Tours of the reserve can be combined with an Islas Ballestas tour to make a full-day excursion (S60).

Established tour operators include **Paracas Explorer** (☎53-1487, 54-5089; www.pparacasexplorer.com; Paracas 9, Paracas) and **Overland** (☎53-3855; www.paracasoverland.com.pe; San Francisco 111, Pisco).

## Sleeping

The best accommodations are located near Paracas.

### Pisco

**HOSTAL VILLA MANUELITA** Hotel **$$**
(**☎53-5218; www.villamanuelitahostal.com; San Francisco 227; s/d/tr incl breakfast S70/95/125; @**) Heavily renovated postearthquake, this hotel still achieves the grandeur of its colonial foundations. Plus, it's conveniently located half a block from the plaza.

**HOTEL RESIDENCIAL SAN JORGE** Hotel **$$**
(**☎53-2885; www.hotelsanjorgeresidencial.com; Barrio Nuevo 133; s/d/tr incl breakfast S85/110/130;**) A breezy, modern entryway sets the tone for an older building that has been added to. There's a bright cafe, and back garden with lounge chairs around a pool. Rooms in the new wing have a splash of tropical color; older ones can be dark and cramped.

### Paracas

**HOTEL PARACAS** Resort **$$$**
(**Map p105; ☎in Lima 01-518-6500; www.starwoodhotels.com; Av Paracas 178; r from US$230;**) A dreamscape plucked from a tourist brochure with gleaming ocean-view rooms, puffed cushions, excellent kid's facilities, a luxuriously raked beach, a permanently smiling staff – not to mention a full spa that offers 24kt-gold facials. Accommodation with all the trimmings is provided in two-story villas surrounded by elegant gardens.

**LA HACIENDA BAHIA PARACAS** Resort **$$$**
(**Map p105; ☎213-1000; www.hoteleslahacienda.com; Santo Domingo lot 25; s/d US$220/260;**) The luxury Hacienda has the air of an all-inclusive resort with some welcome local touches – such as replica Inca murals. Lovely terraces overlook curvaceous swimming pools, and a nice private slice of beach kisses Paracas Bay. There's a restaurant, spa, Jacuzzi and sauna splayed across the well-watered grounds.

**HOTEL GRAN PALMA** Hotel **$**
(**☎665-5933; www.hotelgranpalma.com; Calle 1 lot 3; d S48;**) The newest hotel in on-the-up Paracas is this brain-surgery-clean abode that offers breakfast on a pleasant rooftop terrace. The functional minimalist rooms sparkle, but leave little space for storage.

## Eating & Drinking

### Pisco

**AS DE ORO'S** Peruvian **$$**
(**San Martín 472; mains S30-50; ⏰noon-midnight Tue-Sun**) The plush As de Oro's serves dishes such as spicy mashed potato with octopus, plaice with butter and capers, and grilled prawns with fried *yucca* and tartar sauce on a deck overlooking a small swimming pool.

**TABERNA DE DON JAIME** Bar
(**☎53-5023; San Martín 203; ⏰4pm-2am**) This clamorous tavern is a favorite with locals and tourists alike for its artisanal wines and piscos. On weekends, the crowds show up to dance to live Latin and rock tunes into the small hours.

### Paracas

**EL CHORITO** Seafood **$$**
(**Paracas; mains S20-30; ⏰noon-9pm**) The Italians come to the rescue in the clean, polished Chorito, where a welcome supply of Illy coffee saves you from the otherwise ubiquitous powdered Nescafé. The cooked-to-order fish dishes aren't bad either – all locally caught, of course.

**JUAN PABLO** Seafood **$$**
(**Blvd Turístico; mains S15-40; ⏰7am-9pm**) Probably the best of the restaurants with a waterfront view, Juan Pablo is a winner for fresh seafood and offers breakfast for those departing early to the Islas Ballestas.

## Detour: Ica

If you're visiting Pisco, Paracas or Huacachina, a short trip will take you to Ica, where you can visit bodegas (wineries) and see Peru's famous grape brandy, pisco, being made from scratch. It also offers a good lodging alternative to the tour-group scene at Nazca or the party scene in Huacachina. Following are a few recommended spots:

**Bodega Tacama** (22-8395; www.tacama.com; www.tacama.com; 9am-4:30pm) This sprawling pink hacienda backed by fields of vines is home to a much-lauded winery. It's 11km northwest of Ica.

**Bodega Ocucaje** (40-8011; Av Principal s/n; tastings 9am-noon & 2-5pm Mon-Fri, 9am-noon Sat, tours 11am-3pm Mon-Fri) Some of Peru's finest wines and piscos come from this famous bodega, 30km south of Ica.

**Bodega Vista Alegre** (23-2919; Camino a La Tinguina, Km 2.5; 8am-noon & 1:45-4:45pm Mon-Fri, 7am-1pm Sat) The easiest of the bodegas to visit.

**Museo Regional de Ica** (23-4383; Ayabaca, cuadra 8; admission S11.50, cameras S5; 8am-7pm Mon-Fri, 9am-6pm Sat & Sun) Superb examples of Paracas weavings.

**Hotel Las Dunas Sun Resort** (25-6224; www.lasdunashotel.com; Av La Angostura 400; d/tr from S333/376; ) This sprawling resort is well equipped and organizes area excursions, including visits to bodegas.

**El Otro Peñoncito** (Bolívar 225; mains S9-26; 8am-midnight Mon-Fri) The bartenders at this historic restaurant shake a mean pisco sour.

### Information

There's no tourist office in Pisco, but travel agencies on the main plaza and **police** (53-2884; San Francisco 132; 24hr) help when they can. Everything else you'll need is found around the Plaza de Armas, including internet cafes.

On its knees after the earthquake, the city acquired a reputation for crime, but the curtain is lifting. Commerce-packed streets should be fine during the daytime (there's a notable police presence in the city center). After dark, it's best to utilize taxis.

### Getting There & Around

Pisco is 6km west of the Carr Panamericana Sur, and only buses with Pisco as the final destination actually go there. A number of companies offer service between Lima and the beach district of Paracas, stopping at various points in the area. These include:

**Cruz del Sur** (53-6336)

**Oltursa** (in Lima 01-708-5000; www.oltursa.com.pe)

**Ormeño** (53-2764; San Francisco, Pisco)

These companies also make the journey to points south, such as Ica, Nazca and Arequipa. Onward bus tickets can be purchased via Paracas Explorer (p106).

A short taxi ride around town costs roughly S3. A collective taxi between Pisco and Paracas costs roughly the same and takes 20 minutes. These depart frequently near Pisco's central market.

## Huacachina

056 / POP 200

With its aesthetically perfect desert-oasis proportions – think: lagoon, surrounded by palm trees and dunes – and its long menu of outdoor activities, it's no wonder that Huacachina has become popular among the backpacker set. And while that means plenty of nightlife noise and tie-dye T-shirts, it nonetheless remains a sublime place to stopover.

## Activities

You can rent sandboards for S5 an hour to slide, surf or ski your way down the dunes, getting sand lodged in every bodily orifice. (Though sandboarding is softer and warmer than snowboarding, don't be lulled into a false sense of security – people have injured themselves doing this.) Many hotels offer thrill-rides in *areneros* (dune buggies). They'll drop you off at the top of a slope and then meet you down at the bottom.

The going rate for tours at the time of writing was S45 (plus a S4 fee that must be paid upon entering the dunes). Ask if a sandboard is included in the rate and how long the tour lasts.

Hotels in Huacachina and Ica can all help arrange tours.

## Sleeping & Eating

**HOTEL EL HUACACHINERO** Hotel $$
(☎21-7435; www.elhuacachinero.com; Perotti; s/d/tr incl breakfast S100/110/140; ❄📶🏊) Recently upgraded, the Huacachinero logs the finest restaurant in the oasis, agreeably rustic rooms and a relaxing pool area (no blaring music). There is direct dune access via the back gate if you're up for a 45-degree climb to the sunset of your dreams.

**HOTEL MOSSONE** Historic Hotel $$$
(☎21-3630; Balneario de Huacachina; s/d/ste S200/260/315; ❄@📶🏊) This once posh *balneario* (resort hotel) is equipped with huge rooms that are really two in one: a *sala* (sitting area) and a high-ceiling bedroom. The atmospheric central courtyard with its chipped paving stones and wire-mesh aviary looks like something out of time-warped Cuba. There's a private pool across the road.

## Nazca & Around

☎056 / ELEV 590M

It's hard to say 'Nazca' without following it immediately with the word 'Lines', a reference to the ancient geometric shapes and enigmatic animal geoglyphs that dot the desert area. These great etchings are thought to have been made by a pre-Inca civilization sometime between AD 450 and 600, but question marks still hang over how they were made and by whom.

Lagoon, Huacachina

ANDREW WATSON/GETTY IMAGES ©

## Nazca

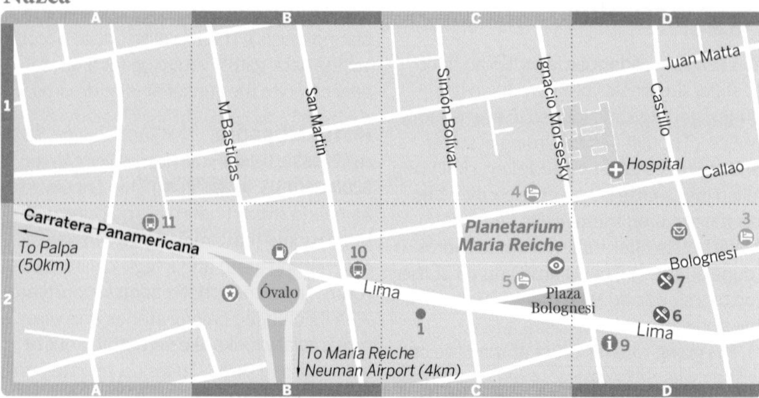


**Nazca**

**Top Sights**

Planetarium Maria Reiche ........ C2

**Activities, Courses & Tours**

1 Alas Peruanas ........ C2
Alegría Tours ........ (see 1)
2 Kunan Tours ........ E1

**Sleeping**

3 Casa Andina ........ D2
4 Hotel Oro Viejo ........ C1
5 Nazca Lines Hotel ........ C2

**Eating**

6 La Taberna ........ D2
7 Via La Encantada ........ D2

**Information**

8 BCP ........ E2
9 DIRCETUR ........ D2

**Transport**

10 Cruz del Sur ........ B2
11 Ormeño ........ A2

Documented for the first time by North American scientist Paul Kosok in 1939 and declared a Unesco World Heritage site in 1994, the lines today are the south coast's biggest tourist attraction. That means the otherwise insignificant desert town of Nazca (population 57,500) can be a bit of a circus. For more information on these mysterious lines, see the boxed text on p112.

## Sights & Activities

**NAZCA LINES** Archaeological Site

The best-known lines are found in the desert 20km north of Nazca. By far the best way to appreciate them is to get a bird's-eye view from a *sobrevuelo* (overflight). For more on the lines and their possible meaning, turn to p112.

Flights are taken in light aircraft (three to nine seats) in the morning and early afternoon. The standard 30-minute overflight starts at about US$80. Many agencies also offer combination flights that include a visit to the glyphs in the nearby community of Palpa. These take an hour or more and are more expensive. Tour packages generally include transportation to the aerodrome, about 4km outside town.

**A word about safety:** in 2010 two *sobrevuelos* crashed in a period of eight months, causing a total of 13 fatalities. This follows an equally catastrophic accident from 2008, in which five French tourists were killed. As a result, some changes have been made: all planes now fly with two pilots and prices have gone up to make sure companies don't cut corners on maintenance. Nonetheless, it pays to put safety before price. Question any company charging less than US$80 for the standard 30-minute excursion.

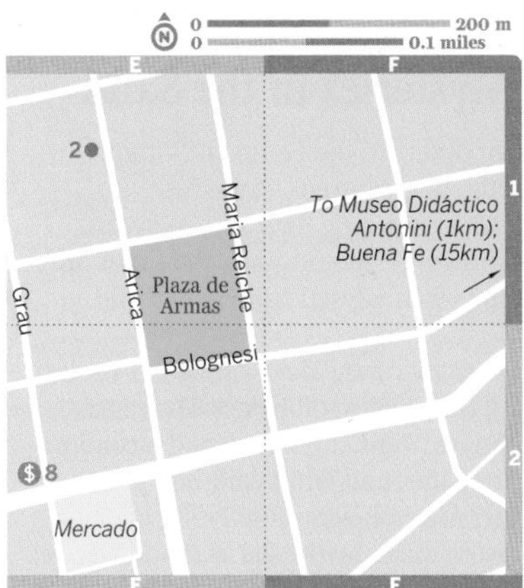


Recommended outfitters include:

**Aeroparacas** (www.aeroparacas.com) One of the better airline companies.

**Aerodiana** (☎444-3057; www.aerodiana.com.pe) Also has overflights departing from Pisco.

**Alas Peruanas** (☎52 2497; www.alasperuanas.com) Another long-time operator.

**MIRADOR** Lookout
**(observation tower; admission S1)** This metal lookout tower on the Pan-American Hwy, about 20km north of Nazca, has an oblique view of three of the figures: the lizard, tree and hands (or frog). If you decide to walk around the desert here, note the signs warning of landmines. These are a reminder that walking on the lines is strictly forbidden: it irreparably damages them.

**MUSEO MARIA REICHE** Museum
**(Museo de Sitio; admission S5; 9am-6pm)** When Maria Reiche, the German mathematician and long-term researcher of the Nazca Lines, died in 1998, her house, which stands another 5km north along Carr Panamericana Sur, was made into a small museum. Though it provides scant information, you can see where she lived, amid the clutter of her tools and sketches, and pay your respects at her tomb.

**MUSEO DIDÁCTICO ANTONINI** Museum
**(http://digilander.libero.it/MDAntonini; Av de la Cultura 600; admission S15, cameras S5; 9am-7pm)** On the east side of town, this excellent archaeological museum has an aqueduct running through the back garden, as well as interesting reproductions of burial tombs, a valuable collection of ceramic pan flutes and a scale model of the Lines. You can get an overview of both the Nazca culture and a glimpse of most of Nazca's outlying sites here.

**PLANETARIUM MARIA REICHE** Planetarium
**(☎52-2293; www.concytec.gob.pe/ipa/inicio_ingles.htm; Nazca Lines Hotel, Bolognesi s/n; admission S20)** This small planetarium in the Nazca Lines Hotel offers scripted evening lectures on the Lines with graphical displays on a domed projection screen.

Quechua woman spinning wool
JOHN WARBURTON-LEE/GETTY IMAGES ©

## The Nazca Lines: Ancient Mysteries in the Sand

Spread across 500 sq km of arid, rock-strewn desert in the Pampa Colorada (Red Plain), the Nazca Lines remain one of the world's great mysteries. Consisting of more than 800 straight lines, 300 geometric figures (geoglyphs) and some 70 spectacular plant and animal drawings (biomorphs), the Lines are almost imperceptible at ground level. It's only when viewed from above that they form their striking network.

They were made by the simple process of removing the dark sunbaked stones from the surface of the desert, thus exposing the lighter soil below. The most elaborate designs represent animals, including a lizard, a monkey and a condor.

Yet questions remain. Who constructed the Lines and why? And how did they do it if the Lines are only visible from the air? Maria Reiche (1903–98), a long-time Nazca researcher, theorized that they were made by the Paracas and Nazca cultures between 900 BC and AD 600, with later additions by Wari settlers in the 7th century. Some have hypothesized that the Lines linked ceremonial sites. Others have suggested they were a giant running track. A more down-to-earth theory, given the value of water in the desert, was suggested by anthropologist Johann Reinhard, who believed that the Lines were involved in mountain worship and a fertility/water cult.

About the only thing that is certain is that when the Nazca set about turning their sprawling desert homeland into an elaborate art canvas, they also began a debate that will keep archaeologists busy for centuries to come.

Call ahead or check the posted schedule. These last about 45 minutes.

**CHAUCHILLA CEMETERY** Cemetery

**(admission S5)** The most popular excursion from Nazca, this cemetery, 30km south of the city, will satisfy any urges you have to see mummies. Dating back to the Ica-Chincha culture, around AD 1000, the mummies were, until recently, scattered haphazardly across the desert, left by ransacking tomb-robbers. Now they are seen carefully rearranged inside a dozen or so tombs. Organized tours last three hours and cost US$10 to US$35 per person.

**CAHUACHI** Ruins

**(⌚9am-4pm)** A dirt road travels 25km west from Nazca to Cahuachi, the most important known Nazca center, which is still undergoing excavation. It consists of several pyramids, a graveyard and an enigmatic site called Estaquería, which may have been used as a place of mummification. Tours from Nazca take three hours and cost US$15 to US$50 per person.

**CERRO BLANCO** Adventure Tour

Located 14km east of Nazca, Cerro Blanco is the highest sand dune in the world. It resides 2078m above sea level and – more importantly – stands 1176m from base to summit, higher than the tallest mountain in England. Trips leave from Nazca at about 4am to avoid the intense heat. The arduous climb to the top of the dune (buggies can't climb this behemoth) takes approximately three hours. Going down is counted more in minutes.

## Tours

These established agencies cover the range of tours, from sandboarding to mountain-biking to visits of the Islas Ballestas:

**Alegría Tours** (☎52-3775; www.alegriatoursperu.com; Hotel Alegría, Lima 168)

**Kunan Tours** (☎52-4069; www.kunantours.com; Arica 419)

## Sleeping

**CASA ANDINA** Boutique Hotel **$$$**
**(☎52-3563; www.casa-andina.com; Bolognesi 367; r incl breakfast buffet from S272; ❄@📶≋)** This newly renovated Peruvian chain hotel offers the best value for money of any of Nazca's upmarket hotels. Earthy rooms have eminently stylish, modern furnishings with bold color schemes, air-con and cable TV.

**NAZCA LINES HOTEL** Hotel **$$$**
**(☎52-2293; www.peru-hotels.com/nazlines.htm; Bolognesi s/n; s/d/tr/q incl buffet breakfast; S288/337/399/459; ❄@📶≋)** Exceedingly tranquil considering its city center location, this lauded hotel is arranged around a large courtyard complete with lovely swimming pool and fountain. There is an on-site planetarium, a shop and a comfy lounge – though not officious service.

**HOTEL ORO VIEJO** Hotel **$$**
**(☎52-3332, 52-1112; www.hoteloroviejo.net; Callao 483; s/d/tr/ste incl buffet breakfast S100/140/170/315; ❄@📶≋)** This charming hotel retains a familial atmosphere and has airy, well-furnished rooms, a welcoming common lounge, an exquisitely tended garden and even a souvenir shop.

**HOTEL NUEVO CANTALLOC** Hotel **$$$**
**(☎52-2283; www.hotelnuevocantalloc.com; s/d incl breakfast S299/516; ❄@📶≋)** The rechristened Nuevo Cantalloc (formerly Hotel Cantayo Spa & Resort) feels less like a hotel and more like a posh retreat. Rooms (some furnished with antiques) are located in a hacienda-style building and the extensive grounds come with peacocks, ostriches and even a meditation circle.

## Eating

**VIA LA ENCANTADA** Peruvian **$$**
**(www.hotellaencantada.com.pe; Bolognesi 282; mains S20-40)** The best restaurant on the 'Boulevard' (Bolognesi), La Encantada sparkles in Nazca's dusty center with well-placed wine displays, great coffee and courteous and friendly wait-staff. The extensive menu features pasta and Peruvian favorites.

**LA TABERNA** Peruvian **$**
**(☎52-3803; Lima 321; menús S6, mains from S15; 🕒lunch & dinner)** Though it's a hole-in-the-wall, the scribbles covering every inch of wall are a testament to its popularity. Try the spicy fish, challengingly named *'Pescado a lo Macho'* ('macho fish') or choose from a list of vegetarian options.

## Information

Internet cafes abound.

**BCP (Lima 495)** Has a Visa/MasterCard ATM and changes US dollars and traveler's checks.

**DIRCETUR (Parque Bolognesi, 3rd fl)** The government tourist information office; can recommend local tour operators.

### Dangers & Annoyances

Nazca is filled with persistent *jaladores* (touts) trying to sell tours or take passengers to hotels. Pay hotel rooms directly at the front desk and never hand money over for a tour unless the company has given you a confirmed itinerary and receipt in writing.

## Getting There & Around

### Bus & Taxi

Nazca is a major destination for buses on the Carr Panamericana Sur and is easy to get to from Lima, Ica or Arequipa. The following long-haul companies are recommended:

**Cruz del Sur** (☎52-3713)

**Ormeño** (☎52-2058)

A taxi from central Nazca to the aerodrome, 4km from the town, costs about S4.

## Detour: Reserva Nacional Pampas Galeras

This national reserve is a **vicuña sanctuary** high in the mountains 90km east of Nazca on the road to Cuzco. It is the best place to see these shy animals, which are the threatened wild relatives of alpacas. Every year in late May or early June is the *chaccu,* when hundreds of villagers round up vicuñas for shearing and three festive days of traditional ceremonies. Full-day or overnight tours from Nazca cost US$30 to US$90 per person.



# Arequipa

054 / POP 864,300 / ELEV 2350M

Peruvians joke that you need a different passport to enter Peru's second-largest city, a metropolis that is one-tenth the size of Lima but pugnaciously equal to it in terms of cuisine, historical significance, and confident self-awareness. Guarded by not one, but three dramatic volcanoes, it is renowned for its formidable ensemble of baroque-*mestizo* buildings crafted out of *sillar* – a white volcanic rock that is common to the region. Certainly, the sight of the gigantic cathedral, with the ethereal image of the 5825m El Misti rising behind it, is worth the visit alone.

The city is also an important cultural center: Nobel laureate Mario Vargas Llosa was born here, and the city's spicy cuisine has played a fundamental role in the country's gastronomic renaissance.

### History

Evidence of pre-Inca settlement by indigenous peoples from the Lake Titicaca area leads some scholars to think the Aymara people first named the city (*ari* means 'peak' and *quipa* means 'lying behind' in Aymara; hence, Arequipa is 'the place lying behind the peak' of El Misti). However, another oft-heard legend says that the fourth *inca* (king), Mayta Cápac, was traveling through the valley and became enchanted by it. He ordered his retinue to stop, saying, '*Ari, quipay,*' which translates as 'Yes, stay.' The Spaniards refounded the city on August 15, 1540 – a date that is remembered with a weeklong fair.

## Sights

**MUSEO SANTUARIOS ANDINOS** Museum

**(20-0345; www.ucsm.edu.pe/santury; La Merced 110; admission S20; 9am-6pm Mon-Sat, to 3pm Sun)** This small museum is dedicated to preserving the body of 'Juanita,' the so-called 'Ice Maiden' – the remains of a 12-year-old Inca girl sacrificed atop Nevado Ampato many centuries ago. Visits begin with a beautifully shot 20-minute film and are followed by a guided tour of a series of dimly lit rooms filled with artifacts related to her burial. The climax is the vaguely macabre sight of the girl, now eerily preserved in a glass refrigerator.

**PLAZA DE ARMAS** Square

Arequipa's main plaza is a monument to the city's *sillar* architecture – white, muscular and aesthetically unique. Impressive colonnaded balconies line three sides. The fourth is given over to the cathedral, a humungous edifice with two soaring towers.

**LA CATEDRAL** Cathedral

**(7-11:30am & 5-7:30pm Mon-Sat, 7am-1pm & 5-7pm Sun)** Originally built in the 17th century (and rebuilt many times since), the cathedral's luminous interiors contain 12 Italian marble columns (symbolizing the 12 Apostles) and a Byzantine-style brass lamp from Spain. In 1870 Belgium provided the organ, said to be the largest in South America – though damage dur-

ALEX E. PROIMOS/GETTY IMAGES ©

## Don't Miss Monasterio de Santa Catalina

Occupying a whole block in Arequipa is one of the most fascinating religious buildings in Peru. This **convent** – really a 20,000-sq-meter citadel – is a disorienting place with twisting passageways, ascetic living quarters, period furnishings and religious art. In other words: a photographer's paradise.

Santa Catalina was founded in 1580 by a rich widow, Doña María de Guzmán, who chose her nuns from only the best Spanish families. Traditionally, going into a nunnery meant living a chaste life of poverty. However, in this privileged convent, nuns had servants or slaves and would often invite musicians to parties. After three centuries of these hedonistic goings-on, Pope Pius IX sent a strict Dominican nun to straighten things out. Sister Josefa Cadena arrived like a hurricane in 1871, sending rich dowries back to Europe and freeing the myriad servants and slaves, some of whom stayed on as nuns.

Today, visitors can examine several **cloisters** – including the **Great Cloister**, which is bordered by a chapel – as well as unusual sights such as the **Profundis Room**, a mortuary where the dead were mourned. (Lining the walls here are portraits of deceased nuns, all painted posthumously.) Other sights include the **communal kitchen**, a small square (called **Zocodober Square**) and the **cell** of the legendary Sor Ana, a nun known for her eerily accurate predictions.

### NEED TO KNOW

**☎22-9798; www.santacatalina.org.pe; Santa Catalina 301; admission S30; ⌚9am-5pm, last entry 4pm, plus 7-9pm Tue & Thu**

ing shipping condemned the devout to wince at its distorted notes for more than a century. It is the only cathedral in Peru that stretches the length of a plaza.

**IGLESIA DE LA COMPAÑÍA** Church
**(⌚9am-12:30pm & 3-6pm Mon-Fri, 11:30am-12:30pm & 3-6pm Sat, 9am-noon & 5-6pm Sun)**
This diminutive Jesuit church on the

## Arequipa

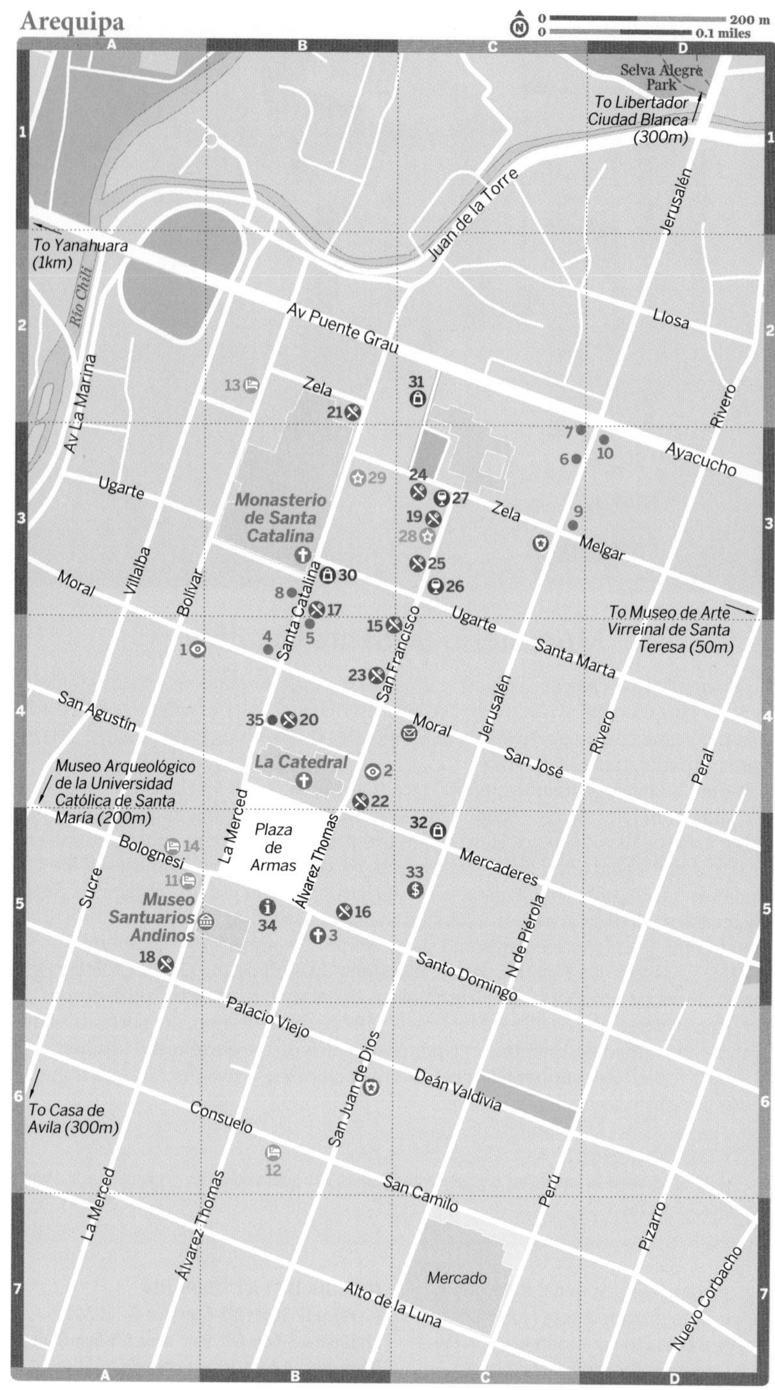

200 m
0.1 miles
Selva Alegre Park
To Libertador Ciudad Blanca (300m)
To Yanahuara (1km)
Río Chili
Juan de la Torre
Jerusalén
Av Puente Grau
Llosa
Av La Marina
Zela
Rivero
Ayacucho
Ugarte
Monasterio de Santa Catalina
Melgar
Moral
Villalba
Bolívar
Santa Catalina
To Museo de Arte Virreinal de Santa Teresa (50m)
San Francisco
Santa Marta
San Agustín
Moral
San José
Peral
La Catedral
Museo Arqueológico de la Universidad Católica de Santa María (200m)
La Merced
Plaza de Armas
Álvarez Thomas
Mercaderes
Bolognesi
Sucre
Museo Santuarios Andinos
N de Piérola
Santo Domingo
Palacio Viejo
San Juan de Dios
Deán Valdivia
To Casa de Avila (300m)
Consuelo
San Camilo
Perú
Pizarro
Mercado
Alto de la Luna
Nuevo Corbacho

## Arequipa

**Top Sights**
La Catedral ... B4
Monasterio de Santa Catalina ... B3
Museo Santuarios Andinos ... B5

**Sights**
1 Casa de Moral ... A4
2 Casa Ricketts ... B4
3 Iglesia de La Compañía ... B5

**Activities, Courses & Tours**
4 Al Travel Tours ... B4
5 Carlos Zárate Adventures ... B4
6 Colca Trek ... C3
7 Ecotours ... C3
8 Naturaleza Activa ... B3
9 Pablo Tour ... C3
10 Peru Camping Shop ... D3

**Sleeping**
11 Casablanca Hostal ... A5
12 Hostal Casona Solar ... B6
13 La Hostería ... B2
14 Los Tambos Hostal ... A5

**Eating**
15 Cafe Fez-Istanbul ... B4
16 Café Restaurant Antojitos de Arequipa ... B5
Chicha ... (see 30)
17 Crepisimo ... B3
18 Cusco Coffee Company ... A5
19 El Viñedo ... C3
20 Inkari Pub Pizzeria ... B4
21 La Trattoria del Monasterio ... B2
22 Manolo's ... B4
23 Nina-Yaku ... B4
24 Zig Zag ... C3
25 Zingaro ... C3

**Drinking**
26 Brujas Bar ... C3
27 Déjà Vu ... C3

**Entertainment**
28 Casona Forum ... C3
29 Las Quenas ... B3

**Shopping**
30 Casona Santa Catalina ... B3
31 Fundo El Fierro ... C2
32 Patio del Ekeko ... C5

**Information**
33 BCP ... C5
34 iPerú ... B5

**Transport**
35 LAN ... B4

southeast corner of the Plaza de Armas has a facade that is an intricately carved masterpiece of the *churrigueresque* style (think Spanish baroque – and then some). It has an equally detailed altar completely covered in gold leaf. To the left of it is the **San Ignacio chapel** (admission S4), with a polychrome cupola smothered in jungle inspired murals of tropical flowers, fruit and birds.

**MONASTERIO DE LA RECOLETA** Monastery

**(La Recoleta 117; admission S5; 9am-noon & 3-5pm Mon-Sat)** This musty monastery was constructed on the west side of the Río Chili in 1648 by Franciscan friars. Bibliophiles will delight in the huge library, which contains more than 20,000 dusty books and maps. There is also a well-known museum of Amazonian artifacts collected by the missionaries, and an extensive collection of preconquest artifacts and religious art of the Cuzco School.

**MUSEO DE ARTE VIRREINAL DE SANTA TERESA** Museum

**(Melgar 303; admission S10; 9am-5pm Mon-Sat, to 1pm Sun)** This gorgeous 17th-century Carmelite convent and museum is filled with priceless votive objets d'art, murals, precious metal works, colonial-era paintings and other historical artifacts. A charming shop at the front of the complex sells baked goods and rose-scented soap made by the nuns.

**CASA DE MORAL** Historic Building

**(Moral 318; admission S5; 9am-5pm Mon-Sat)** Built in 1730, this stylized baroque-*mestizo* house is named after the 200-year-old mulberry tree in its central courtyard. Owned by the BCP bank, it serves essentially as a museum, notable for its antique maps, heavy furniture, religious art, and extensive coin and banknote collection.

**CASA RICKETTS** Historic Building
**(Casa Tristán del Pozo; San Francisco 108; ⌚9:15am-12:45pm & 4:30-6:30pm Mon-Fri, 9:30am-12:45pm Sat)** Built in 1738, the ornate Casa Ricketts has served as a seminary, archbishop's palace, school and home to well-to-do families. Today it is the most splendiferous working bank in the city – possibly in Peru. Even if you're not here for a transaction, it's worth nosing around the interior courtyards with their puma-head fountains.

## Activities

### Trekking

The spectacular canyons around Arequipa offer many excellent hiking options. Most agencies can arrange an array of routes to suit your timeline and fitness level, through canyons, gorges and charming rural villages. Although it is possible to trek year-round, the best (driest) time is from May to November. There is more danger of rockfalls in the canyons during the wet season (between December and April). Easier treks in the Cañón del Colca can be beautifully lush during the wet season, however, while more remote trails, especially those in the Cañón del Cotahuasi, become inaccessible.

For detailed information on the area's canyons, turn to p124.

### River Running

The **Río Chili**, about 7km from Arequipa, is the most frequently run local river, with a half-day trip suitable for beginners leaving almost daily from April to November (from US$35). You can also do relatively easy trips on the **Río Majes**, into which the Río Colca flows. The most commonly run stretches pass Class II and III rapids.

The **Río Colca** is a dangerous, difficult trip, not to be undertaken lightly. A few

**Left:** Plaza de Armas (p114), Arequipa;
**Below:** Guide at the Monasterio de Santa Catalina (p115), Arequipa
(LEFT) ANDRAS JANCSIK/GETTY IMAGES ©; (BELOW) HUGHES HERVÉ© / HEMIS.FR/GETTY IMAGES ©



outfitters will do infrequent trips to the easier sections, which can be found upriver.

Many trips are unavailable during the rainy season (between December and March), when water levels can be dangerously high.

Tour companies offering river running include the following:

**Casa de Mauro** (☎9-59-336-684; www.lacasademaurotoursperu.com; Ongoro Km 5) Almost 200km out of Arequipa, this Río Majes base camp offers trips of all lengths and levels.

**Majes River** (☎83-0297, 9-59-797-731; www.majesriver.com) A simple lodge has a variety of rafting options.

## Mountain Biking

**Peru Camping Shop** (www.perucampingshop.com; Jerusalén 410) rents bikes by the half-day for S35 including helmet, gloves and a map of the area. It also organizes downhill cycling blasts in the vicinity of El Misti for S68 (one day) with transport.

## Mountaineering

Looming 5822m above Arequipa, the city's guardian volcano El Misti is the most popular climb in the area. It is technically one of the easiest ascents of any mountain of this size in the world, but it's hard work nonetheless. The ascent generally takes two days (one day to reach a base camp at 4500m; another day to reach the summit). While this is not a technical climb, it does require you to be in excellent physical condition with some acclimatization to the altitude. You may also need an ice axe and crampons (supplied by area outfitters).

The best months for climbing are between April and December, with the peak months being between July and November. Even in the drier months, temperatures drop to -29°C at the highest camps, necessitating very warm clothing. In addition, the Association of Mountain Guides of Peru warns that many guides offering journeys are uncertified and untrained. Climbers should go well informed about medical and wilderness survival issues.

## Tours

Dozens of travel agencies offer excursions. While some agencies are professional, there are plenty of carpetbaggers, so shop carefully. As a general rule, never accept tours from street touts.

See the following agencies:

**AI Travel Tours** (☎22-2052; www.aitraveltours.com; Santa Catalina 203) Standard city tours and unique excursions, such as a visit to a neighborhood of stonemakers.

**Carlos Zárate Adventures** (☎20-2461; www.zarateadventures.com; Santa Catalina 204) Founded in 1954 by Carlos Zárate, the great-grandfather of climbing in Arequipa, this reputable outfit offers all manner of treks and climbs. It also rents gear.

**Colca Trek** (☎20-6217, 9-60-0170; www.colcatrek.com.pe; Jerusalén 401-B) Run by the English-speaking Vlado Soto, Colca organizes trekking tours, mountaineering, mountain biking and river running. It also sells topographic maps.

**Naturaleza Activa** (☎69-5793; Santa Catalina 211) A multilingual agency offering a range of trekking, climbing and mountain-biking options.

**Pablo Tour** (☎20-3737; www.pablotour.com; Jerusalén 400 AB-1) Consistently recommended by readers for trekking and cultural tours.

**Ecotours** (☎20-2562; Jerusalén 409) In business for 20 years, this agency organizes half-day rafting trips on the Río Chili, among other excursions.

## Sleeping

**HOSTAL CASONA SOLAR** Hotel $$
(☎22-8991; www.casonasolar.com; Consuelo 116; r from S104; wifi) Live like a colonial *caballero* (gentleman) in this 'secret garden' of gorgeousness situated – rather incredibly, given its tranquility – only three blocks from the main square. Grand 18th-century rooms are crafted from *sillar,* the service is excellent and then there's price: the best bargain in the city, if not Peru.

Iglesia de la Compañía (p115), Arequipa

HUGHES HERVÉ© / HEMIS.FR/GETTY IMAGES ©

**LOS TAMBOS HOSTAL** Boutique Hotel **$$$**
(☎60-0900; www.lostambos.com.pe; Puente Bolognesi 129; d S219-289; ❄@📶) Breaking the mold in historic Arequipa is this modern boutique hotel, a marble roll from the main square, where above-and-beyond service justifies every *sol* of the asking price. This includes free bottles of water, chocolates on the pillow, aromatic soaps, huge gourmet breakfasts and airport transfers.

**LIBERTADOR CIUDAD BLANCA** Luxury Hotel **$$$**
(☎21-5110; www.libertador.com.pe; Plaza Bolívar s/n, Selva Alegre; r S400-600, ste S500-775; ❄@📶🏊) The grand dame of Arequipa hotels consists of a stylish building perfectly set amid gardens with a pool and playground. It has spacious rooms, opulent public areas and a spa and fitness room. The sedate restaurant serves a fine Sunday brunch.

**CASABLANCA HOSTAL** Hotel **$$**
(☎22-1327; www.casablancahostal.com; Puente Bolognesi 104; s/d/tr incl breakfast S80/120/160; @) The *New York Times*' 'Frugal Traveler' wasn't the only budget-seeker to marvel at this place. Bank on prime corner-of-main-plaza location, beautiful *sillar* brickwork, and rooms large enough to keep a horse (or two). Breakfast is taken in a lovely sun-filled café.

**LA HOSTERÍA** Hotel **$$**
(☎28-9269; www.lahosteriaqp.com.pe; Bolívar 405; s/d incl breakfast S140/165; 📶) This picturesque colonial hotel has a flower-bedecked courtyard, light rooms (with minibar), carefully chosen antiques, a sunny terrace and a lounge. Some units suffer from street noise, so request one in the back. Apartment-style suites (US$68) on the upper floors have stellar views. Airport pickup included.

**CASA AREQUIPA** Boutique Hotel **$$**
(☎28-4219; www.arequipacasa.com; Av Lima 409, Vallecito; s/d S150/235; 📶) Inside a cotton-candy pink colonial mansion in the gardens of suburban Vallecito, this gay-friendly B&B offers more than half a dozen guest rooms with fine design touches such as richly painted walls, pedestal sinks, antique furnishings and alpaca wool blankets.

## Eating

**ZINGARO** Novo Andino **$$**
(www.zingaro-restaurante.com; San Francisco 309; mains S25-45; ⏰noon-11pm Mon-Sat) In an old *sillar* building with wooden balconies, stained glass and a resident pianist, Zingaro is the ideal place to try out nouveau renditions of Peruvian standards, including alpaca ribs, ceviche, or perhaps your first *cuy* (guinea pig).

**ZIG ZAG** Fusion **$$**
(☎20-6020; www.zigzagrestaurant.com; Zela 210; mains S33-40; ⏰6pm-midnight) Inhabiting a two-story colonial house with an iron stairway designed by Gustave Eiffel, Zig Zag is a Peruvian restaurant with European inflections. The menu classic is a meat selection served on a volcanic stone grill, accompanied by various sauces. The fondues are also good.

**CHICHA** Novo Andino **$$$**
(☎28-7360; www.chicha.com.pe; Santa Catalina 210; mains S26-58; ⏰noon-midnight Mon-Sat, to 9pm Sun) Peru's most famous chef, Gastón Acurio, owns this experimental place which offers a menu that never veers too far from Peru's roots. River prawns are a highlight in season (April to December), as are the alpaca burgers and the fresh pastas. But there are plenty of staples, too: *tacu tacu* (pan-fried rice and beans), *lomo saltado* (beef strips stir-fried with onion, tomatoes, potatoes and chilli), ceviche – all prepared with panache.

**CREPISIMO** Creperie **$**
(www.crepisimo.com; Alianza Francesa, Santa Catalina 208; mains S6-16; ⏰8am-11pm Mon-Sat, noon-11pm Sun; 📶) This great little cafe offers good service, great ambience and a 100 different types of crepes, from Chilean smoked trout to exotic South American fruits. Bonus: excellent coffee.

# If You Like... Arequipeño Cooking

With an exquisite range of local cooking that includes dishes such as the explosive *rocoto rellenos* (red peppers stuffed with ground beef and cheese) and spicy-succulent *chupe de camarones* (shrimp bisque), Arequipa is a food-lovers' paradise. You can find excellent cuisine at all price ranges, but if you really want to eat like a local, hit a *picantería* – the homestyle country restaurants that are typical of the region.

1 **TRADICIÓN AREQUIPEÑA**
**(☎42-6467; www.tradicionarequipena.com; Av Dolores 111; meals S18-40; ⏰11:30am-6pm Mon-Fri, 11:30am-1am Sat, 8:30am-6pm Sun)** A locally famous restaurant that has mazelike gardens, live folk music and offers a Sunday-morning breakfast of *adobo de cerdo*, traditional slow-cooked pork.

2 **LA NUEVA PALOMINO**
**(Leoncio Prado 122; mains S14-29; ⏰lunch)** Definitely a local favorite, the atmosphere at this *picantería* can be boisterous even during the week.

3 **CAFÉ RESTAURANT ANTOJITOS DE AREQUIPA**
**(Moran Cuadra 1; mains S14-32; ⏰24hr)** Expect unadulterated Arequipa cookery. Hone in on the *rocoto rellenos* and anything with potatoes in it.

4 **SOL DE MAYO**
**(☎25-4148; www.restaurantsoldemayo.com; Jerusalén 207, Yanahuara; menú S14, mains S18-47; ⏰11:30am-6pm)** Serving good Peruvian food in the Yanahuara district, this *picantería* has live folk music every afternoon. Reserve in advance.

5 **EL VIÑEDO**
**(www.vinedogrill.com; San Francisco 319; mains S20-50; ⏰noon-midnight)** A Calle San Francisco stalwart offering an *Americano* sampler platter that includes multiple local specialties, including *ocopa* (potatoes in spicy peanut sauce) and *pastel de papas* (like potatoes au gratin).

**LA TRATTORIA DEL MONASTERIO** Fusion **$$$**
**(☎20-4062; www.latrattoriadelmonasterio.com; Santa Catalina 309; mains S18-33; ⏰lunch from noon daily, dinner from 7pm Mon-Sat)** A helping of epicurean delight has descended upon the Monasterio de Santa Catalina. The menu of Italian specialties was created with the help of Gastón Acurio and is infused with the flavors of Arequipa. Reservations essential.

**CAFE FEZ-ISTANBUL** Middle Eastern **$**
**(San Francisco 229; mains S6-11; ⏰7:30am-11pm)** Falafels, hummus and fresh-cut fries are the draw, served in a trendy resto-bar with a people-watching mezzanine.

**NINA-YAKU** Novo Andino **$$**
**(San Francisco 211; menús S35, mains S25-36; ⏰3-11pm)** Nina Yaku offers an atmosphere of whispered refinement along with affordable Arequipa specialties such as broccoli soufflé, potatoes in *huacatay* (Andean mint) sauce and fettuccine with alpaca.

**MANOLO'S** Peruvian **$**
**(Mercaderes 107 & 113; mains S10-30; ⏰7:30am-midnight)** Seeing double? Well, yes, actually. There are two Manolo's 20m apart in Arequipa's pedestrian Calle Mercaderes. Shagged-out shoppers find it hard to resist the hiss of the cappuccino maker and the glint of the glass display case stuffed with thickly sliced cakes.

**INKARI PUB PIZZERIA** Pizzeria **$**
**(Pasaje Catedral; pizzas from S14; ⏰8am-midnight)** You're pretty much guaranteed to meet a gringo at this predictably popular place behind the cathedral which pampers Western palates with a happy-hour special of a personal pizza and a *copa de vino* (glass of wine) for S14.

**CUSCO COFFEE COMPANY** Cafe
**(La Merced 135; drinks S5-11; ⏰8am-10pm Mon-Sat, noon-7pm Sun; 📶)** If you're missing chocolate chip muffins, bucket-sized

lattes and sofas full of noncommunicative wi-fi nerds, this will be your bag.

## Drinking

Many of the bars along Calle San Francisco offer happy-hour specials.

**DÉJÀ VU** Bar

**(San Francisco 319B; 9am-late)** With a rooftop terrace overlooking the church of San Francisco, this eternally popular haunt has crazy cocktails and a lethal happy hour. After dark, decent DJs keep the scene alive.

**BRUJAS BAR** Bar

**(San Francisco 300; 5pm-late)** Nordic-style pub with Union Jack flags, happy hour cocktails and plenty of local and expat action.

## Entertainment

On weekends, Calle San Francisco offers a concentration of nightlife.

**LAS QUENAS** Live Music

**(Santa Catalina 302; Mon-Sat)** This traditional folk music *peña* features performances almost nightly, starting around 9pm.

**CASONA FORUM** Club

**(www.casonaforum.com; San Francisco 317)** A five-in-one excuse for a good night out, incorporating a pub (Retro), pool club (Zero), sofa bar (Chill Out), nightclub (Forum) and restaurant (Terrasse).

## Shopping

**CASONA SANTA CATALINA** Mall

**(www.santacatalina-sa.com.pe; Santa Catalina 210; most shops 10am-6pm)** This polished tourist complex has several shops, some with major export brands, such as Sol Alpaca knits and Biondi piscos.

**PATIO DEL EKEKO** Mall

**(21-5861; www.patiodelekeko.com; Mercaderes 141; 10am-9pm Mon-Sat, 11am-8pm Sun)** This high-end tourist mall has good alpaca and vicuña knits, jewelry and ceramics.

Cañón del Colca (p125)

**FUNDO EL FIERRO** Craft Market
The city's primary craft market – located in a beautiful *sillar* courtyard – has garments, knits, paintings and jewelry, as well as rare alpaca carpets from Cotahuasi.

##  Information

Internet (via wi-fi and in internet cafes) is widely available and generally costs less than S2 per hour.

### Emergency

**Policía de Turismo** (Tourist Police; 20-1258; Jerusalén 315-317; 24hr)

### Medical Services

**Clínica Arequipa** (25-3424, 25-3416; Bolognesi at Puente Grau; 8am-8pm Mon-Fri, to 12:30pm Sat) Arequipa's best.

**Hospital Regional Honorio Delgado Espinoza** (21-9702, 23-3812; Av Daniel Alcides Carrión s/n; 24hr)

**Paz Holandesa Policlinic** (43-2281; www.pazholandesa.com; Av Jorge Chávez 527; 8am-8pm Mon-Sat) An appointment-only travel clinic with English-speaking doctors.

### Money

**BCP** (San Juan de Dios 125) Visa ATM; changes American dollars.

### Tourist Information

**Indecopi** (21-2054; Hipólito Unanue 100A, Urb Victoria; 8:30am-4pm Mon-Fri) Handles complaints against local operators.

**iPerú** Airport (44-4564; 1st fl, Main Hall, Aeropuerto Rodríguez Ballón; 10am-7:30pm); Plaza de Armas (22-3265; iperuarequipa@promperu.gob.pe; Portal de la Municipalidad 110; 8:30am-7:30pm) Government-supported source of information.

##  Getting There & Away

### Air

Arequipa's **Rodríguez Ballón International Airport** (code AQP; 44-3458) is about 8km northwest of the city center.

**LAN** (20-1224; www.lan.com; Santa Catalina 118C) has daily flights to Lima and Cuzco.

### Bus

Most bus companies have departures from the *terminal terrestre* or the smaller Terrapuerto bus terminal, which stand next to each other on Av Andrés Avelino Cáceres, 3km south of the city center (take a taxi for S5). Check in advance which terminal your bus leaves from and keep a close watch on your belongings. There's a S1 departure tax from either terminal.

Some regional bus routes are useful for sightseeing in canyon country. These generally travel to Chivay (three hours), in the Cañón del Colca, with some continuing to Cabanaconde (six hours). Travel times and costs vary. It is best to purchase tickets in advance. During the wet season (December to April), expect delays. The following are the best companies:

**Andalucía** (44-5089)

**Reyna** (43-0612)

Comfortable long-haul services are available to Puno, Cuzco, Nazca and Lima. Recommended operators:

**Cruz del Sur** (42-7375)

**Ormeño** (42-3855)

## Getting Around

A short taxi ride around town usually costs around S3 to S4. An official taxi from downtown Arequipa to the airport costs around S15. Local taxi companies:

**Tourismo Arequipa** (45-8888)

**Taxitel** (45-2020)

# CANYON COUNTRY

Going to Arequipa and missing out on the Cañón del Colca is like going to Cuzco and neglecting to visit Machu Picchu. For those with more time there's a whole load of other excursions, including climbing the city's guardian volcano El Misti, rafting in the Majes canyon and visiting the petroglyphs at Toro Muerto. Most of these places can be visited on organized trips or by hiring a driver.

## Canyon Country

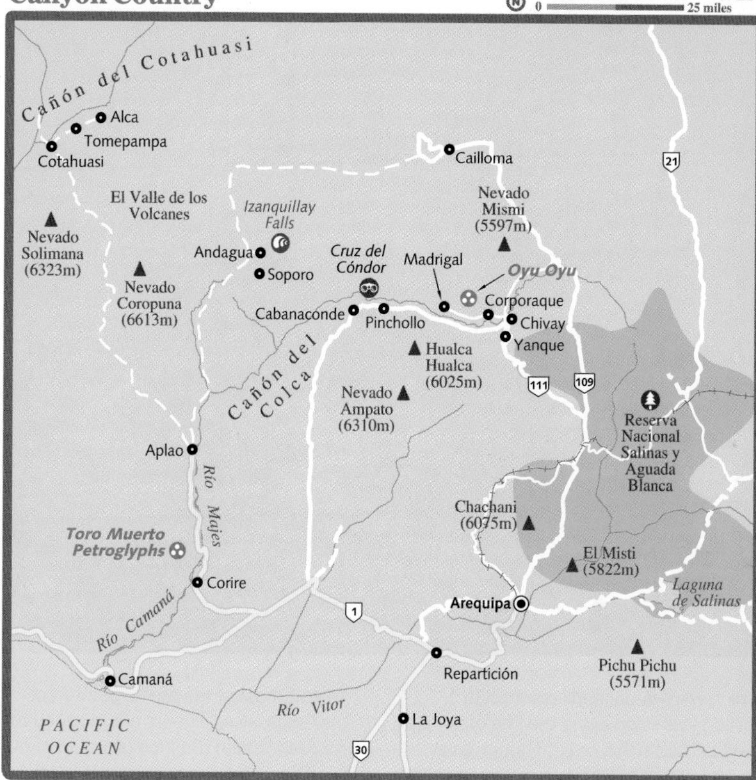


# Reserva Nacional Salinas y Aguada Blanca

One of southern Peru's finest **reserves** (**054-25-7461; admission free; 24hr**) consists of a vast Andean expanse of dozing volcanoes and brawny wildlife forging an existence several kilometers above sea level. Drives here take you to an oxygen-deprived 4910m where, in between light-headed gasps for air, you can ponder weird wind-eroded rock formations, trek on old Inca trails and watch fleet-footed vicuñas run across the desolate pampa. The reserve was designed to protect a rich raft of high-altitude species such as vicuñas, *tarucas* (Andean deer), *guanacos* (a camelid) and various birds, most notably flamingos.

Both El Misti and Chachani volcanoes are included in the reserve.

# Cañón del Colca

It's not just the vastness and depth of the Colca that make it so fantastical, it's the shifts in its mood. There's more scenery changes along its 100km passage than there are in most European countries – from the barren steppe of Sibayo, through the ancient terraced farmland of Yanque and Chivay, into the steep-sided canyon proper beyond Cabanaconde that wasn't thoroughly explored until the 1980s. Of course one shouldn't turn a blind eye to the vital statistics: the Colca is the world's second-deepest canyon, a smidgeon shallower than its neighbor, the Cotahausi, and roughly twice as deep as the more famous Grand Canyon in the US.

Despite its depth, the canyon is geologically young. The Río Colca has cut into beds of mainly volcanic rocks,

which were deposited less than 100 million years ago along the line of a major fault in the earth's crust. Though cool and dry in the hills above, the deep valley and generally sunny weather produce frequent updrafts on which soaring condors often float by at close range. Viscachas (burrowing rodents closely related to chinchillas) are also common around the canyon rim, darting furtively among the rocks. Cacti dot many slopes and, if they're in flower, you may be lucky enough to see tiny nectar-eating birds braving the spines to feed. In the depths of the canyon it can be almost tropical, with palm trees, ferns and even orchids in some isolated areas.

The local people are descendants of two conflicting groups that originally occupied the area, the Cabanas and the Collagua. These two groups used to distinguish themselves by performing cranial deformations, but nowadays use distinctively shaped hats and intricately embroidered traditional clothing to denote their ancestry.

To visit most of the points of interest in the Colca, all foreigners are required to purchase a *boleto turístico* (tourist ticket; S70). If you are taking an organized tour, this expense is generally not included. If you are traveling independently, tickets can be purchased on most public buses entering or leaving Chivay or Cabanaconde.

For more information on trekking and outfitters, see p118.

## Chivay

054 / POP 6300 / ELEV 3630M

Chivay is the Cañón del Colca's unashamedly disheveled nexus, a traditional town that has embraced tourism without losing its high-country identity. It is equipped with enchanting views of snowcapped peaks and terraced hillsides, and serves as a logical base from which to explore the canyon.

The market area and main square are good places to catch a glimpse of the decorative clothing worn by local women.

**Left:** Cañón del Colca (p125); **Below:** Condor
(LEFT) CUTE KITTEN IMAGES/GETTY IMAGES ©; (BELOW) JESSIE REEDER/GETTY IMAGES ©

## Sights & Activities

Chivay is a good starting point for canyon hikes, both short and long. Likewise, you could hit the trails on a bike. **BiciSport** (**☎9-58-807-652; Zaramilla 112; ⏰9am-6pm**), behind the market, rents wheels for about S5 per day.

**ASTRONOMICAL OBSERVATORY** Observatory
(**Huayna Cápac; admission S25**) No light pollution equals excellent Milky Way vistas. The Casa Andina hotel has a tiny observatory which holds nightly sky shows. The price includes a 30-minute explanation and chance to peer into the telescope.

**LA CALERA HOT SPRINGS** Thermal Baths
(**admission S15; ⏰4:30am-7pm**) A 3km stroll to the northeast, these alfresco springs provide warm water – as well as the whoops of ziplines as they sail overhead.

**COLCA ZIP-LINING** Ziplining
(**☎95-898-9931; www.colcaziplining.com; 2/4 cables S50/100**) Dangle terrifyingly over the Río Colca while entertaining bathers in the hot springs below.

## Sleeping & Eating

**HOTEL POZO DEL CIELO** Hotel $$
(**☎34-6547; www.pozodelcielo.com.pe; Huascar; d/ste S88/135;** Wi-Fi) Looking a bit like something Gaudí might have crafted, 'Heaven's Well', as the name translates, is all low doorways, weirdly shaped rooms and winding paths. Surrealism aside, this is a functional, comfortable abode with individually crafted rooms and a fine *mirador* (lookout) restaurant.

**CASA ANDINA** Boutique Hotel $$$
(**☎53-1020, 53-1022; www.casa-andina.com; Huayna Cápac; s/d incl breakfast from S250;** Wi-Fi) Purposefully rustic rooms inhabit thatched-roof stone cottages in neatly

sculpted grounds, but the main grab-you features here are the unusual extras which include an observatory, oxygen (should you be feeling light-headed) and coca-leaf readings.

**INNKAS CAFÉ** Peruvian $

**(Plaza de Armas 705; mains S12-20; 7am-11pm)** This old building with cozy window nooks is warmed by modern gas heaters. Maybe it's the altitude, but the *lomo saltado* tastes Gastón Acurio–good here. The sweet service is backed up by even sweeter cakes and coffee.

## Information

There's a helpful **information office (53-1143; Plaza de Armas 119; 8am-1pm & 3-7pm)** right on the main plaza. Here, you'll also find the police station (next to the *municipalidad* – town hall) and various internet cafes.

## Getting There & Around

Most visitors arrive in Chivay with a hired driver or via organized tours. The bus terminal is a 15-minute walk from the plaza. There are almost hourly departures to Arequipa. Buses to Cabanaconde leave four times daily.

## Chivay to Cabanaconde

The road following the south bank of the upper Cañón del Colca leads past several villages that still use the Inca terracing that surrounds them.

### Yanque

054 / POP 1900

Of the canyon's dozen or so villages, Yanque, 7km west of Chivay, has the prettiest and liveliest main square, and sports its finest church: the **Iglesia de la Immaculada Concepción**. Its ornate baroque-*mestizo* facade has an almost *churrigueresque* look. Also on the plaza is the excellent **Museo Yanque (admission S5; 9am-5pm Mon-Sat)**, which contains displays about the culture of the Colca Canyon, Inca textiles, cranial deformation and ecclesial architecture.

From here, a 30-minute walk down to the river brings you to the hot springs, **Baños Chacapi (admission S5; 3am-7pm)**.

## Sleeping

**HOTEL COLLAHUA** Hotel $

**(22-6098; www.hotelcollahua.com; Av Collahua Cuadro 7; s/d/tr S65/85/95; )** Bright rooms are encased in independent bungalows over large-ish grounds where alpacas roam. There's a comprehensive restaurant on-site.

**SUMAQ HUAYTA WASI** Guesthouse $

**(83-2174; www.casabellaflor.com; Cusco 303)** A number of simple, family-run guesthouses scattered around town offer lodging from S15 per night. This one – also known as 'Casa Bella Flor' – provides an excellent balance between tradition and comfort. It is two blocks from the main plaza.

### Coporaque to Madrigal

Across the river from Yanque, the non-commercialized Coporaque has the valley's oldest church and not much else – unless you count the splendiferous views of canyon slopes covered in terraced fields.

Between the two villages, there is a sign marking the ruins of **Oyu Oyu**. The remnants of this pre-Inca settlement are reached by a half-hour hike uphill. Afterwards you can continue to a waterfall, the source of which is the runoff from Nevado Mismi.

## Sleeping

**COLCA LODGE** Luxury Hotel $$$

**(53-1191; www.colca-lodge.com; d/ste incl breakfast S546/852; )** This utterly romantic hotel is set among artistically manicured grounds alongside the rippling Río Colca. Lavish rooms come loaded with Noel Coward–esque dressing gowns, wood-burning stoves, candles, coffee machines and king beds, but the real carrot is the alfresco thermal baths (37°C to 39°C) sculpted into whimsical pools alongside the river. Reserve in advance.

Nonguests can use the thermal baths for S30.

**LA CASA DE MAMAYACCHI** Inn **$$**
**(www.lacasademamayacchi.com; d/tr incl breakfast from S192/250)** Presiding over terraced valley views, this cozy inn – built from traditional materials, has 28 simple rooms, a games library, fireplace and bar. Reserve in advance via its **Arequipa office** (☎**24-1206; Jerusalén 606**).

## Yanque to Pinchollo

Further along the main road on the south side of the canyon, the spreading landscape is remarkable for its Inca and pre-Inca terracing, which goes on for many kilometers and is some of the most extensive in Peru.

The next big village along the main road is Pinchollo, about 30km from Chivay. From here, a trail climbs toward **Hualca Hualca** (a snowcapped volcano of 6025m) to an active geothermal area set amid wild and interesting scenery.

## Cruz del Cóndor

Some overhyped travel sights are anticlimactic in the raw light of day. This is not one of them. No advance press can truly sell **Cruz del Cóndor (admission with boleto turístico)**, the famed condor viewpoint. Located about 50km west of Chivay, a large family of Andean condors nest at a rocky outcrop here and – weather and season permitting – can be seen riding the currents between 8am and 10am on most days. It's a mesmerizing scene, heightened by the 1200m drop to the river below and the sight of **Nevado Mismi** standing 3000m above the canyon floor on the other side.

## Cabanaconde

☎054 / POP 2700 / ELEV 3290M

Only a fraction of visitors to Cañón del Colca make it to ramshackle Cabanaconde, but for those seeking greater tranquility, its attractions are obvious. The Colca is significantly deeper here with steep, zigzagging paths tempting the fit and the brave to descend 1200m to the eponymous river.

### Activities

The most popular hike in the area is the spectacular two-hour descent from Cabanaconde down to **Sangalle**, where there are **natural pools (per person S5)** for swimming, as well as food and drink. Note

Leading a domesticated alpaca past a colonial church, Cañón del Colca (p125)

that the return trek is a steep and thirsty climb – 1½ to three hours, depending on your level of fitness.

Local guides and mules can be hired by consulting with your hostel or the *municipalidad* in Cabanaconde. The going rate for guides is S30 to S60 per day.

## Sleeping & Eating

Accommodation options are extremely limited. There are a couple of cheap local restaurants near the main plaza.

**LA POSADA DEL CONDE** Hotel **$$**
(**☎40-0408, 83-0033; www.posadadelconde.com; San Pedro s/n; s/d/tr incl breakfast US$25/30/40**) This small, modern hotel mostly has double rooms, but they are well cared for with clean bathrooms. Rates often include a welcome *mate* (herbal tea) or pisco sour in the downstairs restaurant.

**HOTEL KUNTUR WASSI** Hotel **$$**
(**☎81-2166; www.arequipacolca.com; Cruz Blanca s/n; s/d/ste incl breakfast US$45/55/70; @**) Built into the hillside, this charming hotel has stone bathrooms, trapezoidal windows overlooking the gardens and a nouveau-rustic feel. Suites boast enormous bathtubs. Plus, there's a bar, restaurant, library, laundry and currency exchange.

**RESTAURANTE LAS TERRAZAS** International **$**
(**☎958-10-3553; www.villapastorcolca.com; Plaza de Armas; snacks S10-15; @**) Pizza, pasta, sandwiches and cheap Cuba Libres are offered here overlooking the main square and its bucolic donkey traffic. There's also a computer terminal charitably offering free internet.

## Information

There are no ATMs here, so stash some cash.

## Getting There & Away

Buses for Chivay and Arequipa, via Cruz del Cóndor, leave Cabanaconde from the main plaza seven times per day. Departure times change regularly; inquire locally.

**Left:** El Valle de los Volcanes;
**Below:** Culpeo fox, Cañón del Colca (p125)
(LEFT) GRANT DIXON/GETTY IMAGES ©; (BELOW) MARK JONES/GETTY IMAGES ©



## Toro Muerto Petroglyphs

A fascinating, mystical site in the high desert, Toro Muerto (meaning 'Dead Bull') is named for the herds of livestock that commonly died from dehydration as they were escorted from the mountains to the coast. A barren hillside is scattered with white volcanic boulders carved with stylized people, animals and birds. Archaeologists have documented more than 5000 such petroglyphs spread over several square kilometers of desert. Though the cultural origins of this site remain unknown, most archaeologists date the mysterious drawings to the period of Wari domination, about 1200 years ago.

The petroglyphs are visited most conveniently on full-day 4WD tours from Arequipa. But if you're traveling independently, you can catch a taxi from the village of Corire (due south of the Cañón del Colca) to where the petroglyphs start (from S40 round-trip). Bring plenty of water, sunblock and insect repellent.

## El Valle de los Volcanes

El Valle de los Volcanes is a broad valley, west of the Cañón del Colca and at the foot of Nevado Coropuna (6613m), famed for its unusual geological features. The valley floor is carpeted with lava flows from which rise many small (up to 200m high) cinder cones, some 80 in total, aligned along a major fissure, with each cone formed from a single eruption. Given the lack of erosion of some cones and minimal vegetation on the associated lava flows, the volcanic activity occurred no more than a few thousand years ago, and some was likely very recent – historical accounts suggest as recently as the 17th century.

The 65km-long valley surrounds the village of **Andagua**, near the snowy summit of Coropuna. Visitors seeking a destination full of natural wonders and virtually untouched by travelers will rejoice in this remote setting. From

Andagua, a number of sites can be visited by foot or car. Popular hikes are to a nearby *mirador* at 3800m and to the 40m-high **Izanquillay Falls**, which are formed where the Río Andahua runs through a narrow lava canyon to the northeast of town. There are some *chullpas* (funerary towers) at **Soporo**, a two-hour hike or half-hour drive to the south of Andagua. En route to Soporo are the ruins of a pre-Columbian city named **Antaymarca**.

There are several basic hostels and restaurants in Andagua. Some tour companies visit El Valle de los Volcanes as part of multiday 4WD tours that may include visits to the Cañón del Cotahuasi and Chivay.

## Cañón del Cotahuasi

While the Cañón del Colca has stolen the limelight for many years, it is actually this remote canyon, 200km northwest of Arequipa as the condor flies, that is the deepest known canyon in the world. It is around twice the depth of the Grand Canyon, with stretches dropping below 3500m. While the depths of the ravine are only accessible to experienced river runners, the rest of the fertile valley is also rich in striking scenery and trekking opportunities. The canyon also shelters several traditional rural settlements that currently see only a handful of adventurous travelers.

### Sights & Activities

The main access town is appropriately named **Cotahuasi** (population 3800) and is at 2620m above sea level on the southeast side of the canyon. Northeast of Cotahuasi and further up the canyon are the villages of **Tomepampa** (10km away; elevation 2500m) and **Alca** (20km away; 2660m), which also have basic accommodations. En route you'll pass a couple of **thermal baths** (admission S2).

From the Sipia Bridge, about an hour outside of town, you can begin a number of interesting hikes into the deepest parts of the canyon. Forty-five minutes up the trail, the **Sipia waterfall** is formed where the Río Cotahuasi takes an impressive 100m tumble. Another 1½ hours on a well-trodden track brings you to Chaupo, an oasis of towering cacti and remnants of pre-Inca dwellings.

## Mountain Highs

If your red blood cells are up to it, you can disembark into the rarefied air of **Paso de Patopampa**, which lies at a staggering 4910m above sea level, on the road between Arequipa and Chivay. This almost lifeless mountain pass is significantly higher than Europe's Mt Blanc and any points in North America's Rocky Mountains. Some of the best volcano views in the Andes more than make up for the high-altitude gasping.

From the *mirador de volcanes* (volcano lookout), it is possible to see a muscular consortium of eight snow-capped volcanoes: **Ubinas** (5675m), **Misti** (5822m), **Chachani** (6075m), **Ampato** (6310m), **Sabancayo** (5976m), **Huacca Huacca** (6025m), **Mismi** (5597m) and **Chucura** (5360m).

Less spectacular but no less amazing is the scrubby yareta, one of the few plants that can survive in this harsh landscape. Yaretas can live for several millennia and their annual growth rate is measured in millimeters rather than centimeters. Also hardy are the ladies in traditional dress who discreetly ply their wares here during the day – the world's highest shopping center?

Cotahuasi (p132), Cañón del Cotahuasi

JOHNNY HAGLUND/GETTY IMAGES ©



Trekking trips of several days' duration can be arranged in Arequipa (p118). Some can be combined with the Toro Muerto petroglyphs, and, if you ask, they may return via a collection of dinosaur footprints on the west edge of the canyon.

## Sleeping & Eating

**HOTEL VALLEHERMOSO** Hotel $$
(054-58-1057; www.hotelvallehermoso.com; Calle Tacna 106-108, Cotahuasi; s/d S70/100) Just what you probably wanted after a dusty 12-hour bus ride, Cotahuasi's poshest joint offers divine comfort in the middle of nowhere while never straying far from rustic tradition. An on-site restaurant even tries its spin on *cocina novoandina* (new Andean cuisine).

**HOSTAL HATUNHUASI** Hotel $
(054-58-1054, in Lima 01-531-0803; www.hatunhuasi.com; Centanario 309, Cotahuasi; s/d S25/50) A notch above the other options in town, this friendly guesthouse has plenty of rooms situated around a sunny inner courtyard and hot water most of the time. Food can be made upon request, and the owners are good sources of hard-to-get travel information.

## Getting There & Away

The 420km bus journey from Arequipa, half of which is on unpaved roads, takes 12 hours (S25). Three-quarters of the way there, the road summits a 4500m pass between the huge glacier-capped mountains of Coropuna and Solimana (6323m) before dropping down to Cotahuasi. Reyna (43-0612) and Transportes Alex (42-4605) both offer services.

# Laguna de Salinas

This lake (4300m above sea level), east of Arequipa below Pichu Pichu and El Misti, is a salt lake that becomes a white **salt flat** during the dry months of May to December. Its size and the amount of water in it vary from year to year depending on the weather. During the rainy season it is a good place to see all three flamingo species, as well as myriad other Andean water birds.

One-day minibus tours from Arequipa cost about S150 per person; mountain-biking tours are also available.

# Lake Titicaca

**In Andean belief, Lake Titicaca is the birthplace of the sun.** It's also the largest lake in South America and the highest navigable body of water in the world. Banner blue skies contrast with bitterly cold nights. Enthralling and singular, the shimmering deep blue lake is the longtime home of highland cultures steeped in the old ways.

Pre-Inca Pukara, Tiwanaku and Collas all left their mark upon the landscape. Today the region is a mix of crumbling cathedrals, desolate altiplano and checkerboard fields backed by rolling hills and high Andean peaks. In this world, crops are still planted and harvested by hand. *Campesinos* (peasants) wear sandals recycled from truck tires, women work in petticoats and bowler hats, and llamas are tamed as pets.

Life here might appear austere, but ancient holidays are marked with riotous celebrations where elaborately costumed processions and brass bands rip cord a frenzy that lasts for days.

Shallows of Lake Titicaca, near Puno (p146)
ERIC L. WHEATER/GETTY IMAGES ©

# Lake Titicaca

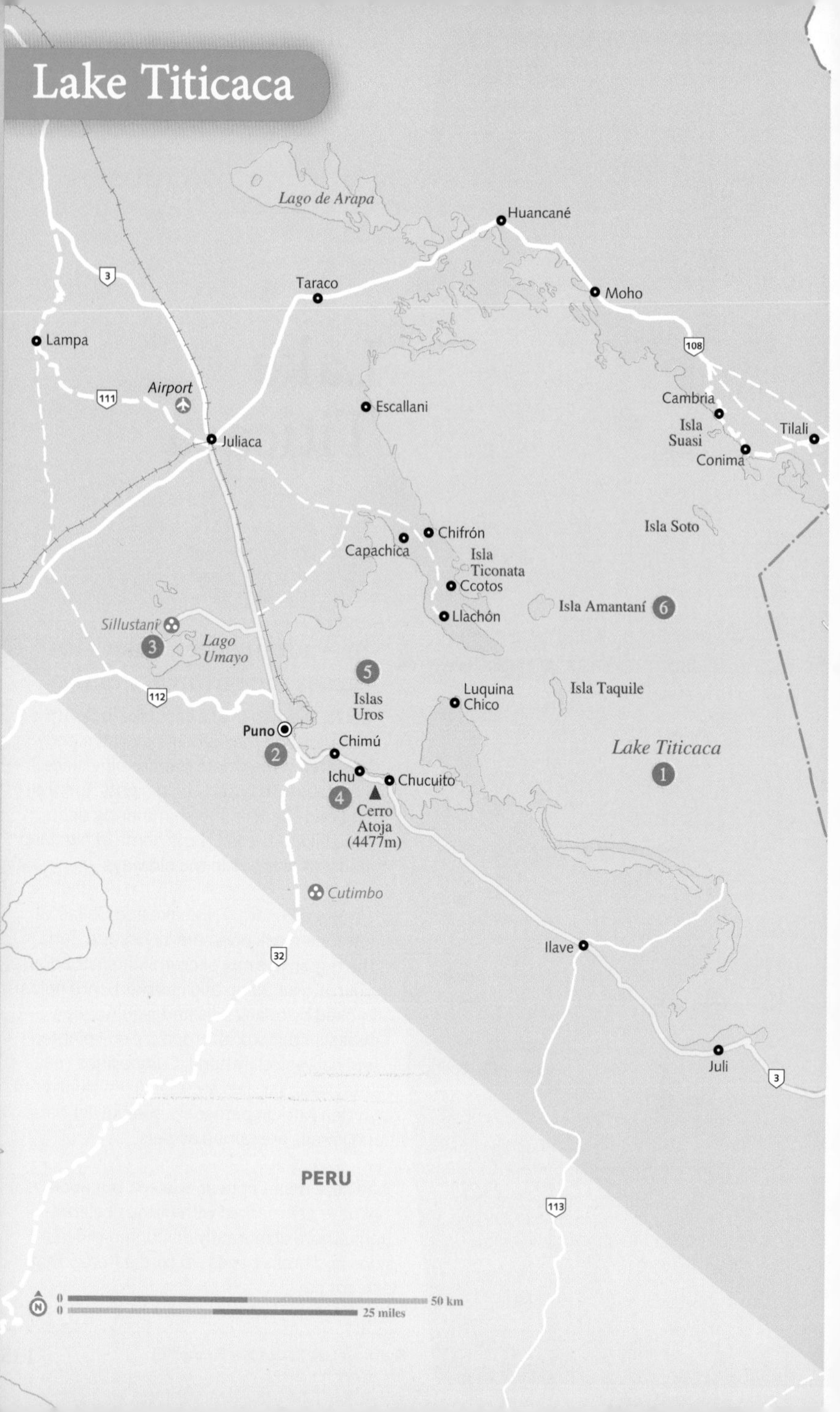

Lago de Arapa
Huancané
Taraco
Moho
3
108
Lampa
111
Airport
Escallani
Cambria
Isla Suasi
Tilali
Juliaca
Conima
Isla Soto
Chifrón
Capachica
Isla Ticonata
Ccotos
Isla Amantaní 6
Llachón
Sillustani
3
Lago Umayo
5
Islas Uros
Luquina Chico
Isla Taquile
112
Puno
2
Chimú
Lake Titicaca
1
Ichu
Chucuito
4
Cerro Atoja (4477m)
Cutimbo
32
Ilave
Juli
3
PERU
113
0 50 km
0 25 miles

1 Lake Titicaca
2 Costumes, Puno
3 Funerary Towers, Sillustani
4 Ruins, Ichu
5 Islas Uros
6 Isla Amantaní
Puerto Acosta
BOLIVIA
Isla Campanario
Isla del Sol
Isla de la Luna
Yampupata
Copacabana
Estrecho de Tiquina
Chua
Huatajata
Sahuiña
Yunguyo
Pomata
Punta Hermosa
Isla Taquiri
Anapia
Laguna de Wiñaymarca
Zepita
Desaguadero
LA PAZ

# Lake Titicaca Highlights

1

## Around Lake Titicaca

Islands that float. A glittering lake. Ancient sites littered with towering tombs that once held entire clans. The Puno and Lake Titicaca area offer the traveler some truly wondrous, surreal sites. Who needs novels laced with magical realism, when you can see it all live? **Above:** *Totora-*reed boat; **Top right:** Isla del Sol (p159); **Bottom right:** Isla Amantaní (p158)

### Need to Know

**HIGH SEASON** June to August is driest, but very cold. **ALTITUDE ADJUSTMENT** The area is very high up. Allow extra time to acclimatize. **For further coverage, see p345.**

Local Knowledge

# Lake Titicaca Don't Miss List

BY BEN ORLOVE, ANTHROPOLOGIST RESEARCHING THE ANDES SINCE THE '70S AND AUTHOR OF *LINES IN THE WATER: NATURE AND CULTURE AT LAKE TITICACA*

## 1 HIT THE ISLANDS INDEPENDENTLY

If you go on a tour, you're going to be with lots of people, making it difficult to explore. If you can, hire a boat independently. In addition to seeing less-visited islands, you'll be able to poke in and out of the reeds, where you'll find incredible birdlife – such as the flightless grebe, which is endemic to the area. They can hold their breath underwater for what seems like an impossible length of time. But they will surface – keep an eye out for them!

## 2 TAKE A MORNING WALK AROUND CHUCUITO

If you start at the main plaza in Chucuito (p155), you can hike up Cerro Atoja. It's not a hard walk and there are plenty of trails. You'll get views of the lake, but the best part is this extraordinary contrast of densely settled agricultural areas with the more isolated pastures higher up. Within hours, you can experience different worlds.

## 3 VISIT LAMPA

This is an extraordinary little town (p152) to the northwest of Puno, via Juliaca. It's one of those places that is preserved in amber – the center of town is lined with low, two-story buildings with balconies. It offers a real flavor for how things once were in the Andes.

## 4 EAT ADVENTUROUSLY

A particularly good local dish is *ajíde lengua,* a spicy stew made with beef tongue. Pay close attention to the potatoes you're served – there will likely be different kinds, each with a unique flavor.

## 5 DON'T BE AFRAID TO GO IN THE RAINY SEASON

In the dry season, the roads are better. But in the rainy season, the entire area feels incredibly alive. If you take walks in rural areas, you'll see these slow-flying iridescent beetles and sometimes even hummingbirds.

## Gaze Upon Elaborate Costumes

Puno is Peru's *capital folklórica* (folkloric capital), where colorful processions can take over the city's streets for days – especially in early February, during the fiesta in honor of the Virgen de la Candelaria. Have a look at some of the extravagant costumes worn during these elaborate street parades at Puno's tiny, quirky Coca Museum (p147).

2

3

## Visit Awe-Inspiring Funerary Towers

Massive towers of granite dot the altiplano around Sillustani (p154), where various pre-Columbian civilizations built massive cylindrical tombs in which entire family groups were interred. Known as *chullpas*, some of them reached a staggering height of 12m. In a country chock-full of unusual sights, this is bound to be somewhere near the top of the list.

## Hike to a Peaceful Ruin

4

Just south of Puno, the diminutive lakeside community of Ichu (p155) offers the opportunity for a short hike up to a multilayered temple complex with unimpeded 360-degree views – totally unencumbered by tour groups. (A great photo op.) The walk will take you through sleepy farmlands to an overgrown complex, a rare opportunity to have an ancient site to yourself. Traveling from Puno to Ichu

5

## Set Foot on a Floating Island

The Islas Uros (p156) offer an experience like no other: the opportunity to visit buoyant islands crafted entirely out of layers of *totora* reeds. These inhabited floating settlements were begun by the Uros people centuries ago – as a way of getting away from the conquering Collas and Incas. Just remember: you're not on solid ground. Watch your step!

6

## Shack Up with a Local Family

You haven't quite experienced a country until you've broken bread with its people. Isla Amantaní (p158), in the middle of Lake Titicaca, offers an opportunity to do more than that: live with them for a night or two. You'll be cooking over open fires, joining them as they do their chores and perhaps even jumping in on a traditional dance – all of it totally unforgettable!

# Lake Titicaca's Best...

## Hotels & Restaurants

- **Titilaka** (p149) A luxurious lodge on a secluded patch of Titicaca shoreline
- **Casa Andina Isla Suasi** (p159) Occupying a private island in the lake, it's as exclusive as resorts get
- **Casa Panq'arani** (p149) This traditional Puno home with a flower-filled courtyard offers a restful B&B
- **Mojsa** (p151) A thoughtful range of Andean and international foods in Puno

## Churches

- **Catedral de Puno** (p146) Puno's majestic baroque cathedral, completed in 1757
- **Iglesia de Santiago de Apostol** (p152) Lampa's main church contains the odd sight of St James on a taxidermied horse and a replica of Michelangelo's Pietà
- **Templo de Santo Domingo** (p155) In Chucuito, see the altiplano's oldest church, founded in 1534

## Pre-Columbian Sites

- **Sillustani** (p154) Cylindrical funerary towers that predate the Incas
- **Isla Taquile** (p156) A small island with Inca terraces – and a small set of ruins, like a cherry on top
- **Chucuito** (p155) More stone phalluses than you can, er, shake a stone phallus at
- **Cutimbo** (p155) Funerary towers, some featuring ancient carvings

## Vistas

- **Sillustani** (p154) Funerary towers on a spit of land partially encircled by the Lago Umayo
- **Isla Taquile** (p156) The hillsides of this fabled island offer views of the Bolivian Andes in the distance
- **Ichu** (p155) 360-degree views from an abandoned temple site
- **Islas Uros** (p156) See starry skies and the twinkling lights of Puno in the distance

**Left:** Selling textiles on the Islas Uros (p156);
**Above:** Templo de la Fertilidad, Chucuito (p155)



# Need to Know

### ADVANCE PLANNING

- **One month before** Make arrangements for a homestay on one of the many islands in Lake Titicaca
- **Three weeks before** Reserve a hotel in Puno – especially during high season (June through August)
- **One day before** Arrange day trips to Sillustani, and other pre-Columbian sites in the area

### RESOURCES

- **Chucuito Travel Information** (www.chucuito.org)
- **Pachamama Radio** (www.pachamamaradio.org) Local news

### GETTING AROUND

- **Air** Daily flights from and to Lima arrive and depart from the airport in Juliaca, about an hour north of Puno
- **Boat** Tour companies and ferries make jaunts to the most popular islands
- **Bus** Minibuses connect the disparate points around town and beyond, while long-haul operators make the journey to Cuzco and Arequipa
- **Train** Thrice-weekly service to Cuzco – a popular tourist attraction, complete with glass-walled observation car
- **Walk** The way to get around the narrow streets of Puno – and Lake Titicaca's many carless islands

### BE FOREWARNED

- **Stay warm** Weather conditions are extreme; bring extra warm clothes – especially if you are doing a homestay on one of the islands
- **Altitude** The heights are staggering – allow time to acclimatize, eat light and refrain from drinking alcohol
- **Photography** Locals don't like being photographed without permission; be respectful and be prepared to pay for the privilege
- **Operating hours** These can be erratic – especially in tiny villages
- **Safety** Pickpocketing and muggings have been an issue at some tourist sites; stay aware and travel in groups

# Puno & Lake Titicaca Itineraries

*From jaunts to see ancient ruins to boat tours of unusual islands on the world's highest commercially navigable lake – you can cover the area's top spots in three days. Opt for five if you want to do some real exploring.*

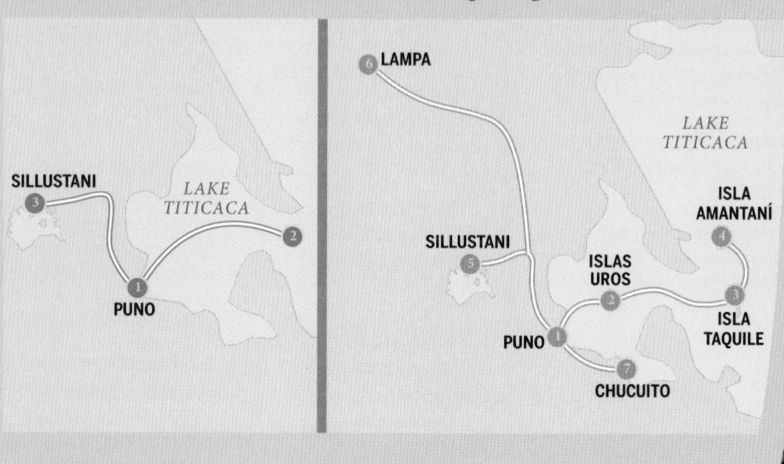

AROUND PUNO

## Highland Jaunts

Using the city as your base, this itinerary is perfect if you want a quick survey of the major sights in and around Lake Titicaca.

On the first day, take it easy (you're up high!). Leisurely explore the splendid sights of **(1) Puno**, such as its baroque cathedral and the charming Coca Museum, which in addition to providing all manner of information on coca, has excellent exhibits on the costumes worn during religious fiestas. If you're not winded, make a final stop at the Casa del Corregidor for a little colonial splendor and some fair-trade arts and crafts.

On day two, go on a tour of the remarkable, inhabited **(2) islands of Lake Titicaca**. These generally include quick visits to the floating islands of the Uros, as well as the dry-land Inca settlements of Amantaní or Taquile. While you're exploring, look for intricate crafts made out of reeds – these are local to the area. In the evening, retire to Puno for a little bit of highland nightlife.

The last day will be all about ruins – specifically *chullpas*, the massive funerary towers that look like spaceship capsules. Find them in abundance at **(3) Sillustani**, which also happens to have excellent views of the sapphire blue Lago Umayo.

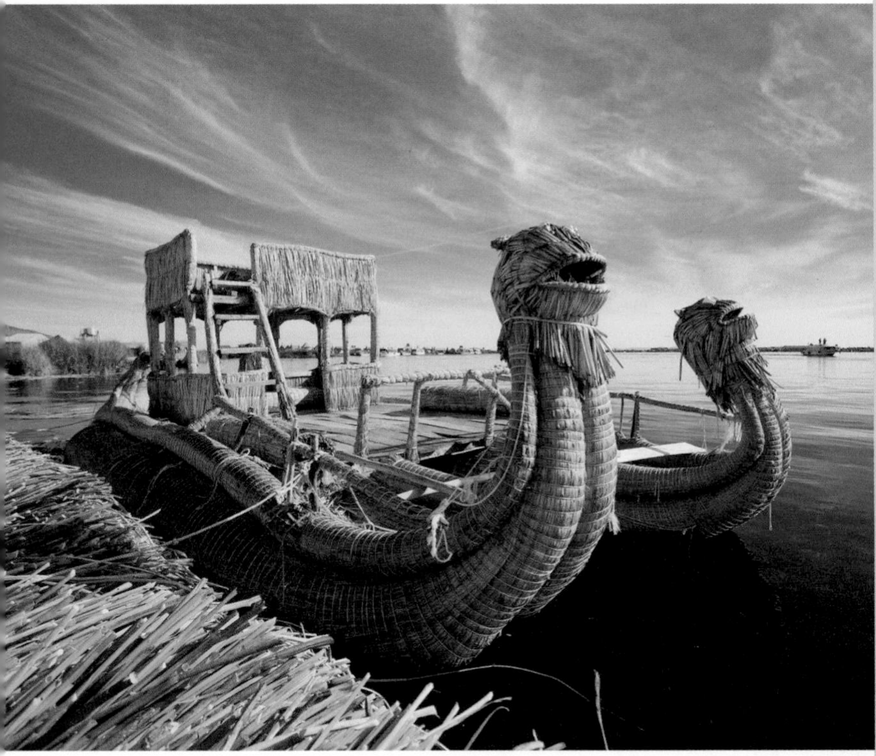

5 DAYS

PUNO TO THE ISLANDS

## Living Like a Local

Spend the first day engaged in leisurely activities in **(1) Puno**, given its literally breathtaking altitude of 3830m. Hit its cultural highlights, including the cathedral and the Coca Museum.

The next day, set out for a one- to two-night homestay on one of the Lake Titicaca islands. If you like your islands to float, then make arrangements to stay on the **(2) Islas Uros**. Otherwise, boat over to **(3) Isla Taquile** or, better yet, the less-visited **(4) Isla Amantaní**. Here, you'll cook over an open flame, watch the moon rise over the lake and generally enjoy a simple, rural existence.

Afterwards, return to Puno for some land-lubbing. Spend a day taking in the nearby pre-Columbian site of **(5) Sillustani**, and, if you have time, visit the village of **(6) Lampa**, where a graceful church contains a lovely baroque facade and some highly unusual decor. (Hello, taxidermy!).

For your last full day in the area, head south to **(7) Chucuito**, where you can admire the stone phalluses at the Templo de la Fertilidad. Spend the last night back in town enjoying Puno's hospitable watering holes – and maybe a *cerveza* (beer), or two.

*Totora*-reed boat, Puno (p146)

TRAVELER1116/GETTY IMAGES ©

# Discover Lake Titicaca

## At a Glance

- **Puno** A bustling highland city in view of Lake Titicaca.
- **Sillustani** (p154) A site dotted with ancient funerary towers.
- **Chucuito** (p155) A diminutive lakeside village, home to a temple with very large phalluses.
- **Lake Titicaca Islands** (p156) Tiny islands that protect traditional ways of life.

Colonial church, Puno

J P DE MANNE/GETTY IMAGES ©

## PUNO

☎051 / POP 120,200 / ELEV 3830M

With a regal plaza, concrete block buildings and crumbling bricks that blend into the hills, Puno has its share of both grit and cheer – a jangling commercial center that also serves as Peru's *capital folklórica* (folkloric capital). The city's Virgen de la Candelaria parades are televised across the nation and the associated drinking is the stuff of legend.

While the colonial core harbors a few worthy sights, for most travelers Puno serves primarily as a jumping-off point for visiting the sights of Lake Titicaca.

### Sights & Activities

**CATEDRAL DE PUNO** Church

**(admission free; 8am-noon & 3-6pm)** On the western flank of the Plaza de Armas is Puno's baroque cathedral, which was completed in 1757. The interior is more spartan than you'd expect from the well-sculpted facade, but the ornate, silver-plated altar is worth a look.

**CASA DEL CORREGIDOR** Historic Building

**(☎35-1921; www.casadelcorregidor.pe; Deustua 576; 9:30am-7:30pm Mon-Fri, 12:30-7pm Sat)** An attraction in its own right, this 17th-century house is one of Puno's oldest residences. A former community center, it now houses a small fair-trade arts-and-crafts store.

**MUSEO CARLOS DREYER** Museum

**(Conde de Lemos 289; admission with English-speaking guide S15; 9:30am-7pm Mon-Sat)** Around the corner from Casa del Corregi-

BRENT WINEBRENNER/GETTY IMAGES ©

## Don't Miss Yavari

The oldest steamship on Lake Titicaca, the famed *Yavari* has turned from 19th-century British gunship into a museum and recommended bed and breakfast, with bunk-bed lodging and attentive service. And no, you don't have to be a navy buff – it's probably the most tranquil spot in Puno.

This storied vessel began its life in Europe – and its passage to Peru was no easy task. Built in 1862, in Birmingham, England, the *Yavari* (and its sister ship, the *Yapura*), were shipped in parts around Cape Horn to Arica (now northern Chile), before being moved by train to Tacna, then hauled over the Andes by mule to Puno. The odyssey took six years and the ship was finally launched on Christmas Day in 1870. Due to a shortage of coal, it was fueled with dried llama dung.

After years of service, it was decommissioned by the Peruvian Navy and the hull was left to rust on the lakeshore. In 1982 Englishwoman Meriel Larken decided to save this piece of Peruvian history. The Yavari Project was formed to buy and restore the vessel. Now it is moored behind the Sonesta Posada Hotel del Inca, about 5km from the center of Puno.

Its devoted crew happily gives guided tours. With prior notice, enthusiasts may even be able to see the engine fired up. The ship also motors across the lake seven times a year – though you will have to find out for yourself if it's still powered by llama dung.

### NEED TO KNOW

**☎36-9329; www.yavari.org; admission by donation; ⏰8am-1pm & 3-5:30pm; per person incl breakfast S99**

dor, this museum houses a fascinating collection of Puno-related archaeological artifacts and art. Upstairs there are three mummies and a full-scale fiberglass *chullpa* (funerary tower).

**COCA MUSEUM** Museum

**(☎36-5087; Deza 301; admission S5; ⏰9am-1pm & 3-8pm)** Tiny and quirky, this museum offers lots of interesting (if not well-presented) information about the coca

## Puno

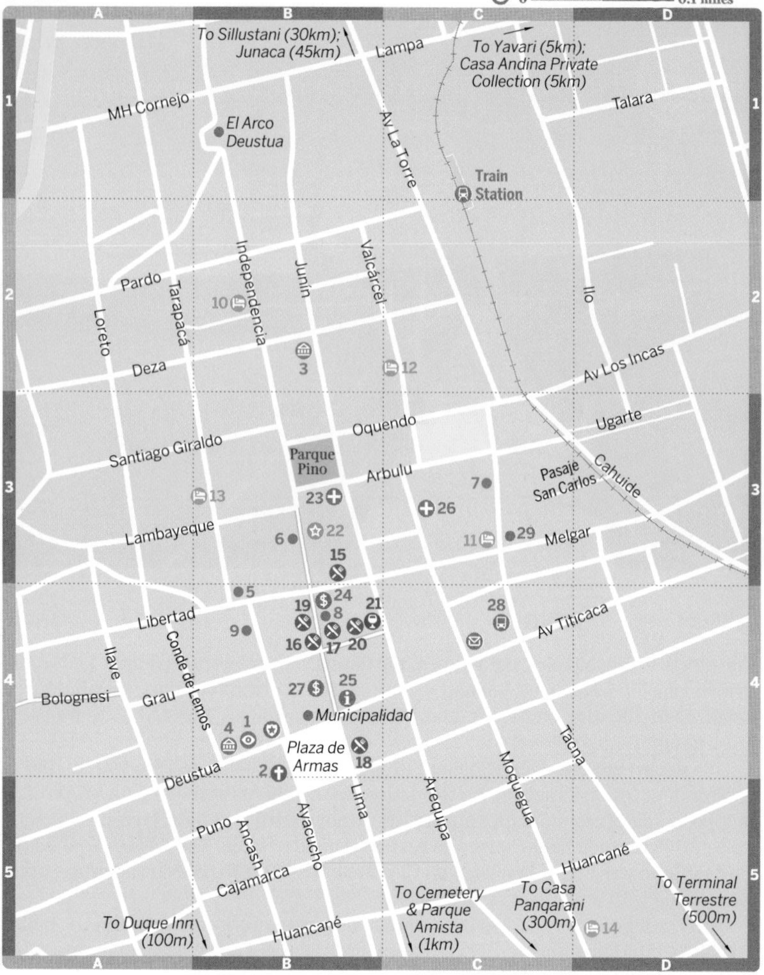

To Sillustani (30km); Junaca (45km)
To Yavari (5km); Casa Andina Private Collection (5km)
El Arco Deustua
Train Station
Parque Pino
Municipalidad
Plaza de Armas
To Duque Inn (100m)
To Cemetery & Parque Amista (1km)
To Casa Panqarani (300m)
To Terminal Terrestre (500m)

plant and its many uses. What makes it truly worthwhile, however, are the colorful displays of traditional costumes worn in Puno's vibrant street parades.

## Tours

Agencies abound and competition is fierce, leading to touting in streets and bus terminals, undeliverable promises, and prices so low as to undercut fair wages. Several of the cheaper tour agencies have reputations for ripping off islanders, with whom travelers stay overnight. Island-hopping tours, even with the better agencies, can be formulaic.

The following agencies offer responsible tours:

**All Ways Travel** (☎35-3979; www.titicacaperu.com; Deustua 576, 2nd fl) Has both classic and 'non-touristy' tours.

**Edgar Adventures** (☎35-3444; www.edgaradventures.com; Lima 328) Longtime agency with positive community involvement.

## Puno

**Sights**

1 Casa del Corregidor ........ B4
2 Catedral de Puno ........ B4
3 Coca Museum ........ B2
4 Museo Carlos Dreyer ........ B4

**Activities, Courses & Tours**

All Ways Travel ........ (see 1)
5 Crillon Tours ........ B4
6 Edgar Adventures ........ B3
7 Las Balsas Tours ........ C3
8 Nayra Travel ........ B4
9 Transturin ........ B4

**Sleeping**

10 Casa Andina Classic ........ B2
11 Colón Inn ........ C3
12 Hotel Italia ........ C2
13 Intiqa Hotel ........ B3
14 Mosoq Inn ........ D5

**Eating**

15 Balcones de Puno ........ B3
16 Café Tunki ........ B4
Colors ........ (see 6)
17 La Casona ........ B4
18 Mojsa ........ B4
19 Tulipans ........ B4
20 Ukuku's ........ B4

**Drinking**

21 Kamizaraky Rock Pub ........ B4

**Entertainment**

22 Ekeko's ........ B3

**Information**

23 Botica Fasa ........ B3
24 Interbank ........ B4
25 iPerú ........ B4
26 Medicentro Tourist's Health Clinic ........ C3
27 Scotiabank ........ B4

**Transport**

28 Inka Express ........ C4
29 LAN ........ C3
Star Peru ........ (see 16)

**Las Balsas Tours** (**☎36-4362; www.balsastours.com; Tacna 240**) Offers classic tours on a daily basis.

**Nayra Travel** (**☎36-4774, 975-1818; www.nayratravel.com; Lima 419, Office 105**) Local package tour operator.

## Sleeping

The following listings include hotels located outside the city, including lodges around the lake.

**TITILAKA** Luxury Hotel **$$$**
(**☎in Lima 1-700-5105; www.titilaka.com; Lake Titicaca; s/d with full board from US$301/530; @ wifi**) Located one hour south of Puno, on a secluded piece of rugged shore, Titilaka is a destination in itself. The look is contemporary Euro-Andino, with a palette that ranges from neutral to flirty (think blushing rose and purples). Touches of exquisite folk art combine with black-and-white photography of well-known Peruvian artists. Huge picture windows drink in the serene landscapes in every direction. Rooms sport king-sized beds warmed by hot water bottles, deep tubs, iPod docks and window ledge seating. There are games for kids, a spa and gourmet restaurant. The staff is groomed to please. While most guests go for the three-day packages, the nightly rate includes full board and local excursions like walks and kayaking.

**CASA PANQ'ARANI** B&B **$$**
(**☎36-4892, 951-677-005; www.casapanqarani.com; Jirón Arequipa 1086; s/tw/d incl breakfast S70/120/130; wifi**) This traditional Puno home has a flower-filled courtyard and inviting rooms lining a 2nd-floor balcony. But the real draw is the sincere hospitality of owners Edgar and Consuelo. Rooms are ample, sporting comfortable beds with crochet bedspreads and fresh flowers. There are also sunny spots for lounging. Don't miss the opportunity to try Consuelo's gourmet altiplano cooking (meals S30 with advance request).

## If You Like... Fiestas & Folklore

If you like festivals, you've come to the right place. Puno is the folkloric capital of Peru, boasting as many as 300 traditional dances and celebrating numerous fiestas throughout the year. Dazzling outfits can range from strikingly grotesque masks and animal costumes to glittering sequined uniforms. Accompanying music uses a host of instrumentation, from Spanish-influenced brass and string instruments to percussion and wind instruments that have changed little since Inca times.

1 **LA VIRGEN DE LA CANDELARIA**
The festival in honor of Puno's patron virgin is celebrated over several days with masses and processions. It culminates with a thunderous street party on February 2, when thousands of splendidly attired dancers perform.

2 **PUNO WEEK**
Centered on Puno Day (November 5), this festival is celebrated in style and marks the birth of the Inca Empire, when Manco Cápac and Mama Ocllo first emerged from Lake Titicaca.

3 **EPIPHANY**
Masked paraders take to the streets for the festival better known as Día de los Reyes (Three Kings Day), when celebrants honor the magi who bestowed gifts on the baby Jesus. It takes place on January 6.

4 **FIESTA SAN JUAN DE DIOS**
On March 8 a more demure religious procession honors St John of God, the patron saint of the sick.

5 **FIESTA DE SANTIAGO**
The Feast of St James on July 25 is a big feast day on Isla Taquile, when dancing, music and general carousing lasts several days, and islanders make offerings to Pachamama (Mother Earth).

**CASA ANDINA PRIVATE COLLECTION** Luxury Hotel **$$$**
(**☎213-9739; www.casa-andina.com; Av Sesqui Centenario 1970; d incl breakfast from US$446; @📶**) On the outskirts of Puno, with a lovely lakeside ambience, this upmarket outpost managed by the Peruvian hotel chain has 46 rooms, rambling gardens and a gourmet restaurant. It even has its own train stop for those coming from Cuzco. The look is rustic chic, with impeccable white linens and subtle decor. All rooms come with oxygen.

**COLÓN INN** Hotel **$$**
(**☎35-1432; www.coloninn.com; Tacna 290; s/d/tr incl breakfast S150/180/225; @📶**) This elegant European-owned option is housed in a Republican-era building featuring Cuzco-school paintings and a covered courtyard. Rooms are smallish but stocked with amenities, while shared spaces are sumptuously colonial. The onsite restaurant specializes in Belgian and French cuisine; reservations recommended.

**CASA ANDINA CLASSIC** Hotel **$$$**
(**☎213-9739; www.casa-andina.com; Jirón Independencia 143; d incl breakfast S258; @📶**) Casa Andina's midrange option features snappy service and 50 tasteful rooms with muted colors, decorated with Andean folk motifs. Rooms have heat, lockboxes, blackout curtains and flat-screen TVs. Guests also get free oxygen and *mate* (herbal tea) to help acclimate.

**MOSOQ INN** Hotel **$$**
(**☎36-7518; www.mosoqinn.com; Jr Moquegua 673; s/d/tr incl breakfast S106/133/172; @📶**) This modern hotel features 15 rooms distributed over three stories. High-quality mattresses ensure sound sleeping in ample, tangerine-hued rooms. There are also big closets, cable TV and space heaters. Recommended.

**HOTEL ITALIA** Hotel **$$**
(**☎36-7706; www.hotelitaliaperu.com; Valcárcel 122; s/d/tr S110/150/190; @📶**) Snug rooms have parquet floors, cable TV, hot

showers and heating but vary in quality at this large, well-established spot. The long-serving staff is efficient, and the delicious buffet breakfast includes salty black olives and Puno's own triangular anise bread.

**INTIQA HOTEL** Hotel **$$**
(☎36-6900; www.intiqahotel.com; Tarapacá 272; s/d incl breakfast S159/186; @ 📶) Finally, a midrange Puno hotel with a sense of style. The 33 large, earth-tone rooms feature snug duvets, extra pillows, desks, flat-screen TVs and a safe box. The elevator is somewhat of a rarity in Puno. It can arrange free pickups at the bus station.

## Eating

Many restaurants don't advertise their *menús* (set meals), which are cheaper than ordering à la carte. For a cheap snack, try *api* (hot, sweet corn juice) – a serious comfort food found in several places on Calle Oquendo between Parque Pino and the *supermercado*. Order it with a paper-thin, wickedly delicious envelope of deep-fried dough.

**MOJSA** Peruvian **$$**
(☎36-3182; Lima 394; mains S18-35; ⏲8am-10pm) The go-to place for locals and travelers alike, Mojsa lives up to its name – which is Aymara for 'delicious.' It has a thoughtful range of Peruvian and international food, including innovative trout dishes and a design-your-own salad option. All meals start with fresh bread and a bowl of olives. In the evening crisp brick-oven pizzas are on offer.

**LA CASONA** Peruvian **$$**
(☎35-1108; http://lacasona-restaurant.com; Lima 423, 2nd fl; mains S12-36) Another solid choice, with upscale *criollo* (spicy Peruvian fare with Spanish and African influences) and international food and portions on the small side. Trout comes bathed in garlic or chili sauce, and there's also pasta, salad and soup.

**TULIPANS** Pizzeria **$$**
(☎35-1796; Lima 394; mains S12-22) Highly recommended for its yummy sandwiches, big plates of meat, and piled-high vegetables, this cozy spot is warmed by the pizza oven in the corner. The courtyard patio is attractive for warm days – whenever those happen! Pizzas are only available at night.

**CAFÉ TUNKI** Cafe **$**
(Lima 394; ⏲10am-7pm Mon-Sat) This closet-sized cafe serves hot cups of coffee, brewed with acclaimed beans from the tropical side of Puno province that are available for purchase by the kilo.

**BALCONES DE PUNO** Peruvian **$$**
(☎36-5300; Libertad 354; mains S14-32) A dinner-show venue that also serves up traditional local food. The nightly show (7:30pm to 9pm) stands out for its quality and sincerity – no panpipe butchering of *El Cóndor Pasa* here. Save room for dessert, a major focus of dining here. Reserve ahead.

**UKUKU'S** Peruvian **$$**
(Grau 172, 2nd fl; mains from S20) Crowds of travelers and locals thaw out in this toasty restaurant, which dishes up good local and Andean food (try alpaca steak with baked apples, or the quinoa omelet), as well as pizzas, pastas, Asian-style vegetarian fare and espresso drinks.

**COLORS** Fusion **$$**
(☎36-9254; Lima 342; mains S16-28; ⏲7am-11pm; 📶) A couch cafe with free wireless, Colors also caters to travelers with a slick look and fusion food. The menu is so extensive it's hard to root out the specialties, and the staff may not be much help.

## Drinking & Entertainment

Central Puno's nightlife is geared toward tourists, with lively bars scattered around the bright lights on Jirón Lima (where touts hand out free-drink coupons) and next to the plaza on Jirón Puno.

## Detour: Lampa

Known as La Ciudad Rosada (the Pink City) for its dusty, pink-colored buildings, the charming little town of Lampa is an attractive old Spanish outpost. A significant commercial center in colonial days, it still shows a strong Spanish influence. Following are some of the key sattractions:

**Iglesia de Santiago de Apostol** (Plaza de Armas; tours S10; ⌚9am-12:30pm & 2-4pm) A lovely baroque church, well worth seeing for its life-size sculpture of St James (Santiago) on a real stuffed horse, returning from the dead to trample the Moors. Oh, and did we mention the huge domed tomb topped by a copy of Michelangelo's *Pietá*? Sublime.

**Municipalidad de Lampa** (Town Hall; admission S2; ⌚8am-12:45pm & 1:30-4pm Mon-Fri; 9am-1pm Sat & Sun) A historic spot that has a little museum honoring Peruvian expressionist painter Victor Humareda (1920–86), as well as another copy of Michelangelo's *Pietá*.

**Casa Romero** (☎952-65-1511, 952-71-9073; casaromerolampa.com; Aguirre 327; s/d/tr incl breakfast S50/80/120) This friendly guesthouse has well-appointed rooms with down duvets. It can provide full board with advance booking or you can drop in on the restaurants around the plaza.

Lampa is located northwest of Puno, via Juliaca. It's an excellent place for a day trip or to kill a few hours before flying out of Juliaca. You can also hire a taxi for the day to drive you over from Puno and wait around while you see the sights.

**KAMIZARAKY ROCK PUB** Pub

(Grau 158) With a classic-rock soundtrack, unbelievably cool bartenders and liquor-infused coffee drinks to keep you warm during Puno's bone-chilling nights, Kamizaraky may be a hard place to leave.

**EKEKO'S** Club

(Lima 355, 2nd fl) Travelers and locals alike gravitate to this tiny, ultraviolet dance floor splashed with psychedelic murals. It moves to a thumping mixture of modern beats and old favorites, from salsa to techno, which can be heard several blocks away.

## Shopping

*Artesanías* (handicrafts) – from musical instruments and jewelry to scale models of reed islands to wool and alpaca sweaters – are sold in every second shop in the town center. For household goods and clothes, head to **Mercado Bellavista** on Av El Sol (though watch out for pickpockets).

## Information

### Dangers & Annoyances

There are scenic lookouts on the hills above town, but since assaults and robberies have been reported (even by groups), it's not recommended to visit them unless there is a drastic improvement in security. If you are the victim of a crime, you can file a report with the **Policía de Turismo** (Tourist Police; ☎35-3988; Deustua 558; ⌚24hr). There is also a policeman on duty at the bus terminal.

### Medical Services

**Botica Fasa** (☎36-6862; Arequipa 314; ⌚24hr) A well-stocked pharmacy that's attended 24 hours, though you may have to pound on the door late at night.

**Medicentro Tourist's Health Clinic** (☎36-5909, 951-62-0937; Moquegua 191; ⏰24hr) English and French spoken; will also come to your hotel.

## Money

Various banks have 24-hour ATMs that dispense soles and US dollars.

**Interbank** (Lima at Libertad)

**Scotiabank** (Jirón Lima 458)

## Tourist Information

**iPerú** (☎36-5088; Plaza de Armas cnr Lima & Deustua; ⏰9am-6pm Mon-Sat, to 1pm Sun) Puno's helpful and well-informed tourist office also runs Indecopi, the tourist-protection agency, which can register complaints.

# Getting There & Away

## Air

The nearest airport is in Juliaca, about an hour away. Hotels can book you a shuttle bus for around S15. Airlines with offices in Puno include **LAN** (☎36-7227; Tacna 299) and **Star Peru** (Lima 154).

## Boat

Ferries for the various Lake Titicaca islands depart daily from the **port** (Av del Puerto). See islands coverage (starting on p156) for costs and times.

## Bus

The **terminal terrestre** (☎36-4737; Primero de Mayo 703) houses Puno's long-distance buses traveling to Cuzco, Arequipa and beyond. Recommended companies include:

**Cruz del Sur** (☎in Lima 01-311-5050; www.cruzdelsur.com.pe)

**Ormeño** (☎36-8176; www.grupo-ormeno.com.pe)

**Tour Peru** (☎35-2991; www.tourperu.com.pe)

Islanders wearing traditional dress, Isla Taquile (p156)



The most enjoyable way to get to Cuzco is via **Inka Express** (☎36-5654; www.inkaexpress.com; Tacna 346), which offers luxury buses with panoramic windows, as well as an English-speaking guide and oxygen. The trip takes eight hours and costs S143.

There is a departure tax of S1.

## Train

The fancy Andean Explorer train, which includes a glass-walled observation car and lunch, costs US$150. Trains depart from Puno's **train station** (☎36-9179; www.perurail.com; Av La Torre 224; ⏰7am-noon & 3-6pm Mon-Fri, 7am-3pm Sat) at 8am, arriving at Cuzco around 6pm. Services run on Monday, Wednesday and Saturday from November to March, with an extra departure on Friday from April to October. Tickets can be purchased online.

# Getting Around

A short taxi ride anywhere in town (and as far as the transport terminals) costs S4. *Mototaxis* are a bit cheaper at S2.

Right: *Chullpas* (funerary towers), Sillustani;
Below: *Totora*-reed homes, Islas Uros (p156)

# AROUND PUNO

## Sillustani

Standing on rolling hills on the Lago Umayo peninsula, the *chullpas* of **Sillustani (admission S10; ⌚8am-5pm)** can be seen for kilometers against the desolate altiplano landscape.

The ancient Colla people who once dominated the area were a fearsome, Aymara-speaking ethnicity, later integrated into the southeastern part of the Inca empire. They buried their nobility in *chullpas,* which can be seen scattered widely around the region. The most impressive of these are at Sillustani, where the tallest reach a height of 12m. The cylindrical structures housed the remains of complete family groups, along with plenty of food and belongings for the journey into the next world.

Nowadays, nothing remains of the burials, but the *chullpas* are well preserved. The area is partially encircled by the sparkling **Lago Umayo** (3890m), which is home to a wide variety of plants and Andean waterbirds, plus a small island with vicuñas (threatened, wild relatives of llamas).

Tours to Sillustani leave Puno at around 2:30pm daily and cost from S35. The round-trip takes about 3½ hours and allows you about 1½ hours at the ruins. If you'd prefer more time at the site, hire a private taxi for S70 with one hour waiting time. Take sunscreen and a hat. There is no shade to speak of.

For overnight stays in the area, **Atun Colla (☎951-90-5006, 951-50-2390; www.turismovivencialatuncolla.com)** offers *turismo vivencial* (homestays). You can help your host family with farming, hike to lookouts and lesser-known archaeological sites, visit the tiny museum and eat dirt – this area is known for its edible *arcilla* (clay). Served up as a sauce on boiled potato, it goes down surprisingly well.

## Cutimbo

The dramatic site of **Cutimbo (admission S6; 8am-5pm)** has an extraordinary position atop a table-topped volcanic hill surrounded by a fertile plain. Its modest number of well-preserved *chullpas,* built by the Colla, Lupaca and Inca cultures, come in both square and cylindrical shapes. Look closely and you'll find several monkeys, pumas and snakes carved into the structures.

A little more than 20km from Puno, this place receives few visitors, which can make it problematic for independent travelers, who have been assaulted here. Go in a group. A taxi will cost approximately S70.

## Ichu

Ten kilometers out of Puno, on the lake's southern shore, this rural community is spread across a gorgeous green valley that is home to a little-known ruin with superb views – a multilayered temple complex with breathtaking 360-degree vistas. It's a great place for a hike.

To get there, leave the Panamericana at Ichu's second exit (after the service station) and head inland past the house marked 'Villa Lago 1960.' Continue on for 2km, bearing left at the junction, aiming for the two small, terraced hills you can see in the left of the valley. After bearing left at a second junction (you'll pass the school if you miss it), the road takes you between the two hills. Turn left again and head straight up the first one. Fifteen minutes of stiff climbing brings you to the hilltop complex.

This can be done as an easy half-day trip from Puno. Taxis from Puno can take you to the top of the hill and wait while you hike. Take plenty of water and food; there are no facilities.

## Chucuito

About 19km south of Puno, this little village (population 1100) on Lake Titicaca's south shore offers one outlandish attraction: the **Templo de la Fertilidad (Inca Uyu;**

admission S5; ⌚8am-5pm). Its dusty grounds are scattered with large stone phalluses, some up to 1.2m in length. Local guides tell entertaining stories about the carvings, including tales of maidens sitting atop the stony joysticks to increase their fertility.

Further uphill from the main road is the **main plaza**, which has two attractive colonial churches, **Santo Domingo** and **Nuestra Señora de la Asunción**. (Ask around for the elusive caretakers if you want to get a glimpse inside.)

If you fancy spending the night, try the unmissable **Taypikala Hotel** (☎79-2252; www.taypikala.com; Km18 Panamericana Sur), a new-age confusion of model condors and artificial rocks. Rooms have lake and garden views. Across the highway, its swanky new sister hotel **Taypikala Lago** (☎79-2266; www.taypikala.com; Calle Sandia s/n; s/d/tr S$201/254/320) offers better views, with understated luxury and more subtle architecture.

Otherwise, agencies in Puno offer day trips.

# LAKE TITICACA ISLANDS

Lake Titicaca's islands are world famous for their peaceful beauty and the living tradition of their agrarian cultures, which date to pre-Columbian times. All travel agencies in Puno offer island-hopping tours of the major islands. Travelers often complain that these offer only a superficial view of the islands.

For more insight into the culture, it's recommended to stay overnight at a homestay or travel independently. Regular ferries from Puno travel to all the major islands and tickets are valid for 15 days, so you can island-hop at will.

Be aware that not all islanders welcome tourism, since not all benefit from it. Plus, many see the frequent intrusions into their daily life as disruptive. It's important to respect the privacy of islanders and show courtesy. Our advice: go with a recommended operator (p148).

## Islas Uros

Just 5km east of Puno, the unique floating **Islas Uros** (admission S5) are Lake Titicaca's top tourist attraction. They're built using the buoyant *totora* reeds that grow abundantly in the shallows of the lake. The lives of the Uros people are interwoven with these reeds, which are used to make their homes, their boats and the crafts they create for tourists. The reeds are even partially edible.

Always a small ethnic group, the Uros began their unusual floating existence centuries ago in an effort to isolate themselves from the aggressive Collas and Incas. The islands are constructed from many layers of *totora*, which are constantly replenished from the top as they rot from the bottom, so the ground is always soft and springy. (Be careful where you step.) Some islands also have elaborately designed versions of traditional reed boats. Be prepared to pay for a ride or to take photographs.

An outstanding option for staying overnight is in the reed huts of **Isla Khantati** (☎951-69-5121, 951-47-2355; uroskhantati@hotmail.com; per person full board S165). Managed by Cristina Suaña, an Uros native, the island has a number of impeccable semitraditional huts (with solar power and outhouses). The rates include transfers from Puno, fresh and varied meals, fishing, some cultural explanations and the pleasure of Cristina's effervescent company. The relaxed pace may not be ideal for those with little time on their hands.

### Getting There & Away

Getting here independently is easy. Ferries leave from the port in Puno (S12) at least once an hour from 6am to 4pm. The community-owned ferry service visits two islands, on a rotation basis. Ferries to Taquile and Amantaní can also drop you off in the Uros.

## Isla Taquile

Inhabited for thousands of years, **Isla Taquile** (admission S5), 35km east of Puno, is a tiny 7-sq-km island with a population of about 2000 people – and natural beauty that makes it a standout. The Quechua-speaking islanders are distinct from most of the surrounding Aymara-speaking communities and maintain a strong sense of group identity.

The island has a fascinating tradition of handicrafts, and the creations are made according to a system of deeply ingrained social customs. Men wear tightly woven woolen hats that resemble floppy nightcaps, which they knit themselves. They wear red hats if they are married and red and white hats if they are single; different colors can denote a man's current or past social position.

Taquile women weave thick, colorful waistbands for their husbands, which are worn with roughly spun white shirts and thick, calf-length black pants. Women wear eye-catching outfits comprising multilayered skirts and delicately embroidered blouses. These fine garments are considered some of the best-made traditional clothes in Peru, and can be bought in the cooperative store on the island's main plaza.

## Sights & Activities

Visitors are free to wander around, explore the ruins and enjoy the tranquility. The island is a wonderful place to catch a sunset and gaze at the moon, which looks twice as bright in the crystalline air, rising over the breathtaking peaks of the Cordillera Real in the distance. Take in the lay of the land while it's still light – with no roads, streetlights or big buildings to use as landmarks, travelers have been known to get lost in the dark.

A stairway of more than 500 steps leads from the dock to the center of the island. The climb takes a breathless 20 minutes if you're acclimatized – more if you're not.

## Festivals & Events

The **Fiesta de Santiago** (Feast of St James; July 25), Easter and New Year's Day are festive and rowdy.

Islanders on Islas Uros

AXEL FASSIO/GETTY IMAGES ©

## Sleeping & Eating

*Hospedajes* (small, family-owned inns) offer basic accommodations for around S20 a night. Meals are additional (S10 to S15 for breakfast; S20 for lunch). Options range from a room in a family house to small guesthouses. Most have indoor toilets and electric showers. Lodgings can be booked with a tour operator or on your own once you arrive. Since the community rotates visitors to lodgings, there is little room for choosing.

Restaurants all offer the same fare of *sopa de quinua* (quinoa soup) – absolutely delicious everywhere on Lake Titicaca – and lake trout. Dishes start at S20. Consider eating in the **Restaurante Comunál**, Taquile's only community-run food outlet.

## Information

Bring small bills in local currency, since change is elusive and there is no place to exchange foreign money. There is limited electricity, but it's not always available. Pack a flashlight for overnight stays.

## Getting There & Away

**Ferries** (round-trip S20) leave from the port of Puno for Taquile starting at about 6:45am. If the ferry stops at the Islas Uros, you will also have to pay the admission there. There's a ferry from Amantaní to Taquile every morning.

# Isla Amantaní

The more remote **Isla Amantaní** (admission S5), population 4000, is a few kilometers north of Taquile. The island is very quiet (no dogs allowed!), boasts great views and has no roads or vehicles. Several hills are topped by ruins, among the highest and best known of which are **Pachamama** (Mother Earth) and **Pachatata** (Father Earth). These date to the Tiwanaku culture, a largely Bolivian culture that appeared around Lake Titicaca and expanded rapidly between 200 BC and AD 1000.

Trips generally involve an overnight stay, in which guests help cook on open fires in dirt-floor kitchens. The villagers sometimes organize rousing traditional dances, letting travelers dress in their traditional party gear to dance the night away. Don't forget to look up at the starry

Isla Amantaní

STEPHEN COLLECTOR/GETTY IMAGES ©

## Detour: In Bolivia: Islands of the Sun and Moon

The most famous islands in Lake Titicaca are located on the Bolivian side of the lake: the Islas del Sol y de la Luna. **Isla del Sol** (Island of the Sun) is the legendary birthplace of Manco Cápac and Mama Ocllo. Here, a series of Inca remains include the **Chincana** (a labyrinth complex), the fortresslike **Pilkokayna** and the gorgeous **Inca Stairway** in the south. The less-visited **Isla de la Luna** (Island of the Moon) has some partially rebuilt ruins that once housed virgins of the sun, women chosen at a young age to serve the sun god Inti.

Sunshine and altitude can take their toll, so bring extra water, food and sunblock. You can visit the main sights on organized trips from Puno, but it is also possible to spend the night via homestays.

Puno-based operators such as **Transturin** (35-2771; www.transturin.com; Ayacucho 148; 2-day tour US$241) and **Crillon Tours** (35-2771; www.titicaca.com; Ayacucho 148) offer one- and two-day tours that include visits to these islands, as well as to the Bolivian coastal settlement of Copacabana. Note that these require immigration proceedings – for which you will need a passport and, in some cases, a visa.



night sky as you stagger home. It is an unforgettable experience.

### Sleeping & Eating

When you arrive, **Amantani Community Lodging** (36-9714), basically the island families, will allocate you to your accommodation according to a rotating system. Please respect this process. There's no problem asking for families or friends to be together. A bed and full board starts at S30 per person per night.

### Getting There & Away

**Ferries** (round-trip S30; admission to island S5) leave from the Puno port for Amantaní at 8am every day. There are departures from Amantaní to Taquile and Puno around 4pm every day. Sometimes there is a boat to Puno at around 8am subject to demand. Check locally; times vary.

## Isla Suasi

This private island harbors the luxurious **Casa Andina Isla Suasi** (1-213-9739; www.casa-andina.com; per person all-inclusive 2 days & 1 night S1090), a remote lodge that is as exclusive as it gets in the area. Terraced rooms are well appointed, with down duvets, fireplaces, peaked ceilings and lake views. Lush gardens have trails, wild vicuñas and spots for swimming (yes, people do swim here!) There is a spa, games and a bevy of private tours, including kayaking on the lake. The lodge has more of a natural-history focus than a cultural one – so it's good if you're looking to be outdoorsy.

The island is a five-hour boat trip from Puno or over a three-hour drive on dirt roads. Reserve in advance.

# Cuzco & Machu Picchu

**The former heart of the Inca empire effortlessly enchants.** Sure enough, a visit to Cuzco tumbles you into the cosmic realm of ancient Andean culture – ladies with llamas walk cobblestone streets, while coca-chewing honchos parade to church in ornate regalia for Catholic mass in Quechua. Welcome to the capital of the former Inca empire, of which Cuzco is only the gateway. Beyond lies the Sacred Valley, dotted with ruins and trails, all of which lead to the country's biggest draw – Machu Picchu.

Though tourism is a booming industry here, this is a place where old ways aren't forgotten. Colorful textiles link to the past. Wild fiestas combine the indigenous tradition with the Catholic. And the landscape careens from Andean peaks to orchid-rich cloud forest. Explore it on foot or fat tire. There's a lot to be seen in this dust-worn corner of the Andes.

Machu Picchu (p217)

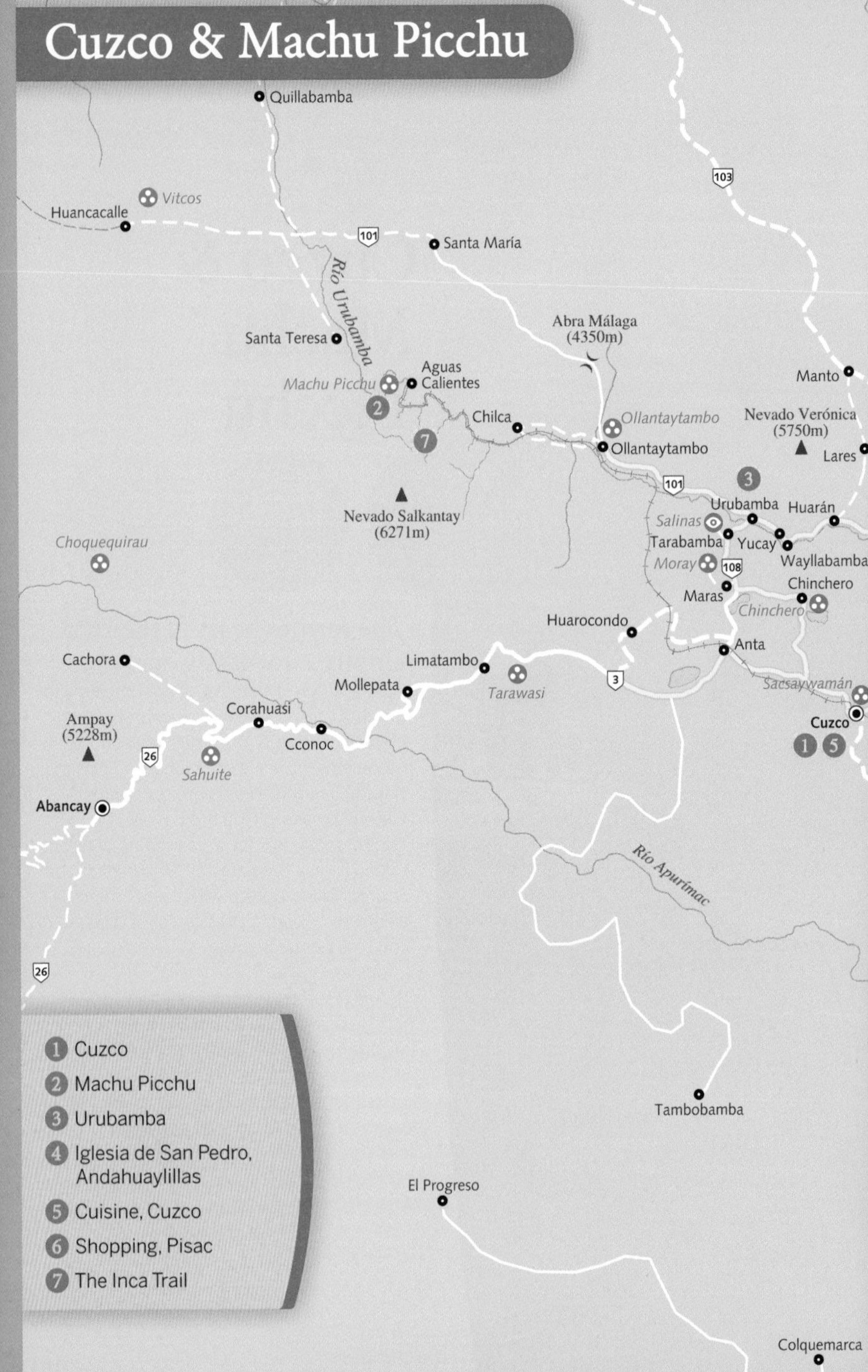

Cuzco & Machu Picchu
Quillabamba
103
Vitcos
Huancacalle
101
Santa María
Río Urubamba
Abra Málaga
(4350m)
Santa Teresa
Aguas
Calientes
Machu Picchu
Manto
Chilca
Ollantaytambo
Nevado Verónica
(5750m)
Ollantaytambo
Lares
101
Nevado Salkantay
(6271m)
Urubamba
Huarán
Salinas
Choquequirau
Tarabamba
Yucay
Moray
108
Wayllabamba
Chinchero
Maras
Chinchero
Huarocondo
Anta
Cachora
Limatambo
Mollepata
Tarawasi
3
Sacsaywamán
Corahuasi
Cuzco
Ampay
(5228m)
Cconoc
26
Sahuite
Abancay
Río Apurímac
26
1 Cuzco
2 Machu Picchu
3 Urubamba
4 Iglesia de San Pedro, Andahuaylillas
5 Cuisine, Cuzco
6 Shopping, Pisac
7 The Inca Trail
Tambobamba
El Progreso
Colquemarca

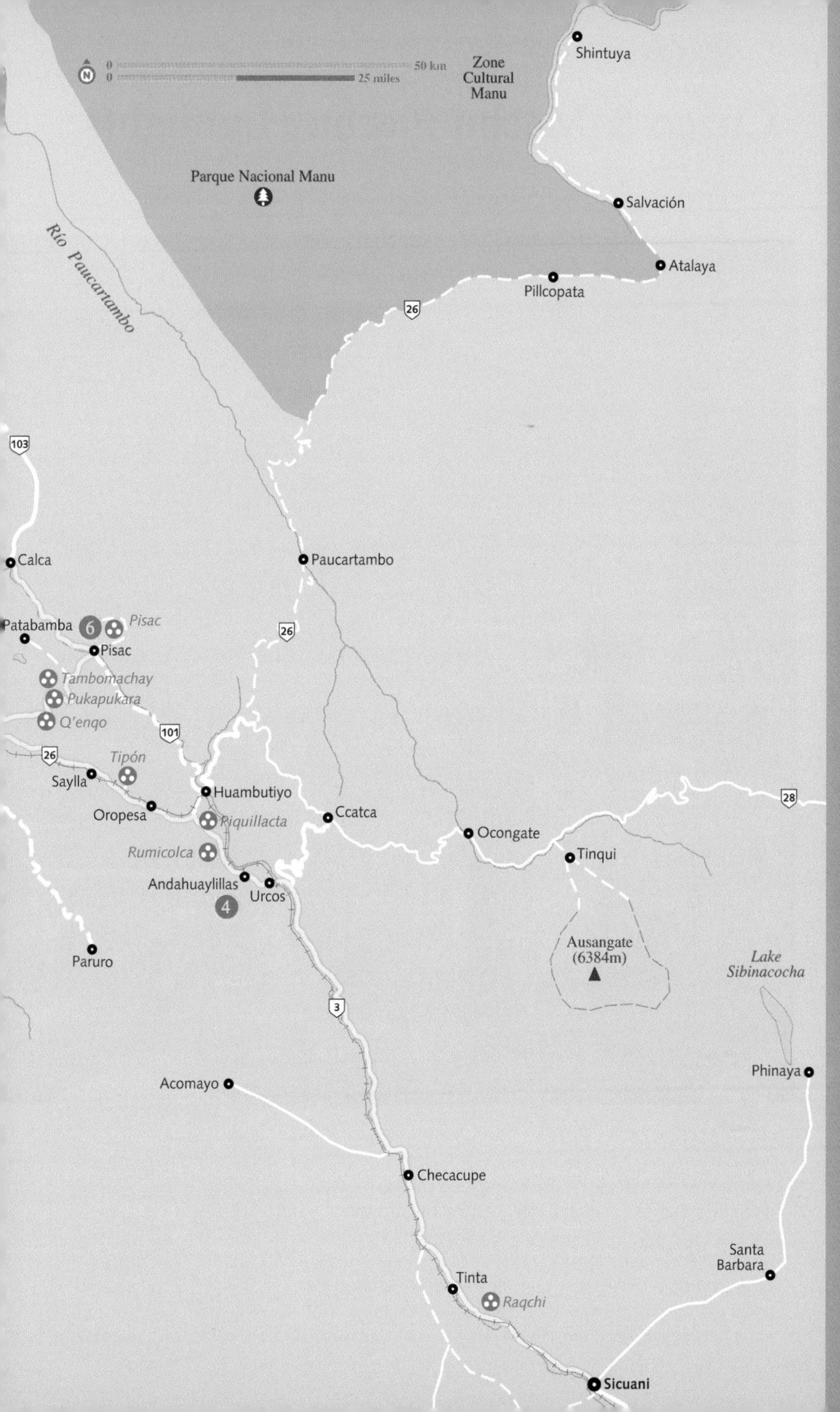

0 50 km
0 25 miles
Zone Cultural Manu
Shintuya
Parque Nacional Manu
Río Paucartambo
Salvación
Atalaya
Pillcopata
26
103
Calca
Paucartambo
Patabamba
6
Pisac
Pisac
26
Tambomachay
Pukapukara
Q'enqo
101
26
Tipón
Saylla
Huambutiyo
28
Oropesa
Ccatca
Piquillacta
Ocongate
Tinqui
Rumicolca
Andahuaylillas
Urcos
4
Ausangate (6384m)
Paruro
Lake Sibinacocha
3
Phinaya
Acomayo
Checacupe
Santa Barbara
Tinta
Raqchi
Sicuani

# Cuzco & Machu Picchu Highlights

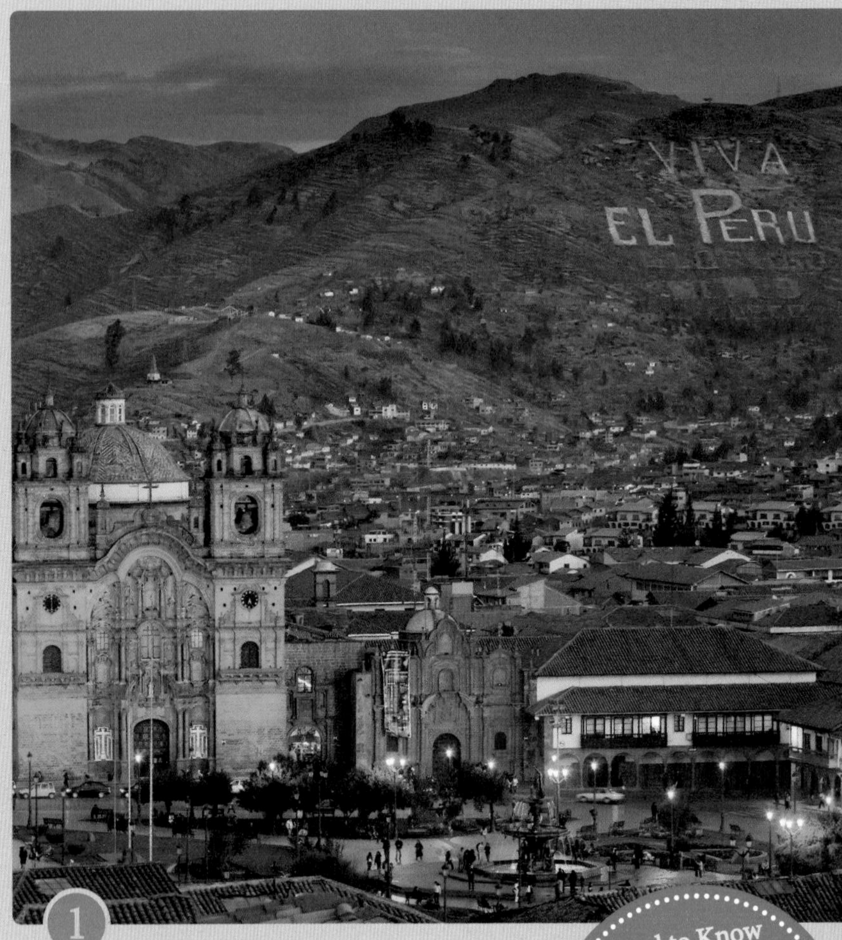


1

## Cuzco

The former capital of the sprawling Inca empire remains a capital of sorts – a global village attracting travelers far and wide with its mix of outstanding pre-Columbian architecture, ornate baroque churches and ring of stunning mountains. The lively cuisine and nightlife make it a good place to linger. **Above:** Cusco; **Top right:** Dancing in traditional dress; **Bottom right:** Selling corn at the market

### Need to Know

**NAME GAME** In Quechua, Cuzco is spelled Qosq'o. **ALTITUDES** Cuzco sits at a dizzying 3362m. Rest and stay hydrated if arriving from sea level. **For further coverage, see p174.**

Local Knowledge

# Cuzco Don't Miss List

BY ANDREA CONFALONIERI, FORTUNATA HUAMAN AND ADA LUZ CARDENAS, THE TRAVEL TEAM AT TURISMO CAITH, A LOCAL NONPROFIT ORGANIZING COMMUNITY TOURS

## 1 MERCADO SAN PEDRO

In Cuzco, a market isn't just for shopping – it's a place where people come to socialize. A great time to visit the *mercado* (p200) is on a weekend, when vendors from the surrounding communities gather to buy and sell goods. It's an event where the modern and the traditional, the rural and the urban, all mix.

## 2 SAN JERÓNIMO

Explore neighborhoods beyond the city center. At the eastern end of Cuzco, the area of San Jerónimo has a beautiful plaza and narrow streets. Life here is lived in a more traditional Andean way. Go with a well-informed guide who can fill you in on the town's history and traditions.

## 3 EAT LOCAL FOODS

Cuzco offers incredible international dining, but we suggest finding a *picantería* (informal homestyle restaurant) and sampling local foods (p196). Some of the best: *cuy* (guinea pig), tamales (corn cakes) or *chiriuchu* (a sampler of meats and other items) – served with a glass of *chicha amarilla* (yellow corn beer).

## 4 WANDER THE STREETS

For a couple of hours, scrap the itinerary and just let yourself amble around Cuzco. Check out the community centers, see the local libraries, admire the murals at the Almudena cemetery (on the southern edge of town). Above all, be sure to fully explore the area around San Blas (p184), both during the day and at night, when it's illuminated and provides incredible views of the city.

## 5 EXPLORE THE AREA'S LIVING HISTORY

Archaeological sites such as Sacsaywamán are impressive, but we also recommend getting to know the city's living culture. Visit the markets, interact with the locals – and if you're in town during a religious holiday, join a procession. One of the most remarkable is held every June, for Corpus Christi.

## Machu Picchu

A sublime stone citadel. A staggering cloud-forest perch. And a backstory that's out of a movie. The extraordinary Inca settlement (and Unesco World Heritage site) of Machu Picchu (p217) came to light in the early 1900s, when an American explorer by the name of Hiram Bingham extolled its presence to the world. **Below and top right:** Machu Picchu; **Bottom right:** Train arriving in Aguas Calientes

**Need to Know**

**WHEN TO GO** June to August are the sunniest months. **AVOID** February, when it's wet and the Inca Trail is closed. **TIP** Pack insect repellent. **For further coverage, see p217.**

2

Local Knowledge

# Machu Picchu Don't Miss List

BY CHRISTOPHER HEANEY, AUTHOR OF *CRADLE OF GOLD: THE STORY OF HIRAM BINGHAM, A REAL-LIFE INDIANA JONES, AND THE SEARCH FOR MACHU PICCHU*

## 1 WATCH THE SUN RISE OVER MACHU PICCHU

The best time to visit Machu Picchu is very early in the morning or late in the day, when the trains have come and gone. This means spending the night in Aguas Calientes. It's worth it: at dawn, the light is especially beautiful.

## 2 EXPLORE THE EAST SIDE

The tours will take you to key sights like the Intihuatana (an astronomical point), but be sure to go east, where the terraces meet the jungle. You'll get a feel for what it was like to live at Machu Picchu, either as an *inca* (king) or one of their servants.

## 3 VISIT THE MUSEO DE SITIO MANUEL CHÁVEZ BÁLLÓN

This museum (p214) might seem small, but it's worthwhile. It has the only gold found at Machu Picchu, as well as excellent displays that chronicle the history of the site and how it fit into a larger entire network of Inca settlements.

## 4 HIKE UP TO THE RUINS FROM AGUAS CALIENTES

There's a little footpath (p223) that leads up the side of the mountain to the ruins. It's a little steep, but in terms of experience, you'll put yourself right in the mindset of the explorers. Hiram Bingham used to see if he could beat his personal best every time he climbed.

## 5 READ A GOOD BOOK BEFOREHAND

John Hemmings' *Conquest of the Incas* is a classic. But for fun, I recommend *Plunder of the Sun,* by David Dodge. It's a noir novel about bruisers fighting for an Inca treasure and will give you a good sense of what Cuzco was like in the 1950s. Machu Picchu is rich with history – these books will make it come alive.

## Enjoy Tranquility in Urubamba

If Cuzco's staggering heights and noisy streets make you feel light-headed, the laid-back country town of Urubamba (p208), surrounded by beautiful countryside, offers a comfortable base for exploring the Sacred Valley. Expect chilled-out lodges, excellent horse ranches, restaurants serving tasty food, and one of the area's most magnificent spas. Are you ready to relax? You've found your spot.

3

4

## See the 'Sistine Chapel of Latin America'

A sleepy village east of Cuzco contains one of the most surprisingly extravagant churches in the region. The Iglesia de San Pedro (p184) in Andahuaylillas doesn't look like much from the outside, but on the inside, it's layered with some of the finest examples of Andean baroque design. Be sure to look up: the ceiling is laced in an array of intricate, indigenous-influenced patterns. Divine.

CAROLINA MIRANDA

## 5 Dig into the Rich Cuisine

Crackling *chicharrones* (deep-fried chunks of pork). Starchy Andean corn with squeaking hunks of cheese. Brothy soups that warm the bones on chilly highland nights. Oh, and did we mention the roasted guinea pigs? Every region in Peru offers a bounty of regional cooking and the Cuzco area is no exception (p196). Get ready to be enriched – not just your mind, but also the belly.

MARGIE POLITZER/GETTY IMAGES ©

## 6 Shop 'til You Drop in Pisac

Who knew a single highland town could have so much to offer? Magnificent ruins, tasty food at local restaurants and one of the most bustling outdoor markets in the entire region. In Pisac (p205), dedicated shoppers can find bright, hand-woven textiles, finely painted ceramics, alpaca knits and a mind-boggling assortment of fresh local produce. You've never seen so many potatoes!

## 7 Trek the Inca Trail

The world's most famous ancient roadway (p224) offers adventurous travelers a four-day bonanza of sumptuous cloud forest, remote Inca ruins, mind-bending passes with extravagant views, and crystalline waterfalls – not to mention the bragging rights of saying that you made it to the lost city of Machu Picchu the old-fashioned way: by walking.

# Cuzco & Machu Picchu's Best...

## Inca Ruins

- **Qorikancha** (p181) The remains of a graceful Inca sun temple
- **Sacsaywamán** (p203) A hillside fortress that is also a feat of masonry and engineering
- **Pisac** (p206) A hilltop citadel that sits astride two gorges in the Sacred Valley
- **Ollantaytambo** (p212) A fort and ceremonial center that is soaked in history
- **Machu Picchu** (p217) The fabled mountaintop citadel

## Churches

- **Iglesia de La Compañía de Jesús** (p180) Cuzco's splendorous baroque Jesuit church
- **Iglesia de San Blas** (p183) A simple adobe house of worship containing a pulpit that is allegedly encrusted with the skull of its carver
- **Cuzco's Cathedral** (p178) An incredible repository of colonial art containing a *Last Supper* in which Christ feasts on *cuy* (guinea pig)
- **Iglesia de San Pedro** (p184) In Andahuaylillas, this church is lavishly decorated in an earthy Andean baroque style

## Restaurants

- **Cicciolina, Cuzco** (p194) Out of this world Andean-Mediterranean fusion
- **La Bodega 138, Cuzco** (p194) Scrumptious clay-oven pizza
- **Huacatay, Urubamba** (p209) This hidden spot serves well-rendered Peruvian specialties
- **Indio Feliz, Aguas Calientes** (p216) Peru meets France at this candlelit eatery
- **Chicha, Cuzco** (p195) Gastón Acurio's top-flight *novoandina* (new Andean cuisine) outpost

## Adventures

- **River running** (p185) The waterways around Cuzco contain heart-pounding white-water runs
- **Trekking the Inca Trail** (p224) The continent's most famous stone road
- **Ziplining** (p227) About 2500m of vertigo-inducing lines in Santa Teresa

Left: Fresco in Iglesia de San Pedro (p184), Andahuaylillas; **Above:** Pisac (p205), the Sacred Valley

(LEFT) JEFFREY BECOM/GETTY IMAGES ©; (ABOVE) RALPH HOPKINS/GETTY IMAGES ©

# Need to Know

### ADVANCE PLANNING

- **Six months before** Make a reservation for trekking the Inca Trail
- **Three months** Buy domestic airplane tickets within Peru
- **One month** Make hotel reservations for Cuzco and Aguas Calientes
- **One day** Book day tours around Cuzco

### RESOURCES

- **Exploring Cuzco** By Peter Frost; the best source of historical and archaeological information on the area
- **Municipalidad del Cusco** (www.municusco.gob.pe) The city's official website
- **Diario del Cusco** (www.diariodelcusco.com) Online edition of the local daily newspaper, in Spanish
- **Jack's Guide** (www.jacksguide.com) Good bilingual information for visitors and calendar of events

### GETTING AROUND

- **Walk** The best way to explore the compact (often Inca-designed) settlements that dot the Sacred Valley
- **Bus** Local service connects disparate points in Cuzco as well as outside towns; long-haul services are available to Puno and Arequipa, among other points
- **Train** Tourist services to Aguas Calientes, at the base of Machu Picchu, as well as Puno
- **Taxis** Plentiful in Cuzco, and other larger towns

### BE FOREWARNED

- **Inca Trail** Closes for maintenance the entire month of February
- **Solo women** Watch out for 'Cuzco Casanovas' on the hunt for ladies who will pay their way
- **Robberies** Crowded locales bring out pickpockets; late-night muggings are not unheard of
- **Altitude** It's not uncommon for travelers who fly in from the coast to be struck by altitude sickness; give yourself time to acclimatize

# Cuzco & Machu Picchu Itineraries

*The heart of the Inca empire can keep you occupied for weeks with extravagant mountainscapes, traditional rural villages and more ruins than you can shake an ancient textile at.*

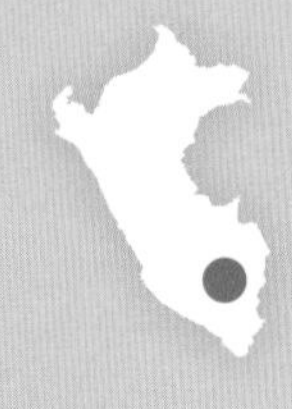

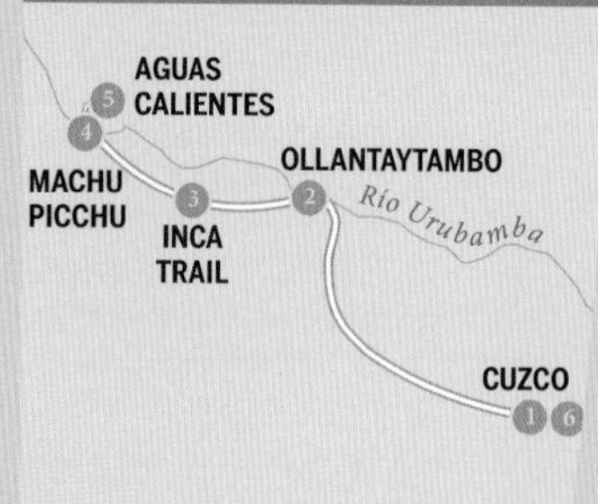

5 DAYS

**CUZCO TO MACHU PICCHU**

## Heart of the Inca Empire

Start with a leisurely couple of days acclimatizing in **(1) Cuzco**, strolling around the Plaza de Armas and visiting the area's churches and ruins. Highlights include the ruins of Qorikancha (the remains of a temple) and Sacsaywamán (a sawtooth shaped fortress), as well as a visit to the baroque cathedral, which contains a trove of colonial art. While you're in Cuzco, be sure to enjoy the area's delicious highland cooking.

Head out of the city to somewhat lower altitudes in **(2) Pisac**, a charming Sacred Valley town with a bustling market and a set of ancient ruins precariously perched on the mountain above it. Travel on to **(3) Ollantaytambo**, an amiable Quechua village criss-crossed by ancient canals and capped by an impressive Inca fortress. Spend the night here then continue by train to **(4) Aguas Calientes**. This cloud-forest village serves as the base for exploring **(5) Machu Picchu**. Spend at least two days here – one seeing the most important ruins, and one exploring the myriad hiking trails.

**Top Left:** Market in Pisac (p205);
**Top Right:** View over Wiñay Wayna (p226) on the Inca Trail

1
WEEK

CUZCO TO MACHU PICCHU ON FOOT

## To Machu Picchu along the Inca Trail

Arrive in **(1) Cuzco** and allow for a leisurely first day of strolling and acclimatization amid the city's labyrinthine cobblestone streets. Afterwards, transfer by car or train to the Sacred Valley village of **(2) Ollantaytambo**, a rural settlement that is home to an important Inca fortress. (A hike here is a good warm-up for the big trek.)

From Ollantaytambo, spend the next four days walking along one of Peru's most renowned footpaths, the **(3) Inca Trail**. Built by the Incas to connect the points in their empire, this incredible trek will take you over high passes and along steamy cloud forest, with views of majestic Andean peaks in the distance. It's studded with plenty of lesser Inca ruins, too.

On the last day, you will emerge at the so-called Sun Gate mountain pass where you will get your first glimpse of the majestic **(4) Machu Picchu**. Spend a day or two exploring the site, overnighting in **(5) Aguas Calientes**, before taking the train back to **(6) Cuzco**. Here, you can do some leisurely urban exploring before you depart. As a reward, treat yourself to a well-deserved meal at one of Cuzco's of-the-moment eateries and do a little crafts shopping in the artisan quarter of San Blas.

# Discover Cuzco & Machu Picchu

## At a Glance

- **Cuzco** The picturesque capital of the former Inca Empire.
- **Pisac** (p205) A highland village with excellent ruins and a renowned crafts market.
- **Urubamba** (p207) Rural idyll at lower elevations in the Sacred Valley.
- **Machu Picchu** (p217) The magnificent mountaintop citadel made famous by explorer Hiram Bingham.
- **The Inca Trail** (p224) Peru's most fabled ancient roadway.

Machu Picchu (p217)
DAVID MADISON/GETTY IMAGES ©

## CUZCO

☎084 / POP 350,000 / ELEV 3326M

The cosmopolitan capital of Cuzco (also Cusco, or Qosq'o in Quechua) today thrives with a measure of contradiction. Ornate cathedrals squat over Inca temples, massage hawkers ply the narrow cobblestone streets, a woman in traditional skirt and bowler hat might offer bottled water to a pet llama while the finest boutiques hawk alpaca knits for small fortunes. The foremost city of the Inca empire is now the undisputed archaeological capital of South America, as well as the continent's oldest continuously inhabited city. Few travelers to Peru will skip visiting this premier South American destination, which also serves as gateway to Machu Picchu.

As with any bustling global destination, Cuzco is not all ancient culture. (Note the Western fast-food chains on the Plaza de Armas.) In recent years the city has gentrified and as rents soar in the colonial core, *cuzqueños* are increasingly pushed to the margins – which may mean getting out of the city center if you want to experience local life.

### History

For almost 200 years beginning in the 12th century, the Incas were a relatively small ethnicity confined to the Cuzco Valley. This changed in the 14th century, under the ninth *inca* (king) Pachacutec, a fervent expansionist who extended the limits of Inca territory to include much of the central Andes as well as the area around Lake Titicaca. Cuzco was the capital of his sprawling empire and the city owes much of its physical glory to him: Pachacutec was the one who allegedly gave the city its layout in the shape of a puma and built some of the area's most magnificent stone monuments, such as Sacsaywamán and quite possibly Machu Picchu.

Inca expansion came to an abrupt end with the arrival of the Spanish. Francisco Pizarro entered the city on November 8, 1533, after dispatching emperor Atahualpa in the northern highland city of Cajamarca. By that point, the Spanish had already gotten to work demolishing indigenous monuments and stripping Cuzco's temples of their silver and gold. All of this was followed, in 1536, by a fierce indigenous rebellion led by Manco Inca, Atahualpa's half-brother, who had originally served as the Spaniard's puppet leader. Manco would lay siege to the city for almost a year, but was ultimately unsuccessful in wresting control from the Spanish.

After the Spanish moved the nation's capital to Lima, Cuzco's importance as an urban center declined. Even so, it remained an important cultural center – and the heart of indigenous life in Peru. During the 16th century, the city produced one of the continent's most renowned chroniclers: El Inca Garcilaso de la Vega (1539–1616), the son of an Inca princess and a Spanish military captain, and author of the vital historical document *The Royal Commentaries of the Incas*. Cuzco was also the birthplace of the remarkable 16th-century art movement known as the *escuela cuzqueña* (Cuzco School), a religious art movement that blended Spanish and indigenous iconography and styles.

The city was at the heart of the last major indigenous uprising, in 1780. Led by the grandson of an Inca noble, José Gabriel Condorcanqui (known as Túpac Amaru II), it didn't last long. Condorcanqui was captured by colonial authorities and violently executed in the city's main square.

Apart from devastating earthquakes in 1650 and 1950, the city remained a quiet provincial capital until the early 20th century, when an American explorer by the name of Hiram Bingham broadcast the existence of Machu Picchu to the world.

## Sights

A resurgence of indigenous pride means that many streets have been signposted with Quechua names, though they are still commonly referred to by their Spanish titles. The most prominent example is Calle Triunfo, now labeled Sunturwasi.

To visit Cuzco's principal historic sights, foreign travelers have to purchase a **boleto turístico** (adult/student with ISIC card S130/70), a ticket that covers the entry fee into a dozen spots. There is

Panpipe playing at the Mercado de Artesanía (p205), Pisac
BARTOSZ HADYNIAK/GETTY IMAGES ©

# Cuzco

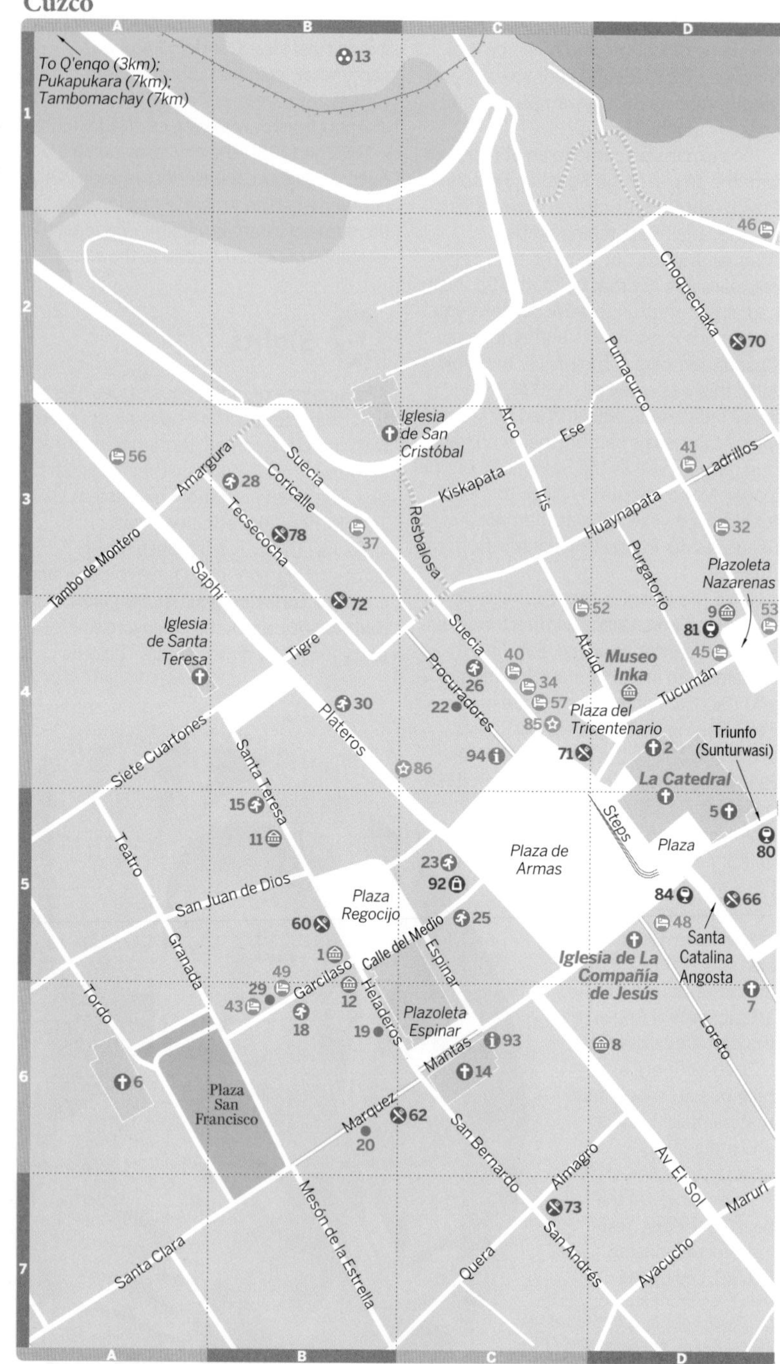

To Q'enqo (3km); Pukapukara (7km); Tambomachay (7km)
Iglesia de San Cristóbal
Iglesia de Santa Teresa
Museo Inka
Plaza del Tricentenario
La Catedral
Triunfo (Sunturwasi)
Plazoleta Nazarenas
Plaza de Armas
Plaza Regocijo
Plazoleta Espinar
Iglesia de La Compañía de Jesús
Santa Catalina Angosta
Plaza San Francisco
Steps
Plaza
Amargura
Tambo de Montero
Saphi
Suecia
Coricalle
Tecsecocha
Resbalosa
Kiskapata
Arco
Iris
Ese
Pumacurco
Choquechaka
Ladrillos
Huaynapata
Purgatorio
Ataúd
Tucumán
Procuradores
Tigre
Plateros
Siete Cuartones
Santa Teresa
Teatro
San Juan de Dios
Granada
Tordo
Garcilaso
Calle del Medio
Espinar
Heladeros
Mantas
Marquez
San Bernardo
Almagro
San Andrés
Quera
Av El Sol
Maruri
Ayacucho
Loreto
Mesón de la Estrella
Santa Clara

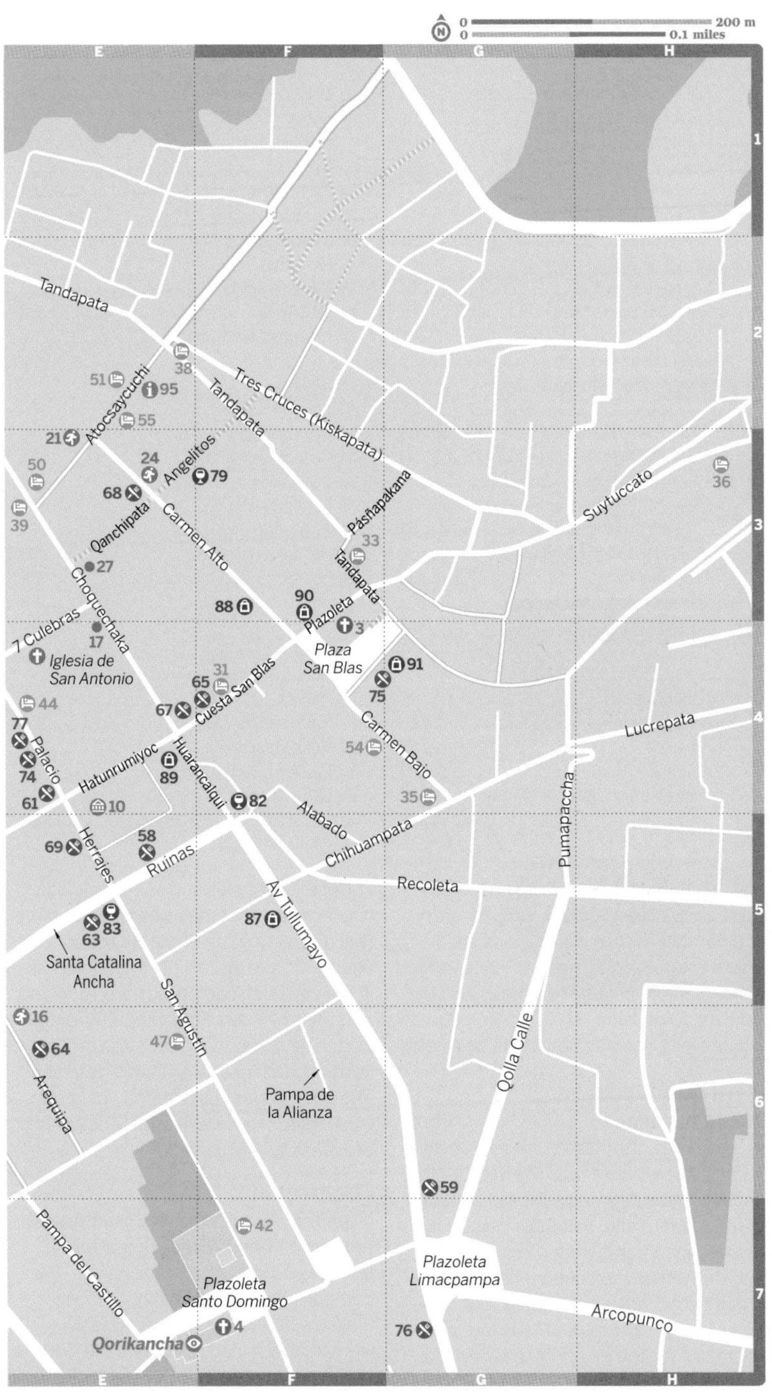

0
200 m
0
0.1 miles
Tandapata
Tres Cruces (Kiskapata)
Tandapata
Atocsaycuchi
Angelitos
Qanchipata
Carmen Alto
Pásñapakana
Suytuccato
Choquechaka
7 Culebras
Iglesia de San Antonio
Plazoleta
Tandapata
Plaza San Blas
Cuesta San Blas
Carmen Bajo
Palacio
Hatunrumiyoc
Huarancalqui
Lucrepata
Alabado
Chihuampata
Pumapaccha
Herrajes
Ruinas
Recoleta
Av Tullumayo
Santa Catalina Ancha
San Agustín
Qolla Calle
Arequipa
Pampa de la Alianza
Pampa del Castillo
Plazoleta Santo Domingo
Plazoleta Limacpampa
Arcopunco
Qorikancha

## Cuzco

**Top Sights**
- Iglesia de La Compañía de Jesús ........D5
- La Catedral ........D5
- Museo Inka ........D4
- Qorikancha ........E7

**Sights**
1. Choco Museo ........B5
2. Iglesia de Jesús María ........D4
3. Iglesia de San Blas ........F4
4. Iglesia de Santo Domingo ........F7
5. Iglesia del Triunfo ........D5
6. Iglesia San Francisco ........A6
7. Iglesia y Monasterio de Santa Catalina ........D6
8. Museo de Arte Popular ........D6
9. Museo de Arte Precolombino ........D4
10. Museo de Arte Religioso ........E4
11. Museo de Plantas Sagradas, Mágicas y Medicinales ........B5
12. Museo Histórico Regional ........B6
13. Sacsaywamán ........B1
14. Templo y Convento de La Merced ........C6

**Activities, Courses & Tours**
15. Action Valley ........B5
16. Andina Travel ........E6
17. Antipode ........E4
18. Apumayo ........B6
19. Asociación de Guías Oficiales de Turismo ........B6
20. Chiquity Club Cusco ........B6
21. Eco Trek Peru ........E3
22. Fertur ........C4
    Gravity Peru ........(see 83)
23. Mayuc ........C5
24. Party Bike ........E3
25. Peruvian Highland Trek ........C5
26. Quechua's Expeditions ........C4
27. Respons ........E3
28. Samana Spa ........B3
29. SAS Travel ........B6
30. X-treme Tourbulencia ........B4

**Sleeping**
31. Amaru Hostal ........F4
32. Casa Cartagena ........D3
33. Casona les Pleiades ........F3
34. Del Prado Inn ........C4
35. Eureka Hostal ........G4
36. Hospedaje Inka ........H3
37. Hostal Corihuasi ........B3
38. Hostal Pensión Alemana ........E2
39. Hostal Rumi Punku ........E3
40. Hostal Suecia I ........C4
41. Hotel Arqueólogo ........D3
42. Hotel Libertador Palacio del Inka ........F7
43. Hotel los Marqueses ........B6
44. Hotel Monasterio ........E4
45. Inkaterra La Casona ........D4
46. La Encantada ........D2
47. La Lune ........E6

also a **boleto religioso** **(religious tourist ticket; adult/student S50/25)**, valid for entry at a number of Cuzco's religious sites. These are sold on-site at the city's various historic and religious attractions and are valid for 10 days.

Note that opening hours can be erratic.

## Central Cuzco

### PLAZA DE ARMAS — Plaza

In Inca times, the plaza – called Huacaypata or Aucaypata – was the heart of the capital. Today it remains the nerve center of the modern city. Two flags usually fly here – the red-and-white Peruvian flag and the rainbow-checkered flag of Tahuantinsuyo, representing the four quarters of the Inca empire. (Many foreigners mistake it for the gay-pride banner.)

Colonial arcades surround the plaza, which in ancient times was twice as large (encompassing the **Plaza Regocijo** to the south). On the plaza's northeastern side is the imposing cathedral, flanked by the churches of Jesús María and El Triunfo. On the southeastern side is the ornate Jesuit church of La Compañía de Jesús. The quiet pedestrian alleyway of Loreto, which has Inca walls, is a historic means of access to the plaza.

### LA CATEDRAL — Church

**(Plaza de Armas; admission S25 or with boleto religioso; ⏲10am-5:45pm)** A squatter on the site of Viracocha Inca's palace, the cathedral was built starting in 1559 with blocks pilfered from nearby Sacsaywamán. It is joined by **Iglesia del Triunfo** (1536) to its right and **Iglesia de Jesús**

**María** (1733) to the left. El Triunfo, Cuzco's oldest church, houses a vault containing the remains of renowned Inca chronicler Garcilaso de la Vega.

The cathedral is one of the city's great repositories of colonial art, especially for works from the *escuela cuzqueña*, a style that combined European devotional painting styles with the earthy color palette and iconography of indigenous Andean art. One of the most famous paintings here is the **Last Supper** by Quechua artist Marcos Zapata, in the northeast corner of the cathedral, which depicts Christ and the disciples feasting on *cuy* (guinea pig).

Also look for the **oldest surviving painting** in Cuzco, showing the entire city during the great earthquake of 1650. The inhabitants can be seen parading around the plaza with a crucifix, praying for the earthquake to stop. This precious crucifix, called **El Señor de los Temblores** (The Lord of the Earthquakes), can still be seen in the alcove to the right of the door leading into El Triunfo.

Other worthwhile points include the **sacristy**, which is covered with paintings of Cuzco's bishops, the **wooden altar** (behind the present silver altar) and the magnificently carved **choir**, dating from the 17th century.

The doors are open for Mass between 6am and 10am. If you decide to attend, keep your camera stowed (or you might not be let in) and remain seated for the duration of the mass.

**IGLESIA DE LA COMPAÑÍA DE JESÚS** Church

**(Plaza de Armas; admission S15 or with boleto religioso; ⌚9-11:30am & 1-5:30pm)** Built upon the palace of Huayna Cápac, the last Inca to rule an undivided empire, this fabulously ornate church was originally built by the Jesuits in 1571 (and restored after the 1650 earthquake). At the time of construction, the Jesuits planned to make it the most magnificent of Cuzco's churches. But Cuzco's archbishop complained that its splendor should not rival that of the cathedral, and the squabble grew to a point where Pope Paul III was called upon to arbitrate. His decision was in favor of the cathedral, but by the time word reached Cuzco, La Compañía was just about finished, complete with an incredible baroque facade and Peru's biggest altar, all crowned by a soaring dome.

Two large canvases near the main door show early marriages in Cuzco and are worth examining for their wealth of period detail.

Local student guides are available to show you around the church, as well as the grand view from the choir on the 2nd floor, reached via rickety steps. Tips are gratefully accepted.

**MUSEO INKA** Museum

**(☎23-7380; Tucumán at Ataúd; admission S10; ⌚8am-6pm Mon-Fri, 9am-4pm Sat)** A steep block north from the plaza, a restored colonial house serves as the best museum in town for those interested in the Incas. The displays are modest, but the collection of artifacts is significant, including goldwork, jewelry, pottery, mummies, models, an impressive collection of *queros* (ceremonial drinking cups) and historic textiles – including one that depicts the violent quartering death of Túpac Amaru II in Cuzco's main plaza.

The building itself has some noteworthy architectural embellishments: a massive stairway is guarded by sculptures of mythical creatures and a corner window column looks like a statue of a bearded man from the inside, but outside appears to be a naked woman.

Spanish- and English-speaking guides are usually available for a small fee.

**MUSEO DE PLANTAS SAGRADAS, MÁGICAS Y MEDICINALES** Museum

**(☎22-2214; Calle Santa Teresa 351; admission S15; ⌚10am-7pm Mon-Sat, noon-6pm Sun)** A fascinating new museum that leaves no leaf unturned, exploring the history and workings of Peruvian medicinal and sacred plants. Highlights include displays on coca's 8000 years of cultivation and trippy multilayered visuals that emulate the ayahuasca experience. The dioramas are in Spanish, but English-speaking guides are available (S4 per person).

A lauded cafe resides in an upstairs patio.

**MUSEO DE ARTE RELIGIOSO** Museum

**(cnr Hatunrumiyoc & Herrajes; admission S15 or with boleto religioso; ⌚8-11am & 3-6pm Mon-Sat)** Originally the palace of Inca Roca, the foundations of this museum were converted into a grand colonial residence and later became the archbishop's palace. It is now home to an important religious art collection that provides a unique window into life in the colony. The building also contains some impressive ceilings and colonial-style tile work.

**TEMPLO Y CONVENTO DE LA MERCED** Church

**(☎23-1821; Mantas 121; admission S6; ⌚8am-noon & 2-5pm Mon-Sat)** Cuzco's third most important colonial church, La Merced has a beautiful **cloister** (⌚**8-11am**) hung with paintings that chronicle the life of San Pedro Nolasco. The far side contains the **tombs** of conquistadors Diego de Almagro and Gonzalo Pizarro (brother of Francisco). Here, you'll also find a small **religious museum** displaying vestments that allegedly belonged to conquistador and friar Vicente de Valverde. The exhibit's most famous piece is a priceless solid-gold monstrance, 1.2m high and covered with rubies, emeralds and no fewer than 1500 diamonds and 600 pearls. (Ask to see it if the display room is locked.)

The entrance to the monastery and museum is located to the left of the church, at the back of a small courtyard.

MICHAEL LANGFORD/GETTY IMAGES ©

## Don't Miss Qorikancha

If you visit only one site in Cuzco, make it this former **Inca temple**, which now forms the base of the colonial church and priory of Santo Domingo. Once the richest temple in the empire, Qorikancha (Quechua for 'Golden Courtyard') was once literally covered in gold. Walls were lined with solid-gold sheets and the building housed life-sized gold and silver replicas of llamas and corn, as well as a massive gold sculpture of the sun. Moreover, it has been reported that the mummified bodies of deceased *incas* (kings) were kept here, brought out into the sunlight each day and offered food and drink.

Unfortunately, the only thing that remains is the stonework. Within months of the Spanish arrival, the precious metals were all looted. What remains, however, is some of the finest Inca architecture in Peru – including a curved, perfectly fitted 6m-high retaining wall (known as the Solar Drum Wall) that encircles the site.

The temple was built in the mid-15th century during the reign of the 10th *inca*, Túpac Yupanqui. After the conquest, Francisco Pizarro gave it to his brother Juan, who was unable to enjoy it for long – he died in battle in 1536, leaving it to the Dominicans in his will.

Today's site is a downright postmodern combination of Inca and colonial religious architecture. Spanish walls cut into the remains of trapezoidal pre-Columbian temples. An Inca fountain in the main cloister is surrounded by paintings that depict the life of St Dominic.

Explanatory text is sparse. So it's best to hire one of the multilingual guides in grey jackets who stand by the main door. During the high season, it gets ridiculously crowded in the afternoons. Go in the morning.

### NEED TO KNOW

Plazoleta Santo Domingo; admission S10; ⌚8:30am-5:30pm Mon-Sat, 2-5pm Sun

**IGLESIA SAN FRANCISCO** Church

**(Plaza San Francisco; admission free; ⏰6:30-8am & 5:30-8pm Mon-Sat, 6:30am-noon & 6:30-8pm Sun)** More austere than many Cuzco churches, Iglesia San Francisco dates back to the 16th century and is one of the few that didn't need to be completely reconstructed after the 1650 earthquake. It has a large collection of colonial religious paintings and a well-carved cedar choir. The attached **museum (admission S8; ⏰9am-noon & 3-5pm Mon-Fri, 9am-noon Sat)** houses what is supposedly the largest painting in South America: a 9m by 12m canvas that shows the family tree of St Francis of Assisi, the founder of the order. Also of macabre interest are the two crypts, which contain plenty of carefully arranged human bones.

**IGLESIA Y MONASTERIO DE SANTA CATALINA** Church

**(Arequipa s/n; admission S8; ⏰8:30am-5:30pm Mon-Sat)** This convent houses many colonial paintings from the *escuela cuzqueña,* as well as an impressive collection of vestments and other religious embroidery. It also contains a baroque side chapel with dramatic friezes, and many life-sized (and sometimes startling) models of nuns praying, sewing and going about their lives.

**MUSEO DE ARTE PRECOLOMBINO** Museum

**(☎23-3210; http://map.perucultural.org.pe; Plazoleta Nazarenas 231; admission S22; ⏰9am-10pm)** Inside a Spanish colonial mansion with an Inca ceremonial courtyard, this pre-Columbian art museum showcases a small, varied collection of artifacts drawn from the vast storerooms of Lima's Museo Larco (p69). Highlights include displays of *queros,* the Nazca and Moche galleries of multicolored ceramics, and the dazzling displays of gold and silver jewelry.

The courtyard is home to a contemporary, glass-walled eatery, **MAP Café** **(⏰noon-3pm & 6pm-midnight)**, a fine spot for upscale renditions of Peruvian classics.

**CHOCO MUSEO** Museum

**(☎24-4765; Calle Garcilaso 210; www.chocomuseo.com; admission S2; ⏰10:30am-6:30pm)** While the museum is frankly lite, the best part of this French-owned enterprise is the organic chocolate-making workshop (S70 per person). You can also come for fondue, a fresh cup of fair-trade hot

Chinchero (p184)

## Stargazing with the Ancients

The Incas were the only culture in the world to define constellations of darkness as well as light. Astronomy wasn't taken lightly: some of Cuzco's main streets are designed to align with the stars at certain times of the year. To truly understand this worldview we therefore recommend a visit to the **Cuzco Planetarium** (www.planetariumcusco.com; per person about S30), where you can learn about Inca constellation systems and peek at the planets through a Celestron telescope. Think of how clever you'll feel pointing out the Black Llama to your fellow hikers on the Inca trail.

Reservations are essential. Prices include pickup and drop-off.

cocoa or to book a chocolate farm tour. Multilingual and kid-friendly.

**MUSEO HISTÓRICO REGIONAL** Museum

**(Calle Garcilaso at Heladeros; admission with boleto turístico; 8am-5pm Tue-Sun)** An eclectic museum is housed in the home that once belonged to El Inca Garcilaso de la Vega, the 16th-century *mestizo* (person of mixed indigenous and Spanish descent) chronicler. There are sundry exhibitions from various periods, but the most significant (and moving) are devoted to Túpac Amaru II, the indigenous leader who fomented a series of rebellions in the 18th century – and was heavily influenced by Garcilaso's writings.

Also worthwhile is a dramatic reproduction of a colonial religious statue showing St James (Santiago) slaying an Inca instead of the traditional Moors.

### San Blas

Known as the artists' neighborhood, San Blas is nestled on a steep hillside next to the center. With its narrow passageways and classic colonial architecture, it has become a hip part of town – cluttered with eateries, bars and boutiques.

**IGLESIA DE SAN BLAS** Church

**(Plaza San Blas; admission S15 or with *boleto religioso*; 10am-6pm Mon-Sat, 2-6pm Sun)** This simple adobe church is comparatively small, but you can't help but be awed by the baroque, gold-leaf principal altar. The exquisitely carved pulpit, made from a single tree trunk, has been called one of the finest examples of colonial wood carving in the Americas. Legend claims that its creator was an indigenous man who miraculously recovered from a deadly disease and subsequently dedicated his life to carving this pulpit. Supposedly, his skull is nestled into its topmost reaches.

### Avenida El Sol & Downhill

**MUSEO DE ARTE POPULAR** Museum

**(Av El Sol 103, basement; admission with boleto turístico; 9am-6pm Mon-Sat, 8am-1pm Sun)** Winning entries in Cuzco's annual folk-art competition are displayed in this engaging museum, where the artists of San Blas strut their creative stuff in styles ranging from high art to cheeky cute. Works include small-scale ceramic models that show aspects of everyday life, from drunken debauchery in the *picantería* (homestyle restaurant) to torture in the dentist's chair.

There's also a display of black-and-white photographs of Cuzco by renowned local photographer Martín Chambi (1891–1973).

**IGLESIA DE SANTO DOMINGO** Church

The church of Santo Domingo is adjacent to Qorikancha. Less baroque and ornate than many of Cuzco's churches, it is notable for its charming paintings of archangels depicted as Andean children in jeans and T-shirts. Opening hours are erratic.

# If You Like... Andean Baroque

Cuzco may be home to some resplendent, historic churches, but the region's highland villages shouldn't be overlooked. Though some of these towns may be microscopic, many harbor extravagant houses of worship. These are unique for their rococo embellishments – bringing together the Spanish love of all things ridiculously ornate with an earthy indigenous iconography and color palette. In other words, the type of artistry that could only exist in Peru.

Here are two of the best:

1 **IGLESIA COLONIAL DE CHINCHERO** (8am-5:30pm; admission with boleto turístico) Located 30km west of Cuzco, in the small market town of Chinchero, this turn-of-the-17th-century church is built on the site of an old Inca temple. (In fact, pre-Columbian terraces surround the complex.) Its interiors are draped in colorful murals and the baroque altar is smothered in gold leaf. Be sure to examine the murals on the exterior facade, too – one of which depicts the capture of Túpac Amaru.

2 **IGLESIA DE SAN PEDRO** (admission S10; 7am-5:30pm) In scenic Andahuaylillas (45km southeast of Cuzco), this incredible church is referred to by the locals as the 'Sistine Chapel of Latin America.' It dates to the 17th century and houses countless exquisite works, most notably an Andean baroque ceiling that is a masterpiece of *escuela cuzqueña* (Cuzco School) art. Rumor has it that there are countless gold treasures locked in the church and the villagers all take turns guarding it. Is the rumor true? All we can tell you is they take their job *very* seriously.

## Activities

### Trekking

The Cuzco area is a hiker's paradise, with ecosystems that range from cloud forest to high alpine environments. The most famous trek is the stunning Inca Trail, but it can get crowded and permits are required. If for some reason you can't secure a permit, there are other paths that lead to Machu Picchu – so there are alternatives. Likewise, treks to less-trafficked locations, such as Choquequirau, Ausangate and Vilcabamba, are also available.

There are regular departures from May to September, and private departures can be organized at any time of year. The best trekking months are June to August. In the wettest months (from December to April), trails can be slippery and campsites muddy. In February the Inca trail is closed for maintenance.

If renting equipment, always check it before setting out. In addition, be sure to pack rain gear, insect repellent, sunblock, a flashlight, basic first-aid supplies and water-purification tablets. For the Inca Trail, trekking poles are highly recommended, since you'll be descending a number of cartilage-crunching stone steps.

If you're on a guided trek, take a stash of cash for tipping the guide and porters. (About US$10 per day per trekker is the minimum decent tip for a guide; a similar amount to divide among your porters is appropriate.)

For information on the Inca Trail, turn to p224. For tips on booking a good trek, turn to p188.

For a detailed guide to other treks in the area, we recommend picking up a copy of *Alternative Inca Trails Information Packet* from the South American Explorers Club in Lima (p86) or Cuzco (p201).

The following companies are Cuzco-based trekking specialists often recommended by readers:

**Andina Travel** (25-1892; www.andinatravel.com; Plazoleta Santa Catalina 219)

**Apu's Peru** (23-3691; www.apus-peru.com; Cuichipunco 366)

**Eco Trek Peru** (24-7286; www.ecotrekperu.com; Atocsaycuchi 599)

**Peru Treks** (☎22-2722; www.perutreks.com; Av Pardo 540)

**Peruvian Highland Trek** (☎24-2480; www.peruvianhighlandtrek.com; Calle del Medio 139)

**Quechua's Expeditions** (☎23-7994; www.quechuasexpeditions.com; Suecia 344)

**X-treme Tourbulencia** (☎22-5872; www.x-tremetourbulencia.com; Plateros 358)

## River Running

Cuzco is becoming increasingly popular for river running, with nearby waterways that range in difficulty from Class I to Class V. The most popular of these is one of the many day runs on the **Río Urubamba**, through the Sacred Valley, which offers Class II and Class III runs on the stretch between **Cusipata** and **Quiquihana**. Closer to Cuzco, the section from **Pampa** to **Huambutio** (Class I to II) is beautiful and ideal for small children (ages three and over). There are many more difficult stretches as well. Do note that while the scenery is spectacular, Cuzco and all the villages along its course dispose of raw sewage in the Urubamba, making for a polluted trip. (Seriously, close your mouth if you fall in.)

Tougher runs on more inaccessible waterways – such as the **Río Santa Teresa**, the **Río Apurimac** and **Río Tambopata** – are also available, but generally as part of multiday trips. The area around Ollantaytambo is polluted and is not recommended for rafting.

Note that river running isn't regulated in Peru and fly-by-night operators abound. Go with reputable companies. The following have the best reputations for safety:

**Amazonas Explorer** (☎25-2846; www.amazonas-explorer.com; Av Collasuyu 910, Miravalle)

**Apumayo** (☎24-6018; www.apumayo.com; Jirón Ricardo Palma N-11, Urb Santa Mónica)

**Mayuc** (☎24-2824; www.mayuc.com; Portal Confiturías 211)

**River Explorers** (☎26-0926; www.riverexplorers.com; Urb Kennedy A, B-15)

The Río Urubamba flowing through the Sacred Valley (p205)

## Mountain Biking

Mountain-biking tours are a growing industry in Cuzco, and the local terrain is superb. However, rental bikes are poor quality and it is most common to find *rígida* (single suspension) models, which can make for bone-chattering downhills. If you're a serious mountain biker, consider bringing your own bike from home. Selling it in Cuzco is eminently viable.

Outfitters can organize day trips in the neighboring hillsides, though most folks come for multiday excursions. The following bike operators are recommended:

**Amazonas Explorer** (☎25-2846; www.amazonas-explorer.com) Has kids' bikes available.

**Cusco Aventuras** (☎984-13-7403; cuscoaventura@hotmail.com)

**Gravity Peru** (☎22-8032; www.gravityperu.com; Santa Catalina Ancha 398) The only operator offering double-suspension bikes for day trips.

**Party Bike** (☎24-0399; www.partybiketravel.com; Carmen Alto 246)

## Children

The **Chiquity Club** (☎23-3344; www.chiquityclubcusco.com; Marquez 259; child with parents S15; ⌚9am-8pm Thu-Tue; 📶) is an excellent activity center for children, which offers a great way for young families to decompress. The brainchild of a bilingual Waldorf-trained teacher, this multifaceted space has play areas, a climbing wall, an art room, a library, a dress-up theatre and a rockin' dark mini-*discoteca,* pulsing fun tunes. The ideal age for visitors is one to nine years old. The center also offers babysitting services and activity kits to go.

## Other Activities

These span the range from **horseback riding** (which just about any agency can arrange) to paying a visit to adventure parks such as **Action Valley** (☎24-0835; www.actionvalley.com; Santa Teresa 325; ⌚9am-5pm Sun-Fri, closed mid-Jan to mid-Feb), where you can get the adrenaline pumping with paintball and bungee jumping. It's 11km outside Cuzco on the road to Poroy.

The Sacred Valley (p205)

## Mountain Rites: Q'oyoriti

Life in Peru often comes to a halt during one of the country's myriad religious rituals. One of the most unusual is the celebration of Q'oyoriti.

Held in late May or early June, between the feasts of the Ascension and Corpus Christi, this procession takes worshippers up one of the area's most sacred mountains: Ausangate (6384m), the *pakarina* (sacred place of origin) of llamas and alpacas. Though it's officially about the icy image of Christ that appeared here in 1783, the festival remains an indigenous appeasement of an *apu* (a sacred deity found in the geographical landscape).

The traditional way to go about appeasing an *apu* is to buy an *alacita* (miniature scale model) of what you desire. Sold en route, these included houses, cars and money. You then line up at the church on the mountain to have it blessed by a priest. It's a three-hour trek up the mountain, traditionally in the wee hours to arrive around dawn. It's a fervent belief among many inhabitants of the region that if you attend Q'oyoriti three times, you'll get your heart's desire.

Note that discomfort will be an aspect of the pilgrimage: Q'oyoriti takes place at an altitude of 4750m. It's brutally cold, there's no infrastructure and the temporary toilets are an ordeal. But the whole thing is other-worldly and monumentally striking.

Welcome to Peru – this is the pointy end.



A more soothing option: hit a spa. **Samana Spa** (☎23-3721; www.samana-spa.com; Tecsecocha 536; h10am-7pm Mon-Sat) is one of the most luxurious options in Cuzco, with a menu that includes Peruvian hot stone massages and chocolate body wraps.

Be wary of cheap massages touted in the street. Most practitioners lack formal training and there are reports of massages getting unexpectedly intimate.

## Tours

### Agencies

There are hundreds of registered travel agencies in Cuzco, but things change quickly, so ask other travelers for recommendations. Classic options include half-day tours of the city and/or nearby ruins, half-day trips to visit Sunday markets at neighboring villages and full-day tours of the Sacred Valley. Agents also offer Machu Picchu day trips that include transportation, admission, an English-speaking guide and lunch. Note that these only allow you a few hours at the ruins before it's time to return.

The following agencies are recommended:

**Andina Travel** (☎25-1892; www.andinatravel.com; Plazoleta Santa Catalina 219) Adventure tour operator.

**Antipode** (☎970-440-448; www.antipode-travel.com; Choquechaca 229) Attentive, French-run outfit that has classic tours and treks.

**Chaski Ventura** (☎23-3952; www.chaskiventura.com; Manco Cápac 517) Pioneer of alternative and community tourism.

**Fertur** (☎22-1304; www.fertur-travel.com; San Agustín 317) Long-established, reliable agency for tours and travel.

**Milla Turismo** (☎23-1710; www.millaturismo.com; Av Pardo 800) Conventional tour operator that can also arrange for private tours and drivers.

## Booking a Great Trek

Trekking in the area around Cuzco has become increasingly popular, especially the journey on the Inca Trail. Unfortunately, this has brought out some less-than-stellar operators. Common complaints include minimal food, missing train tickets, leaking tents and overloaded porters. Here's what you need to know to book a great trek:

### INCA TRAIL: REGULATIONS & FEES

Only 500 people each day are allowed on the trail and they must have a permit and be in the company of a licensed guide. Tour prices generally include a tent, food, a cook, porters to carry group gear (you are expected to carry your own pack), one-day admission to the ruins and train fare back to Cuzco. Average price: US$350 to US$500 per person.

Book six months in advance between May and August.

### ALTERNATIVES TO THE INCA TRAIL

If you can't get a permit for the Inca Trail, there are other equally stellar treks that go to Machu Picchu, via the village of Santa Teresa, through the Lares Valley, or along the snowy peak of Salkantay. **Mountain Lodges of Peru** (☎23-6069; mountainlodgesofperu.com) has pioneered a luxury approach to the latter.

### PORTER WELFARE

Poor treatment of porters has been an issue. Any Inca Trail trip priced at less than US$250 means that cost-cutting is occurring – and porter welfare is likely affected. If you don't like what you see, register an official complaint with **iPerú** (www.peru.info).

For a comprehensive list of reputable agencies and guides, turn to the Activities section on p184.

**Respons** (☎23-3903; www.respons.org; Choquechaca 216-C, staircase) High-end sustainable tour operator.

**SAS Travel** (☎24-9194; www.sastravelperu.com; Calle Garcilaso 270) Package tours and treks.

**SATO** (South American Travels Online; ☎22-1304; www.southamericatravelsonline.com; Matara 437, interior-G) A European agency offering trekking, hiking and rafting.

**Turismo Caith** (☎23-3595; www.caith.org; Centro Yanapanakusun, Urb Ucchullo Alto, N4, Pasaje Santo Toribio) A leader in community tourism that also organizes standard trips.

### Guides

**Asociación de Guías Oficiales de Turismo** (Agotur; ☎24-9758; www.agoturcusco.org.pe; Heladeros 157) The Peruvian guides association is a good way to contact licensed guides.

**Adam Weintraub** (☎962-859-000; www.photoexperience.net) A Seattle native leads custom high-end photography tours and workshops.

**Alain Machaca Cruz** (☎984-056-635, 973-220-893; alain_313@hotmail.com) Recommended for interesting alternative city tours where you can make *chicha* (corn beer) or see *cuy* farms.

## Sleeping

Cuzco fills to bursting in June and August, especially during the 10 days before Inti Raymi on June 24 and during Fiestas Patrias (Independence Days) on July 28 and 29. Book well in advance during this time.

### Central Cuzco

**INKATERRA LA CASONA** Boutique Hotel **$$$**

(**23-5873; www.lacasona.info; Atocsaycuchi 616; ste incl breakfast from US$410; @**) Hitting the perfect balance between cozy and high style, this renovated grand colonial home in tiny Plazoleta Nazarenas has a rustic-meets-majestic grace. Original features include oversized carved doors, rough-hewn beams and stone fireplaces, all enhanced with radiant floors, plush divans and gorgeous Andean textiles. The telly is tucked away, but tech isn't far with laptop loans and iPod docks.

Service is impeccable and highly personal.

**NIÑOS HOTEL** Hotel **$$**

(**23-1424, 25-4611; www.ninoshotel.com; Meloc 442; s/d without bathroom S63/126, d/tr incl breakfast S137/200; @**) Long beloved and highly recommended, these hotels are run by a Dutch-founded nonprofit foundation that serves underprivileged children in Cuzco. Both are in rambling colonials with sunny courtyards and refurbished rooms bordered with bright trim. The public cafeteria features homemade cakes and breads as well as box lunches. The other branch is at Fierro 476.

**HOTEL LOS MARQUESES** Hotel **$$**

(**26-4249; www.hotelmarqueses.com; Calle Garcilaso 256; s/d/tr incl breakfast from S196/252/308;**) Romance pervades this 16th-century Spanish colonial villa. Classic features include *escuela cuzqueña* paintings, courtyard fountains and balconies looking out onto the cathedral. Rooms are large and airy, with some brass beds and carved wooden doors. Wi-fi is available only on the patio.

**PALACIO NAZARENAS** Luxury Hotel **$$$**

(**58-2222; www.palacionazarenas.com; Plaza Nazarenas 144; d ste from US$885; @**) Hotels in Cuzco don't get more luxurious than this new Orient-Express property: 55 oxygenated suites are set inside an exquisitely restored, 9000-sq-m Spanish convent that dates back to the 16th century. Amenities include bathrooms with radiant floors, spa massage rooms set over Inca canals and the city's only hotel swimming pool – heated, of course. There are countless other extravagant touches, including a poolside juice bar,

Traditional clothing worn at festivities in Ollantaytambo (p210)

bath pillows scented with local herbs and suites that retain original baroque ceilings.

It's expensive, but if you're looking to blow the wad on something mind-bogglingly special, this would be the place to do it.

**HOTEL ARQUEÓLOGO** Boutique Hotel **$$$**
(**☎23-2569; www.hotelarqueologo.com; Pumacurco 408; d/superior incl breakfast S384/451; @📶**) Feeling luxurious but also lived-in, this antique French-owned guesthouse gives a real feel for Cuzco, with Inca stonework, original murals and tasteful rooms that overlook a vast courtyard. Relax on the lawn out back, pet the three-legged dog or sip a complimentary pisco sour in the fireplace lounge.

**MIDORI** Hotel **$$$**
(**☎24-8144; www.midori-cusco.com; Ataúd 204; s/d incl breakfast S221/280; @📶**) Popular with small tour groups, this small hotel is classic and comfortable. Enormous rooms feature a living area, brocade fabrics and firm beds. Locally recommended.

**LA LUNE** Boutique Hotel **$$$**
(**☎24-0543; www.onesuitehotelcusco.com; San Agustín 275; d incl breakfast US$450-550; @📶**) It's hard to get more exclusive than this: a two-suite hotel with 24-hour concierge service from its French owner, Artur. He wants you to relax – so stays also include drinks from a full bar and a professional massage under a stained-glass window. Suites are luxuriant, with tasteful modern decor and organic Cacharel bedding; the pricier option comes with Jacuzzi (filled with rose petals at your bidding).

**CASA CARTAGENA** Boutique Hotel **$$$**
(**☎in Lima 01-242-3147; www.casacartagena.com; Pumacurco 336; ste from US$450; @📶🏊**) Fusing modern with colonial, this Italian-owned boutique hotel has 16 contemporary suites equipped with king beds, iPod docks, enormous bathtubs and bouquets of long-stemmed roses. Management boasts that both Pablo

**Left:** Moray (p208);
**Below:** Quechua children dressed in traditional clothing
(LEFT) SEAN CAFFREY/GETTY IMAGES ©; (BELOW) JESSICA ANTOLA/GETTY IMAGES ©



Neruda and Che Guevara bedded down in this historic mansion (though it was far simpler back then). There's a lovely on-site spa and room service is free.

**HOTEL MONASTERIO** Luxury Hotel **$$$**
(☎60-4000; www.monasterio.orient-express.com; Calle Palacio 136; d from US$700, ste S2150-5952; @ wi-fi) Set around graceful 16th-century cloisters, this Orient-Express hotel has long been a Cuzco jewel, with majestic public areas and more than 100 irregularly sized rooms that show their Jesuit monastery roots. All in all, an elegant option (even if some of the renovation touches – ie a plasma TV that emerges from the foot of the bed – seem a little gauche).

The fireside bar in the lobby is a perfect place for a cocktail (even if you're not staying in the hotel). Don't miss the baroque chapel with its original gold-leaf paintings.

**TIERRA VIVA** Hotel **$$$**
(☎60-1317; www.tierravivahoteles.com; Saphi 766; s/d/tr incl breakfast S300/330/360; @ wi-fi) With modern stylings and notable service, this new Peruvian hotel chain offers two comfortable midrange options in downtown Cuzco. The **Plaza de Armas location** (Suecia 345) is more spacious, with an interior courtyard. Doubles sport hardwood floors or Berber carpets, white linens and colorful throws. Buffet breakfast is available from 5am on.

**HOSTAL SUECIA I** Hotel **$**
(☎23-3282; www.hostalsuecia1.com; Suecia 332; s/d incl breakfast S60/90; wi-fi) Most rooms in this pint-sized guesthouse are very basic, but location and staff are fabulous and there's a sociable, stony, indoor courtyard. The two newer doubles on the top floor (311 and 312) are good value.

**LORETO BOUTIQUE HOTEL** Hotel $$
(☎22-6352; www.loretoboutiquehotel.com; Loreto 115; s/d/tr incl breakfast S199/252/305) Maybe you're paying for the plaza location, since 'boutique' is an overstatement here. Dimly lit in daytime, Loreto has well-heeled, snug rooms bathed in neutrals. The best feature is the four rooms with surviving Inca walls.

**RENACIMIENTO** Apartment $$
(☎22-1596; www.cuscoapart.com; Ceniza 331; s/d S100/160; wi-fi) An unsigned treasure, this old colonial mansion on a residential street has been converted into 12 individually appointed one- and two-bedroom apartments sleeping one to six people. Quiet and comfortable, it's fabulous for families.

**DEL PRADO INN** Hotel $$$
(☎22-442; www.delpradoinn.com; Suecia 310; s/d/tr incl buffet breakfast S225/390/435; @ wi-fi) A solid option, with efficient staff and just over a dozen snug rooms reached by elevator. Some have tiny balconies with corner views of the plaza. Check out the original Inca walls in the dining room.

**LOS ANDES DE AMERICA** Hotel $$$
(☎60-6060; www.cuscoandes.com; Calle Garcilaso 150; s/d incl breakfast S347/410; wi-fi) A Best Western hotel noted for its buffet breakfast, which includes regional specialties such as *mote con queso* (cheese and corn) and *papa helada* (frozen potato). Rooms are warm and comfortable, bathrooms are big and relatively luxurious, and the atrium features a scale model of Machu Picchu.

**HOSTAL CORIHUASI** Guesthouse $$
(☎23-2233; www.corihuasi.com; Suecia 561; s/d/tr incl breakfast S119/149/178) A brisk walk uphill from the main plaza, this family-feel guesthouse inhabits a maze-like colonial building with postcard views. Ample rooms are outfitted in a warm, rustic style with alpaca-wool blankets and wooden furnishings. Room 1 is the most in demand for its wraparound windows, ideal for soaking up sunsets.

**HOSPEDAJE MONTE HOREB** Guesthouse $$
(☎23-6775; montehorebcusco@yahoo.com; San Juan de Dios 260, 2nd fl; s/d incl breakfast S84/112) With an inner-courtyard entry, this serene and well-cared-for option has big, old-fashioned rooms, an inviting balcony and a curious mix of furnishings.

## San Blas

**SECOND HOME CUSCO** Boutique Hotel $$$
(☎23-5873; www.secondhomecusco.com; Atocsaycuchi 616; d/tr incl breakfast S318/384; @ wi-fi) A cozy lodging with three chic suites has original artwork, adobe walls and skylights. Carlos Delfín, the affable and cosmopolitan English-speaking owner, orchestrates private tours and has even hunted down the best baguettes in town for breakfast.

**LA ENCANTADA** Boutique Hotel $$$
(☎24-2206; www. encantadaperu.com; Tandapata 354; s/d incl breakfast S212/265; @ wi-fi) Bright and cheerful, this modern spot features terraced gardens and immense views from iron-rail balconies. A circular staircase leads to small, tasteful rooms with king-sized beds while an on-site spa helps hikers work out the kinks. Be aware that checkout is at 9am.

**HOSTAL PENSIÓN ALEMANA** Hotel $$
(☎22-6861; www.cuzco-stay.de; Tandapata 260; s/d/tr incl breakfast S154/184/232; @ wi-fi) Attentive and lovely, this polished Swiss-German lodge wouldn't look out of place in the Alps. Nice touches include air purifiers and complimentary tea and fruit, as well terraces with sweeping views. Couples should note there are very few matrimonial beds.

**MADRE TIERRA** B&B $$
(☎24-8452; www.hostalmadretierra.com; Atocsaycuchi 647; d/tr S130/207; @ wi-fi) Warm and supercozy, with plenty of B&B-style luxury comfort touches, Madre Tierra is a vine-entwined, slightly claustrophobic little jewel box. Rooms have skylights and funky dimensions. Good value.

**AMARU HOSTAL** Hotel $$

(☎22-5933; www.cusco.net/amaru; Cuesta San Blas 541; s/d/tr incl breakfast S105/135/189; @ 📶) In a characterful old building in a prime location, flowerpots sit outside well-kept rooms with styles that are a little dated. Some feature rocking chairs from which to admire the rooftop view. Rooms in the outer courtyard are noisy; those at back are newest.

**HOSTAL RUMI PUNKU** Hotel $$$

(☎22-1102; www.rumipunku.com; Choquechaca 339; s/d incl breakfast S223/279; @ 📶) Recognizable by the monumental Inca stonework around the entrance, Rumi Punku (Stone Door) is a stylish complex of old colonial houses, gardens and terraces. The rooftop terraces are utterly charming and the rooms ooze comfort, with central heating, wood floors and European bedding. Sauna and Jacuzzi are available for a minimal charge.

**CASONA LES PLEIADES** B&B $$

(☎50-6430; www.casona-pleiades.com; Tandapata 116; d/tr incl breakfast S165/210; @ 📶) This pleasant French-run B&B has a sunny courtyard featuring fresh flowers and balcony seating, as well as offering a buffet breakfast served in cozy booths. Heaters and lockboxes are supplied in rooms.

**LOS APUS HOTEL & MIRADOR** Hotel $$$

(☎26-4243; www.losapushotel.com; Atocsaycuchi 515; s/d incl breakfast S260/315; ❄ @ 📶) With understated class, this longtime Swiss-run hotel features central heating, large bedrooms with down duvets and colonial *cuzqueño*-style art. A wheelchair-accessible room is available.

**EUREKA HOSTAL** Hotel $$

(☎23-3505; www.peru-eureka.com; Chihuampata 591; s/d/tr S198/231/297; @ 📶) A funky blend of old and new, Eureka's stylish lobby and sun-soaked cafeteria give way to comfortable (if oddly decorated) rooms. Orthopedic mattresses and down quilts, however, make them quite comfortable.

**PANTASTICO** Guesthouse $

(☎95-4387; www.hotelpantastico.com; Carmen Bajo 226; s/d S65/90, dm/s/d/tr without bathroom S30/45/70/90; @ 📶) This newish bed and bakery features fresh bread daily at 5am. But from the looks of it, few of the guests have theirs hot (though breakfast is included). There's also good water pressure and a hard-core hippie groove: if you want to shop for ayahuasca experiences or make organic pizza, it's your spot.

## Av El Sol & Downhill

**HOTEL LIBERTADOR PALACIO DEL INKA** Luxury Hotel $$

(☎23-1961; www.libertador.com.pe; Plazoleta Santo Domingo 259; d/ste US$210/260; ❄ @ 📶) Opulence bedecks this colonial

San Blas neighborhood (p183), Cuzco

mansion. It's built over Inca foundations, with parts of the building dating back to the 16th century, when Francisco Pizarro was an occupant. It's as luxurious and beautiful as you'd expect, with a fine interior courtyard and ample rooms that were recently renovated.

**YANANTIN GUEST HOUSE** Guesthouse **$$**
(**☎25-4205; www.yanantin.com; Ahuacpinta 775; s/d incl breakfast S95/108;** 📶) This small guesthouse has an assortment of well-heeled rooms large enough for desks and coffee tables. Organic toiletries are offered and the comfy beds feature cotton sheets and down bedding. Good value.

**LOS ATICOS** Hotel **$$**
(**☎23-1710; www.losaticos.com; Quera 253, Psje Hurtado Álvarez; d/apt incl breakfast S132/172;** @📶) Hidden in a small passageway, this well-tended spot is off the radar but worth snagging. Rooms have comfy beds and parquet floors. There's also a full guest kitchen. The three mini-apartments sleep up to four – good value for families.

## Eating

### Central Cuzco

**CICCIOLINA** International **$$$**
(**☎23-9510; Triunfo 393, 2nd fl; mains S30-55; ⏲8am-late**) On the 2nd floor of a colonial house, Cicciolina has long held its position as Cuzco's best restaurant. The sophisticated Peruvian-Mediterranean menu is divine, with house-marinated olives, crisp polenta squares with cured rabbit, delectable charred octopus and satisfying mains like squid-ink pasta and tender lamb. The service is impeccable, as is the warmly lit dining room. Reservations recommended.

**LA BODEGA 138** Pizzeria **$$**
(**☎26-0272; Herrajes 138; mains S18-35; ⏲6:30-11pm Mon-Sat**) Sometimes you are homesick for good atmosphere and

**Left:** The Sacred Valley (p205);
**Below:** The Temple of Viracocha, Raqchi (p203)
(LEFT) HUGHES HERVE / HEMIS.FR/GETTY IMAGES ©; (BELOW) KELLY CHENG TRAVEL PHOTOGRAPHY/GETTY IMAGES ©



uncomplicated menus. In comes La Bodega, a fantastic laid-back enterprise run by a family in what used to be their home. Thin-crust pizzas are fired up in the adobe oven, organic salads are fresh and abundant and the prices are reasonable. A true find.

**CHICHA** Novo Andino **$$$**
**(☎24-0520; Regocijo 261, 2nd fl; mains S24-50)** A Gastón Acurio venture serving up haute versions of highland classics, including a beefy *rocoto relleno* (red pepper stuffed with beef), a wonton-style *sopa de gallina* (chicken soup) and a *chicha morada* (purple corn drink) that's beyond fresh. Naturally, debate rages as to whether it's worth the price: our vote is yes.

**LIMO** Peruvian **$$$**
**(☎24-068; Portal de Carnes 236, 2nd fl; mains S24-60; ⏰11am-11pm Mon-Sat)** Start with a tart pisco sour, it's the perfect accompaniment to the fresh Peruvian-Asian seafood creations. The basket of native potatoes with sauces as a starter is a fun change from bread. And *tiraditos,* sashimi-style strips of fish, simply melt on the tongue. Other hits are the creamy *causas* (potato terrines) and *sudadito,* a brothy mix of greens, corn and seared scallops.

**EL HADA** Ice Cream **$**
**(Arequipa 167; ice creams from S6; ⏰11am-8pm Mon-Sat)** Served in fresh-made cones with a hint of vanilla or lemon peel, these exotic ice creams are ecstasy. The rotating flavors – like Indonesian cinnamon, bitter chocolate or roasted apples – do not disappoint.

**GREEN'S ORGANIC** Cafe **$$**
**(☎24-3399; Santa Catalina Angosta 235, 2nd fl; mains S21-44; ⏰11am-10pm; )** With all-organic food and a bright farmhouse feel, Green's Organic serves up inventive salads (such as roasted fennel, goat cheese,

## A Guide to Cuzco Cuisine

Steaming soups, fresh-grilled meats and an ice-cold *chela* (that's Peruvian slang for beer). Here are some local dishes not to miss when you're in Cuzco.

**Anticucho** The Peruvian answer to the lollipop is beef heart on a stick, with a potato on the end for punctuation. Much more delicious than it sounds – many who try it without realizing it's heart end up addicted.

**Caldo de gallina** It's impossible to find bad soup in Cuzco, but simple, healthy, hearty *caldo de gallina* (chicken soup) is a standout, and a local favorite for hangovers. It also goes down well if the altitude has you dizzy.

**Chicharrones** Deep-fried chunks of pork, served with corn, mint leaves and onion. This one is definitely more than the sum of its parts: get a bit of each ingredient on your fork and you'll experience coronary-inducing heaven.

**Choclo con queso** *Choclo* are the huge, pale cobs of corn that are typical of the area. Served with a teeth-squeaking chunk of cheese, it's a great, cheap snack. Look for it in the Sacred Valley.

**Cuy** Yes, they really do eat guinea pig. Nothing to be afraid of (it tastes like chicken – honestly!), though it's often served complete with head, which can be, er, disconcerting.

**Lechón** Suckling pig with plenty of crackling, generally served with tamales (corn cakes). Another shortcut to a heart attack, but what a way to go.

beets and spring greens) and heartier fare such as pasta and alpaca dishes.

**TRUJILLO RESTAURANT** Peruvian **$**
(☎23-3465; Av Tullumayo 542 at Plaza Limacpampa; mains S15-28; ⏲8am-8pm Mon-Sat, noon-6pm Sun) Run by a northern Peruvian family, this simple dining hall by Qorikancha nails northern classics such as *aji de gallina* (a creamy chicken stew served with rice and potatoes).

**CBC BAKERY** Bakery **$**
(☎23-4035; http://qosqomaki.org/taller panaderia; Tullumayo 465; pastries S3; ⏲7:30am-8pm Mon-Sat) The best chocolate croissants in town, plus other scrumptious baked goods – all crafted by a charitable foundation.

**UCHU PERUVIAN STEAKHOUSE** Peruvian **$$**
(☎24-6598; Calle Palacio 135; S22-48; ⏲12:30-11pm) With a cozy, cavernous ambience of low-lit adobe, dark tables and bright turquoise walls, this chic eatery has a simple menu of meat (steak, alpaca or chicken) and fish cooked on hot volcanic stones at your table. The staff is knowledgeable and quick to serve – a real treat.

**LOS PERROS** Fusion **$**
(Tecsecocha 436; mains S17-24) You'll find Asian-slanted bar food at good prices in this intimate couch bar. Try the sesame chicken sandwich – which is tender, and served with a dollop of guacamole, all of it big enough for two.

**SENZO** Fusion **$$$**
(☎58-2222; Plaza Nazarenas 144; lunch mains US$19-27, dinner tasting menu per person US$84; 🍷) Located inside the Palacio Nazarenas hotel, this sedate poolside eatery has a menu designed by Lima celebrity chef Virgilio Martinez. And the focus is all local: tender alpaca medallions are seared with *palo santo* (a type of fragrant wood), local potatoes are smashed and blended with Andean herbs and red quinoa salad comes in a bright citrus–passion-fruit

dressing. It's not cheap, but the market-fresh cooking and excellent service make it a singular treat.

Note that lunch is à la carte and dinner is served as a tasting menu (with vegetarian option).

**ALDEA YANAPAY** Cafe **$**

**(☎25-5134; Ruinas 415, 2nd fl; menú S15, mains from S22; 🕒9am-11:30pm; 🌶)** Stuffed animals, board games and decor perfectly evoke the circus you dreamed of running away to as a child. Pitched at families, but with wide appeal, the menu includes burritos, falafel and tasty little fried things to pick at. Plus, there's a whole separate menu for vegetarians.

**EL ENCUENTRO** Vegetarian **$**

**(Santa Catalina Ancha 384; menu S8; 🕒6:30am-10pm; 🌶)** This economical vegetarian restaurant offers set lunches with a salad-bar starter, rib-sticking barley soup and mains like tofu and wilted veggies with rice. What it lacks in subtlety, it makes up for in abundance.

**EL AYLLU** Cafe **$**

**(Marquez 263; mains S10; 🕒6:30am-10pm)** This old-fashioned café is beloved by *cuzqueños* for its inky coffee and traditional pastries, like the puff pastry *lengua de suegra*. It's a great spot for breakfast.

**LOS TOLDOS** Peruvian **$**

**(cnr Almagro & San Andrés; mains S12-20; 🕒lunch & dinner Mon-Sat)** A local favorite for abundant cheap eats, this rotisserie restaurant features a worthwhile salad bar (try the black olive sauce). While the menu lists an abundance of specialties, most people don't get past the Peruvian classic *cuarto de pollo* (quarter chicken), done to perfection.

**VICTOR VICTORIA** Peruvian **$$**

**(☎25-2854; Tecsecocha 466; mains from S15; 🕒7am-10pm)** Serving princely portions of Peruvian food, this restaurant serves deliriously good quinoa laced with cheese, as well as tasty roasted *cuy*. (For the latter, order ahead.)

**MARCELO BATATA** Peruvian **$$**

**(Calle Palacio 121; mains from S21-38; 🕒2-11pm)** A sure bet for Peruvian food with a twist, such as the exquisite chicken soup with *hierbaluisa* (lemongrass). It's also a good spot for a cocktail: the heated rooftop deck is the best outdoor venue in Cuzco.

## San Blas

**JACK'S CAFÉ** Cafe **$**

**(☎25-4606; Choquechaca 509; mains S12-20; 🕒7:30am-11:30pm)** A line often snakes out the door at this Western-style eatery serving fresh juices, strong coffee and eggs in myriad ways, heaped with smoked salmon or roasted tomatoes.

Andean corn

**JUANITO'S** Sandwiches **$**

**(Qanchipata 596; sandwiches S15; ⏰8am-8pm)** With the griddle hopping, this sandwich shop churns out extravagant made-to-order numbers with hand-cut fries and homemade sauces. Vegetarians can feast on big fried-egg sandwiches.

**GRANJA HEIDI** Cafe **$$**

**(☎23-8383; Cuesta San Blas 525, 2nd fl; mains S18-38; ⏰11:30am-9:30pm Mon-Sat)** A cozy Alpine café serving healthy meals, some of it provided from the small farm of the German owner. In addition to Peruvian fare (*rocoto relleno* is served vegetarian, with peanuts), there are crêpes, huge soups and salads. Save room for dessert.

**MEETING PLACE** Cafe **$**

**(☎24-0465; Plazoleta San Blas; mains S15-21; ⏰8:30am-4pm Mon-Sat; 📶)** Owned by Idaho natives, this cafe nails gringo breakfast, with organic coffee, loose-leaf teas, and puffy waffles. Service is swift and friendly.

**LA QUINTA EULALIA** Peruvian **$$**

**(☎22-4951; Choquechaca 384; mains S25-50)** A Cuzco classic that has been in business for over half a century, La Quinta has a charming courtyard patio that's a score on a sunny day. The chalkboard menu features tender roast lamb, alpaca and traditional sides like the phenomenal *rocoto relleno*.

## Avenida El Sol & Downhill & Beyond

**DON ESTÉBAN AND DON PANCHO** Cafe **$$**

**(☎25-2526; Av El Sol 765A; snacks S5-15; ⏰8am-10pm)** A local favorite for *cuzqueño* breakfasts, cinnamon raison rolls and empanadas – the *empanada de ají de gallina* is especially scrumptious.

**TRADICIONES CUSQUEÑAS** Peruvian **$$**

**(☎23-1988; Belén 835; mains S20-40; ⏰11am-10pm)** Located outside the city center, this traditional spot is the home of a good Sunday lunch – Cuzco-style. It features jolly, utilitarian decor, huge piles of meat and potatoes, and delicious homemade *limonada* (lemonade). Come hungry, be prepared to linger and don't expect to hear a language other than Spanish.

## Drinking & Entertainment

**MUSEO DEL PISCO** Cocktail Bar

**(museodelpisco.org; Santa Catalina Ancha 398; ⏰11am-1am)** This chic tapas bar and lounge goes far beyond the standard pisco sour, whipping up original cocktails like the *valicha* (pisco with ginger, spearmint and tart apple) and delicious tapas, including alpaca miniburgers and *tiradito* marinated in cumin-chile.

**7 ANGELITOS** Bar

**(Siete Angelitos 638; ⏰6pm-late Mon-Sat)** A tiny hillside haunt is the city's unofficial hipster lounge and late-night backup: when everything else has closed and the sun has come up, knock on the door.

**FALLEN ANGEL** Cocktail Bar

**(☎25-8184; Plazoleta Nazarenas 221; ⏰6pm-late)** This relentlessly decorated lounge redefines kitsch with glitter balls, fake fur and bathtub-cum-aquarium tables complete with live goldfish. It isn't cheap, but the hallucinatory interiors are worth seeing at least once.

**NORTON RATS** Pub

**(cnr Santa Catalina Angosta & Plaza de Armas, 2nd fl; ⏰7am-late)** Run by a motorcycle enthusiast, this unassuming expat pub overlooks the Plaza de Armas. It's a boon for people-watching, if you can get a balcony seat. Though known for delicious burgers, it's also got TVs, darts and billiards to help you work up a thirst. Avoid the burritos.

**CROSS KEYS** Pub

**(Triunfo 350; ⏰10am-late; 📶)** This typical British pub has all the trappings, with leather barstools and dark wood – as well as a long list of imported beer and excellent wi-fi.

**FROGS** Lounge

**(Huarancalqui 185)** Gloriously glamorous and run by high-profile hipsters, Frogs offers a bit of everything: café service during the day and live music at night that ranges from acoustic to reggae to funk.

Textiles at the market in Pisac (p205)

STEVE ALLEN/GETTY IMAGES ©



**UKUKU'S** Live Music

(☎24-2951; Plateros 316; 8pm-late) The most consistently popular nightspot in town, Ukuku's plays a winning combination of rock, reggae, *reggaetón*, salsa and hip-hop, and often hosts live bands. Usually full to bursting after midnight.

**INKA TEAM** Club

(Portal de Carnes 298; 8pm-late) Though it may change names, this place usually has the latest electronic music collection, with trance, house and hip-hop mixed in with mainstream standards. It has chill-out sofas upstairs but this isn't the place for chat.

**CENTRO QOSQO DE ARTE NATIVO** Performing Arts

(☎22-7901; Av El Sol 604; admission with boleto turístico) Has performances of Andean music and dance at 6:45pm every night.

## Shopping

### Artisan Workshops

San Blas, Cuzco's artisan quarter, is a top spot for shopping – with the workshops and showrooms of the city's top artisans. Some of the best:

**Taller Olave** (☎23-1835; Plaza San Blas 651) Sells reproductions of colonial sculptures and precolonial ceramics.

**Taller Mendivil** (☎23-3247); city center (cnr Hatunrumiyoc & Choquechaca); San Blas (Cuesta de San Blas, Plaza San Blas) Nationally famous for its giraffe-necked religious figures and sun-shaped mirrors.

**Taller and Museo Mérida** (☎22-1714; Carmen Alto 133) Striking earthenware statues that straddle the border between craft and art.

### Textiles

**CENTRO DE TEXTILES TRADICIONALES DEL CUZCO** Handicrafts

(☎22-8117; www.textilescusco.org; Av El Sol 603A; 7:30am-8:30pm Mon-Sat, 8:30am-8:30pm Sun) This nonprofit organization, founded in 1996, promotes the survival of traditional weaving. It also stocks some of the most exquisite textiles around – hand-crafted, from sheep or alpaca wool (no synthetic fibers here). On some days, there are shop-floor demonstrations. This is the real deal – so expect to pay top-shelf prices.

**INKAKUNAQ RUWAYNIN** Handicrafts
(☎26-0942; www.tejidosandinos.com; inside CBC, Tullumayo 274; ⌚9am-7pm) This weaving cooperative selling high-quality goods is run by 12 mountain communities from Cuzco and Apurímac and sells everything from *chullos* (earflap hats) to *chuspas* (coca leaf bags) to more moderns designs. Find the shop at the far end of the inner courtyard. There is also an online catalog.

**CASA ECOLÓGICA** Handicrafts
(☎25-5646; www.casaecologicacusco.com; Triunfo 393; ⌚9am-9pm Mon-Sun) Handmade textiles from 29 communities as far away as Ausangate, plus homemade jams and essential oils.

## Additional Shopping

**MERCADO SAN PEDRO** Market
(Plazoleta San Pedro) Cuzco's central market is a must-see. Stalls plying pig heads for *caldo* (soup), frogs (to enhance sexual performance), mountains of cheese and roasted *lechón* (suckling pig) are surrounded by traditional clothes, textiles, crafts and enough other random products to keep you entertained for hours.

**CENTRO ARTESANAL CUZCO** Crafts Market
(cnr Avs El Sol & Tullumayo; ⌚9am-10pm) You'll find everything from jewelry to textiles to alpaca rugs and knockoff pre-Columbian ceramics at this vast crafts center.

**TATOO** Outdoor Equipment
(☎25-4211; Calle del Medio 130; ⌚9am-9:30pm) Brand-name outdoor clothing and technical gear at high prices.

# Information

## Dangers & Annoyances

Like any big city, Cuzco has crime. Pickpocketing can be a problem in crowded areas. It is advisable to avoid walking around by yourself late at night. Lastly, there are occasional reports of spiked drinks. Solo women travelers should only accept drinks from people they trust.

**Left:** Sacsaywamán (p203);
**Below:** Golden-headed quetzal
(LEFT) ANDRAS JANCSIK/GETTY IMAGES ©; (BELOW) TED CHEESEMAN/GETTY IMAGES ©

That said, your biggest concern during your visit will likely be the altitude. Take it easy the first few days. (For advice on dealing with altitude sickness, see p345).

## Emergency

**Policía de Turismo** (Tourist Police; ☎23-5123; Plaza Túpac Amaru s/n; ⏰24hr) Can issue police reports for stolen items.

## Internet Access

Internet cafes are found on almost every street corner. Many hotels and cafes offer free wireless.

## Medical Services

Pharmacies abound along Av El Sol. Cuzco's medical facilities are limited; head to Lima for serious procedures.

**Clínica Pardo** (☎24-0997; Av de la Cultura 710; ⏰24hr) Well equipped, but expensive.

**Clínica Paredes** (☎22-5265; Lechugal 405; ⏰24hr) Consultations S60.

## Money

ATMs are plentiful in and around the Plaza de Armas and are also available at the airport, Huanchac train station and the bus terminal. *Casas de cambio* (foreign-exchange bureaus) give better exchange rates than banks, and are scattered around the main plazas and Av El Sol.

## Tourist Information

**Dirección Regional de Cultura Cusco** (Directur; ☎58-2030; www.drc-cusco.gob.pe; Av de la Cultura 238; ⏰7:15am-6:30pm Mon-Sat) The place in Cuzco to purchase Machu Picchu entry tickets; closed on holidays. Take cash and be ready to stand in line.

**iPerú** (www.peru.travel) airport (☎23-7364; Aeropuerto, Main Hall; ⏰6am-4pm); city center (☎25-2974; Portal de Harinas 177, Plaza de Armas; ⏰8am-8pm) Excellent source of tourist information on both the region and the country.

**South American Explorers Club** (☎24-5484; www.saexplorers.org; Atocsaycuchi 670;

9:30am-5pm Mon-Fri, to 1pm Sat) Gives unbiased advice and sells information booklets on alternatives to the Inca Trail. There is also a book exchange. Some services are for members only.

## Getting There & Away

### Air

**Aeropuerto Internacional Alejandro Velasco Astete** (CUZ; 22-2611) is Cuzco's main airport and offers daily flights to and from Lima, Puerto Maldonado (in the Amazon) and Arequipa. Check in two hours before your flight. During the rainy season (December to April), flights to Puerto Maldonado may be seriously delayed. Departure taxes are included in the ticket.

### Bus

Buses to major cities, including Puno, Arequipa and Lima, leave from the **terminal terrestre** (22-4471, Vía de Evitamiento 429), about 700m out of town towards the airport. Buses for more unusual destinations leave from elsewhere. Check carefully.

Recommended long-haul companies include:

**Cruz del Sur** (24-3621; www.cruzdelsur.com.pe)

**Ormeño** (26-1704; www.grupo-ormeno.com.pe)

**Tour Peru** (24-9977, www.tourperu.com.pe)

A couple of luxury services make daily runs to Puno with scenic stops along the way and the services of an English speaking guide:

**Inka Express** (24-7887; www.inkaexpress.com; Av La Paz C32, El Óvalo)

**Turismo Mer** (24-5171; www.turismomer.com; Av La Paz A3, El Óvalo)

A network of minibuses connects Cuzco to other towns in the region. Stops are scattered around the city. Inquire locally.

### Taxi

*Colectivos* (collective taxis) to Andahuaylillas, Tipón and Piquillacta leave from the middle of the street outside Tullumayo 207.

It is easy to hire private taxis for day trips to nearby villages and the Sacred Valley. Be sure to negotiate rates in advance.

### Car & Motorcycle

Given all the hazards of driving yourself around, it is highly recommended to consider hiring a taxi for the day – it's cheaper and safer than renting a car. Otherwise, you'll find a couple of rental agencies at the bottom of Av El Sol. Motorcycle rentals are offered by a couple of agencies in the first block of Saphi heading away from the Plaza de Armas.

### Train

Cuzco has two train stations:

**Estación Poroy** (58-1414, Av Pachacutec s/n) On the outskirts of the city, it serves travelers headed to Ollantaytambo and Machu Picchu.

**Estación Huanchac** (58-1414; 7am-5pm Mon-Fri, to midnight Sat & Sun) Near the end of Av El Sol, this is for passengers headed to Puno and Lake Titicaca.

You can buy tickets at Estación Huanchac, but it's best to reserve in advance directly through **PeruRail** (www.perurail.com) – especially during high season. Downtown's Estación San Pedro is used only for local trains, which foreigners cannot board.

## Getting Around

### To/From the Airport

The airport is about 6km south of the city center. A taxi to or from the city center to the airport costs S10. An official radio taxi hailed at the airport costs S12 to S25. With advance reservations, many hotels offer free pickup.

### Bus

Local rides on public transportation cost only S0.60, though it's easier to walk or just take a taxi than to figure out where any given *combi* is headed.

### Taxi

There are no meters in taxis, so negotiate rates in advance. At the time of writing, trips within the city center cost S4. Destinations further afield usually run S8. Check with your hotel whether this is still correct. Official taxis, identified by a lit company telephone number on the roof, are more expensive than taxis flagged down on the street, but they are safer.

Unofficial 'pirate' taxis, which only have a taxi sticker in the window, have been complicit in crimes. Approach with caution.

**AloCusco** (22-2222) A reliable company to call.

## Tram

The **Tranvía** is a free-rolling tourist tram that conducts a 1½ hour hop-on, hop-off city tour (S15). It leaves at 8:30am, 10am, 11:30am, 2pm, 3:30pm, 5pm and 6:30pm from the Plaza de Armas.

# AROUND CUZCO

The four ruins closest to Cuzco are Sacsaywamán, Q'enqo, Tambomachay and Pukapukara. They can all be visited in a day – far less if you're whisked through on a guided tour. If you wish to visit these independently, a taxi will charge roughly S40 to take you to all four sites. If you only have time to visit one, Sacsaywamán is the most important (and spectacular), and less than a 2km trek uphill from the Plaza de Armas in central Cuzco.

Each site can only be entered with the *boleto turístico* and is open daily from 7am to 6pm. Local guides hang around offering their services. Agree on a price before beginning any tour.

Robberies at these places are uncommon but not unheard of. It is best to visit in daylight hours, between 9am and 5pm.

## Sacsaywamán

This **immense ruin** of both religious and military significance is the most impressive in the immediate area around Cuzco. The long Quechua name means 'Satisfied Falcon,' though tourists will inevitably remember it by the mnemonic 'sexy woman.'

The site is composed of three different areas, the most striking being the magnificent three-tiered **zigzag fortifications**. One stone, incredibly, weighs more than 300 tons. It was the ninth *inca*, Pachacutec, who envisioned Cuzco in the shape of a puma, with Sacsaywamán as the head and these 22 zigzagged walls as its teeth.

In 1536 the fort was the site of one of the bitterest indigenous rebellions of the conquest. More than two years after Pizarro's entry into Cuzco, Manco Inca recaptured the lightly guarded Sacsaywamán and used it as a base to lay siege to the conquistadors in Cuzco. Manco was on the brink of defeating the Spaniards when a desperate last-ditch attack by 50 Spanish cavalry succeeded in retaking Sacsaywamán and putting an end to the uprising. Manco Inca survived,

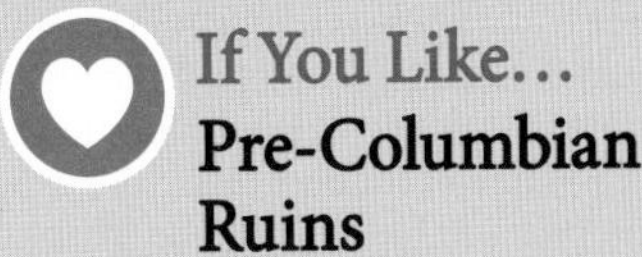

## If You Like... Pre-Columbian Ruins

If you enjoy clambering around ruins – and would like to do it with some measure of peace – a number of less-trafficked sites around Cuzco offer just that:

**1 TIPÓN**
**(admission with boleto turístico; 7am-6pm)** About 30km east of Cuzco you'll find this impressive site, which contains some exceptional terracing and an ingenious irrigation system. The steep dirt road at the turnoff has some excellent spots for eating *cuy* (guinea pig). Taxis from Cuzco can bring you here.

**2 PIQUILLACTA & RUMICOLCA**
**(admission with boleto turístico; 7am-6pm)** Literally translated as 'the Place of the Flea,' Piquillacta is the only major pre-Inca ruin in the area. Built around AD 1100 by the Wari (another empire-building culture), it consists of a large ceremonial center surrounded by a defensive wall. On the opposite side of the road about 1km further east is the huge Inca gate of Rumicolca, built on Wari foundations. These sites are located east of Tipón.

**3 RAQCHI**
**(admission S10)** About 125km southeast of Cuzco is this ruin that looks from the road like a strange alien aqueduct. These are the remains of the Temple of Viracocha, one of the holiest shrines in the Inca empire. Twenty-two columns made of stone blocks helped support the largest-known Inca roof. Unfortunately, most were destroyed by the Spanish – though there is a reconstruction process underway. The surrounding village is known for its ceramics.

and retreated to Ollantaytambo, but most of his forces were killed. Thousands of dead littered the site after the Incas' defeat, attracting swarms of carrion-eating Andean condors. The tragedy was memorialized by the inclusion of eight condors in Cuzco's coat of arms.

Opposite is the hill called **Rodadero**, with retaining walls, polished rocks and a finely carved series of stone benches known as the Inca's Throne. Three towers once stood above these walls. Only the foundations remain, but the 22m diameter of the largest, **Muyuc Marca**, gives an indication of how big they must have been. With its perfectly fitted stone conduits, this tower was probably used as a huge water tank for the garrison. Other buildings within the ramparts provided food and shelter for an estimated 5000 warriors.

Between the zigzag ramparts and the hill lies a large, flat parade ground that is used for the colorful tourist spectacle of **Inti Raymi**, held every June 24.

## Q'enqo

The name of this small but fascinating **ruin** means 'zigzag.' It's a large limestone rock riddled with niches, steps and extraordinary symbolic carvings, including the zigzagging channels that probably gave the site its name. These channels were likely used for the ritual offering of *chicha* or, perhaps, blood. Up top you'll find a flat surface used for ceremonies and, if you look carefully, some laboriously etched representations of a puma, a condor and a llama. Back below you can explore a mysterious subterranean cave with altars hewn into the rock.

Q'enqo is about 4km northeast of Cuzco, on the left of the road as you descend from Tambomachay.

## Tambomachay

In a sheltered spot about 300m from the main road, this site consists of a beautifully wrought ceremonial stone bath channeling crystalline spring water through fountains that still function today. It is thus popularly known as *El Baño del Inca* (The Bath of the Inca), and theories connect the site to an Inca water cult. Pukapukara can be seen from the small signaling post opposite.

## Pukapukara

Just across the main road from Tambomachay is this commanding structure looking down on the Cuzco valley. In some lights the rock looks pink, and the name literally means 'Red Fort,' though it is more likely to have been a hunting lodge, a guard post or a stopping point for travelers. It is composed of several lower residential chambers, storerooms and an upper esplanade with panoramic views.

Salt pans, Salinas (p208)
JON ARNOLD IMAGES/GETTY IMAGES ©

# THE SACRED VALLEY

Tucked under the tawny skirts of formidable foothills, the beautiful Río Urubamba Valley, known as El Valle Sagrado (The Sacred Valley), is about 15km north of Cuzco as the condor flies, via a narrow road of hairpin turns. Long the home of attractive colonial towns and isolated weaving villages, in recent years it has become a destination in its own right. Star attractions are the markets, as well as the lofty Inca citadels of Pisac and Ollantaytambo.

It's famous for some high-adrenaline activities, from rafting to trekking to rock climbing. Most activities can be organized in Cuzco and at some Urubamba hotels.

## Pisac

☎084 / POP 900 / ELEV 2715M

It's not hard to succumb to the charms of sunny Pisac, a bustling colonial village at the base of a spectacular Inca fortress perched on a mountain spur. Its pull is universal and recent years have seen an influx of expats and new age followers in search of an Andean Shangri-la. Located 33km northeast of Cuzco by a paved road, it's the most convenient starting point to the Sacred Valley.

### Pisac

**Sights**
1 Horno Colonial San Francisco ........... B1
2 La Capilla ........... A1

**Sleeping**
3 Hospedaje Kinsa Ccocha ........... B2
4 Hotel Pisac Inca ........... B2
5 Pisac Inn ........... B1

**Eating**
6 Mullu ........... B1
Restaurante Cuchara de Palo ..... (see 5)
7 Ulrike's Café ........... A2

## Sights & Activities

**MERCADO DE ARTESANÍA** Market

Pisac is known far and wide for its market, by far the biggest and most touristy in the region. Official market days are Tuesday, Thursday and Sunday, when tourist buses descend on the town in droves. However, the market has taken over Pisac to such an extent that it fills the Plaza de Armas and surrounding streets every day; visit on Monday, Wednesday, Friday or Saturday if you want to avoid the worst of the crowds.

**HORNO COLONIAL SAN FRANCISCO** Landmark

**(Mariscal Castilla s/n; snacks S2.50; 🕘6am-6pm)** Huge clay ovens for baking empanadas and other goodies and *castillos de cuyes* (miniature castles inhabited by guinea pigs) are found in many nooks and crannies, particularly in Mariscal Castilla. This bakery and store is the town's most authentic – a colonial oven dating back to 1830 – plying hot cheese and oregano empanadas with *chicha morada*.

**LA CAPILLA** Church

In recent times the Instituto Nacional de Cultura (INC), in a characteristically controversial move, demolished the church in the main square in order to reconstruct it in colonial style. Masses, which have moved to a nearby chapel, are nonetheless worth visiting. On Sunday,

OLIVER J DAVIS PHOTOGRAPHY/GETTY IMAGES ©

## Don't Miss Pisac Ruins

This **hilltop Inca citadel** lies high above the village on a triangular plateau with a plunging gorge on either side. It's a truly awesome sight – one that, on most days, is relatively uncrowded. This dominating structure guards not only the Urubamba Valley below, but also a pass leading into the jungle to the northeast.

The most impressive element is the **agricultural terracing**, which sweeps around the south and east flanks of the mountain in huge and graceful curves, almost entirely unbroken by steps. Instead, the terracing is joined by diagonal flights of stairs made of flagstones set into the terrace walls. Above the terraces are cliff-hugging footpaths, watched over by caracara falcons and well defended by massive stone doorways, steep stairs and a short tunnel carved out of the rock. Vendors meet you at the top with drinks.

Topping the terraces is the site's **ceremonial center**, with an *intihuatana* (literally 'hitching post of the sun'; an Inca astronomical tool), several working water channels, and some painstakingly neat masonry in the well-preserved **temples**. A path leads up the hillside to a series of ceremonial **baths**. Looking across the Kitamayo gorge from the back of the site, you'll also see hundreds of holes honeycombing the cliff wall. These are **Inca tombs** that were plundered by *huaqueros* (grave robbers) and are now off-limits.

Many travelers arrive on group tours from Cuzco, but it's easy to get here independently. You can walk the steep – but *spectacular* – 4km trail from town. (The walk begins on the west side of the church and takes more than two hours up; 1½ hours back.) Likewise, you can take a taxi. The easiest, most scenic option: have a taxi drop you off at the top, then hike down.

### NEED TO KNOW

admission with boleto turístico; ⏲dawn-dusk

services are held in Quechua, attracting traditionally dressed locals blowing horns, and *varayocs* (local authorities) with silver staffs of office.

## Sleeping

**PISAC INN** Inn $$
(☎20-3062; www.pisacinn.com; Plaza de Armas; d incl breakfast from S146; @ wi-fi) This lovely plaza hotel features an inviting courtyard and romantic rooms with goose-down bedding, dark blue walls and Andean decor. Rooms with king-sized beds are a slight upgrade. The location means it may get noisy early when merchants are setting up outside.

**LA CASA DEL CONDE** Guesthouse $$
(☎78-7818; www.cuzcovalle.com; s/d S50/70, s/d/tr incl breakfast S119/159/212; wi-fi) Guests rave about this lovely country house, nestled into the foothills with blooming flower patches. Family-run and brimming with personality, its lovely rooms feature down duvets, heat and cable TV. There's no car access. It's a 10-minute walk uphill from the plaza, but a mototaxi can leave you at the chapel, five minutes away.

**HOTEL PISAC INCA** Guesthouse $
(☎43-6921; www.hotelpisacinca.com; Vigil 242; s/d 35/70, s/d/tr without bathroom S25/50/75; @ wi-fi) Sisters Tatiana and Claudia run this small, cheerful lodging with a handful of colorful rooms around a tiny courtyard. Kitchen use is extra but it's a steal.

**ROYAL INKA HOTEL PISAC** Hotel $$
(☎20-3064, 20-3066; www.royalinkahotel.com; s/d incl breakfast S154/212; wi-fi pool) Once a large hacienda, this surprisingly unpretentious hotel has generous rooms – many of which offer views of the ruins – as well as well-tended flower gardens. Guests can access the facilities of Club Royal Inka across the road, plus the on-site spa and Jacuzzi. The wi-fi only works in some areas. This hotel is a highly worthwhile splurge.

It's about 1.5km from the plaza up the road to the ruins.

**HOSPEDAJE KINSA CCOCHA** Hotel $
(☎20-3101; Arequipa 307A; s/d S50/70, s/d without bathroom S25/50) With a fertile fig tree in its stony patio, this simple lodging has a nice vibe and thoughtful touches, such as plenty of power plugs, good towels and strong, hot showers. Breakfast is not offered.

## Eating

**ULRIKE'S CAFÉ** Cafe $
(☎20-3195; Manuel Prado s/s; veg/meat menú S17/20, mains from S11; ⊙9am-9pm; wi-fi vegetarian) A sunny cafe serving up a great vegetarian *menú*, plus homemade pasta and melt-in-your-mouth cheesecake and brownies.

**MULLU** Fusion $$
(☎20-3073; www.mullu.pe; San Francisco s/n, 2nd fl; mains S14-44; ⊙9am-9pm) Josip welcomes his guests with high-octane hospitality and a menu of wanderlust (think: Thai meets Amazon and flirts with highland Peruvian). Chilled and very welcoming, and the traditional lamb is tender to falling-off-the-bone.

**RESTAURANTE CUCHARA DE PALO** International $$
(☎20-3062; Plaza de Armas; mains S15-38; ⊙7:30-9:30am & noon-8pm) Inside Pisac Inn, this fine-dining restaurant has organic salads and original dishes like pumpkin ravioli drizzled with corn and cream. It doesn't always hit the mark but it has great ambience.

### Information

There's an ATM in the Plaza de Armas. There are slow cybercafes around the plaza.

### Getting There & Away

Buses to Urubamba and Cuzco leave frequently from the downtown bridge. Many travel agencies in Cuzco also operate tour buses to Pisac, especially on market days.

# Detour: Moray

South of Salinas, via the village of Maras, you'll find the impressively deep amphitheater-like terracing of this **ancient Inca site** (admission S10; dawn to dusk). If you have the time, it is a fascinating spectacle. Different levels of concentric terraces are carved into a huge earthen bowl, each layer of which has its own microclimate. For this reason, some theorize that the Incas used them as a kind of laboratory to determine the optimal conditions for growing crops of each species. There are three bowls, one of which has been planted with various crops as a kind of living museum.

Taxis from Urubamba to visit Moray (with a stop at the salt pans at Salinas) will cost around S80.



## Urubamba & Around

084 / POP 2700 / ELEV 2870M

Though the town of Urubamba has little of historical interest, it is surrounded by beautiful countryside and enjoys great weather, making it a convenient base from which to explore some of the surrounding sites in the Sacred Valley. (This attribute has made it a popular pit stop for tour groups.) Located at a significantly lower altitude than Cuzco, it's also an idyllic place to acclimatize prior to visiting Machu Picchu.

### Sights & Activities

**SALINAS** Salt Pans

(admission S5; 9am-4:30pm) This is one of the most spectacular sights in the area: thousands of salt pans that have been used for salt extraction since Inca times. A hot spring at the top of the valley discharges a small stream of heavily salt-laden water, which is then diverted into these mountainside pans and evaporated to produce salt for cattle licks. It may sound pedestrian, but the visuals are beautiful and surreal.

Most folks arrive on tours, but it's just as easy to get here by taxi. It's 4km southwest of Urubamba.

**PEROL CHICO** Horseback Riding

(984-62-4475; www.perolchico.com; overnight packages from US$510) Run by Dutch-Peruvian Eduard van Brunschot Vega, this excellent ranch outside of Urubamba has Peruvian *paso* horses. Eduard organizes horseback-riding tours that last up to two weeks. Advance bookings are required.

**CUSCO FOR YOU** Horseback Riding

(79-5301, 987-841-000; www.cuscoforyou.com; day trips US$165) Another ranch offering horseback riding and trekking trips from one to eight days long. Ask about special rates for families and groups.

### Sleeping

**LAS CHULLPAS** Cabins $$

(20-1568; www.chullpas.pe; Pumahuanca Valley; s/d/tr/q S120/150/180/220; @ ) Hidden 3km above town, these rustic woodland cottages are nestled among thick eucalyptus trees. Rooms feature comfortable beds and fireplaces. There is also a lounge with hammocks, an open kitchen serving vegetarian food, holistic treatments and a sweat lodge. Much of the food is grown organically on-site, and efforts are made towards composting and recycling. The affable Chilean owner also guides treks. Come with good directions, the roads are unmarked and not all taxi drivers know it.

Highly recommended.

**GREENHOUSE** B&B **$$**
(**☎984-770-130; www.thegreenhouseperu.com; Km 60.2, Carr Pisac-Ollantaytambo, Huarán; s/d/tr S165/210/335; @ 📶**) For a stint of serious relaxation, stay at this recommended retreat, on the road between Urubamba and Pisac. Replete with dogs lounging on their pillows, the hotel has large rustic-modern rooms and a social area that overlooks the garden. As green as its name, it features solar panels, composting and recycling, uses recycled river water for gardening and offers guests water refills.

**RÍO SAGRADO HOTEL** Luxury Hotel **$$$**
(**☎20-1631; www.riosagradohotel.com; d incl breakfast from S1311; @ 📶**) A design haven of cottage-style rooms with rough-hewn beams and exquisite accents of Ayacucho embroidery, this Orient-Express property is the epitome of understated luxury. The steep hillside location affords privacy for rooms set on terraced pathways perfumed with jasmine blooms. Or enjoy the river view from hammocks set amid cascading waterfalls. Service is smooth and top-notch.

Facilities include a spa, hot tubs, a sauna, restaurant, and breakfast in a hot-air balloon suspended above the lawn.

**SOL Y LUNA** Boutique Hotel **$$$**
(**☎20-1620; www.hotelsolyluna.com; Fundo Huincho lote A-5; @ 📶 🏊**) Fans of folk art will be overwhelmed by this luxury property, with 43 casitas featuring original murals and comic, oversized sculptures by Peruvian artist Federico Bauer. Avant-garde circus productions with former Cirque de Soleil artists provide evening entertainment. For daytime fun, Peruvian *paso* horses can be ridden on the 15ha property. Its acclaimed restaurant, **Wayra**, is the creation of Pedro Miguel Schiaffino, of Malabar fame in Lima.

**TAMBO DEL INKA** Luxury Hotel **$$$**
(**☎58-1777; www.libertador.com.pe; d from US$689; @ 📶 🏊**) Stark and commanding, this Leed-certified hotel occupies an immense riverside spread dotted with giant eucalyptus trees. The resource does not go unnoticed: eucalyptus is a staple of interior decor and even spa treatments. Features include an indoor-outdoor pool which changes colors at night, a hipster lounge backlit by an immense mural of fractured onyx and a private train station for morning jaunts to Machu Picchu. Rooms are appealing and comfortable, but it seems cheeky that standards like breakfast and wi-fi cost extra.

**CASA ANDINA** Luxury Hotel **$$$**
(**☎in Lima 1-213-9739; www.casa-andina.com; d incl breakfast S555; @ 📶**) In a lovely countryside setting, this Peruvian chain has 92 rooms in townhouse-style buildings on manicured lawns. The main lobby and restaurant occupies an inviting high-ceiling glass lodge. Rooms offer all the standard amenities, as well as plasma TVs.

## Eating

**HUACATAY** Peruvian **$$**
(**☎20-1790; Arica 620; mains S28-42; ⏰1-9:30pm Mon-Sat**) In a little house tucked down a narrow side street, Huacatay is worth hunting down. The tender alpaca steak, served in a port reduction with quinoa risotto, is the stuff memories are made of. Not every dish is a hit (the trout is on the dry side), but it makes for a lovely night out.

**TRES KEROS RESTAURANT GRILL & BAR** Novo Andino **$$**
(**☎20-1701; cnr hwy & Señor de Torrechayoc; mains from S26; ⏰lunch & dinner**) Garrulous chef Ricardo Behar smokes his own trout and imports steaks from Argentina for his tasty gourmet fare. Food is taken seriously here, and enjoyed accordingly. It's 500m west of town.

## Shopping

**SEMINARIO CERÁMICAS** Ceramics
(**☎20-1002; www.ceramicaseminario.com; Berriozabal 405; ⏰8am-7pm**) Well-known local potter Pablo Seminario creates original

work with a preconquest influence. His workshop is open to the public and offers a well-organized tour through the entire ceramics process.

## Information

**Banco de la Nación** (Mariscal Castilla s/n) Changes US dollars. There are ATMs at the *grifo* (gas station) on the corner of the highway and the main street, Mariscal Castilla, and along the highway to its east.

## Getting There & Away

Urubamba is quite spread out, so expect to do a lot of walking or pay for *mototaxis* (three-wheeled motorcycle rickshaw taxis).

Buses leave the terminal on the main highway about 1km west of town for Cuzco every 15 minutes. Here, you'll also find regular buses to Ollantaytambo.

# Ollantaytambo

084 / POP 700 / ELEV 2800M

Dominated by two massive Inca ruins, the quaint village of Ollantaytambo (known to locals and visitors alike as 'Ollanta') is the best surviving example of Inca city planning, with narrow cobblestone streets that have been continuously inhabited since the 13th century. After the hordes passing through on their way to Machu Picchu die down around late morning, Ollanta is a lovely place to be. It's perfect for wandering along mazy byways of stone and babbling irrigation channels, pretending you've stepped back in time. It also offers access to excellent hiking and biking.

## Activities

**KB TAMBO** Mountain Biking
(20-4091; www.kbperu.com; Ventiderio s/n) Considered the best tour operator in town for mountain biking. Recommended for families.

**SOTA ADVENTURE** Adventure Sports
(63-4003; www.sotaadventure.com) Sota Adventure comes highly recommended by readers, particularly for horseback riding. The family-run business also offers mountain biking and multiday hikes.

## Sleeping

**APU LODGE** Inn $$
(79-7162; www.apulodge.com; Lari s/n; s/d/q incl breakfast S140/160/240; @ wi-fi) Backed against the ruins, this modern lodge with a sprawling lawn has ample, cozy rooms with powerful hot showers. Wi-fi is available in the common area. Breakfast includes yogurt, cereal, fresh fruit and eggs.

Ollantaytambo
LEW ROBERTSON/GETTY IMAGES ©

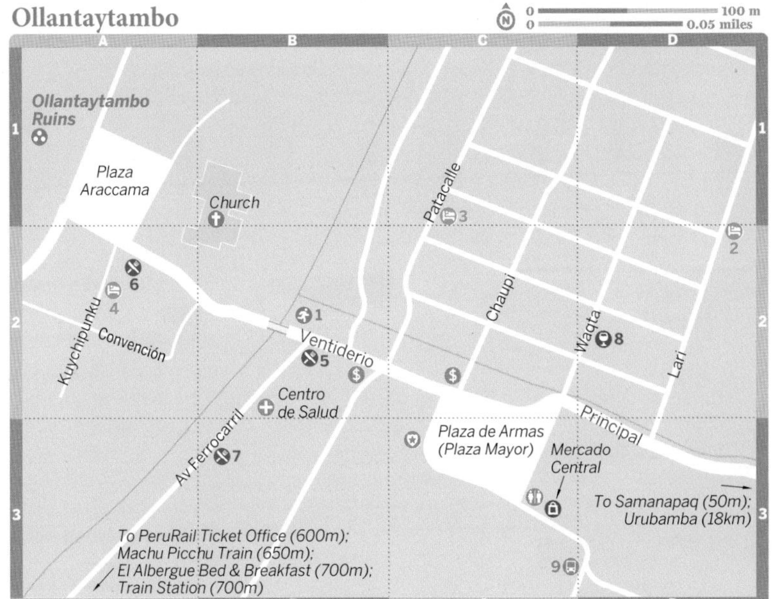


## Ollantaytambo

**Top Sights**

Ollantaytambo Ruins .......... A1

**Activities, Courses & Tours**

1 KB Tambo .......... B2

**Sleeping**

2 Apu Lodge .......... D2
3 Casa de Wow .......... C1
4 K'uychi Punku Hostal .......... A2

**Eating**

5 Hearts Café .......... B2
6 Puka Rumi .......... A2
7 Tutti Amore .......... B3

**Drinking**

8 Ganso .......... D2

**Transport**

9 Buses to Urubamba & Cuzco .......... C3

**EL ALBERGUE BED & BREAKFAST** B&B $$$

(☎20-4014; www.elalbergue.com; Estación de Tren; d/tr incl breakfast S204/259, d superior S303; @ 📶) On the train platform, this romantic pit stop is full of Andean charm. Tasteful tile rooms feature dark hardwood trim, tapestries and quality linens – and there are also games for kids. It's 800m uphill from the village center but there's an excellent on-site restaurant.

**SAMANAPAQ** Inn $$

(☎20-4042; www.samanapaq.com; cnr Principal & Alameda de las Cien Ventanas; s/d/tr S199/244/318) Recommended entirely for the tireless charm of Don Jaime and his mellow Great Dane Venus, this sprawling complex features lawns for kids to run on, comfortable shared spaces and 20 motel-style rooms with massage-jet showers.

**K'UYCHI PUNKU HOSTAL** Hotel $$

(☎20-4175; Kuyuchipunku s/n; s/d/tr incl breakfast S75/105/135; 📶) Run by the wonderful Bejar-Mejía family, these recommended lodgings are in an Inca building with 2m-thick walls, as well as a modern section with less personality. A breakfast including eggs and fresh juice is served in Ollanta's most photographed outdoor dining room. Recommended.

EMIL VON MALTITZ/GETTY IMAGES ©

## Don't Miss Ollantaytambo Ruins

The huge, steep terraces that guard Ollantaytambo's spectacular **Inca ruins** mark one of the few places where the Spanish conquistadors lost a major battle. It was to this **fortress** that the rebellious Manco Inca retreated after his defeat at Sacsaywamán. In 1536 Hernando Pizarro (Francisco Pizarro's younger half-brother) led a force of 70 cavalrymen here, supported by large numbers of indigenous and Spanish foot soldiers, in an attempt to capture Manco.

Pizarro's men were showered with arrows, spears and boulders from atop the steep terracing and were unable to climb to the fortress. They were further hampered when Manco Inca, in a brilliant move, flooded the plain below the fortress through previously prepared channels. The Spaniards' horses were bogged down in the water and Pizarro ordered a hasty retreat, which almost became a rout when the conquistadors were followed down the valley by thousands of Manco Inca's victorious soldiers. The Inca victory was short-lived, however. The Spanish forces soon returned with reinforcements and Manco was forced to flee to the jungle stronghold at Vilcabamba.

Though Ollantaytambo was a highly effective fortress, it was also a temple. A finely worked **ceremonial center** is at the top of the terracing. In addition, you'll find some extremely well-engineered walls – which were under construction at the time of the conquest and therefore never completed. The stone for these was quarried from the mountainside 6km away, high above the opposite bank of the Río Urubamba. Transporting the huge stone blocks to the site was a stupendous feat: rather than move the massive blocks through the river, the Incas diverted the entire river channel around them.

### NEED TO KNOW

admission with boleto turístico; 🕒7am-5pm

**CASA DE WOW** Hostel $

(☎20-4010; www.casadewow.com; Patacalle s/n; d S110, dm/s/d without bathroom S40/55/90; @☎) A cozy little home away from home, thanks to the caring attention of Winn and her partner Wow. Bunks are snug and couples have a shot at the fantastic handmade Inca royalty bed (though unlike the original, the raw beams are held together with rope, not llama innards).

## Eating

**EL ALBERGUE RESTAURANTE** International $$

(☎20-4014; Estación de Tren; mains S19-45; ⏲5am-9pm) This whistle-stop café inside the Albergue hotel serves elegant dinners that include *causas* with organic greens, lamb medallions with *chimichurri* (herb sauce) and *molle* pepper steak – the spice comes from the tree outside. For train passengers, it may be worth stopping by the patio option, Café Mayu, for an espresso and homemade *aguantamayo* (gooseberry) cheesecake.

**PUKA RUMI** Cafe $$

(☎20-4091; Ventiderio s/n; mains S5-32; ⏲7:30am-10pm) A tiny locale where locals rave about the steaks, travelers melt over the breakfasts, and everyone enjoys the fresh, nontraditional burritos, presented with pancakelike tortillas and a wide array of ingredients in separate bowls.

**HEARTS CAFÉ** Cafe $

(☎20-4078; cnr Ventiderio & Av Ferrocarril; sandwiches S10-14, menú S18; ⏲7am-9pm; ✎) Serving healthy and hearty food, beer and wine and fabulous coffee, Hearts is a longtime local favorite, with some organic produce and box lunches for excursions. Breakfasts like huevos rancheros target the gringo palate perfectly.

**TUTTI AMORE** Ice Cream $

(Av Ferrocarril s/n; ice creams S5; ⏲8:30am-7pm) Homemade gelato-style ice cream comes in flavors such as *dulce de leche* (caramel) and banana split, as well as worthwhile jungle fruit flavors. It's halfway down the hill to the train station.

## Drinking

**GANSO** Bar

(☎984-30-8499; Waqta s/n; ⏲2pm-late) Treehouse meets circus meets Batman! The hallucinatory decor in tiny, friendly Ganso is enough to drive anyone to drink. The firemen's pole and swing seats are the icing on the cake.

### Information

There are a couple of internet cafes and ATMs in and around plaza. There are no banks, but several places change money.

### Getting There & Away

Frequent minibuses and *colectivos* shuttle between Urubamba and Ollantaytambo. To get to Cuzco, it's easiest to change in Urubamba, though there are occasional departures direct to Cuzco's Puente Grau.

The local train station offers service to Aguas Calientes (for Machu Picchu), as well as to Cuzco. **PeruRail** (www.perurail.com; ⏲5am-8pm) has numerous departures each way every day. In addition, **Machu Picchu Train** (www.machupicchutrain.com; Av Ferrocarril s/n) has a new service with panoramic view trains, only from Ollantaytambo, three times daily in high season. Reserve in advance.

# MACHU PICCHU & THE INCA TRAIL

Shrouded by mist and surrounded by lush vegetation and steep escarpments, the sprawling Inca citadel of Machu Picchu is one icon that lives up to every expectation. Like the Mona Lisa, the pyramids and San Francisco's Golden Gate Bridge, it has been seared into our collective consciousness – yet nothing can diminish the thrill of seeing it. If you have the time and the interest, hiking to Machu Picchu via the scenic Inca Trail, as its ancient inhabitants once did, offers a full-immersion experience.

# Aguas Calientes

084 / POP 1000 / ELEV 2410M

Located in a deep gorge below the ruins, Aguas Calientes is enclosed by stone cliffs, towering cloud forest and two rushing rivers. Despite its gorgeous location, it has always been a bit of a no-man's land, with a large itinerant population, slack services that count on one-time customers and an architectural tradition of rebar and unfinished cement. Your best bet is to go without expectations.

However, spending the night offers one distinct advantage: early access to Machu Picchu, which turns out to be a very good reason to stay.

## Sights & Activities

**MUSEO DE SITIO MANUEL CHÁVEZ BALLÓN** Museum

**(admission S22; 9am-5pm)** This museum has superb information in Spanish and English on the archaeological excavations of Machu Picchu and Inca building methods. Stop here to get a sense of context – and to enjoy the air-conditioning after hours in the sun! There's a small botanical garden outside, down a nifty, nerve-testing set of Inca stairs. It's by Puente Ruinas, at the base of the footpath to Machu Picchu.

**LAS TERMAS** Hot Springs

**(admission S10; 5am-8:30pm)** Weary trekkers soak away their aches in the town's hot springs, 10 minutes' walk up Pachacutec from the train tracks. These tiny, natural springs are nice enough but get scummy by late morning. Towels can be rented cheaply outside the entrance.

**PUTUCUSI** Mountain

For those who still have energy left for trekking, the steep hike up this toothy mini-mountain, directly opposite Machu Picchu, is highly recommended. Follow the railway tracks about 250m west of town and you'll see a set of stairs; this is the start of a well-marked trail. Parts of the walk are up ladders, which get slippery in the wet season, but the view across to Machu Picchu is worth the trek. Allow three hours.

## Sleeping

Because of its strategic location, expect to pay more for lodgings here than on average.

**MACHU PICCHU PUEBLO HOTEL** Lodge $$$

**( in Lima 01-610-0400; www.inkaterra.com; d casitas from S1640, villas from S2532;** ) Set amid tropical gardens, these chic Andean-style cottages (many with their own private pool) are pure indulgence, featuring iPod docks, subtle decor, and showers with glass walls looking out onto the vegetation. The onsite spa features a bamboo-eucalyptus sauna, but the best feature are the guided excursions included in your stay. Rates include half-board and kids under 12 stay free.

**RUPA WASI** Hotel $$$

**( 21-1101; www.rupawasi.net; Huanacaure s/n; d incl breakfast S472;** ) Hidden away up a steep flight of stairs, Rupa Wasi clings to the hillside with wooden stairways and moss-strewn stone pathways. It's quaint and a little wild, but the price only reflects its proximity to Machu Picchu. Cabin-style rooms feature down duvets and views. A nice American breakfast is served in the Tree House café.

**WIRACOCHA INN** Hotel $$

**( 21-1088; wiracochainn.com; Wiracocha s/n; s/d incl breakfast S172/225)** On a side street crowded with midrange hotels, this newer option has well-kept, polished rooms with down bedding, amiable service and a sheltered patio area near the river.

**EL MAPI** Design Hotel $$$

**( 21-1011; www.elmapihotel.com; Pachacutec 109; d casitas from S1640, villas from S2532;** ) The stark, all-white rooms at this new design hotel have lofty ceilings, burnished steel and oversized nature photos. Perks include a welcome pisco sour at the stylish bar and the enormous buffet breakfast. There's a full-service

# Aguas Calientes

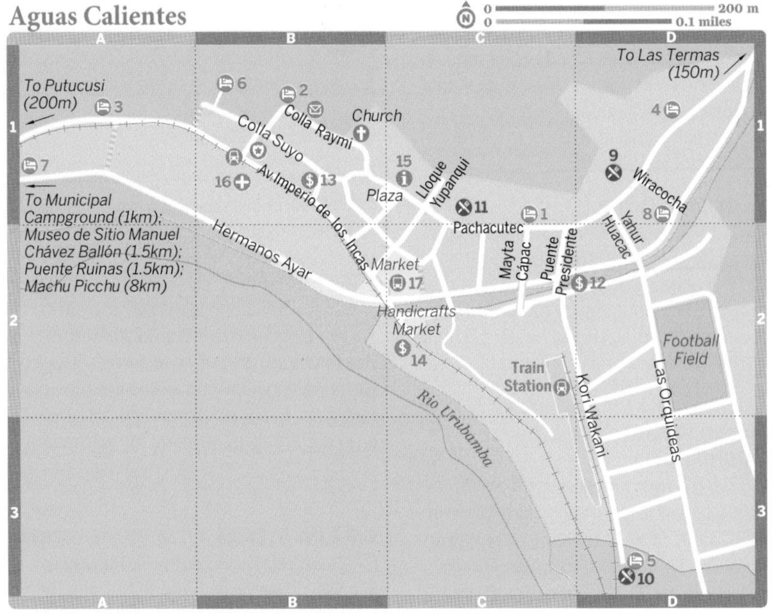


## Aguas Calientes

**Sleeping**

1 El Mapi ............ C1
2 Gringo Bill's ............ B1
3 Hospedaje los Caminantes ............ A1
4 La Cabaña Hostel ............ D1
5 Machu Picchu Pueblo Hotel ............ D3
6 Rupa Wasi ............ B1
7 Sumaq Machu Picchu Hotel ............ A1
8 Wiracocha Inn ............ D1

**Eating**

9 Café de Paris ............ D1
10 Café Inkaterra ............ D3
11 Indio Feliz ............ C1
Tree House ............ (see 6)

**Information**

12 ATM ............ D2
13 ATM ............ B1
14 BCP ............ C2
15 iPerú ............ C1
Machu Picchu Ticket Office ............ (see 15)
16 Medical Center ............ B1

**Transport**

17 Machu Picchu Bus Tickets & Bus Stop ............ C2

restaurant and a warm landscaped pond for dips.

**GRINGO BILL'S** Hotel $$$

(**☎21-1046; www.gringobills.com; Colla Raymi 104; d/tr/ste incl breakfast S199/278/358;** @ 🛜 🏊) One of the original Aguas Calientes lodgings, friendly Bill's has smart, well-heeled rooms equipped with thick cotton quilts and large bathrooms. Suites feature massage jet tubs and TVs. Larger suites easily accommodate families.

**HOSPEDAJE LOS CAMINANTES** Guesthouse $

(**☎21-1007; los-caminantes@hotmail.com; Av Imperio de los Incas 140; per person with/without bathroom S35/20;** 🛜) The best bargain digs are in this big, multistory guesthouse.

Rooms are dated, but clean with laminate floors, reliable hot water and a few balconies. The train whistling directly outside your window at 7am is an unmistakable wake-up call. Breakfast isn't included but available (S8 to S10) at the strangely upscale in-house café.

**LA CABAÑA HOTEL** Hotel **$$$**
(**21-1048; www.lacabanamachupicchu.com; Pachacutec s/n; s/d incl breakfast S336/392; @**) Further uphill than most of the hotels, this popular spot has woody, cozy rooms, down duvets and heaters. There is buffet breakfast and complimentary tea and fruit round the clock.

**SUMAQ MACHU PICCHU HOTEL** Hotel **$$$**
(**21-1059; www.sumaqhotelperu.com; Hermanos Ayar s/n; s/d with some meals from S1312/1594; @**) Though ungainly on the outside, the soothing light-flooded interior gives this hotel a modern feel that's luxurious without being pompous. Rooms boast views of either the river or the mountains and there are multiple eating and drinking areas – as well as a full spa. Rates include a buffet breakfast, afternoon tea and either lunch or dinner.

## Eating

Touts standing in the street will try to herd you into their restaurant, but take your time making a selection.

**INDIO FELIZ** French **$$$**
(**21-1090; Lloque Yupanqui 4; mains from S38, menú S50; 11am-10pm**) It's hard to overstate the pleasures of this candle-lit restaurant. There are Peruvian classics, such as *sopa criolla* (noodle soup with beef and peppers), served with hot bread and butter. But the menu also nods to French cooking, with Provençal tomatoes and melt-in-your-mouth *tarte aux pommes*. The S50 menú is an extremely good value for a decadent dinner. At the time of writing, it was adding a rooftop bar geared at grown-ups.

**CAFÉ INKATERRA** Peruvian **$$$**
(**21-1122; Machu Picchu Pueblo Hotel; mains S25-60; 11am-9pm**) Second to none for ambience, this tucked-away riverside restaurant is housed in elongated thatched rooms with views of water tumbling over the boulders. The prices are quite reasonable for perfectly executed *lomo saltado*, the traditional Peruvian stir-fry.

Aguas Calientes (p214)

CUAN HANSEN/GETTY IMAGES ©

**TREE HOUSE** Fusion **$$$**

(☎21-1101; Huanacaure s/n; S32-59; ⌚4:30am-10pm) With just a few tables, the rustic ambience of Tree House provides a cozy setting for its inviting fusion menu. Dishes like chicken soup with wontons and ginger, red quinoa risotto and crispy trout are lovingly prepared. For dessert order the lip-smacking fruit crumble. Reserve ahead.

**CAFÉ DE PARIS** Bakery **$**

(Plaza Wiyawaina s/n; pastries S1-4; ⌚7am-9pm) We don't know how these Frenchmen got here, we're just thankful they did. This open-air stand sells *pain au chocolat*, fresh croissants and desserts. The upstairs bakery offers community classes, which should leave an interesting imprint on rural Andean baking.

## Information

There's a helpful branch of **iPerú** (☎21-1104; Pachacutec, cuadra 1; ⌚9am-1pm & 2-6pm) near the **Machu Picchu ticket office** (⌚5:20am-8:45pm). If the ATM at **BCP** (Av Imperio de los Incas s/n) runs out of money, there are four others in town, including one on Av Imperio de los Incas. Pay phones and cybercafes are scattered around the town and there's a **medical center** (☎21-1005; Av Imperio de los Incas s/n; ⌚emergencies 24hr) by the train tracks.

## Getting There & Away

There are only three options to get to Aguas Calientes, and hence to Machu Picchu: trek it, catch the train via Cuzco and the Sacred Valley, or travel by road and train via Santa Teresa. It is advisable to buy train tickets in advance, especially in high season.

**PeruRail** (www.perurail.com) Has service to Cuzco, with stops in the Sacred Valley.

**Machu Picchu Train** (☎in Cuzco 22-1199; www.machupicchutrain.com) Travels to Ollantaytambo.

# Machu Picchu

For many visitors to Peru and even South America, a visit to the Inca city of Machu Picchu is the sweet cherry on top of their trip. One of the best-known archaeological sites on the continent, this awe-inspiring ancient city was never revealed to the conquering Spaniards and was virtually forgotten until the early part of the 20th century. In the high season (late May until early September), an estimated 2500 people arrive daily. Despite this influx, Machu Picchu nonetheless retains an air of grandeur and mystery.

For any visitor to Peru, this is a must.

## History

Machu Picchu is not mentioned in any of the chronicles of the Spanish conquistadors. Apart from a couple of German adventurers in the 1860s, who apparently looted the site with the Peruvian government's permission, few apart from local Quechua people knew of its existence until American historian Hiram Bingham was guided to it by locals in 1911.

The Machu Picchu site was initially overgrown with thick vegetation, forcing Bingham's team to be content with roughly mapping the site. He returned in 1912 and 1915 to carry out the difficult task of clearing the thick forest. It was at this point that he also mapped some of the ruins on the so-called Inca Trail. (Read Bingham's own account in *Inca Land: Explorations in the Highlands of Peru*, first published in 1922.) Peruvian archaeologist Luis E Valcárcel undertook further studies in 1934, as did a Peruvian-American expedition under Paul Fejos in 1940–41.

Bingham's search was originally for the lost city of Vilcabamba, the last stronghold of the Incas, and he thought he had found it at Machu Picchu. (In fact, he died believing he had.) But we now know that the remote ruins at Espíritu Pampa, much deeper in the jungle, are actually the remains of Vilcabamba. Despite scores of more recent studies, knowledge of Machu Picchu remains sketchy. Even today archaeologists are forced to rely heavily on speculation as to its function. Some believe that it was founded in the waning years of the Inca empire, while others think it was a royal retreat or country palace abandoned at the time of the Spanish

# Machu Picchu

This great 15th century Inca citadel sits at 2430m on a narrow ridge top above the Urubamba River. Traditionally considered a political, religious and administrative center, new theories suggest that it was a royal estate designed by Pachacutec, the Inca ruler whose military conquests transformed the empire. Trails linked it to the Inca capital of Cuzco and important sites in the jungle. As invading Spaniards never discovered it, experts still dispute when the site was abandoned and why.

At its peak, Machu Picchu was thought to have some 500 inhabitants. An engineering marvel, its famous Inca walls have polished stone fitted to stone, with no mortar in between. The citadel took thousands of laborers 50 years to build – today its cost of construction would exceed a billion US dollars.

Making it inhabitable required leveling the site, channeling water from high mountain streams through stone canals and building vertical contention walls that became agricultural terraces for corn, potatoes and coca. The drainage system also helped combat heavy rains (diverting them for irrigation), while east-facing rooftops and farming terraces took advantage of maximum sun exposure.

The site is a magnet to mystics, adventurers and students of history alike. While its function remains hotly debated, the essential grandeur of Machu Picchu is indisputable.

**TOP TIPS**

**Visit** before mid-morning crowds

**Allow** at least three hours

**Wear** walking shoes and a hat

**Bring** drinking water

**Gain** perspective walking the lead-in trails

CAROLYN MCCARTHY

**Intihuatana**

'Hitching Post of the Sun', this exquisitely carved rock was likely used by Inca astronomers to predict solstices. It's a rare survivor since invading Spaniards destroyed *intihuatanas* throughout the kingdom to eradicate pagan blasphemy.

**Temple of the Three Windows**

Enjoy the commanding views of the plaza below through the huge trapezoidal windows framed by three-ton lintels. Rare in Inca architecture, the presence of three windows may indicate special significance.

CAROLYN MCCARTHY

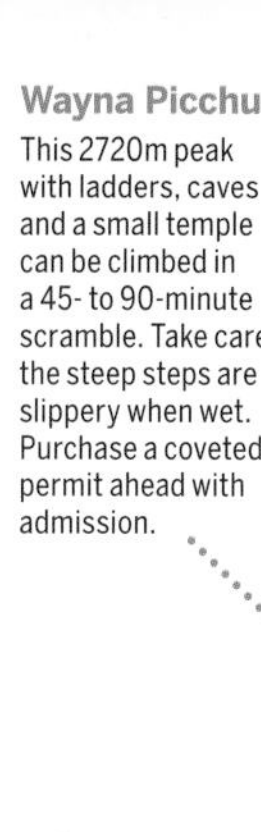

### Wayna Picchu

This 2720m peak with ladders, caves and a small temple can be climbed in a 45- to 90-minute scramble. Take care, the steep steps are slippery when wet. Purchase a coveted permit ahead with admission.

CAROLYN MCCARTHY

### Central Plaza

This sprawling green area with grazing llamas separates the ceremonial sector of Machu Picchu from the more mundane residential and industrial sectors.

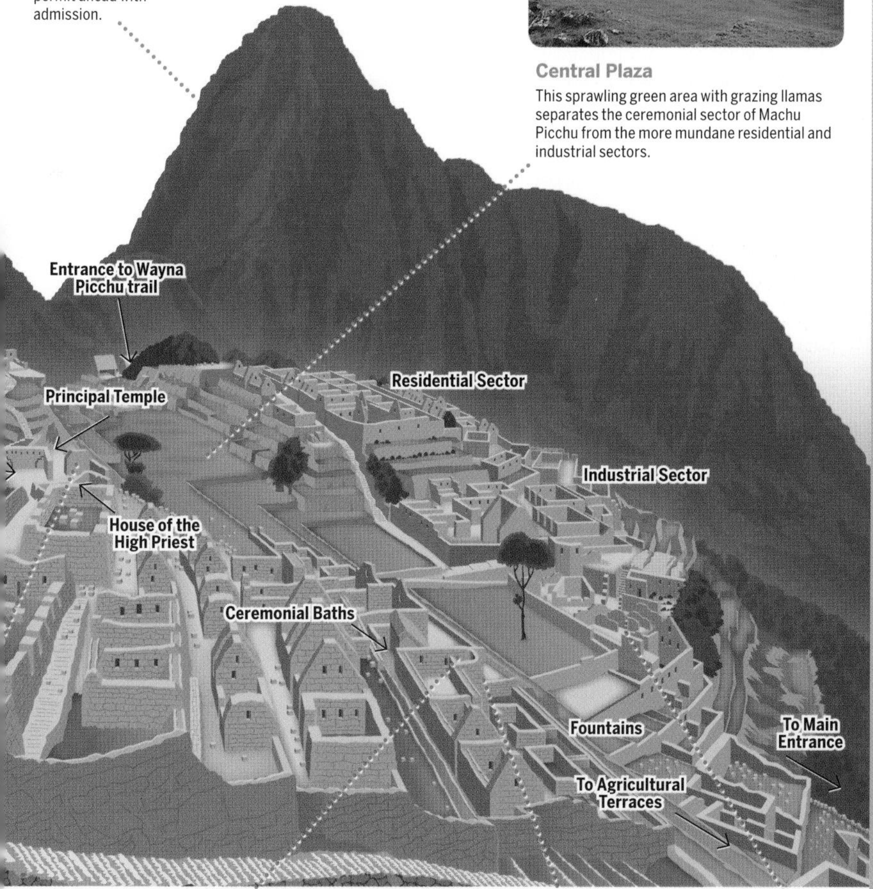

Entrance to Wayna Picchu trail

Principal Temple

Residential Sector

Industrial Sector

House of the High Priest

Ceremonial Baths

Fountains

To Main Entrance

To Agricultural Terraces

### Temple of the Sun

This off-limits rounded tower is best viewed from above. Featuring the site's finest stonework, an altar and trapezoidal windows, it may have been used for astronomical purposes.

CAROLYN MCCARTHY

### Royal Tomb

Speculated to have special ceremonial significance, a natural rock cave sits below the Temple of the Sun. Though off-limits, visitors can view its steplike altar and sacred niches from the entrance.

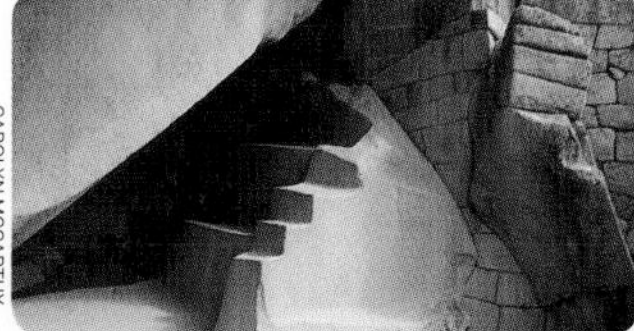

CAROLYN MCCARTHY

### Temple of the Condor

Check out the condor head carving with rock outcrops that resemble outstretched wings. Behind, an off-limits cavity reaches a tiny underground cell that may only be entered by bending double.

invasion. The site's director believes that it was a city and a political, religious and administrative center. Its location, and the fact that at least eight access routes have been discovered, suggests that it was a trade nexus between the Amazon and the highlands.

It seems clear from the exceptionally high quality of the stonework and the abundance of ornamental work that Machu Picchu was vitally important as a ceremonial center. To some extent, it still is: Alejandro Toledo, the country's first full-blooded indigenous president, staged his inauguration here in 2001.

## Sights & Activities

### Inside the Ruins

Unless you arrive via the Inca Trail, you'll officially enter the ruins through a ticket gate on the south side of Machu Picchu. A roughly 100m-long footpath brings you to the mazelike main entrance of Machu Picchu proper, where the ruins lie stretched out before you, roughly divided into two areas separated by a series of plazas.

Note that the names of individual ruins speculate their use – in reality, much is unknown. To get a visual fix of the whole site and snap the classic postcard photograph, climb the zigzagging staircase on the left immediately after entering the complex, which leads to the Hut of the Caretaker.

**HUT OF THE CARETAKER OF THE FUNERARY ROCK** Ruin

An excellent viewpoint to take in everything. It's one of a few buildings that has been restored with a thatched roof, making it a good shelter in the case of rain. The Inca Trail enters the city just below this hut. The carved rock behind the hut may have been used to mummify the nobility, hence the hut's name.

**CEREMONIAL BATHS** Ruin

If you continue straight into the ruins instead of climbing to the hut, you pass through extensive terracing to a beautiful series of 16 connected ceremonial baths that cascade across the ruins, accompanied by a flight of stairs.

**TEMPLE OF THE SUN** Ruin

Just above and to the left of the baths is Machu Picchu's only round building, a curved and tapering tower of exceptional stonework. It appears to have been used for astronomical purposes. Inside are an altar and a curiously drilled trapezoidal window that looks onto the site.

**ROYAL TOMB** Ruin

Below the Temple of the Sun, this almost hidden, natural rock cave was carefully carved by Inca stonemasons. Its use is highly debated; though known as the Royal Tomb, no mummies were actually found here.

Temple of the Sun
GLOWIMAGES/GETTY IMAGES ©

**SACRED PLAZA** Plaza

The stairs above the ceremonial baths lead to a flat area of jumbled rocks, once used as a quarry. Turn right at the top of the stairs and walk across the quarry on a short path leading to the four-sided Sacred Plaza. The far side contains a small viewing platform with a curved wall, which offers a view of the snowy Cordillera Vilcabamba in the far distance and the Río Urubamba below.

**TEMPLE OF THE THREE WINDOWS** Ruin

Important buildings flank the remaining three sides of the Sacred Plaza. The Temple of the Three Windows features huge trapezoidal windows that give the building its name.

**PRINCIPAL TEMPLE** Ruin

The 'temple' derives its name from the massive solidity and perfection of its construction. The damage to the rear right corner is the result of the ground settling below this corner rather than any inherent weakness in the masonry itself.

**HOUSE OF THE HIGH PRIEST** Ruin

Opposite the Principal Temple.

**SACRISTY** Ruin

Behind and connected to the Principal Temple lies this famous small building. It has many well-carved niches, perhaps used for the storage of ceremonial objects, as well as a carved stone bench. The Sacristy is especially known for the two rocks flanking its entrance; each is said to contain 32 angles, but it's easy to come up with a different number whenever you count them.

**INTIHUATANA** Ruin

This Quechua word loosely translates as the 'Hitching Post of the Sun' and refers to the carved rock pillar, often mistakenly called a sundial, which stands at the top of the Intihuatana hill. The Inca astronomers were able to predict the solstices using the angles of this pillar. Thus, they were able to claim control over the return of the lengthening summer days. Exactly how the pillar was used for these astronomical purposes remains unclear, but its elegant simplicity and high craftwork make it a highlight.

## Read Up on the Ruins

If you are wondering what it's like to hike the Inca Trail, or its lesser-known alternatives, pick up Mark Adams' *Turn Right at Machu Picchu* (2010). Not a hero's tale, the humorous travelogue is a first-person account of one adventure editor bumbling out into the wild. On the way, it provides an entertaining layman's look at Inca history and the striving explorations of Hiram Bingham.

**CENTRAL PLAZA** Plaza

At the back of the Intihuatana another staircase descends to the Central Plaza. This separates the ceremonial sector of Machu Picchu from the more mundane (and less well-constructed) residential and industrial sectors.

**PRISON GROUP** Ruin

At the lower end of this latter area is the Prison Group, a labyrinthine complex of cells, niches and passageways, positioned both under and above the ground.

**TEMPLE OF THE CONDOR** Ruin

The centerpiece of the Prison Group is this 'temple' named for a carving of the head of a condor with outstretched wings.

### Ruins Outskirts

**INTIPUNKU** Ruin

From the far eastern edge of the residential sector, a trail leads to a notch in the horizon called Intipunku (Sun Gate). This is where trekkers on the Inca Trail catch their first glimpse of Machu Picchu. From the main ruins sector, it takes about an hour to reach Intipunku, and if you can spare at least half a day for the round-trip, it may be possible to continue as far as Wiñay Wayna, on the Inca Trail itself. If you do the latter, expect to pay a reduced-charge admission fee for the Inca Trail, and be sure to return before 3pm, which is when the checkpoint typically closes.

**INCA DRAWBRIDGE** Ruin

A scenic but level walk from the Hut of the Caretaker takes you right past the top of the terraces and out along a narrow, cliff-clinging trail to the Inca drawbridge. In under a half-hour's walk, the trail gives you a good look at cloud-forest vegetation and an entirely different view of Machu Picchu. This walk is recommended, though you'll have to be content with photographing the bridge from a distance, as someone crossed the bridge some years ago and tragically fell to their death.

**WAYNA PICCHU** Hike

Wayna Picchu is the steep cone-shaped mountain at the back of the ruins. At first glance, it would appear that it's a challenging climb, but it's not technically difficult – although the ascent is steep. The path zigzags up the side of the mountain and lands at a small set of Inca constructions at the top.

Part of the way up, a marked path plunges down to your left, continuing down the rear of Wayna Picchu to the small **Temple of the Moon**. The trail is easy to follow, but involves steep sections, a ladder and an overhanging cave, which is a bit tricky to get past. The descent takes about an hour and the ascent back to the main Wayna Picchu trail is longer. But it's spectacular: the trail drops and climbs steeply as it hugs the sides of Wayna Picchu before plunging into the cloud forest. Suddenly, you reach a cleared area where the small, very well-made ruins are found. From here, another cleared path leads up behind the ruin and steeply onward up the back side of Wayna Picchu.

Access to Wayna Picchu is limited to 400 people per day – the first 200 in line are let in at 7am, and another 200 at 10am. A **ticket** (S24) may only be obtained when you purchase your entrance ticket. These spots sell out a week in advance in low season and far sooner in high season, so plan accordingly.

Cerro Machu Picchu is a very good alternative to this climb.

## Sleeping & Eating

**MACHU PICCHU SANCTUARY** Lodge $$$

**(Map p224; ☎984-81-6956; www.sanctuarylodgehotel.com; standard/mountain view/ste US$975/1400/1750)** Run by Orient-Express, this exclusive hotel is the only place to stay at Machu Picchu. Staff attention is impeccable and rooms are comfortable, with sober decor and docking stations. There is a spa, manicured gardens and personalized guide service. It's popular – so book at least three months ahead. Two restaurants serve meals, and there is a popular **lunch buffet** (S97; 11:30am-3pm) that is open to the public.

## Information

Machu Picchu Historical Sanctuary **(adult/student S128/65; www.machupicchu.gob.pe; 6am-4pm)** Because of the strict limits on the number of visitors, entrance tickets to the ruins often sell out, so buy them in advance in person at the Dirección Regional de Cultura in Cuzco (p200) or via a reputable travel agency.

The ruins are most heavily visited between 10am and 2pm, and June to August are the busiest months. Visitors can enter the site until 4pm, though those inside are not expelled until 5pm. Plan your visit early or late in the day to avoid the worst of the crowds. Early morning visits during the rainy season will guarantee you more room to breathe, especially during February, when the Inca Trail is closed.

Inside the ruins, do not walk on any of the walls – this loosens the stonework and prompts a cacophony of whistle blowing from the guards. Overnighting here is also illegal: guards do a thorough check of the site before it closes. Disposable plastic bottles and food are not allowed. It's best to eat outside the gate, use camping-type drink bottles and pack out all trash, even organic. Water is sold at the cafe just outside the entrance, but only in glass bottles.

JAMES SPARSHATT/CORBIS ©

## Don't Miss Cerro Machu Picchu

A 1½- to two-hour climb brings you to the top of Machu Picchu mountain, to be rewarded with the site's most extensive view – along the Inca trail to Wiñay Wayna and Phuyupatamarka, down to the valley floor and the impressive terracing near Km 104 (where the two-day Inca Trail begins) and across the site of Machu Picchu itself. This walk is more spectacular than Wayna Picchu, and less crowded. Allow yourself plenty of time to enjoy the scenery (and catch your breath!).

Walking sticks or backpacks of over 20L are not allowed into the ruins. There is a **baggage check office (S5 per item; ⌚6am-4pm)** outside the entrance gate and another **baggage office (S3 per item; ⌚6am-5pm)** inside the complex.

Use of the only toilet facilities, just below the cafe, will set you back S1.

Local guides (per guest S100–S150; per guest S20 in groups of 6-10) are readily available for hire at the entrance. Their expertise varies, look for one wearing an official guide ID from DIRSETUR. Agree on a price in advance, clarify whether the fee is per person or group.

### Dangers & Annoyances

Tiny sand fly-like bugs abound. You won't notice them biting, but you may be itching for a week. Use insect repellent.

The weather at Machu Picchu seems to have only two settings: heavy rain or bright, burning sunlight. Don't forget rain gear and sunblock.

### Getting There & Around

From Aguas Calientes, frequent buses for Machu Picchu (S50 round-trip, 25 minutes) depart from a ticket office along the main road from 5:30am to 2:30pm. Buses return from the ruins when full, with the last departure at 5:45pm.

Otherwise, it's a steep walk (8km, 1½ hours) up a tightly winding mountain road. First there's a flat 20-minute walk from Aguas Calientes to Puente Ruinas, where the road to the ruins crosses the Río Urubamba, near the museum. A breathtakingly steep but well-marked trail climbs another 2km up to Machu Picchu, taking about an hour to hike (but less coming down!).

# The Inca Trail

The most famous trek in South America, the Inca Trail, is walked by thousands of travelers every year. Although the total distance is only about 40km, the ancient trail laid by the Incas from the Sacred Valley to Machu Picchu (one of many Inca roadways) winds its way up and down and around the mountains, snaking over three high Andean passes and providing extravagant views of snowy peaks and distant rivers. It is an unforgettable experience.

Excursions vary in length, from two to four days, utilizing different starting points and campsites. The following itinerary serves as a rough guide.

## Day One

Most treks begin at **Km 82** on the railway that leads to Aguas Calientes. After crossing the **Río Urubamba** (2600m), you'll climb gently along the river to the first archaeological site, **Llactapata**. After this, you'll head down a side valley of the Río Cusichaca. The path then leads southwards, 7km to the hamlet of **Wayllabamba** (3000m). Many groups spend their first night camping here, where you can also buy bottled drinks and take in views of the snowcapped **Nevado Verónica** (5750m).

## Day Two

From here, the route crosses the **Río Llullucha**, then climbs steeply up along the

### Inca Trail

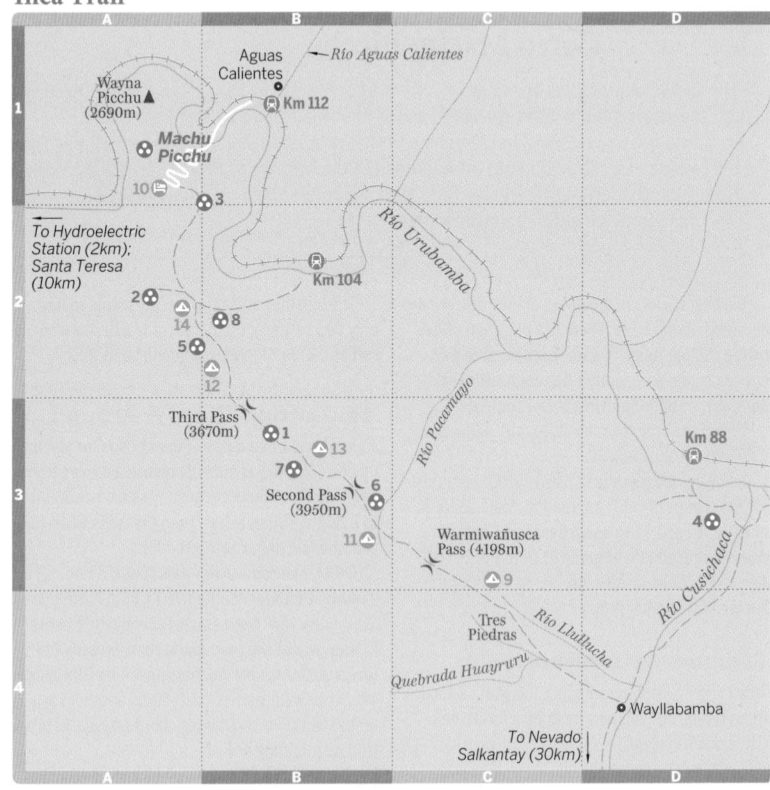

river. This area is known as **Tres Piedras** (Three Stones; 3300m), though the boulders are no longer visible. From here it is a long, very steep 3km climb through humid woodlands. The trail eventually emerges on the bare mountainside of **Llulluchupampa** (3750m), where there is water available and the flats are dotted with campsites. This is as far as you can reasonably expect to get on your first day, though many groups will actually spend their second night here.

From Llulluchupampa, the trail then ascends to **Warmiwañusca Pass** – also colorfully known as 'Dead Woman's Pass.' At about 4200m above sea level, this is the highest point of the trek – leaving many a seasoned hiker gasping. From Warmiwañusca, you can see the Río Pacamayo (Río Escondido) far below, as well as the ruin of Runkurakay halfway up the next hill, above the river.

The trail continues down a long and knee-jarringly steep descent to the river, where there are large campsites at **Paq'amayo** (3600m). The trail then crosses the river over a small footbridge and climbs toward **Runkurakay**, a round ruin with superb views.

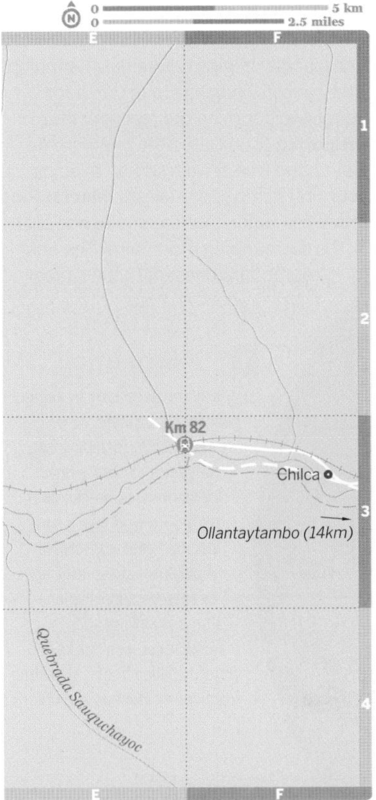


## Day Three

Above Runkurakay the path then climbs to a false summit before continuing past two small lakes, to the top of the **second pass** at 3950m, which has views of the snowcapped Cordillera Vilcabamba. You'll notice a change in ecology as you descend from this pass – you're now on the eastern, Amazon slope of the Andes and things immediately get greener. The path then descends to the ruin of **Sayaqmarka**, a tightly constructed complex on a mountain spur with incredible views, and then continues downward, crossing a tributary of the Río Aobamba.

From here, the walk continues across an Inca causeway and up a gentle climb through some beautiful cloud forest

### Inca Trail

**Top Sights**

Machu Picchu .......... A1

**Sights**

1 Inca Tunnel .......... B3
2 Intipata .......... A2
3 Intipunku .......... B1
4 Llactapata .......... D3
5 Phuyupatamarka .......... A2
6 Runkurakay .......... B3
7 Sayaqmarka .......... B3
8 Wiñay Wayna .......... B2

**Sleeping**

9 Llulluchupampa Campground .......... C3
10 Machu Picchu Sanctuary Lodge .......... A1
11 Paq'amayo Campground .......... B3
12 Phuyupatamarka Campground .......... B2
13 Sayaqmarka Campground .......... B3
14 Wiñay Wayna Campground .......... A2

and an **Inca tunnel** carved from rock. This is a relatively flat section and you'll soon arrive at the **third pass**, at almost 3600m. This spot has grand views of the Río Urubamba valley, as well as campsites where some groups spend their final night. While the sunsets are beautiful, the disadvantage of camping here is having to leave at 3am in the race to reach the Sun Gate in time for sunrise. Be careful in the early morning as the steep incline makes the following steps slippery.

Just below the pass is the well-restored ruin of **Phuyupatamarka** (3570m). The site contains six beautiful ceremonial baths with water running through them. From Phuyupatamarka, the trail makes a dizzying dive into the cloud forest below, following an incredibly well-engineered flight of many hundreds of Inca steps. (It's nerve-racking in the early hours, use a headlamp.) After two or three hours, the trail eventually zigzags its way down to a collapsed red-roofed white building that marks the final night's campsite, which contains a series of ceremonial baths.

A 500m trail behind an old, out-of-use pub leads to the exquisite little Inca site of **Wiñay Wayna** (also spelled Huiñay Huayna), which is variously translated as 'Forever Young,' 'To Plant the Earth Young' and 'Growing Young.' Peter Frost writes that the Quechua name refers to an orchid *(Epidendrum secundum)* that blooms here year-round. The semitropical campsite at Wiñay Wayna boasts one of the most stunning views on the whole trail, especially at sunrise. For better or worse, the famous pub located here is now deteriorated and no longer functioning. A rough trail leads from this site to another spectacular terraced ruin, called **Intipata**, best visited on the day you arrive at Wiñay Wayna. Coordinate with your guide if you are interested.

## Day Four

The last day begins before dawn, winding through cliff-hanging cloud forest for about two hours before reaching the **Intipunku** (Sun Gate), the penultimate site on the trail. It's a tradition to enjoy your first glimpse of majestic **Machu Picchu** while waiting for the sun to rise over the surrounding mountains. The final triumphant descent to the citadel takes about an hour.

### Information

Pack all the necessary trekking gear for hiking in extreme temperatures, including two changes of clothes – one for warm days, one for cold nights – a wool cap, a sun hat, rain gear, sunscreen, repellent, water-purifying tablets, personal hygiene items, a walking stick, headlamps, wool socks and sturdy hiking boots. Also bring cash for incidentals and tips.

Machu Picchu (p217)

For details on finding a reputable operator for the trip – or alternate routes to Machu Picchu – turn to p188.

## Santa Teresa

☎084 / POP 460 / ELEV 1900M

The makeshift feel of Santa Teresa persists even some years after the flooding that has taken place on various occasions – most recently in 2010. In its tiny center, most buildings are prefabricated emergency-relief shells. The most permanent construction is the puzzling Plaza de Armas statue – of a strangely ferocious man threatening some flowers. As more travelers come through on alternate trekking routes to Machu Picchu, however, services here have begun to grow.

### Sights & Activities

**BAÑOS TERMALES COCALMAYO** Hot Springs

**(admission S5; ⏲24 hr)** These stunningly landscaped hot springs are truly a world-class attraction. As if huge, warm pools and a natural shower straight out of a jungle fantasy weren't enough, you can buy beer and snacks. It's 4km from town – an unshaded, dusty walk or a round-trip taxi ride of roughly S36.

**COLA DE MONO** Adventure Sports

**(☎79-2413, 959-743-060; www.canopyperu.com; US$60)** South America's highest zipline is a must for thrill seekers. A total of 2500m of cables with six separate sections whiz high above the spectacular scenery of the Sacsara Valley. The owners, river guides from way back, also run rafting on the spectacular, and so far little-exploited, Santa Teresa river. To get there, it's a pleasant 2km (half-hour) stroll east – just follow the road out of town or take a taxi (S10).

**TOUR DE CAFE** Tour

**(per person S25)** Run by Eco Quechua, this 2½-hour tour visits a family coffee farm steeped in local tradition (see the *cuys* being raised in the kitchen!). You can also pick tropical fruit and see a fish farm in action. Not a modern operation, this is old-style cultivation in transition. Fifty percent of the visitor fees go to help local farmers.

### Sleeping & Eating

**ECO QUECHUA** Lodge $

**(☎63-0877, 984-756-855; www.ecoquechua.com; Sauce Pampa; per person with half-board S75)** Run by a wonderful and energetic young couple, this funky thatched lodge lets you sample the jungle right outside of Santa Teresa. The open-air living room is cloaked in thick vegetation. Rooms feature mosquito nets and the outdoor stall bathrooms are rustic, but this is undoubtedly the most ambient spot in Santa Teresa

**ALBERGUE MUNICIPAL** Hostel $

**(☎984-145-049; dm/d S20/60)** Next to the football field, a gated circular compound is one of the best options in town, with a manicured lawn, cool spacious rooms and doubles with minifridges. Book ahead via the municipality. If the gate is closed, the caretaker may be out.

### Information

There are no banks or ATMs in Santa Teresa – you must bring all the cash you need. You may be able to change dollars at an extremely unfavorable rate. Internet access is poor, but available in a few cafes.

### Getting There & Away

Many travelers arrive in Santa Teresa as part of an organized trek.

You can take the train to Aguas Calientes for visits to Machu Picchu. Tickets for this route are sold only at the Peru Rail ticket office **(⏲6-8am & 10am-3pm daily, 6-8pm Wed & Sun)**, which is located inside the Santa Teresa bus terminal.

# Huaraz, Trujillo & the North

**In the north, expect the unexpected.** Majestic mountains – the highest outside the Himalayas – are bordered by desert coast studded with the remnants of some of the most artful pre-Columbian civilizations to ever inhabit the continent.

To the interior, you'll find the Cordillera Blanca, a mecca for hiking, trekking and mountain climbing – all located within convenient reach of the 3000-year-old ruins at Chavín de Huántar, an ancient ceremonial center whose rise heralded the birth of art. And along the coast you'll find long-forgotten adobe pyramids and splendid museums tucked between bottle-green oases. Oh, and did we mention the pumping surf scene?

The north offers dramatic mountain landscapes, hospitable rural villages, hip-shaking *cumbia* music and delectable regional cuisine. Welcome to Peru.

Basilica Menor Catedral (p255), Trujillo

Cordillera Blanca (p251)

# Huaraz, Trujillo & the North

# Huaraz, Trujillo & the North Highlights

1

## The Cordilleras

Icy mountaintops. Rugged valleys. Crystalline, high-altitude lakes. Hikers and climbers the world over travel to the area around Huaraz (p250) to lay eyes on some of Peru's most majestic vistas – not to mention the Andes' highest, most dramatic peaks. If rugged nature gets you going, this is the place to be.

**Need to Know**

**BEFORE BOOKING** Ask your outfitter about quality of tents, the food served, emergency planning and if national park fees are included. **For further coverage, see p247**.

Local Knowledge

# The Cordilleras Don't Miss List

BY BRAD JOHNSON, AUTHOR OF *CLASSIC CLIMBS OF THE CORDILLERA BLANCA, PERU* AND THE MAN BEHIND THE CLIMBING SITE, HTTP://PEAKSANDPLACES.COM

## 1 MOUNTAIN BIKE AROUND HUARAZ

I highly recommend a ride with Julio Olaza of Mountain Bike Adventures (p243), the first guy to do this in the area. He speaks English, has a good sense of humor and he does a great day trip that takes you to the Cordillera Negra. You'll ride a single-track trail that has views of the Cordillera Blanca in the distance.

## 2 SANTA CRUZ TREK

If you only have five days available for trekking, this is the best trip to do (see p247). To start with, the drive to the drop-off point is beautiful: you'll get marvelous views of Huascarán (6768m), the highest peak in Peru. Once on the trek you'll see incredible valleys, local hamlets and seven peaks over 6000m – including Alpamayo, one of the country's most famous.

## 3 CORDILLERA HUAYHUASH

If you've got 10 days for trekking, then I recommend the complete Cordillera Huayhuash Circuit (p252). I've been in Nepal, Kilimanjaro and China, and this rivals any other trek in the world. Every day you're beneath peaks that are 6000m. It's got a wild feeling and there are lakes where you camp. Plus, you often see condors.

## 4 PISCO

If you're a novice mountain climber, I recommend Pisco (p247), which stands at 5750m. It's a short, relatively easy glaciated climb, though previous experience using crampons and an ice ax is recommended. You can do a round-trip from Huaraz in about three to four days (if you're acclimatized). The views from the top are spectacular.

## 5 CAFÉ ANDINO

In Huaraz, I recommend this café (p250), which has fresh-brewed coffee, good breakfast, lunch and dinner, as well as incredible views of the mountains. There's even wi-fi and a little library – a good spot to rest.

## Kuélap

Matched in grandeur only by Machu Picchu, the fabulous ruins of Kuélap tower over the Río Utcubamba, near Chachapoyas, at 3100m above sea level. The remarkably preserved citadel, dating back to AD 500, is a monumental feat of stonework shrouded in misty cloud forest – and it is nearly always uncrowded.

### Need to Know

**TAKE A TOUR** It's easiest to visit on guided tours from Chachapoyas. **BUS IT** Otherwise, the public bus departs at 4am from Chachapoyas. **For further coverage, see p272.**

## Kuélap Don't Miss List

BY DANIEL FERNANDEZ-DAVILA, ARCHAEOLOGIST, DOCUMENTARY ADVISER

1 **EL TINTERO**
El Tintero (The Inkpot) stands out for the unique structural and ritual features of its inverted cone structure. It's a solid raised round structure with a center hole on the top where offerings were deposited. Don't miss the carved human face at the base of the stone staircase entrance.

2 **PUEBLO ALTO**
As you enter the citadel, walk to the northern part of the site, where a small ramp leads to the upper section. Once there, pay attention to the large rectangular Callanca Inka (dorm room), the small quadrangular ritual temple, and the outstanding view from the northern Torreon (watchtower).

3 **MAIN ENTRANCE (ENTRANCE 1)**
Slow down on your exit via Entrance 1 so you don't miss the small carvings, including a carved face (on your right) and carved figures of a double headed snake, hybrid bird and small faces (halfway down on your left). Almost at the exit, look for the bedrock with a canal that filters water. Here you'll see an impressive carved figure of an inverted feline on your right.

4 **INCA VS CHACHAPOYAS**
Differentiate between Chachapoya (circular) and Inca (squared) structures. You will understand how Incas strategically displayed their structures in order to control access, rituals and administration of the site. The best example of this can be found close to El Tintero looking east. Here lies a platform where a rectangular Inka structure has been superimposed on top of a Chachapoyas round house.

5 **LLAMA HOOF MARKS**
The site has been built over a huge outcrop of sedimentary rock. Entrance 2 has been built to take advantage of a natural bedrock ramp. Over hundreds of years endless caravans of llamas came inside, eroding the sedimentary rock and leaving behind traces of their hooves. These marks are visible as two parallel grooves that clearly stand out as you climb up.

## Hang 10 in Máncora

Peru's beachside hot spot (p274) is the perfect place to indulge in some serious sun, surf and sand – along with plenty of divine seafood eateries and pumping nightspots. On offer is surfing and kitesurfing and every other water activity in between. When you're ready for a break from the scene, just hop over to chill out on one of the solitary beaches nearby.

3

4

## Gaze Upon the Vast Wealth of a Moche Burial Site

Outside the northern oasis of Chiclayo, a powerful Moche lord was entombed in an adobe pyramid amid ornaments, ceramics and even a headless llama. In a rare stroke of luck, his tomb was discovered – largely untouched – 17 centuries later. Now its incredible treasure can be seen almost in its entirety at the Museo Tumbas Reales de Sipán (p273). Do not miss!

ARTURO BULLARD/GETTY IMAGES ©

## Dip into Seafood in Trujillo 5

Citrus-soaked ceviches. Buttery bisques known as *chupe*. Brothy stews stuffed full of fresh fish, mussels and scallops. Peru's north coast is renowned for its well-spiced local cuisine – dishes that tingle the brain as much as the tongue. Trujillo is the place to pull up a chair at an informal *cevichería* (ceviche stand) and dig in (p259). In this part of the world, it's *all* good. Ceviche

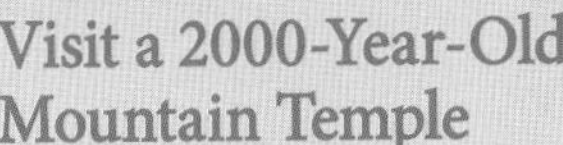

DANITA DELIMONT/GETTY IMAGES ©

## 6 Visit a 2000-Year-Old Mountain Temple

Dating back to 800 BC, the temple structure at Chavín de Huántar (p253) is evidence of one of the oldest cultures in the Andes, but there's more to it than that. The locale is breathtaking and the temple boasts a maze of alleys that deliver the unwary viewer to a terrifying carving of a creature with snakes radiating from its head. A perfect spot to channel your inner Indiana Jones.

## 7 Get Lost in the Ancient City of Chan Chan

The pre-Columbian city of Chan Chan (p261) was, in its heyday, a staggeringly large adobe urban center, covering more than 36 sq km of coastal desert – a remarkable feat of urban planning and construction. Today, the city's remains include reconstructed decorative friezes bearing stylized images that were highly important to the Chimú culture that built it: fish, waves and seabirds.

# Huaraz, Trujillo & the North's Best...

## Museums

- **Museo Nacional de Chavín** (p253) Stone objects from one of Peru's most ancient ruins sites
- **Museo Tumbas Reales de Sipán** (p273) A Moche pyramid's treasure, beautifully showcased
- **Museo Nacional Sicán** (p272) An exhibit devoted to one of Peru's most unusual pre-Columbian burials
- **Museo de Sitio Chan Chan** (p261) Detailed displays explain the Chimú culture and a sprawling ruins site

## North Coast Restaurants

- **La Sirena d'Juan** (p277) Peruvian classics get a serious foodie upgrade in Máncora
- **Mar Picante** (p259) A bamboo-lined joint in Trujillo serves divine *ceviche mixto*
- **Restaurant Big Ben** (p264) Superfresh fish and steamy *sudados* (stews) in Huanchaco
- **Fiesta Chiclayo Gourmet** (p270) Pisco cocktails crafted tableside and flash-seared ceviche are a must in Chiclayo

## Places to Stay

- **Hostal Colonial, Trujillo** (p258) A rose-colored colonial mansion
- **Sunset Hotel, Máncora** (p276) Excellent views of the seascape at this boutique inn
- **Lazy Dog Inn, Huaraz** (p246) A deluxe mountain lodge at the mouth of a waterfall
- **Llanganuco Mountain Lodge, Cordilleras** (p249) A comfortable base for the Santa Cruz Trek

## Adventures

- **Surfing the longest left-hand wave** (p266) In Puerto Chicama, just a 90-minute drive north of Trujillo
- **Trekking to Laguna 69** (p247) Take in the beauty of an impressive array of glistening high-altitude lakes over the course of 48 hours
- **Kitesurfing** (p275) Catch the breeze in Máncora
- **Mountain biking** (p243) Race down the coffee-colored hillsides of the Cordillera Negra

**Left:** Cordillera Blanca (p251); **Above:** Máncora (p274)



# Need to Know

### ADVANCE PLANNING

- **Five months before** Book a Cordillera Blanca trek
- **Three months before** Reserve beachside hotels in Máncora for high season
- **One month before** Arrange a guided side trip to Chachapoyas
- **Three weeks before** Reserve a hotel in Huaraz
- **One day before** Make reservations at the renowned Restaurant Típico La Fiesta in Chiclayo

### GETTING AROUND

- **Air** Huaraz, Trujillo and Chiclayo are all serviced by airports with multiple daily flights to Lima; Máncora is reached by the airport at Talara, 40 minutes away
- **Bus** Minibuses connect points within cities, while comfortable long-haul vehicles offer service all over the region – including from Chiclayo to Chachapoyas
- **Walk** The best way of exploring the narrow town centers of cities such Huaraz, Trujillo and Chiclayo
- **Taxis** Found just about everywhere in bigger cities and towns; some smaller areas may be serviced by *mototaxis* (motorcycle taxis)

### BE FOREWARNED

- **Museum closings** Many museums are closed on Mondays
- **Altitude** The areas around Huaraz get staggeringly high – allow plenty of time to acclimatize before setting out a on a trek
- **Unlicensed operators** Be especially cautious when booking complex adventure activities such as treks and climbs; recommended agencies are best
- **Robberies** As in all places in Peru, they happen – especially in crowded markets and archaeological sites, and even along some remote, but popular, trekking trails

# Huaraz, Trujillo & the North Itineraries

*Desert oases that harbor pre-Columbian ruins, majestic mountains that offer some of the continent's most superlative trekking, and plenty of sunny beaches – allow at least seven days to visit the main sights.*

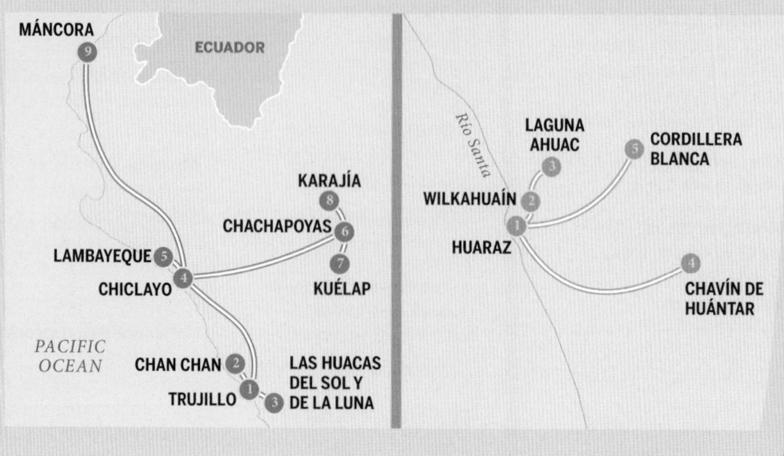

TRUJILLO TO CHACHAPOYAS

## Surf & Turf

Begin in **(1) Trujillo**, where you can admire the colonial architecture, such as the pristinely preserved Casa de Urquiaga. On the second day go back in time with a visit to one of several nearby pre-Columbian ruins: the sprawling adobe city of **(2) Chan Chan**, once the largest city in the Americas, or **(3) Las Huacas del Sol y de la Luna**, a Moche ceremonial complex.

Continue up the coast to **(4) Chiclayo**, taking a day to explore the witch doctors' market and to try the divine local seafood (the flash-seared ceviche at Fiesta Chiclayo Gourmet is a must). Also visit the unparalleled treasures of the Museo Tumbas Reales de Sipán in nearby **(5) Lambayeque**.

Next, head inland to the charming regional capital of **(6) Chachapoyas**. This friendly highland hub is an excellent base for exploring the ancient cloud-forest citadel of **(7) Kuélap** and visiting the highly unusual sarcophagi at **(8) Karajía** – incredible pre-Columbian treasures that happen to be practically tourist-free.

Afterwards, return to Chiclayo and make immediately for the coast, where you can enjoy some beach-itude on the palm-fringed sands of **(9) Máncora** – a popular spot for fresh fish, good waves and hard-core relaxing.

### HUARAZ TO THE CORDILLERAS

## Mountain Majesty in the Andes

Begin with a day of gentle acclimatization in **(1) Huaraz**. Stroll around the town center and pay a visit to the Museo Regional de Áncash, where you'll see mummies with trepanned skulls. You can use your second day in town to do a gentle hike in the area as a way of conditioning your body to the altitude. A short two-hour walk will take you to the Wari ruins at **(2) Wilkahuaín**, but if you'd like to get a full day of walking in, a longer hike (six hours) will take you all the way to **(3) Laguna Ahuac**, a lovely lake. On the third day, organize a day trip to the ancient temple site of **(4) Chavín de Huántar**, one of Peru's earliest ceremonial centers, known for an elaborate stele with fearsome carvings called *El Lanzón*.

Once you are well acclimatized, head out to explore the majestic peaks of the **(5) Cordillera Blanca**. This is best done with on a multiday trek (which run anywhere from quick overnighters to 10-day mountaineering extravaganzas). Expect dizzying mountain passes, beautiful lakes and towering walls of granite – an Andean landscape you will never forget.

Countryside around Monumento Nacional Wilkahuaín (p242)

# Discover Huaraz, Trujillo & the North

## At a Glance

- **Huaraz** The capital of Peruvian highland trekking.
- **Chavín de Huántar** (p253) Otherworldly ruins of Peru's most ancient culture.
- **Trujillo** (p255) Lively colonial center with good proximity to pre-Columbian ruins.
- **Chachapoyas** (p272) Charming mountain town that lies close to an ancient mountaintop citadel.
- **Máncora** (p274) Peru's trendiest, prettiest beaches.

Quechua woman at the market, Huaraz



## Huaraz

☎043 / POP 48,500 / ELEV 3091M

Huaraz is the restless capital of an Andean adventure kingdom and its rooftops command exhaustive panoramas of the city's dominion: one of the most impressive mountain ranges in the world. Nearly wiped out by the earthquake of 1970, the city isn't going to win any beauty contests, but it does have personality – and personality goes a long way.

This is first and foremost a trekking metropolis. During the high season the streets buzz with hikers fresh from the mountains. Dozens of outfits help plan trips, rent equipment and organize adventure sports. And an endless lineup of restaurants and bars keep the belly full and the place lively.

### Sights

**MONUMENTO NACIONAL WILKAHUAÍN** Ruins

**(admission S5; ⏰9am-5pm)** This small Wari ruin about 8km north of Huaraz is remarkably well preserved, dating from about AD 600 to 900. It's an imitation of the temple at Chavín, done in the Tiwanaku style. Wilkahuaín means 'grandson's house' in Quechua. The three-story temple has seven rooms on each floor, each originally filled with bundles of mummies. (The bodies were kept dry using a sophisticated system of ventilation ducts.)

Taxis from town cost about S20. Otherwise, the two-hour walk up is an easy acclimatization jaunt, passing farms and simple *pueblos* (villages). Ask locally if it is safe before you set off. (See Dangers and Annoyances, p248.)

**MUSEO REGIONAL DE ÁNCASH** Museum

**(Plaza de Armas; adult/child S5/1; 8:30am-5:15 Tue-Sat, 9am-2pm Sun)** This small but interesting museum houses the largest collection of ancient stone sculptures in South America, as well as a few mummies, some trepanned skulls and a garden of stone monoliths from the Recuay (400 BC–AD 600) and Wari cultures (AD 600–1100).

**JIRÓN JOSÉ OLAYA** Historic District

East of town on the right-hand side of Raymondi a block beyond Confraternidad, this thoroughfare is the only street that has remained intact through the earthquakes. It provides a glimpse of what old Huaraz looked like. Go on Sunday when a street market sells regional foods.

**MIRADOR DE RETAQEÑUA** Lookout

This lookout is about a 45-minute walk southeast of the center and has great views of the city and its mountainous backdrop. It's best to take a S8 taxi here.

# Activities

## Trekking & Mountaineering

Whether you're arranging a mountain expedition or going for a day hike, Huaraz is the place to start. Numerous outfits can prearrange entire trips so that all you need to do is show up. See the section on trekking (p247) for a list of some popular routes in the area.

## Rock Climbing

Rock climbing is one of the Cordillera Blanca's biggest pastimes. Avid climbers will find some gnarly bolted sport climbs nearby. (For some big-wall action, ask about Torre de Parón, known locally as 'the Sphinx.') Most trekking agencies offer climbing trips for beginners and advanced climbers. Many also rent gear.

In Huaraz, Galaxia Expeditions and Monttrek have indoor *rócodromos* (climbing or bouldering walls).

## Mountain Biking

**MOUNTAIN BIKE ADVENTURES** Mountain Biking

**( 42-4259; www.chakinaniperu.com; Lúcar y Torre 530, 2nd fl; 9am-1pm & 3-8pm)** Owned by Julio Olaza, this company comes well recommended. A lifelong resident of Huaraz, Olaza speaks English and knows the region's single-track possibilities better than anyone. The company offers bike rentals or guided tours, ranging from an easy five-hour cruise to 12-day circuits around the Cordillera Blanca. Rates start at S100 per day either for rentals or for one-day tours.

# Tours

## Day Tours

Dozens of agencies along Luzuriaga can organize outings. One popular tour visits the ruins at Chavín de Huántar; another passes through Yungay to the beautiful **Lagunas Llanganuco**, where there are superb vistas of Huascarán; a third takes you through Caraz to **Laguna Parón**, surrounded by ravishing glaciated peaks; and a fourth travels through Caraz to see the massive *Puya raimondii* plant and then continues on to **Nevado Pastoruri**, to see ice caves, glaciers and mineral springs.

All of these trips cost between S35 and S45 each; prices may vary depending on the number of people going, but typically include transport and a guide (who often doesn't speak English). Admission fees and lunch are extra. Trips take a full day; bring warm clothes, drinking water, sunblock and snacks.

Do not fall for a day trip to Chavín de Huántar on a Monday – the ruins and museum are closed.

Out of the throngs of agencies, these are the most popular with travelers:

**Pablo Tours** **( 42-1145; www.pablotours.com; Luzuriaga 501)**

**Sechín Tours** **( 42-1419; www.sechintours.com; Morales 602)**

## Huaraz

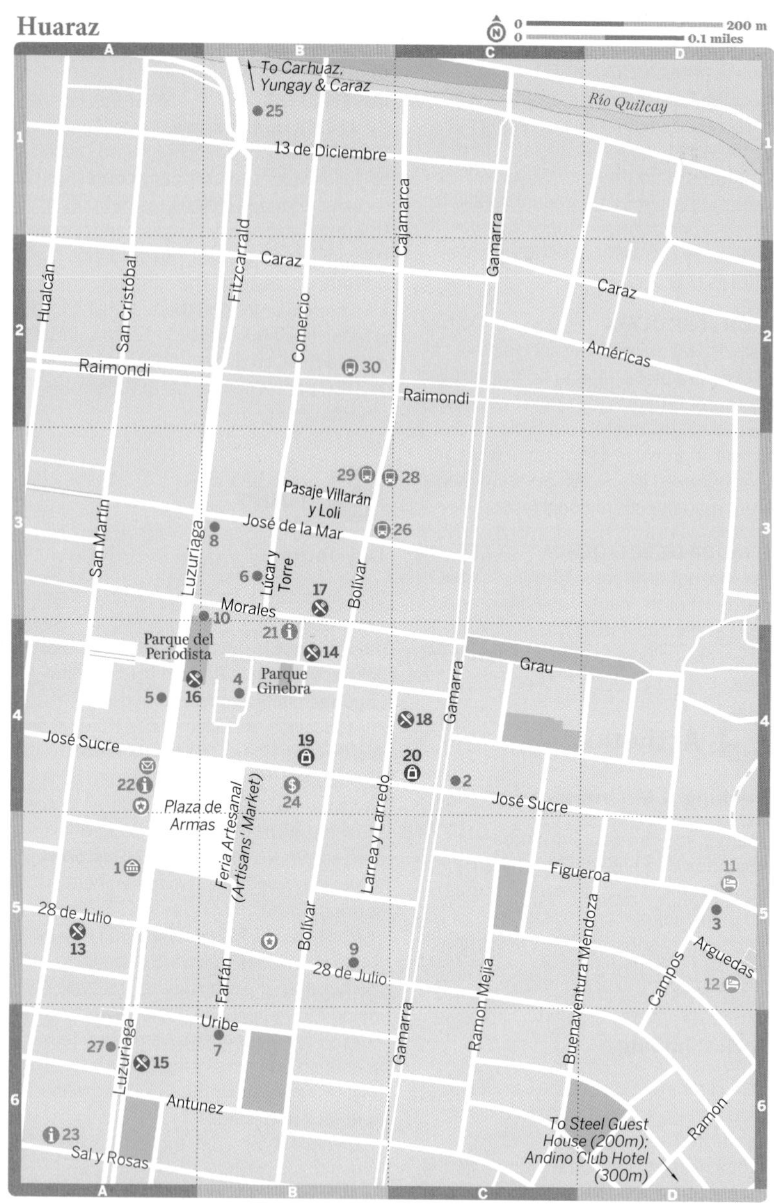


### Trekking & Mountaineering

Mountaineers and trekkers should check out **Casa de Guías** (**☎42-1811; www.casadeguias.com.pe; Parque Ginebra 28G; ⏲9am-1pm & 4-8pm Mon-Sat**), the headquarters of the Mountain Guide Association of Peru, for a list of certified guides. All of the following agencies arrange full trekking and climbing expeditions that include guides, equipment, food, cooks, porters and transport. Depending on the number

## Huaraz

**Sights**

1 Museo Regional de Ancash .......... A5

**Activities, Courses & Tours**

2 Active Peru .......... C4
Casa de Guías .......... (see 21)
Galaxia Expeditions .......... (see 16)
3 Huascarán .......... D5
4 Montañero .......... B4
5 Monttrek .......... A4
6 Mountain Bike Adventures .......... B3
7 MountClimb .......... B6
8 Pablo Tours .......... B3
9 Respons Sustainable Tourism Center .......... B5
10 Sechín Tours .......... B3

**Sleeping**

11 Albergue Churup .......... D5
12 Olaza's Bed & Breakfast .......... D5

**Eating**

Café Andino .......... (see 6)
13 California Cafe .......... A5
14 Chili Heaven .......... B4
15 La Brasa Roja .......... A6
16 Mi Chef Kristoff .......... A4
17 Rinconcito Mineiro .......... B3
18 Taita .......... C4

**Drinking**

Los 13 Buhos .......... (see 14)

**Shopping**

19 Perú Magico .......... B4
20 Tejidos Turmanyé .......... C4

**Information**

21 Casa de Guías .......... B4
22 iPerú .......... A4
23 Parque Nacional Huascarán Office .......... A6
24 Scotiabank .......... B4

**Transport**

25 Combis to Carhuaz, Yungay & Caraz .......... B1
26 Cruz del Sur .......... B3
27 LC Perú .......... A6
28 Línea .......... B3
29 Movil Tours .......... B3
30 Oltursa .......... B2

of people, the length of your trip and what's included, expect to pay from under S90 (for an easy hike) to S670 (technical mountain climbing) per person per day. Try not to base your selection solely on price – you get what you pay for.

The following list is by no means exhaustive; things change, good places go bad and bad places get good. Talk to other travelers about their experiences. Also consult the South American Explorers Club in Lima (p86), which is an excellent source of information.

**Active Peru** (☎99-648-3655; www.activeperu.com; Gamarra 699)

**Galaxia Expeditions** (☎42-5335; www.galaxia-expeditions.com; Parque Periodista)

**Huascarán** (☎42-2523; www.huascarin-peru.com; Campos 711)

**Montañero** (☎42-6386; Parque Ginebra)

**Monttrek** (☎42-1124; www.monttrek.com.pe; Luzuriaga 646, 2nd fl)

**Peaks & Places** (☎in USA 970-626-5251; www.peaksandplaces.com) Though not based in Huaraz, this reputable outfitter has been doing custom treks since 1982. Reserve well in advance.

**Skyline Adventures** (☎42-7097; www.skyline-adventures.com; Pasaje Industrial 137, Huaraz)

### Community Tourism

It is possible to arrange trips in the area to learn about traditional aspects of local life. These agencies are recommended:

**Mountain Institute** (☎42-3446; www.mountain.org; Ricardo Palma 100)

**Respons Sustainable Tourism Center** (☎42-7949; Calle 28 de Julio 821; www.respons.org; ⌚9am-1pm & 3-7:30pm)

## Sleeping

**LAZY DOG INN** Lodge $$
(94-378-9330; www.thelazydoginn.com; s/d without bathroom S135/210, d inside main house from S280, cabins S310, all incl breakfast & dinner; @ ) Run by the rugged Diana and Wayne, this deluxe lodge is at the mouth of the Quebrada Llaca, 8km east of Huaraz. It's hand-built out of adobe and you can stay in either comfortable double rooms in the main lodge or in fancier private cabins, which have fireplaces and bathtubs.

**HOTEL SAN SEBASTIÁN** Hotel $$
(42-6960; www.sansebastianhuaraz.com; Italia 1124; s/d incl breakfast S170/198; @ ) A fetching white-walled, red-roofed urban sanctuary, this four-story hotel is a neocolonial find. Balconies and arches overlook a grassy garden and inner courtyard with a soothing fountain. All rooms have a writing desk, good beds, hot showers and cable TV. Most have balconies, too.

**STEEL GUEST HOUSE** Guesthouse $$
(42-9709; www.steelguest.com; Pasaje Maguina 1467; s/d incl breakfast S110/145; @ ) The perfect midrange choice, with white-glove clean rooms styled with Andean textiles. The owner tends to dote on her guests, making it feel a little like grandma's house. Loads of facilities round out the offerings, including cable TV, outdoor hammocks, billiards, a steam room and a gorgeous roof terrace with views of Huascarán.

**OLAZA'S BED & BREAKFAST** Guesthouse $$
(42-2529; www.olazas.com; Arguedas 1242; s/d/tr incl breakfast S80/100/140; @ ) This smart little hotel has a boutique feel, spacious bathrooms and comfortable beds, but the best part is the big lounge area upstairs, equipped with a massive panoramic terrace. The owner is an established figure in the Huaraz tourism scene.

**ALBERGUE CHURUP** Boutique Hostel $$
(42-4200; www.churup.com; Figueroa 1257; dm S28, s/d incl breakfast S69/99; @ ) An immensely popular family-run hostel that continues to win the top budget-choice accolade. Immaculate and comfortable rooms share cushy, colorful lounging areas on every floor. The building is topped by a massive, fireplace-warmed lounge with magnificent 180-degree views.

Glacier, Nevado Pastoruri (p243)

**HOTEL COLOMBA** Hotel $$
(☎42-1501; www.huarazhotel.com; Francisco de Zela 210; s/d incl breakfast from S150/200; @ 📶) The rooms at this surprising oasis surround a dense and compulsively trimmed hedge forest, which spills out onto a long, relaxing veranda. The area is enclosed, making it a great place for kids to safely run amok.

**ANDINO CLUB HOTEL** Hotel $$$
(☎42-1662; www.hotelandino.com; Pedro Cochachín 357; s/d incl breakfast from S280/338, d with balcony S433; @ 📶) The structure feels a little chain hotel, but this 54-room, Swiss-run hotel has immaculate rooms. Balcony units are worth the splurge for the wood-burning fireplaces and postcard views of Huascarán peak.

## Eating

**MI CHEF KRISTOF** Fusion $$
(Parque del Periodista, 2nd fl; mains S20-29; closed Sun; 📶) The garrulous chef here is known for dishes such as stewed beef in black beer, served on a bed of Belgian fries, or tender chicken with ratatouille and fresh pasta. The pisco-laced *maracuyá* (passion fruit) aperitif is a great way to begin a meal.

**CAFÉ ANDINO** Cafe $
(www.cafeandino.com; Lúcar y Torre 530, 3rd fl; breakfast S8.50-20, mains S7-25; @ 📶 🖉) This modern top-floor cafe has space and light in spades, as well as a crackling fireplace, books and groovy tunes. You can get breakfast anytime (waffles, huevos rancheros), snacks (nachos!), and coffee made from fresh-roasted organic beans.

**CHILI HEAVEN** Asian $$
(Parque Ginebra; mains S18-35) The fiery Indian and Thai curries at this English-run hot spot will seize your taste buds and mercilessly shake them up. They bottle their own hot sauces here and bring in loads of English beers.

## If You Like... Trekking

If trekking is your thing, spend some time tackling the longer hikes around the Cordilleras.

1 **SANTA CRUZ TREK**
The area's most popular trek is a wondrous five-day walk that ascends the spectacular Quebrada Santa Cruz valley and crosses the Punta Unión pass (4760m) before tumbling into Quebrada Huarípampa on the other side. Head-turning sights include emerald lakes, sensational views of many Cordillera peaks, beds of bright alpine wildflowers and stands of red *qeñua* trees.

2 **OLLEROS TO CHAVÍN DE HUÁNTAR**
If you're short on time but still want icy-peak time, try this two- to three-day trek. The 40km trip travels along pretty villages and pre-Inca roads – some with great views of the Uruashraju (5722m), Rurec (5700m) and Cashan (5716m) mountains. Bonus: the hot springs at the end of the route.

3 **QUILCAYHUANCA VALLEY**
Kicking off in Pitec, this three- to four-day hike is only moderately difficult, but you'll need to be well acclimatized. It winds up the Quilcayhuanca Valley through *qeñua* trees and grassy meadows until reaching the Laguna Cuchillacocha and Tullpacocha.

4 **INCA ROADWAY**
A three- to six-day hike between Huari and the city of Huánuco covering well-preserved parts of an old Inca roadway. To book, contact the community tourism agencies in Huaraz.

5 **PISCO**
Pisco (5750m) is one of the most sought-after summits in the Cordillera Blanca, with hundreds of mountain climbers bagging it every summer. The approximately 5km trek takes two to three days and brings you into stone-throwing distance of this thrilling peak. Short, but very challenging.

**TAITA** Peruvian $
(Larrea y Laredo 633, 2nd fl; mains S4.50-15; ⏰10am-3pm) This atmospheric local haunt is a good place to try *chocho* (legumes marinated in citrus), the highland answer

to ceviche. This great spot covered in historical photos, also does fish ceviche and *chicharrones* (deep-fried pork).

**RINCONCITO MINEIRO** Peruvian **$**
**(Morales 757; menú S7-12; ᯤ)** Tuck into cheap Peruvian dishes at this welcoming place decorated with Andean textiles. The daily blackboard of 10 or so options includes an excellent *lomo saltado* (stir-fry of beef and potatoes) as well as grilled trout and *tacu tacu* (pan-fried rice and beans).

**CALIFORNIA CAFÉ** Cafe **$**
**(www.huaylas.com; Calle 28 de Julio 562; breakfast S10-22; ⌚7:30am-6:30pm, to 2pm Sun; ᯤ)** This hip traveler magnet does breakfasts at any time, plus light lunches and salads. It's a funky, chilled-out space where you can spend the day listening to the world-music collection or reading one of the hundreds of books available for exchange.

**LA BRASA ROJA** Peruvian **$**
**(Luzuriaga 915; mains S10-26)** This upscale *pollería* (roasted chicken joint) is the ultimate refueling stop. The chicken is perfect, and you get five sauces (including black olive) – as well as live violin playing.

## Drinking

**SIERRA ANDINA** Brewery
**(Centenario 1690; www.sierraandina.com; pint/pitcher S7/30; ⌚3-10pm)** The S5 taxi ride to nearby Cascapampa is a small price to pay for golden, pale and amber ales brewed at this wonderful microbrewery.

**LOS 13 BUHOS** Bar
**(Parque Ginebra; ⌚5pm-late)** This cool cafe-bar sells home-brewed craft beer in five tasty choices, including red and black ales laced with coca. It's the best place in town for kicking back on comfy lounge sofas.

## Shopping

Inexpensive woolen knits of all kinds are available at the many craft stalls on pedestrian alleys off Luzuriaga or at the *feria artesanal* (artisans' market) off the Plaza de Armas.

**PERÚ MAGICO** Gifts
**(José Sucre btwn Farfán & Bolívar; ⌚9am-2pm & 3-9pm Mon-Sat)** red Offers an assortment of jewelry, textiles and pottery from around Peru.

**TEJIDOS TURMANYÉ** Gifts
**(José Sucre 883; ⌚8am-5pm)** Locally made weavings and knit garments to support a foundation for young mothers.

## Information

Cybercafes are plentiful, as are ATMs.

**Scotiabank** **(José Sucre 760)** Can exchange dollars and euros.

Road to Monumento Nacional Wilkahuaín (p242)
KELLY CHENG TRAVEL PHOTOGRAPHY/GETTY IMAGES ©

## Dangers & Annoyances

Trying to race into the mountains without acclimatizing will likely result in altitude sickness, which can get pretty serious. (See p345 for details.)

Overall, the city is safe, though there have been robberies, especially in the area of the Mirador de Rataquenua and the Wilkahuaín ruins. It is best to go with a group or hire a taxi.

## Emergency

**Policía de Turismo** (**☎42-1351; Plaza de Armas; 🕗8am-8pm**) Some officers speak limited English.

**Clínica San Pablo** (**www.sanpablo.com.pe; Huaylas 172; 🕗24hr**) The best medical care in Huaraz. Some doctors speak English.

## Tourist Information

**iPerú** (**☎42-8812; Plaza de Armas, Pasaje Atusparia, Oficina 1; 🕗9am-6pm Mon-Sat, to 1pm Sun**) Has general tourist information.

**Parque Nacional Huascarán Office** (**☎42-2086; www.sernanp.gob.pe; Sal y Rosas 555; 🕗8:30am-1pm & 2:30-6pm Mon-Fri, to noon Sat**) Limited information about visiting the park.

## Getting There & Around

### Air

The Huaraz **airport** (**code ATA**) is in Anta, 23km north of town. A taxi will cost about S20. **LC Perú** (**☎42-4734; www.lcperu.pe; Luzuriaga 904**) has daily flights from Lima.

### Bus & Taxi

Minibuses go to surrounding villages (such as Monterrey, Yungay and Carhuaz) from near the petrol station on Calle 13 de Diciembre, north of the town center.

For long-haul trips to and from other major cities, the following companies are recommended:

**Cruz del Sur** (**☎42-8726; www.cruzdelsur.com.pe; Bolívar 491**)

**Línea** (**☎42-6666; www.linea.pe; Bolívar 450**)

**Móvil Tours** (**www.moviltours.com.pe**) Terminal (**☎42-2555; Confraternidad Internacional Oeste 451**); Ticket Office (**Bolívar 452**)

**Oltursa** (**☎42-3717; www.oltursa.pe; Raymundi 825**)

A taxi ride around Huaraz costs about S3.

## If You Like... Mountain Retreats

If you like to enjoy your mountains minus the trappings of a noisy city, these cozy lodgings will let you explore the stunning hills by day – and return to a comfortable bed at night. Reserve in advance.

### 1 EL PATIO DE MONTERREY

(**☎42-4965; www.elpatio.com.pe, Monterrey; s/d S189/222; @ 📶**) In the hamlet of Monterrey, 9km north of Huaraz, this colonial-style hacienda has spacious rooms with bathtubs – some with fireplaces (S376). Most units look out onto a bountiful garden.

### 2 LLANGANUCO MOUNTAIN LODGE

(**☎94-366-9580; www.llanganucolodge.com; Yungay; camping S15, dm with/without full board S135/38, s/d with full board from S183/228**) Outside the village of Yungay, this recommended lodge is in a prime position for exploring the Llanganuco Lakes area and charging the Santa Cruz trek (see p247). Lodge rooms have down-feather beds and balconies. The food is excellent.

### 3 HUMACCHUCO COMMUNITY TOURISM PROJECTS

(**☎42-7949; www.respons.org; Yungay; per person incl meals from S108**) A community-tourism program operating a comfy guesthouse in Humacchuco (outside of Yungay). Here, visitors can learn about local culture and savor *pachamanca* (a stew cooked in the ground with rocks).

### 4 ANDES LODGE PERU

(**☎76-5579; www.andeslodgeperu.com; Jirón Gran Chavín s/n, Yanama; s/d S70/120, without bathroom S60/100, all incl breakfast**) A 20-minute drive from the end of the Santa Cruz trek in Yanama, this is one of the best mountain lodges in the Callejón de Huaylas. Expect home-cooked meals, blazing hot showers and snug beds with down comforters.

**Right:** Cordillera Blanca;
**Below:** Donkeys

## The Cordilleras

A pair of dramatic *cordilleras* (mountain chains) run parallel to each other on either side of Huaraz. To the west is the Cordillera Negra, with its coffee-colored soil. To the east is the snow-covered crown of the Cordillera Blanca. Between them, in the valley, runs a paved road known as the Callejón de Huaylas, which furnishes visitors with perfect views of the lofty elevations.

The star of the show here is the Cordillera Blanca. About 20km wide and 180km long, it is an elaborate collection of toothed summits, razor-sharp ridges, emerald-colored lakes and grassy valleys draped with crawling glaciers. More than 50 peaks of 5700m or higher grace this fairly small area. North America, in contrast, has only three mountains in excess of 5700m; Europe has none. Huascarán, at 6768m, is Peru's highest mountain and the highest pinnacle in the tropics anywhere in the world.

South of the Cordillera Blanca is the smaller, more remote, but no less spectacular Cordillera Huayhuash – which contains Peru's second-highest mountain, the 6634m Yerupajá.

### Information

To get the lowdown on trekking and the latest conditions, your first port of call should be Casa de Guías (p243), which has information on weather, trail conditions, guides and mule hire. Some IGN and Alpenvereinskarte topographic maps are sold here.

Trekking and equipment-rental agencies are also good sources of local knowledge and can advise on day hikes. For more impartial advice, be sure to visit popular Huaraz haunts such as Café Andino (p250) and California Café (p248), whose foreign owners keep abreast of local developments and sell hiking maps.

Trekking agencies generally supply everything from ice axes to tents. But if you need to rent gear, see the following agencies:

**Monttrek** (☎42-1124; www.monttrek.com.pe; Luzuriaga 646, 2nd fl, Huaraz)

**MountClimb** (☎42-4322; www.mountclimb.com.pe; Uribe 732, Huaraz)

## Cordillera Blanca

The world's highest tropical mountain range encompasses some of South America's most breathtaking peaks. Andean leviathans include the majestic Nevado Alpamayo (5947m) – once termed 'the most beautiful mountain in the world' by the German Alpine Club. Others include the Nevado Huascarán (at 6768m, Peru's highest), Pucajirca Oeste (6039m), Nevado Quitaraju (6036m) and Nevado Santa Cruz (Nevado Pucaraju; 6241m).

Shorter hikes and treks are listed on p252. For longer, multiday options, turn to p247.

### Sights & Activities

**PARQUE NACIONAL HUASCARÁN** National Park

**(admission per day/week S5/65)** Established in 1975, this 3400-sq-km park encompasses practically the entire area of the Cordillera Blanca above 4000m, including more than 600 glaciers and nearly 300 lakes, and protects extraordinary and endangered species such as the giant *Puya raimondii* plant, the spectacled bear and the Andean condor.

Visitors should bring their passports to register at the park office in Huaraz (see p249) and pay the park fee. You can also do this at one of the control stations. Officials will not sell park permits to trekkers or climbers who are not utilizing the services of a local registered agency or a local licensed guide.

### Artesonraju's 15 Minutes of Fame

If you think the dramatic peak of Artesonraju (5999m) looks familiar, that's because the mountaintop spent a chunk of the '80s and '90s as the peak featured in Paramount Pictures' live-action logo. The famous view is of its northeast face as seen from Quebrada Arhuaycocha (also known as Mirador Alpamayo).

**HUARAZ–WILKAHUAÍN–LAGUNA AHUAC** Hiking

This is a relatively easy, well-marked day hike to Laguna Ahuac (4560m) starting from Huaraz or the Wilkahuaín ruins (p242). From Huaraz, the walk will take six hours; from Wilkahuaín, four. It makes an excellent early acclimatization trip. Look for furry, rabbitlike *vizcachas* sniffing around and the big mountain views of the Cordillera Blanca.

**LAGUNA CHURUP** Hiking

If overnight trekking isn't your bag, but you'd like to experience the sight of some of the area's extravagant high-altitude lakes, this one-day hike is for you. It begins at the hamlet of Pitec (3850m), just above Huaraz, and takes you to the emerald green Laguna Churup (4450m), at the base of Nevado Churup. Note the altitudes and the ascent (it's a steep 600m straight up). The walk takes roughly six hours and is a good acclimatization hike. A taxi from Huaraz to Pitec will cost about S30.

**LAGUNA 69** Hiking

A beautiful overnight trek offering backdrops dripping with marvelous views. The campsite is a true highlight: you'll wake up to morning views of Chopicalqui (6354m), Huascarán Sur (6768m) and Norte (6655m) all around you. From here, you'll then scramble up to Laguna 69, which sits right at the base of Chacraraju (6112m). From there, the journey takes you past the famous Llanganuco lakes – a lot of impressive scenery crammed into 48 hours.

## Cordillera Huayhuash

This more remote mountain range hosts an impressive medley of glaciers, summits, lakes and high-altitude passes (over 4500m), all packed into a hardy area only 30km across. The feeling of utter wilderness is the big draw; you are more likely to spot the graceful Andean condor here than in other parts of the Cordilleras.

Many visitors explore it on the Cordillera Huayhuash Circuit, a stunning 10- to 12-day trek through multiple high-alpine passes with spine-tingling views. The dramatic lakes along the eastern flank provide great campsites and give hikers a wide choice of routes to make this trek as difficult or as easy as they want.

There is no technical climbing, but it does require good acclimatization and physical fitness. Daily ascents range from 500m to 1200m and the average day involves about 12km on the trail, or anywhere from four to eight hours. (Though you may experience at least one 10- to 12-hour day.) Most trekkers take extra rest days along the way because of the length and altitude.

Outfitters in Huaraz (p244) can make arrangements.

## Chavín de Huántar

043 / POP 2000 / ELEV 3250M

The Conchucos Valley (called the Callejón de Conchucos) runs parallel to the Callejón de Huaylas on the eastern side of the Cordillera. Chavín de Huántar, at the south end of the valley, lays claim to one of the most important and mysterious pre-Inca ruins in the Andes. While many folks whiz through on day trips from Huaraz, consider spending the night: if you can see this impressive archaeological site in the morning, chances are you'll have it all to yourself.

## Sights & Activities

**CHAVÍN DE HUÁNTAR** Archaeological Site

**(adult/student S10/5; 9am-5pm Tue-Sun)**

This stupendous complex – a series of large temple structures with labyrinthine underground passageways – was one of many relatively independent ceremonial centers for 700 years starting in 1000 BC. Although squatters built on top of the ruins or carried away stone works, and a huge landslide covered part of the area in 1945, this site is still intact enough to provide a full-bodied glimpse into one of Peru's oldest societies.

At the heart of the complex is a massive sunken **square**, with an intricate and well-engineered system of channels for drainage. From here, a broad staircase leads up to the most important building, the **Castillo**. Built on three different levels, the walls here were at one time embellished with *tenons* (keystones of large projecting blocks carved to resemble human heads with animal traits or perhaps hallucinogen-induced characteristics). A series of **tunnels** underneath this structure comprise a maze of complex alleys and chambers. At the heart of this is an exquisitely carved (somewhat terrifying) 4.5m rock of white granite known as the **Lanzón de Chavín**, which represents a person with snakes radiating from the head.

Several construction quirks, such as the strange positioning of water channels and the use of highly polished minerals to reflect light, led Stanford archaeologists to believe that the complex was used as an instrument of shock and awe. Here, priests could manipulate light and sound, blowing on strombus trumpets and amplifying the rush of running water in the channels. The disoriented were probably given hallucinogens before entering the darkened maze. These tactics endowed religious leaders with an awe-inspiring power.

To get the most from your visit, it's worth hiring a guide to show you around (S30) or go on a guided day trip from Huaraz.



The Cordilleras

## The Art of Chavín

Named after the archeological site at Chavín de Huántar, the era known simply as Chavín (1000 BC to 300 BC) is considered a major turning point in the development of art and culture in Peru. Though not necessarily a full-blown civilization, it was a time when a common culture arose around the deity of a feline (either a jaguar or puma), though condors, eagles and snakes are also represented.

These figures are highly stylized and cover a number of extraordinary objects, including the Tello Obelisk at the Museo Nacional de Chavín (p253), the Lanzón, which stands in mystical glory in the tunnels underneath the Chavín site, and the Raimondi Stela at the Museo Nacional de Antropología, Arqueología e Historia del Perú in Lima (p69).

The latter has carvings of a human figure, sometimes called the Staff God, with a jaguar face and large staffs in each hand – an image that is believed to indicate a belief in a tripartite universe consisting of heavens, earth and underworld. It has shown up at archaeological sites along the coasts of Peru, suggesting a large area of influence.

**MUSEO NACIONAL DE CHAVÍN** Museum

**(admission free; ⌚9am-5pm, closed Mon)** Funded jointly by the Peruvian and Japanese governments, this excellent new museum adjacent to the archaeological site houses most of the intricate *tenons,* as well as the magnificent Tello Obelisk, a stone object with relief carvings of a caiman and other fierce animals.

**QUERCOS THERMAL BATHS** Hot Springs

**(admission S3)** If your muscles need a break, take a soak in one of the four private baths or the larger pool. It's a 30-minute walk south of town.

###  Sleeping & Eating

Restaurants tend to close after sunset, so dig in early.

**HOSTAL CHAVÍN TURÍSTICO** Guesthouse $$

**(☎45-4051; soniavalenciapozo@hotmail.com; Maytacapac 120; s/d S40/80; @)** This family-run option has well-appointed, clean-as-a-whistle rooms and large bathrooms. Although it doesn't offer internet per se, the owners do have a 3G modem that you can use with your either your own laptop or theirs.

**BUONGIORNO** Peruvian $$

**(Calle 17 de Enero Sur s/n; mains S17-38; ⌚7am-7pm)** You'll find sophisticated dishes in a garden setting, including a *lomo a la pimienta* (pepper steak) that is three-star Lima quality. Atmosphere takes a dive at dinner – go at lunch.

**CAFETERÍA RENATO** Cafe $

**(Plaza de Armas; breakfast S3-12; ⌚from 7am)** This cozy place serves yummy local and international breakfasts alongside homemade yogurt, cheese and *manjar blanco* (caramel). The cafe also has a lovely garden.

### Information

Multiple bus companies make the three-hour trip back and forth to Huaraz. Tour agencies in Huaraz also arrange trips to the area (for more information see p243).

# Trujillo

01 / POP 54,000

Stand in the right spot and the glamorously colonial streets of this coastal settlement look like they've barely changed in hundreds of years (except for the honking taxis). Founded by Francisco Pizarro, the city has a reputation for being independent-minded. In 1820 it was the first Peruvian city to declare independence from Spain. And, in the 20th century, it was here that the populist workers' party Alianza Popular Revolucionaria Americana (APRA) was founded, and where many of its members were later massacred.

Today, Trujillo remains a vibrant center of art and culture. (It's the home of Peru's national dance – the *marinera*.) It is also conveniently situated alongside some of the country's most incredible pre-Columbian sites, including the behemoth Chimú capital of Chan Chan and the Moche ceremonial sites of Huacas del Sol y de la Luna (Temples of the Sun and Moon), which date back 1500 years.

## Sights

The downtown area is chock-full of colonial buildings and churches that make for excellent photo ops, only a few of which are listed here. Hours can be erratic.

### PLAZA DE ARMAS — Plaza

Trujillo's spit-shined main square hosts a colorful assembly of preserved colonial buildings. Elegant mansions abound. To the northeast, the plaza is fronted by the **Basilica Menor Catedral** (Cathedral; 10-11am), which dates back to 1647 and contains a **museum** of religious and colonial art.

### CASA GANOZA CHOPITEA — Historic Building

**(Independencia 630)** Northeast of the cathedral, this 18th-century colonial mansion is one of the best preserved in Trujillo. Stunning details include an elaborate gateway entrance, 300-year-old frescoes, Oregon pine pillars and beam ceilings, some of which are tied together with sheepskin. In addition to myriad other treasures, the building is also home to the wonderful café **Casona Deza**.

### CASA DE URQUIAGA — Historic Building

**(Pizarro 446; 9:15am-3:15pm Mon-Fri, 10am-1pm Sat)** Owned and maintained by Banco Central de la Reserva del Perú since 1972, this beautiful colonial mansion's history dates to the 17th century. It now houses exquisite period furniture (and a working bank), including a writer's desk once used by Simón Bolívar.

Frieze of a Moche deity, Huaca de la Luna (p265)

# Trujillo

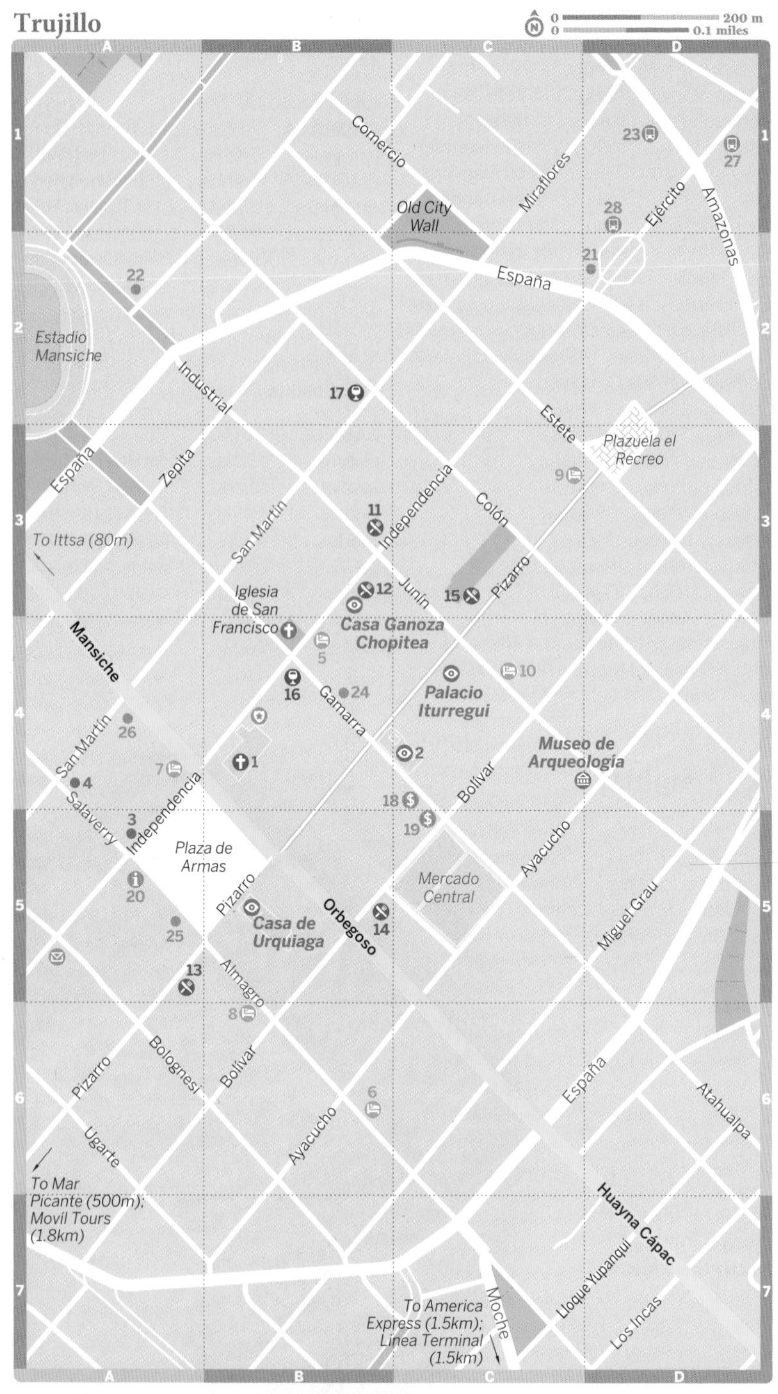
0 200 m
0 0.1 miles
Comercio
Miraflores
Old City Wall
Ejército
Amazonas
España
Estadio Mansiche
Industrial
Estete
Plazuela el Recreo
España
Zepita
Colón
Independencia
San Martín
To Ittsa (80m)
Junín
Pizarro
Iglesia de San Francisco
Casa Ganoza Chopitea
Mansiche
Palacio Iturregui
Gamarra
Museo de Arqueología
San Martín
Bolívar
Salaverry
Independencia
Plaza de Armas
Ayacucho
Mercado Central
Pizarro
Casa de Urquiaga
Orbegoso
Miguel Grau
Almagro
Bolognesi
Bolívar
Pizarro
España
Atahualpa
Ayacucho
Ugarte
To Mar Picante (500m); Movil Tours (1.8km)
Huayna Cápac
Lloque Yupanqui
To America Express (1.5km); Linea Terminal (1.5km)
Moche
Los Incas

## Trujillo

**Top Sights**
- Casa de Urquiaga ..... B5
- Casa Ganoza Chopitea ..... B3
- Museo de Arqueología ..... C4
- Palacio Iturregui ..... C4

**Sights**
1. Basilica Menor Catedral ..... B4
2. Casa de la Emancipación ..... C4

**Activities, Courses & Tours**
3. Chan Chan Tours ..... A5
4. Trujillo Tours ..... A4

**Sleeping**
5. Hostal Colonial ..... B4
6. Hostal Solari ..... B6
7. Hotel Libertador ..... A4
8. Los Conquistadores Hotel ..... B6
9. Pullman Hotel ..... C3
10. Saint Germain Hotel ..... C4

**Eating**
11. Café Bar Museo ..... B3
12. Casona Deza ..... B3
13. Chifa Heng Lung ..... A5
14. Juguería San Agustín ..... B5
15. Restaurant Demarco ..... C3

**Drinking**
16. El Celler de Cler ..... B4
17. Restaurante Turístico Canana ..... B2

**Information**
18. BCP ..... C4
19. HSBC ..... C5
20. iPerú ..... A5

**Transport**
21. Combis to Chan Chan, Huanchaco & Huaca Esmeralda ..... D2
22. Combis to Chan Chan, Huanchaco & Huaca Esmeralda ..... A2
23. Cruz del Sur ..... D1
24. Cruz del Sur Booking Office ..... B4
25. LAN ..... A5
26. Línea Booking Office ..... A4
27. Oltursa ..... D1
28. Ormeño ..... D1

**PALACIO ITURREGUI** Historic Building
**(Pizarro 688; adult S5; 8-10am Mon-Sat)**
A canary yellow 19th-century mansion is impossible to ignore unless you're color-blind. Built in neoclassical style, it has beautiful window gratings, slender interior columns and gold moldings on the ceilings. General Juan Manuel Iturregui lived here after he famously proclaimed independence. Note the limited operating hours.

**MUSEO DE ARQUEOLOGÍA** Museum
**(Junín 682; adult/child S5/1; 9am-5pm Mon-Sat, to 1pm Sun)** This well-curated museum has artifacts from the Moche, Chimú and Inca cultures. But it's worth popping in for the building itself: a restored 17th-century mansion with striking cedar pillars.

**CASA DE LA EMANCIPACIÓN** Historic Building
**(Pizarro 620; 9am-1pm & 4-8pm Mon-Sat)** Now the Banco Continental building, this building is where Trujillo's independence from colonial rule was formally declared on December 29, 1820.

**MUSEO CASSINELLI** Museum
**(N de Piérola 607; admission S7; 9am-1pm & 3-6pm Mon-Sat)** One of the more unusual archaeological museums in Peru, this private collection is housed in the basement of a Repsol gas station. It contains some 2000 ceramic pieces on display – including bird-shaped whistling pots which each produce unique notes.

## Tours

Dozens of agencies offer day tours of the city (S53 per person), as well as group excursions to nearby pre-Columbian sites (S60–S70). Note that admission to archaeological sites is generally *not* included in the tour price. If you prefer a private guide, ask at iPerú for a list of certified guides.

## Detour: Complejo Arqueológico la Huaca el Brujo

This **archaeological complex** (admission negotiable; h9am-5pm) consists of various sites: Huaca Prieta, the recently excavated Moche site of Huaca Cao Viejo and Huaca el Brujo, which is only starting to be excavated. The best site for visitors is the Huaca Cao Viejo, a 27m truncated pyramid with some of the best friezes in the area. They show magnificently multicolored reliefs with stylized life-sized warriors, prisoners, priests and human sacrifices.

The complex is 60km from Trujillo and is hard to find without a guide. It's technically not open to the public, but tour agencies in Trujillo can arrange a visit.



The following agencies are recommended:

**Trujillo Tours** (23-3091; www.trujillotours.com; Almagro 301; 7:30am-1pm & 4-8pm)

**Chan Chan Tours** (24-3016; chanchantourstrujillo@hotmail.com; Independencia 431; 8am-1pm & 3-8pm)

## Sleeping

Hotels can get noisy if you get street-side rooms. Book well in advance in late September, when places fill up for the International Spring Festival.

**HOSTAL COLONIAL** Historic Hotel $$
(25-8261; www.hostalcolonial.com.pe; Independencia 618; s/d/tr S60/90/120; ) The tastefully renovated, rose-colored colonial mansion (now HI-affiliated, though not a hostel) has a great location just a block from the Plaza de Armas. Helpful staff, a popular cafe (with room service) and gorgeous courtyards keep travelers coming back.

**HOTEL LIBERTADOR** Historic Hotel $$$
(23-2441; www.libertador.com.pe; Independencia 485; s/d S475/510, ste from S668.80, all incl breakfast; ) The grand dame of the city's hotels, the 79-room Libertador is in a building that wears its age with refined grace. Set around a bright three-story atrium, the rooms come stocked with all the expected amenities and there are archways aplenty – as well as a lush courtyard pool.

**PULLMAN HOTEL** Hotel $$$
(47-1645; Pizarro 879; s/d S74/92; ) On a pedestrian street near the Plazuela el Recreo, this modern hotel doesn't suffer much from street noise. Neat and spotless, the parquet- or tile-floored rooms feature modern amenities, including LCD televisions. The front desk couldn't be friendlier and the pottery-walled atrium is pleasant.

**LOS CONQUISTADORES HOTEL** Hotel $$
(48-1650; www.losconquistadoreshotel.com; Almagro 586; s/d incl breakfast S200/240; ) A few steps away from the Plaza de Armas, this discerning, 54-room choice got a modern makeover in 2012. New rooms ooze contemporary elegance, dressed up in soft creams and whites, and there's a classic hotel bar for a pisco sour nightcap.

**HOSTAL SOLARI** Hotel $$
(24-3909; www.hostalsolari.com.pe; Almagro 715; s/d with breakfast S80/130; ) A borderline contemporary spot, this place has massive, sensibly decorated rooms, which feature polished floorboards, a separate sitting/luggage-storage area, fine mattresses, Aquos LCD TVs and minifridges. A cafe provides room service and the helpful front-desk staff can arrange tours.

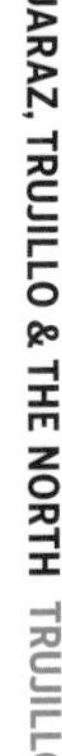
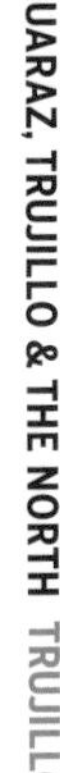


## Eating

**MAR PICANTE** Seafood **$$**

**(Húsares de Junín 412; www.marpicante.com; mains S18-30; 10am-5pm)** Don't leave Trujillo without sampling the *ceviche mixto* at this bamboo-lined seafood palace. A mound of citrus-marinated shrimp, fish, crab, scallops and onions are piled on top of yucca and sweet potato with a side of toasted *cancha* (corn). Service is swift and friendly – no small feat considering it's always packed. A taxi here costs S4.

**CASONA DEZA** Cafe **$**

**(Independencia 630; mains S10-25; )** This atmospheric cafe occupies one of the city's most fiercely preserved colonial homes: the Casa Ganoza Chopitea. Expect excellent espresso, house-made desserts and tasty pizzas, served in an airy courtyard or in one of the antiques-lined rooms.

**JUGUERÍA SAN AUGUSTÍN** Juice Bar **$**

**(Bolívar 526; juices S2-5, sandwiches S6-7; 8:30am-1pm & 4-8pm Mon-Sat, 9am-1pm Sun)** You can spot this place by the near-constant lines snaking around the corner as locals queue for the drool-inducing juices and *lechón* (suckling pig) sandwiches, slathered with all the fixings.

**RESTAURANT DEMARCO** Peruvian **$$**

**(Pizarro 725; mains S10-45; 7:30am-11pm; )** With veteran cummerbund-bound waiters, this elegant classic offers a long list of sophisticated meat and seafood dishes, along with some good-value lunch specials. It has mouthwatering *chupe de camarones* (a gumbo of shrimp simmering in a buttery broth), and the mile-high *tres leches* cake is excellent.

Chimú reliefs on Huaca Arco Iris (p263), Chan Chan

DEA / G. DAGLI ORTI/GETTY IMAGES ©

**CHIFA HENG LUNG** Chinese **$$**

**(Pizarro 352; mains S10.50-42.50; to 11:30pm)** Owned by a Chinese family of veteran chefs, this vaguely upscale, tasty option features a menu of Cantonese dishes that is long on options and flavors.

**CAFÉ BAR MUSEO** Cafe **$**

**(cnr Junín & Independencia; mains S6-15, cocktails S18-22; closed Sun)** The tall, wood-paneled walls and classic marble-top bar make this place feel like a cross between an English pub and a Left Bank café.

## Drinking & Entertainment

**EL CELLER DE CLER** Bar

**(cnr Gamarra & Independencia; cocktails S12-18; 6pm-1am)** The perfect atmospheric spot for a drink on a 2nd-story colonial balcony that dates to the early 1800s. There is food (mains S12–S24), but it's the cocktails that shine, with contemporary renditions of classic drinks.

Chimú ruins, Chan Chan (p261)

MARC SHANDRO/GETTY IMAGES ©

**RESTAURANTE TURÍSTICO CANANA** Live Music

(San Martín 791; admission S20; from 11pm Thu-Sat) It's a restaurant, but go late – from Thursday to Saturday – when local musicians and dancers perform, starting at around 11pm. You just might find yourself joining in...

## Information

### Dangers & Annoyances

Single women tend to receive a lot of attention from males in Trujillo – to exasperating levels. Firmly state you aren't interested. Inventing a boyfriend or husband sometimes helps. See p351 for more advice.

Like many other cities, noise pollution levels are high.

### Emergency

**Policía de Turismo** (Tourist Police, Poltur; 29-1770; Independencia 572)

### Medical Services

**Clínica Americano-Peruano** (24-5181; Mansiche 810) The best general medical care in town.

### Money

Numerous banks change foreign currency and come equipped with 24-hour ATMs.

**BCP** (Gamarra 562) Has the lowest commission for changing traveler's checks.

**HSBC** (Gamarra 574) Fee-less ATM.

### Tourist Information

**iPerú** (29-4561; cnr Almagro 420; 9am-6pm Mon-Sat, 10am-2pm Sun) Provides tourist information and a list of certified guides and travel agencies.

## Getting There & Away

### Air

The **airport** (code TRU; 46-4013) is 10km northwest of town. Both **LAN** (22-1469; www.lan.com; Almagro 490) and **Taca** (0-800-1-8222; www.taca.com; César Vallejo Oeste 1345, Real Plaza) have multiple daily flights.

### Bus

Buses fill up, so buy tickets in advance.

Some companies depart from the north end of town, at España and Amazonas, while others, going to southern destinations, have terminals on the Panamericana Sur, separate from the ticket office. Double-check the point of departure when buying a ticket. The following are recommended long-haul companies:

**Cruz del Sur** (**☎26-1801; www.cruzdelsur.com.pe; Amazonas 437**) It also has a **booking office** (**Gamarra 439; ⏱9am-9pm Mon-Sat**) in the city center. Travels all over Peru.

**Ittsa** (**☎25-1415; www.ittsabus.com; Mansiche 143**) Buses for Máncora and Lima.

**Línea** (**☎24-5181; cnr San Martín & Orbegoso; ⏱8am-8pm Mon-Fri**) Good for points north.

**Móvil Tours** (**☎28-6538; www.moviltours.com.pe; America Sur 3959, Óvalo Larco**) Also good for the north; travels to Chachapoyas.

**Oltursa** (**☎26-3055; www.oltursa.pe; Ejército 342**) Travels all over the country.

**Ormeño** (**☎25-9782; www.grupo-ormeno.com.pe; Ejército 233**) Major company covering all of Peru, including Máncora.

## Getting Around

A taxi to the airport from the city center will cost about S15, while taxis for sightseeing charge S20 to S25 an hour.

One-way taxi rides to the pre-Columbian ruins that surround Trujillo generally cost S10 to S15.

A minivan bus system connects points around the city. These also go past some of the big archeological sites. Fares are only S2, but watch for pickpockets.

# Around Trujillo

The Moche and Chimú cultures left the greatest marks on the Trujillo area, but they were by no means the only cultures in the region. In a March 1973 *National Geographic* article, Drs ME Moseley and CJ Mackey claimed knowledge of more than 2000 sites in the Río Moche valley and many more have been discovered since.

Five of these sites are of interest to travelers, including the adobe city of Chan Chan and the Moche pyramids of Las Huacas del Sol y de la Luna. The entrance ticket for Chan Chan is valid for the Chimú sites of Huaca Esmeralda and Huaca Arco Iris, as well as the Chan Chan museum, but it must be used within two days. Tickets are sold at every site, except La Huaca Esmeralda.

For the most part, the ruins are best reached via taxi or group tour.

## Sights

**CHAN CHAN** Ruins

(**admission S11; ⏱9am-4:30pm**) Built around AD 1300 and covering 36 sq km, Chan Chan is the largest pre-Columbian city in the Americas and the largest adobe city in the world. At the height of the Chimú empire, it housed an estimated 60,000 inhabitants and contained a vast wealth of gold, silver and ceramics (which the Spanish quickly looted). Over time,

### Around Trujillo

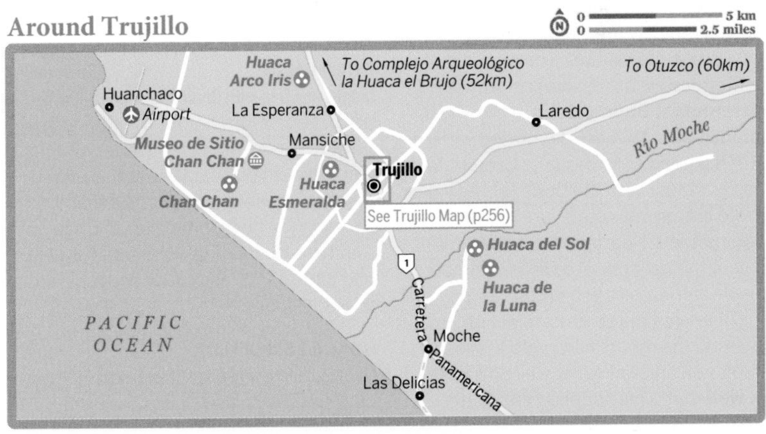

**Right:** *Caballitos de totora* (reed boats), Huanchaco;
**Below:** Seashell necklaces
(BELOW) ANDREW WATSON/GETTY IMAGES ©; (RIGHT) ANDREW WATSON/GETTY IMAGES ©

devastating El Niño floods and heavy rainfall have severely eroded the mud walls of the city – you'll need an active imagination to fill in the details. Today the most impressive aspect of the site is its sheer size.

The area known as the **Tschudi Complex** – also called the Palacio Nik-An – is the only area within the site that is open to visitors. The complex's centerpiece is a massive restored **Ceremonial Courtyard**, with 4m-thick interior walls that are decorated with re-created geometric designs. Ground-level designs closest to the door, representing three or four sea otters, are the only originals left. Nearby, an outside wall – one of the best restored in the complex – displays friezes of fish and seabirds.

Other elements include a set of labyrinthine rooms filled with friezes of birds, fish and waves, as well as a **walk-in well** that once supplied the daily water needs of the royal compound. Also on view is a **Mausoleum**, where a king was buried with human sacrifices, as well as the fascinating **Assembly Room**, a large rectangular room with 24 seats set into niches in the walls. Its acoustic properties are such that speakers sitting in any one of the niches can be clearly heard all over the room.

**MUSEO DE SITIO CHAN CHAN** Museum

**(admission free with Chan Chan ticket)** On the main road, 500m before the Chan Chan turnoff, you'll find this museum, which contains exhibits explaining the Chimú culture. The aerial photos and maps showing the huge extension of Chan Chan are fascinating. Here you will also find bathrooms, as well as souvenir and snack vendors.

**HUACA ESMERALDA** Ruins

**(admission free with Chan Chan ticket)** Halfway between Trujillo and Chan Chan, this

temple was discovered, buried in the sand, by an unsuspecting landowner in 1923. Although little restoration work has been done to its adobe friezes, it is still possible to make out the characteristic Chimú designs of fish, seabirds, waves and fishing nets.

Note: thieves reportedly prey on unwary tourists wandering around. It is best to go with a group or guide.

**HUACA ARCO IRIS** Ruins

**(Rainbow Temple; admission free with Chan Chan ticket)** Also known locally as Huaca del Dragón, this temple is in the suburb of La Esperanza, about 4km northwest of Trujillo. Dating from the 12th century, it is one of the best preserved of the Chimú temples – simply because it was buried under sand until the 1960s.

The *huaca* (tomb) used to be painted, but these days only faint traces of its yellow hues remain. It consists of a defensive wall more than 2m thick enclosing an area of about 3000m square, which houses the temple itself. The walls are slightly pyramidal and covered with repeating rainbow designs, most of which have been restored. A ramp leads to the very top of the temple, from where a series of large bins, found to contain the bones of infants – possibly human sacrifices – can be seen.

There is a tiny on-site **museum**, and local guides are available to show you around.

## Huanchaco

044 / POP 41,900

This once-tranquil fishing hamlet, 12km outside Trujillo, woke up one morning to find itself an international beach destination. Though the beach is distinctly average, it nonetheless manages to retain a certain village-y appeal. In fact, things change slowly here – so slowly that local fishermen are still using the very same narrow reed boats depicted on 2000-year-old Moche pottery. Fishers ride these neatly crafted boats like seafaring cowboys, with their legs dangling on either side – which explains the boats' nickname:

*caballitos de totora* (little reed horses). The inhabitants of Huanchaco are among the few remaining people on the coast who known how to construct and use them.

## Sights & Activities

**SANTUARIO DE LA VIRGEN DEL SOCORRO** Church

(9am-12:30pm & 4-7pm) This church above town is worth a visit. Built between 1535 and 1540, it is said to be the second-oldest church in Peru. There are sweeping views from the restored belfry.

**SURFING & SWIMMING** Water Sports

The curving, gray-sand beach is fine for swimming from December to April; expect serious teeth-chatter during the rest of the year. The surf is good for beginners and has its regular followers.

You can rent surfing gear (S15 to S30 per day for a wet suit and surfboard) or take lessons from several places, including **Muchik** (63-4503; www.escueladetablamuchik.com; Larco 650) and **Un Lugar** (94-957-7170; www.unlugarsurfschoolperu.com; Atahualpa 225), two blocks back from the beach road.

## Sleeping

**HOSTAL CABALLITO DE TOTORA** Boutique Hotel $$

(46-1154; www.hotelcaballitodetotora.com.pe; La Rivera 348; s S35, d/ste from S90/360, all incl breakfast; ) Although regular rooms can be a little stuffy, the suites here are the best single rooms in Huanchaco, decked out in modern motifs that wouldn't be out of place in Miami. They offer perfect sea views; wide, circular tubs and private patios to boot. A cozy bar adds to the ambience.

**HOTEL BRACAMONTE** Hotel $$

(46-1162; www.hotelbracamonte.com.pe; Los Olivos 160; s/d/tr incl breakfast from S124/150/197; ) Though it resides behind high walls and a locked gate, this is a welcoming spot. Nice gardens, a games room, barbecue, restaurant, bar and toddlers' playground make it great for families. The most resortlike of the bunch.

**HOSPEDAJE OCEANO** Guesthouse $

(46-1653; www.hospedajeoceano.com; Los Cerezes 105; r/tr from S40/60; ) Ideally situated between one of town's most lush and pleasant *plazoletas* and the ocean, this superbly welcoming family-run spot has great Mediterranean-tilted rooms that feel like a pleasant surprise. Best of all? The family makes addictive homemade *cremoladas* (Italian ices; S2).

## Eating & Drinking

Huanchaco has oodles of seafood restaurants, especially near the *caballitos de tortora* stacked at the north end of the beach. On weekends, *trujillanos* descend on the town and things are a little more lively.

**RESTAURANT BIG BEN** Seafood $$

(Larco 836; www.bigbenhuanchaco.com; mains S17-40; 11:30am-5:30pm; ) This sophisticated seafooder at the north end of town specializes in lunchtime ceviches (S39 to S46). The menu is also heavy on fresh fish, *sudados* (seafood stews) and prawn dishes, all of which go down even better on the umbrella-dotted 3rd-floor patio with views.

**OTRA COSA** Vegetarian $

(Larco 921; dishes S6-13; from 8am; ) This Dutch-Peruvian beachside pad serves up yummy vegetarian victuals like falafel, crepes, Spanish tortillas, Dutch apple pie and tasty curry-laced burritos. The coffee is organic.

**MOCOCHO** Seafood $$

(Bolognesi 535; 3-course meal S45; 1-3pm, closed Mon) In a secluded walled garden, the legend of chef Don Victor is carried on by his widow and son, Wen. Local fishers stop by every morning to announce the catch of the day, and Wen, the only Chinese-Peruvian restaurateur in town, serves up just two dishes with whatever's fresh that day. It's not cheap, but it's fresh and excellent.

DANITA DELIMONT/GETTY IMAGES ©

## Don't Miss Huacas del Sol y de la Luna

The Temples of the Sun and the Moon are a pair of **adobe pyramids** that reside on the south side of the Río Moche. Built by the Moche culture, 700 years prior to the construction of Chan Chan, the **Huaca del Sol** is the largest single pre-Columbian structure in Peru (though a third of it has been washed away). It was built with an estimated 140 million adobe bricks, many of them marked with symbols representing the workers who made them.

At one time the pyramid consisted of several different levels connected by steep flights of stairs, huge ramps and walls sloping at 77 degrees. Unfortunately, the last 1500 years have wrought their inevitable damage. But the size alone makes this an awesome sight and the views from the top are excellent.

The smaller, but more interesting, **Huaca de la Luna** is about 500m away across the open desert. This structure is riddled with rooms that contain ceramics, precious metals and some of the beautiful polychrome friezes for which the Moche were famous. The *huaca* (tomb) was built over six centuries to AD 600, with six succeeding generations completely covering the previous structure. Archaeologists are currently onion-skinning selected parts of the *huaca* and have discovered that there are friezes of stylized figures on every level. It's well worth a visit; you'll see newly excavated friezes every year.

As you leave, check out the souvenir stands, some of which sell pots made using the original molds found at the site. Also look around for a *perro biringo,* the native Peruvian hairless dogs that hang out here.

The site is about 10km southeast of Trujillo via a rough road. The entrance price includes a guide.

**NEED TO KNOW**

admission S11; 🕒9am-4pm

## If You Like... Beach Towns

It's no Caribbean, but if you're going to beach it in Peru, the north coast is the place to do it. The main season runs from December to April, though you'll see surfers out all year. A couple of points of interest:

1 **PUERTO CHICAMA**
This old sugar port, about 90 minutes north of Trujillo, lays claim to one of the longest left-hand waves in the world. The town's not much to look at, but it attracts a bevy of international surfers and is home to Peru's National Surfing Championship. Waves can be found year-round, but the best time to ride is between March and June. Surf shops in Huanchaco arrange day trip trips. Otherwise, **El Inti** (☎57-6138; www.intisurfcamp.com; s/d/ste S45/80/150; @📶) has good rooms and impressive gourmet fare (S20 to S35).

2 **PUNTA SAL**
The long, curvy bay at Punta Sal, 25km north of Máncora, has fine sand and is dotted with rocky bits, but it's still great for a dip in the ocean. The sea here is calm, which means the area is particularly popular with families. The seaside **Hotel Punta Sal** (☎59-6700; www.puntasal.com.pe; s/d per person incl full board from S280/479, bungalows for 2 from S582; ❄@📶🏊) is a great option for those with little ones, full of distractions such as minigolf, banana-boat rides, table tennis, billiards and a wooden-decked pool. Grown-ups will dig the rainbow-colored bungalows with fabulous terraces.

**JUNGLE BAR BILY** Bar, Restaurant
**(Larco 420; cocktails S12-18; closed Mon;** 📶) Travelers gravitate to this quasi-Polynesian-themed bar due to location (across from the pier), good music and popular S15 ceviche.

### Information

See www.huanchacovivo.com for useful tourist information. Next to the *municipalidad* (town hall) are three ATMs that accept MasterCard and Visa cards.

### Getting There & Away

*Combis* (minibuses) between Huanchaco and Trujillo are frequent and cost about S2. A taxi costs S9 to S14.

## Chiclayo

☎074 / POP 256,900

Spanish missionaries founded this small rural community at a dusty oasis in the 16th century, and it has prospered ever since. In one of the first sharp moves in Peruvian real estate, the missionaries chose a spot that sits at the hub of vital trade routes connecting the coast, the highlands and the deep jungle. The result: a bustling coastal city that shows no signs of slowing down.

The town is light on tourist attractions, but its unique combination of exquisite regional cooking and surrounding pre-Columbian sites may inspire you to hang around for a couple of days.

### Sights

**PLAZA DE ARMAS AREA** Plaza
The central plaza is a great place to amble as it fills nightly with sauntering couples, evangelical preachers and an army of underemployed shoe shiners. To the east, find the **cathedral**, which was built in the late 19th century.

**MERCADO MODELO** Market
**(cnr Arica & Balta; ⏲9am-5pm)** This fascinating market sprawls for several blocks and is a thick maze of fresh produce, woven goods, live animals, fish, meats and, most interestingly, the *Mercado de Brujos* (witch doctors' market) in the southwest corner – a one-stop shop for whale bones, amulets, snake skins and vials of indeterminate tonics. This is a good spot to buy *huayruros* (red and black seeds that bring good fortune) as well as *seguros* (religious charms meant to ward off evil). As in any crowded market: watch your pockets.

**PASEO DE LAS MUSAS** Park

One of the stranger sights you'll see in northern Peru: a park chock-full of massive statues that pay homage to Greek mythology. It's a favorite photo-op spot for local newlyweds.

## Tours

Agencies offer frequent inexpensive tours of Sipán, Túcume, Ferreñafe and the museums in Lambayeque. Tours cost between S50 and S130, depending on whether entrance fees to museums are included.

**MOCHE TOURS** Guided Tour

(**23-4637; www.mochetourschiclayo.com.pe; Calle 7 de Enero 638; 8am-8pm Mon-Sat, to noon Sun)** Highly recommended for cheap daily tours with Spanish- or English-speaking guides.

**SIPÁN TOURS** Guided Tour

(**22-9053; www.sipantours.com; Calle 7 de Enero 772; 8:30am-1:30pm & 4:30-8:30pm)** Offers guided tours in Spanish.

## Sleeping

**HOTEL MOCHIKS** Boutique Hotel **$$**

(**20-6620; www.hotelmochiks.com; Tacna 615; s/d incl breakfast S135/180;** ) This newcomer made an immediate impression on the hotel scene in the city with its sense of style: public spaces are decked out in chromes and moody reds, which contrast perfectly with the 25 soothing (and smallish) beige-toned rooms. Everything is new and well maintained – and the trendiness is held in check with indigenous Moche touches.

**COSTA DEL SOL** Business Hotel **$$$**

(**22-7272; www.costadelsolperu.com; Balta 399; s/d incl breakfast S285/350;** ) This fully loaded business hotel (now part of the Ramada chain) is one of Chiclayo's best, with comfortable, modern rooms, swimming pool, gym, sauna and massage rooms.

**LATINOS HOSTAL** Hotel **$$**

(**23-5437; latinohotelsac@hotmail.com; Igaza 600; s/d S90/140;** ) An excellent

Produce at the *Mercado de Brujos* (witch doctors' market), Mercado Modelo

NIGEL HICKS/GETTY IMAGES ©

## Chiclayo

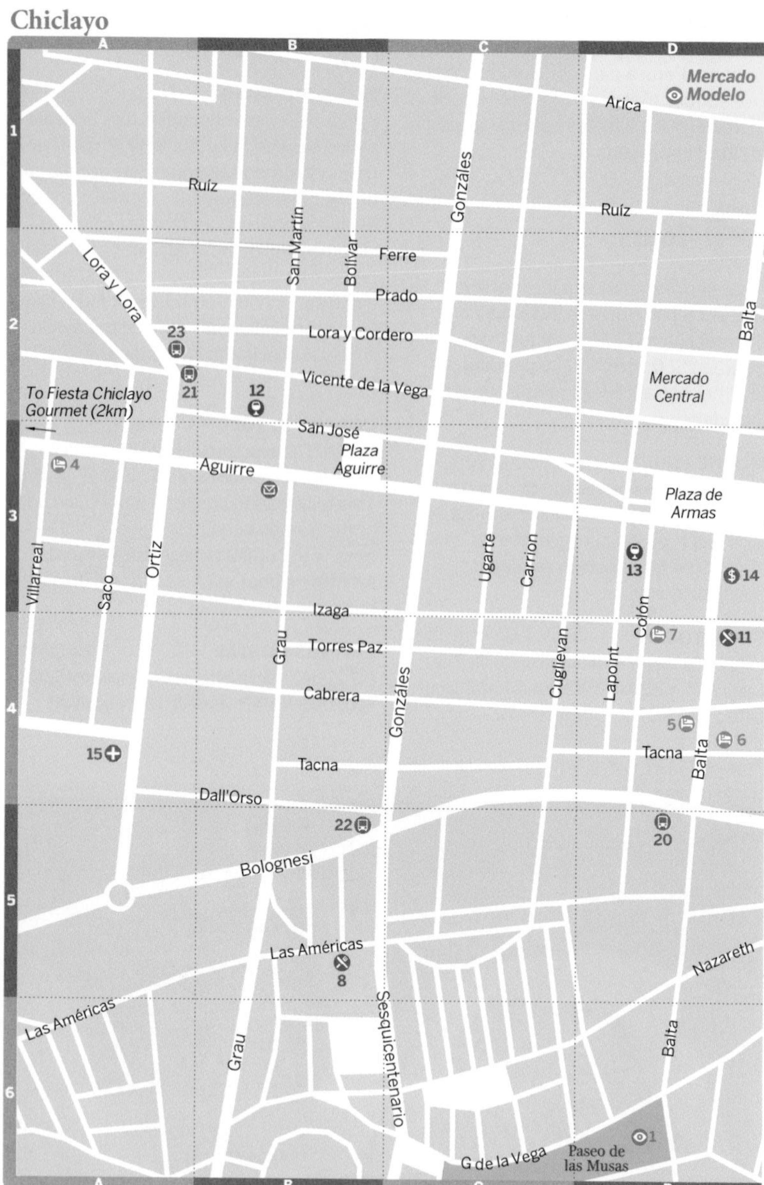


choice, this hotel is well maintained with perfect little rooms. Some of the corner units have giant curving floor-to-ceiling windows for great street views and plenty of light. The staff is very helpful.

**CASA ANDINA SELECT CHICLAYO** Boutique Hotel **$$$**
(**23-4911; www.casa-andina.com; Villarreal 115; r/ste incl breakfast S616/788;** ) The Peruvian boutique chain Casa Andina swooped in and gobbled up this aging

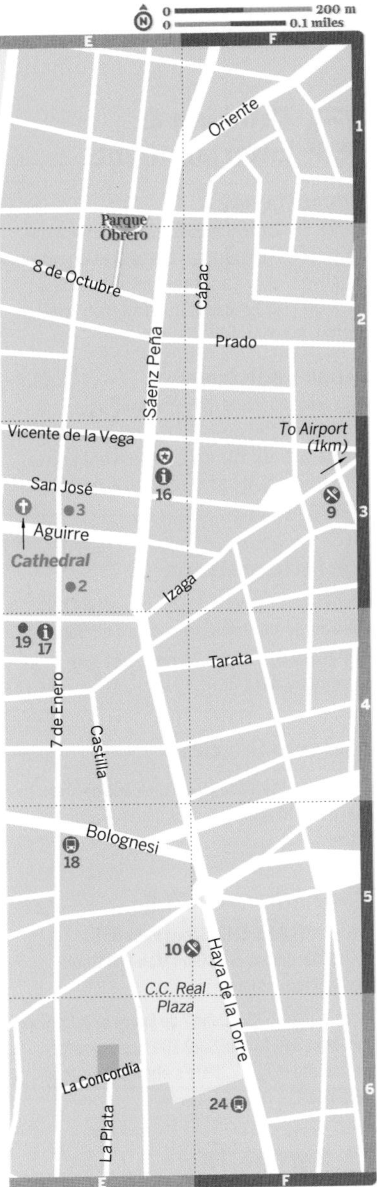


## Chiclayo

**Top Sights**

| | |
|---|---|
| Cathedral | E3 |
| Mercado Modelo | D1 |

**Sights**

| | |
|---|---|
| 1 Paseo de las Musas | D6 |

**Activities, Courses & Tours**

| | |
|---|---|
| 2 Moche Tours | E3 |
| 3 Sipán Tours | E3 |

**Sleeping**

| | |
|---|---|
| 4 Casa Andina Select Chiclayo | A3 |
| 5 Costa del Sol | D4 |
| 6 Hotel Mochiks | D4 |
| 7 Latinos Hostal | D4 |

**Eating**

| | |
|---|---|
| 8 El Ferrocol | B5 |
| 9 El Pescador | F3 |
| 10 Heladaría Hoppy | E5 |
| 11 Restaurant Romana | D4 |

**Drinking**

| | |
|---|---|
| 12 Sabor y Son Cubano | B2 |
| 13 Tribal Lounge | D3 |

**Information**

| | |
|---|---|
| 14 BCP | D3 |
| 15 Clínica del Pacífico | A4 |
| 16 Dircetur | E3 |
| 17 iPerú | E4 |

**Transport**

| | |
|---|---|
| 18 Cruz del Sur | E5 |
| 19 LAN | E4 |
| 20 Línea | D5 |
| 21 Minibuses to Lambayeque & Pimentel | A2 |
| 22 Móvil Tours | B5 |
| 23 Oltursa | A2 |
| Oltursa Sales Office | (see 11) |
| 24 Ormeño | F6 |

relic, formerly the Gran Hotel Chiclayo. A 100% makeover was underway during our visit (expected completion 2014). Presume superswankiness (for Chiclayo), including room service, spa, cappuccino bar, casino, fitness center, parking and a plaza sports bar.

## Eating

Chiclayo is a top dining destination on the north coast. *Arroz con pato a la chiclayana* (duck and rice cooked in cilantro and beer) and *tortilla de manta raya* (Spanish omelet made from stingray) are favorites.

**FIESTA CHICLAYO GOURMET** Peruvian $$$

(☎20-1970; www.restaurantfiestagourmet.com; Salaverry 1820; mains S35-49) Few things are as satisfying as scraping those last bits of slightly charred rice off the bottom of an iron-clad pan and savoring all that's great about a rice dish like *arroz con pato a la chiclayana*. But there's more: Fiesta also makes delectable tableside cocktails and a blindingly good *ceviche a la brasa* – the traditional dish served warm after a last-minute searing. The service is exquisite and the menu offers the best of this region's world-famous cuisine. Reserve ahead (especially on weekends).

A taxi here costs S5 from the center.

**EL PESCADOR** Seafood $

(San José 1236; mains S10-20; 11am-6pm) A local haunt that has outstanding seafood and regional dishes. The ceviches here are every bit as good as the expensive joints – and weekend specials like *cabrito con frijoles* (goat with beans; Saturday) and *arroz con pato* (duck with rice; Sunday) are steals.

**EL FERROCOL** Seafood $

(Las Américas 168; mains S13-27; 9am-7pm) This brash hole-in-the-wall, a little out of the center, is well worth the trip (though not for the service or atmosphere). Chef Lucho prepares some of the best ceviche in all of Chiclayo, served here with lovely *fried tortitas de choclo* (corn fritters).

**RESTAURANT ROMANA** Peruvian $$

(Balta 512; mains S13-25; 7am-1am; ) This popular place serves a bunch of different dishes, all of them local favorites. If you're feeling brave, try the *chirimpico:* stewed goat tripe and organs. If not, the *humitas* (a steamed fresh-corn cake) are tasty, plus there's an extensive egg menu, steaks, seafood, pasta, chicken and *chicharrones*.

**HELADARÍA HOPPY** Desserts $

(www.heladoshoppychiclayo.blogspot.com; Haya de la Torre, CC Open Plaza; scoops S3-7) If you're jonesin' for something other than industrialized ice cream, they do a decent job here with the homemade stuff. Good flavors include pisco sour and *lúcuma* (an earthy Andean fruit).

## Drinking & Entertainment

**TRIBAL LOUNGE** Bar

(Lapoint 682; cocktails S12-22; closed Mon) This rock-themed bar has good cocktails and live music (acoustic on Thursday, rock on Friday and Saturday from midnight). A great spot for a tipple.

**SABOR Y SON CUBANO** Bar, Club

(San José 155; cover S10; closed Sun) This spot gives the over-35 crowd somewhere to shake their rumps on the weekends, with tropical, classic salsa and merengue setting the pace.

## Information

Internet cafes abound, ATMs are plentiful and there are several banks off *cuadra 6* off Balta.

**BCP** (Balta 630) Has a 24-hour Visa and MasterCard ATM.

### Medical Services

**Clínica del Pacífico** (www.clinicadelpacifico.com.pe; Ortiz 420) The best medical assistance in town.

### Tourist Information

**Dircetur** (☎23-8112; Sáenz Peña 838; 7:30am-1pm & 2-4:30pm Mon-Fri) Good regional tourist info.

**iPerú** (☎20-5703; Calle 7 de Enero 579; 9am-6pm Mon-Sat, to 1pm Sun) The best spot for tourist info in town; there's another booth at the airport.

## Getting There & Away

### Air

The **airport** (CIX) is 1.5km east of town; a taxi ride there is S5. Among other airlines, **LAN** (☎27-4875; www.lan.com; Izaga 770) and **Taca** (☎0-800-1-8222; www.taca.com; Cáceres 222, CC Real Plaza) have daily flights to and from Lima.

## Bus

The minibus terminal at the corner of San José and Lora y Lora has regular buses to Lambayeque to visit the museums.

The following companies are recommended for long-distance travel:

**Cruz del Sur** (☎23-7965; www.cruzdelsur.com.pe; Bolognesi 888) Destinations around Peru.

**Ittsa** (☎23-3612; www.ittsabus.com; Grau 497) Destinations all over the northern coast.

**Línea** (☎23-2951; www.linea.pe; Bolognesi 638) Serves the north.

**Móvil Tours** (☎27-1940; www.moviltours.com.pe; Bolognesi 199) Daily buses to Chachapoyas and other northern points.

**Oltursa** (☎22-5611; www.oltursa.pe) Sales Office (cnr Balta & Izaga); Terminal (Vicente de la Vega 101) Serves destinations around Peru.

**Ormeño** (☎23-4206; www.grupo-ormeno.com.pe; Haya de la Torre 242) One of the bigger companies, with comfortable vehicles.

# Around Chiclayo

Given the doubling of guide prices in the last few years, it hardly makes sense to travel independently to most of the archaeological sites around Chiclayo – you'll find the organized tours far more convenient.

## Sights

**SIPÁN** Ruins

(Huaca Rayada; ☎80-0048; www.huacarajada sipan.cb.pe; admission S8; ⏲9am-5pm) Located about an hour east of Chiclayo, Sipán was initially discovered by grave robbers; in 1987 sharp-eyed archaeologist Walter Alva noticed an influx of pre-Columbian artifacts on the black market and realized that a burial site in the area was being ransacked. Careful questioning led him to this series of earthen mounds, which were actually disintegrating adobe pyramids that date back to AD 300. This discovery led to the untouched tomb of a major Moche leader known as El Señor de Sipán (Lord of Sipán), who was buried with hundreds of precious objects and numerous sacrificial beings.

Though little remains of the pyramids beyond a mound of earth, some of the tombs have been restored with replicas to show what they looked like more than 1500 years ago. Opposite the entrance is the **Museo de Sitio Sipán** (admission S8; entrance incl in site ticket; ⏲9am-5pm Mon-Fri), opened in 2009, which is worth a visit. Note that the most impressive artifacts were placed in the Museo Tumbas Reales de Sipán (p273) in Lambayeque.

Spanish- and English-speaking guides can be hired (S15). Daily guided tours are available from tour agencies in Chiclayo for around S50.

*Caballitos de totora* (reed boats), Huanchaco (p263)

ANDREW WATSON/GETTY IMAGES ©

**BRUNING MUSEUM** Museum

(☎28-2110, 28-3440; www.museobruning.com; Av Huamachuco s/n, Lambayeque; admission S8; ⏲9am-5pm) Situated in Lambayeque, this regional museum, once a regional archaeological showcase, is now greatly overshadowed by the Museo Tumbas Reales de Sipán. However, it still houses a good collection of artifacts from the Chimú, Moche, Chavín and Vicus cultures. Architecture and sculpture lovers may find some interest in the Corbusier-inspired building, bronze statues and tile murals adorning the property. Models of several important sites are genuinely valuable for putting the archaeology of the region into perspective. English-speaking guides charge S30.

**MUSEO NACIONAL SICÁN** Museum

(☎28-6469; http://sican.perucultural.org.pe; Av Batán Grande Cuadra 9 s/n, Ferreñafe; admission S8; ⏲9am-5pm Tue-Sun) Situated in Ferreñafe, about 18km north of Chiclayo, this splendid museum displays replicas of the 12m-deep tombs found in the area. These were among the largest ever found in South America, and the most enigmatic: the Lord of Sicán was buried upside down, in a fetal position, with his head separated from his body. Produced by the Sicán culture, which had its apogee in the Lambayeque area from AD 750 to 1375, these unusual exhibits are worth a trip.

Guided tours from Chiclayo travel here as part of a package deal that includes a visit to the nearby archaeological site of Túcume (which contains remnants of adobe pyramids) for about S50 per person.

## Chachapoyas

☎041 / POP 22,900 / ELEV 2335 M

From Chiclayo, a winding day's drive inland through the Andes brings you to the charming settlement of Chachapoyas. Also known as 'Chachas,' this laid-back little town, washed in white and insulated by a buffer of unpaved roads, is an excellent point from which to explore the awesome ancient ruins left behind by the Chachapoyas civilization ('People of the Clouds').

The Chachapoyas culture was never fully subdued by the Incas. As a result, the area has a stunning lack of Inca influence – a rarity in the Andes.

### Sights

Though Chachapoyas is charming, sights are few. Most travelers in the area use it as a base for exploring the surrounding countryside on day tours.

**KUÉLAP** Ruins

(adult/student/child S15/8/2; ⏲8am-5pm) Matched in grandeur only by the ruins of Machu Picchu, this mountaintop citadel 2½ hours southwest of Chachapoyas is the best preserved and most accessible of the district's extraordinary archaeological sites. Bonus: this monumental stone fortification, crowning a craggy limestone mountain, receives remarkably few visitors.

Constructed between AD 500 and 1493, and rediscovered in 1843, the site consists of a 700m-long fortress surrounded by an imposing, near-impenetrable wall that towers on average nearly 20m high. Though the stonework is not as elaborate as that of the Inca, there are some incredible structures here. The most impressive is named **El Tintero** (Inkpot), in the shape of a large inverted cone. There are also traditional **round houses** and a **lookout tower** with excellent 360-degree vistas. The mountain summit on which the whole city sits is surrounded by abundant greenery, towering bromeliad-covered trees and exotic orchids.

**KARAJÍA** Ruins

(admission S5) Less than an hour from Chachapoyas, a 45-minute hike from the village of Cruz Pata, this extraordinary funerary site hosts six sarcophagi perched high up a sheer cliff face. Each is constructed from wood, clay and straw and stares intently over the valley below. Only important individuals, such as shamans, warriors and chieftains, were buried with such reverence. The skulls on some sarcophagi are thought to have been trophies of enemies or possibly human sacrifices.

DANITA DELIMONT/GETTY IMAGES ©

## Don't Miss Museo Tumbas Reales de Sipán

Opened in 2002, this exceptional museum is the pride of northern Peru, containing all of the discoveries made in the Sipán tombs. This includes impossibly fine turquoise-and-gold ear ornaments, spectacularly reconstructed beadwork, dazzling pectoral plates representing sea creatures such as the octopus and crab, and mass amounts of ceramics – some of them displayed as they were found. Also on show: *narigueras* (nose shields). Since emperors were considered animal-gods, these served the purpose of concealing their all-too-human teeth.

The signage is all in Spanish, but English-speaking guides are available for S20. The museum lies in the town of Lambayeque, about 10km northwest of Chiclayo. A taxi here will cost about S12.

### NEED TO KNOW

**28-3977, 28-3988; www.tumbasreales.org; Vizcardo y Guzmán s/n, Lambayeque; adult/child S10/3; 9am-5pm Tue-Sun, last admission 4pm**

**CATARATA DE GOCTA** Waterfall

**(adult/child S5/1; 6am-4pm)** This 771m waterfall (the fifth tallest in the world) is dripping in lore about a mermaid who guards lost treasure. You might not see the mermaid, but you might see the bizarre orange bird called the Andean Cock-of-the Rock or, better yet, the rare and endemic Yellow-tailed Woolly Monkey. The falls are less than two hours from Chachapoyas.

**MUSEO LEIMEBAMBA** Museum

**(www.museoleymebamba.org; admission adult/student S15/8; 10am-4:30pm)** Located 2½ hours from Chachapoyas, in the village of Leimebamba, this small – surprisingly good – museum contains a trove of mummies and other artifacts from a tomb unearthed at Laguna de los Cóndores. Recommended.

## Tours

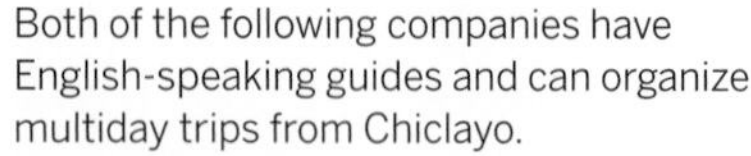

Both of the following companies have English-speaking guides and can organize multiday trips from Chiclayo.

**Chachapoyas Tours** (☎94-196-3327; www.kuelapperu.com; Santo Domingo 432) These guys get rave reviews for their day tours of the area. Reserve ahead.

**Turismo Explorer** (☎47-8162; www.turismoexplorerperu.com; Grau 509) A company with a great reputation specializing in multiday treks.

## Sleeping

**HOSTAL LAS ORQUÍDEAS** Guesthouse **$$**
(☎47-8271; www.hostallasorquideas.com; Ayacucho 1231; s/d incl breakfast S60/100; @ 📶) Friendly and good value, this upscale guesthouse offers bright, open and renovated tile-floor rooms, and a public area decorated with wood and artsy accents.

**CASA VIEJA HOSTAL** Boutique Guesthouse **$$**
(☎47-7353; www.casaviejaperu.com; Chincha Alta 569; s/d incl breakfast from S95/145; @ 📶) These very comfortable quarters in a converted mansion have handcrafted wood accents, fireplaces and big windows facing onto the verdant garden.

**CASA ANDINA** Hotel **$$**
(☎96-933-5840; www.casa-andina; Km 39 Carretera Pedro Ruíz; r/ste from S208/281; @ 📶 🏊) This Peruvian chain's latest offering is in a 21-room colonial-style hacienda in a sublime location down in the Utcubamba Valley surrounded by cherimoya plantations. Rooms aren't very interesting. But it doesn't really matter – this place is all about the riverside veranda.

## Eating

**EL TEJADO** Peruvian **$$**
(Santo Domingo 426; mains S15-25) It may not look like much from the outside, but a lovely courtyard dining room awaits inside. The specialty is *tacu tacu*, seen here in nine varieties. The *lomo saltado* is conversation-stopping good, especially when doused in the house hot pepper sauce.

**LA TUSHPA** Steakhouse **$**
(Ortiz Arrieta 753; mains S12-30) Service is infamously slow but always worth the wait at this classic Chachapoyas grill house. Try the *cuadril* (tri-tip), a succulent beef cut, and interesting creations such as *lomo fino* (sirloin) with a spicy pisco sauce.

**CAFÉ FUSIONES** Cafe **$**
(Chincha Alta 445; snacks S1.50-4.50, breakfast S6-9; ⏲from 7am Mon-Sat; 📶) The traveler congregation gathers at this artsy cafe serving organic coffee and great breakfasts.

## Information

There are internet cafes around town. BCP (Ortiz Arrieta) changes US dollars and traveler's checks and has an ATM. iPerú (☎47-7292; Arrieta 582; ⏲8am-7pm) has information and maps.

## Getting There & Away

Although Chachapoyas has an airport, at the time of writing no carriers flew in or out of it. Most travelers arrive via organized tours from Chiclayo, or on one of the long-haul bus services (also from Chiclayo). The following services are recommended:

Civa (☎47-8048; Salamanca 956)

Móvil Tours (☎47-8545; La Libertad 464)

# Máncora

☎073 / POP 9700

Peru's worst-kept secret, Máncora is the place to see and be seen along the Peruvian coast. In the summer months foreigners flock here to rub sunburned shoulders with the frothy cream of the local Peruvian jet set. You won't find it hard to see why – the best of Peru's sandy beaches stretches for several kilometers in the sunniest region of the country, while dozens of plush resorts offer up rooms within meters of the lapping waves. On shore, a plethora of restaurants provide seafood straight off the boat and

Beach football, Máncora

ANDREW WATSON/GETTY IMAGES ©



the raucous nightlife keeps visitors busy well after the sun dips into the sea.

Máncora has the Pan-American Hwy passing right through its middle, within 100m of the surf. Addresses are not used much here – just look for signs in the center.

## Activities

### Surfing & Kitesurfing

Surf here is best from November to February, although good waves are found year-round. You can rent surfboards from several places at the southern end of the beach in Máncora (per hour/day S10/20).

A few recommended outfitters:

**Máncora Surf Shop** (Piura 352) Sells boards, surf clothing and organizes lessons for about S50 per hour.

**Laguna Camp** (☎41-1587; www.vivamancora.com/lagunacamp) The friendly Pilar does surf lessons for S50 for 90 minutes of instruction, including board rental.

**Del Wawa** (☎25-8427; www.delwawa.com) Ask about kitesurfing lessons (per six hours S624).

### Other Activities

About 11km east of town, up the wooded Fernández valley, a natural **hot spring** (admission S2) has bubbling water and powder-fine mud – perfect for a face pack. It's slightly sulfurous, but is said to have curative properties. It can be reached by *mototaxi* (S35, including waiting time).

There are remote, deserted beaches around Máncora; ask your hotel to arrange a taxi. Just be prepared to walk – not all beaches lie right off the road.

## Tours

**IGUANA'S** Tour Company
(☎63-2762; www.iguanastrips.com; Piura 245) Organizes all manner of trips, from horseback riding to visits to the mud baths to sea kayaking.

## Sleeping

In the December to March summer period, accommodation prices tend to double, but year-round sun means that this is one of

the few coastal resort towns that doesn't turn into a ghost town at less-popular times. High-season rates are given here.

**SUNSET HOTEL** Boutique Hotel $$$
(☎25-8111; www.sunsetmancora.com; Antique Panamericana 196; s/d incl breakfast S180/250; ) The intimate, boutique-styled Sunset wouldn't be out of place on the cover of a glossy travel mag. It has aqua-themed rock sculptures and good-sized rooms with solid mattresses, hot showers, balconies and views of the seascape. The pool, however, is tiny and the ocean access, rocky. Though a short walk brings you to a sandy beach – if you can tear yourself away from the hotel's Italian restaurant, one of the area's best.

**CASA DE PLAYA** Resort $$
(☎25-8005; www.casadeplayamancora.net; Antigua Panamericana Km 1217; s/d incl breakfast S180/220; ) A wonderfully friendly place offering up slick dwellings colored in warm orange and yellow tones and constructed with lots of gently curving lines. Half the room interiors are dressed in smoothed exposed concrete – all have hot water, arty bits and a balcony with a hammock. An inviting two-story lounge hangs out over the sea.

**CLARO DE LUNA** Hotel $$
(☎25-8080; www.clarodelunamancora.com; Antigua Panamericana Km 1216; s/d incl breakfast S130/220; @) This spot gets rave reviews for its cozy, down-home atmosphere. Of the nine rooms, five face the sea and four face a small garden. The whole place channels a vague Santorini aesthetic. Two pools, a movie projection room, kayaks and an oceanside patio/lounge round out the picture.

**HOTELIER** Hotel $$
(☎25-8702; www.hotelier.pe; Antigue Panamericana Km 1217; s/d incl breakfast from S150/220; ) If you travel for food, this artsy choice is for you. The owner, Javier Ruzo, is the son of one of Peru's most famous chefs, Teresa Ocampo. He carries on the family tradition at the fabulous restaurant here, but beyond that, he's also an artist and photographer whose work gives unique personality to each of the rooms.

**DCO SUITES** Boutique Hotel $$$
(☎25-8171; www.hoteldco.com; ste incl breakfast from S710; @) This relative newcomer remains the discerning choice of jetsetters, rock stars, honeymooners and deep-pocketed nomads. The color scheme is a love-it-or-hate-it turquoise and white, but the spacious rooms come with his and her kimono-style robes, rain showers and lovely curved sandstone walls. Service, privacy and luxury are the trump cards here, whether it's on the curtained beach cabanas, at the remarkable outdoor spa or in the infinity pool.

Beachside souvenirs, Máncora
ANDREW WATSON/GETTY IMAGES ©

**HOSTAL LAS OLAS** Hotel **$$**
(☎25-8099; www.lasolasmancora.com; s/d/tr incl breakfast from S80/140/220; 📶) A great couples spot dons an olive skin tone on the outside and has minimalist white rooms with wood accents on the inside. Newer 2nd- and 3rd-floor rooms are larger with expansive terraces and ocean views. But avoid the cheapest rooms, which sit under a noisy staircase. The restaurant looks onto the beach's best breaks.

**LAGUNA SURF CAMP** Bungalow **$**
(☎99-401-5628; www.vivamancora.com/lagunacamp; Veraniego s/n; r per person S40; 📶🏊) This laid-back pad one block back from the beach is a rustic oasis, with older Indonesian-style bamboo bungalows set around a pleasant sandy garden. Shady hammocks comprise the entertainment. Four newer bungalows are more spacious. A pool is in the works.

## Eating & Drinking

Seafood rules the culinary roost in Máncora, with all manner of good and fresh ceviches, *majariscos* (a mix of seafood nibbles), *sudados* and just plain *pescado* (fish) on offer.

**LA SIRENA D'JUAN** Seafood **$$**
(☎25-8173; Piura 316; mains S30-35; 🕐closed Tue; 📶) Yellowfin tuna fresh from Máncora's waters is the showstopper here, whether it's prepared as a *tiradito* (Peruvian sashimi) in yellow curry or grilled with a mango-*rocoto*-red pepper chutney. It also offers creative ravioli and Peruvian classics (which have been given a food upgrade). Reserve ahead in the high season.

**DONDE TERESA** Seafood **$$$**
(☎25-8702; Antigue Panamericana Km 1217, Hotelier; mains S32-70; 📶) Before Gastón Acurio, there was Teresa Ocampo, Peru's most recognizable celebrity chef. She lives in Texas now, but her son, Javier, keeps the dream alive with smoked *ají de gallina* (spicy chicken and walnut stew), stir-fried seafood rice, yellowfin tuna, and a memorable pisco-dunked bread pudding. Call ahead in January, February and July.

**LAS GEMELITAS** Seafood **$$**
(Bastidas 154; mains S15-20) Three blocks off the Pan-American Hwy behind the Cruz del Sur office, this cane-walled restaurant does a bang-up ceviche – with an emphasis on spicy for a nice kick in the pants.

**GREEN EGGS AND HAM** Breakfast **$**
(Grau 503; meals S15 & S18; 🕐7:30am-4:30pm) This Dr Seuss–inspired breakfast spot serves battalions of gringos homesick-remedy breakfasts such as pancakes, French toast and hash browns. But the real coup is the 2nd-floor patio: a straight shot through a thatch of tall palms to the crashing waves.

**JUGERÍA MI JANETT** Juice Bar
(Piura 677; juices S3-6) The best juice place in town – come here for massive jugs of your favorite tropical fruit squeeze.

## Information

There is no information office, but the website www.vivamancora.com has tons of useful information. Two ATMs (no bank) accept Visa and MasterCard.

**Banco de la Nación** (Piura 625; 🕐8:30am-2:30pm Mon-Fri) Change US dollars here.

**Medical Center** (www.medicalcentermancora.com; Panamericana s/n; 🕐24 hr) If you get stung by a ray or break a bone, head to this full-service clinic at the north end of town.

## Getting There & Away

### Air

The nearest airport is in Piura, a 2 ½-hour ride south of Máncora. **LAN** (www.lan.com) and **Peruvian Airlines** (www.peruvian.pe) have regular service.

### Bus

Many bus offices are in the center, with regular minibuses running between Máncora and Punta Sal (30 minutes). The following companies are recommended for long-haul trips:

**Cruz del Sur** (☎25-8232; Grau 208)

**Oltursa** (☎25-8276; Piura 509)

**Tepsa** (☎25-8672; Grau 113)

# Iquitos & the Amazon

**It is a strange, sweltering, seductive country-within-a-country.** Peru's Amazon Basin has a vastness and an impenetrability that has long shielded it from the outside world. Remote tribes still exist in its depths and uncatalogued plants still grow in the tropical mist. In fact, more plant types flourish in a single hectare here than in any European country. And the fauna? Totally sci-fi.

But as the 21st century dawns on this expanse of wilderness, exploitation of the rainforest's abundant natural resources – be it oil or ranch land – threatens to irreversibly damage it. For now though, this lush wilderness is still a paradise for adventure-seekers. It offers phenomenal wildlife-spotting, exquisite forays into untamed forest and raucous city life unlike anything you'll experience elsewhere in Peru. Forge through it by road or river and you'll feel like the explorers who first brought international attention to this region.

Canopy walk in the Amazon Basin

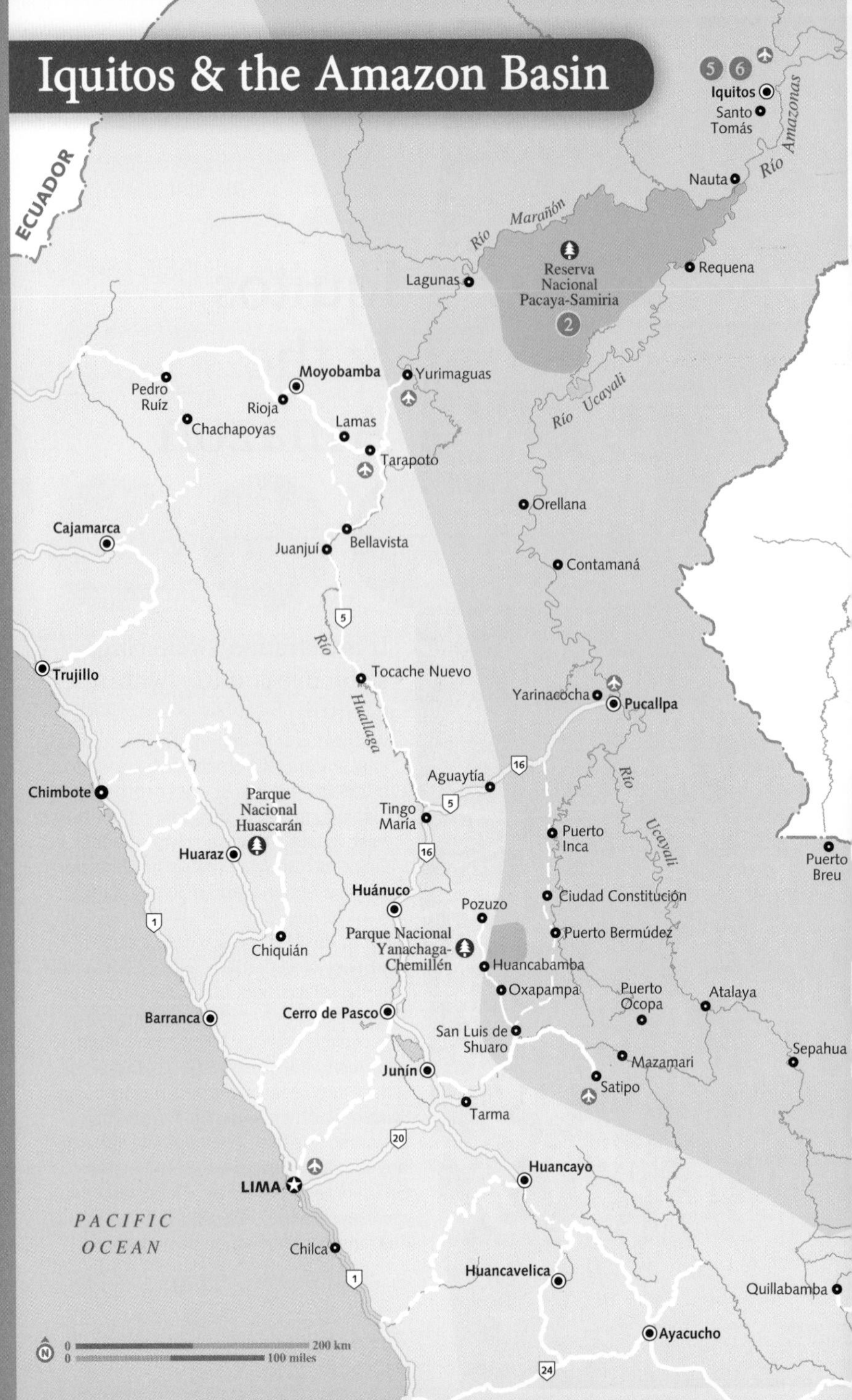

Iquitos & the Amazon Basin
ECUADOR
Iquitos
Santo Tomás
Río Amazonas
Nauta
Río Marañón
Reserva Nacional Pacaya-Samiria
Requena
Lagunas
Moyobamba
Yurimaguas
Pedro Ruíz
Rioja
Chachapoyas
Lamas
Tarapoto
Río Ucayali
Orellana
Cajamarca
Bellavista
Juanjuí
Contamaná
Río Huallaga
Trujillo
Tocache Nuevo
Yarinacocha
Pucallpa
Aguaytía
Chimbote
Parque Nacional Huascarán
Tingo María
Río Ucayali
Puerto Inca
Huaraz
Puerto Breu
Huánuco
Ciudad Constitución
Pozuzo
Parque Nacional Yanachaga-Chemillén
Puerto Bermúdez
Chiquián
Huancabamba
Oxapampa
Puerto Ocopa
Atalaya
Barranca
Cerro de Pasco
San Luis de Shuaro
Sepahua
Mazamari
Junín
Satipo
Tarma
Huancayo
LIMA
PACIFIC OCEAN
Chilca
Huancavelica
Quillabamba
Ayacucho
200 km
100 miles

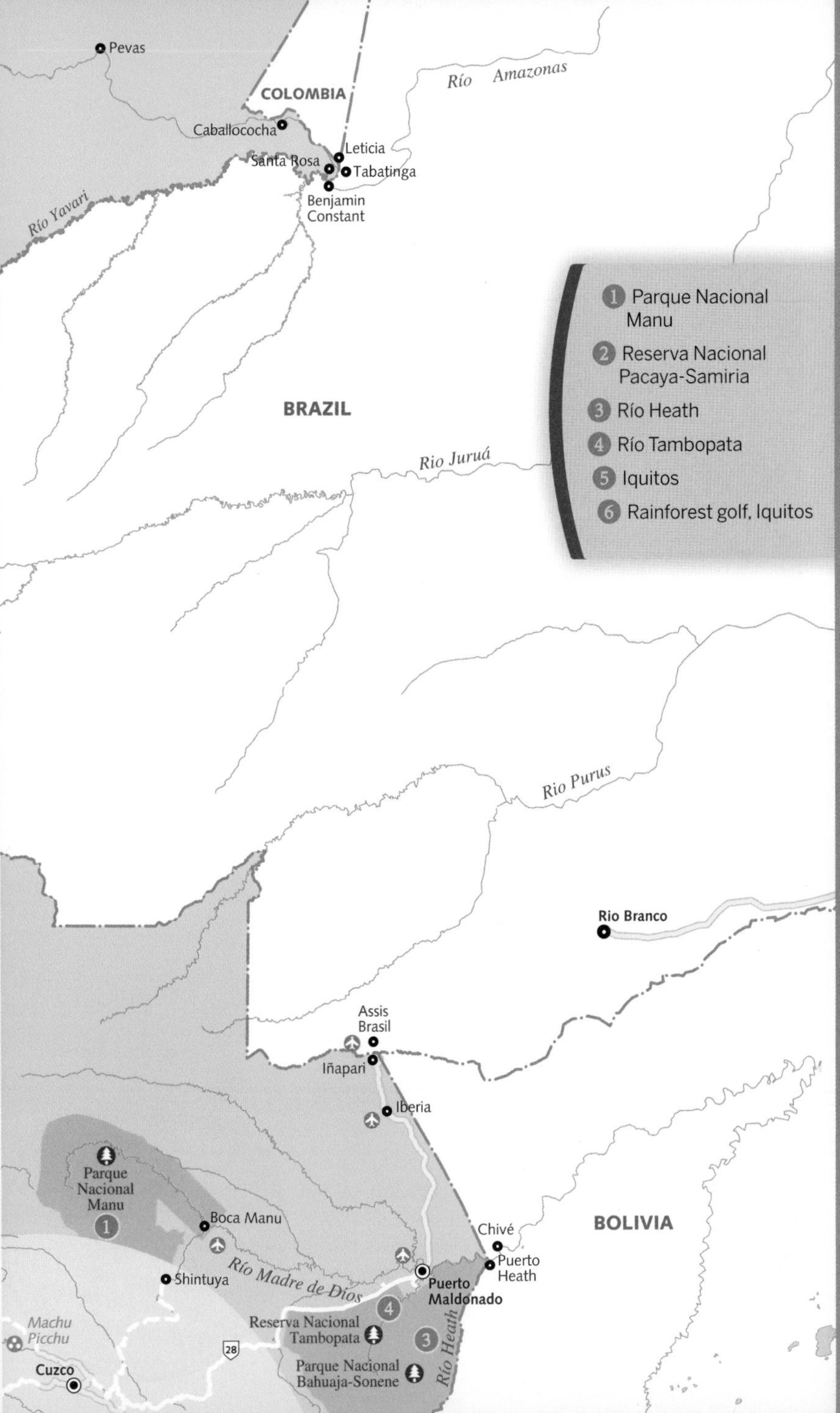

Pevas
COLOMBIA
Río Amazonas
Caballococha
Leticia
Santa Rosa
Tabatinga
Benjamin Constant
Río Yavari
1 Parque Nacional Manu
2 Reserva Nacional Pacaya-Samiria
3 Río Heath
4 Río Tambopata
5 Iquitos
6 Rainforest golf, Iquitos
BRAZIL
Rio Juruá
Rio Purus
Rio Branco
Assis Brasil
Iñapari
Iberia
Parque Nacional Manu
Boca Manu
Chivé
Puerto Heath
BOLIVIA
Shintuya
Río Madre de Dios
Puerto Maldonado
Machu Picchu
Reserva Nacional Tambopata
Río Heath
28
Cuzco
Parque Nacional Bahuaja-Sonene

# Iquitos & the Amazon Highlights

1

## Parque Nacional Manu

At more than 20,000 sq km, this expansive rainforest park (p307) is larger than many countries. It is also Peru's most fiercely protected tract of wilderness, with 80% of it off-limits to outsiders. What you can see, however, is fantastic: this is one of the best places on earth to see wildlife. **Above:** White-lined leaf frog; **Top right:** Caiman; **Bottom right:** Macaw plumage

### Need to Know

**WHEN TO GO** July and August are driest. **MUST-HAVE** A good pair of binoculars. **RECOMMENDED READING** *One River*, by Wade Davis. **For more coverage, see p307.**

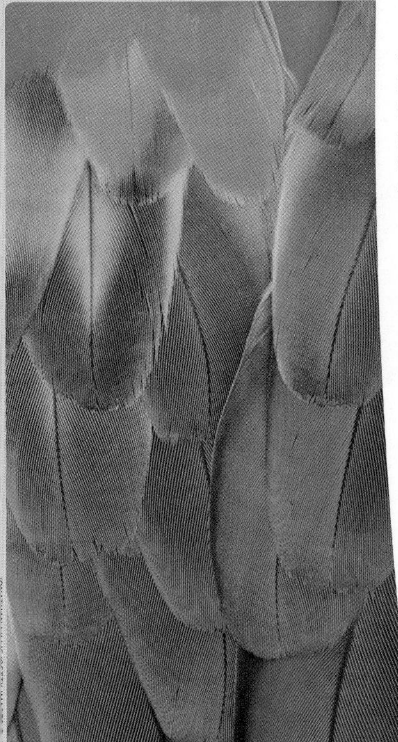

Local Knowledge

# Parque Nacional Manu Don't Miss List

BY RYSE HUAMANI CHOQUEPUMA, MANU NATIVE AND RAINFOREST GUIDE AT LOCALLY OWNED BONANZA TOURS

## 1 GIANT OTTER

Parque Nacional Manu remains the only place with a large population of the endangered giant otter, a fish-eating mammal than can reach almost 2m in length. They can be quite territorial and aggressive. They build extensive campsites, clearing large amounts of vegetation. There they construct dens, which are holes dug into riverbanks, with multiple entrances and chambers. Many can be seen around the area of Cocha Juárez.

## 2 JAGUARS

The jaguar is the Amazon jungle's main predator – they're at the top of the food chain. They are a big draw in Manu, and we regularly see them on riverbanks from boats in our tours. I myself have seen many jaguars in Manu's protected *zona reservada*. Once we saw five jaguars in a seven-day tour.

## 3 CLAY LICKS

It's not just humans who know how to use medicine. Some mammals have the bizarre habit of eating clay – this neutralizes toxins produced by fungi found on fruits they eat. Of the creatures that are known for this the most famous is the tapir, the Amazon's biggest mammal. Other animals that use clay licks are deer and small rodents. In Parque Nacional Manu, three of these can be visited to observe wildlife: the Bonanza Ecological Reserve (Map p304), the Manu Wildlife Center (Map p304) and the nearby Reserve Maquisapayoj.

## 4 INDIGENOUS PEOPLE

Manu is home to about 100 indigenous tribes and their members live throughout the reserve. Some are remote groups that still live in the traditional way. My brother William recently saw at least 10 members of the remote Mashco Piro tribe from a boat – and one attacked it with arrows. The tribe normally lives in the heart of Parque Nacional Manu but they might have been fighting with another tribe, which forced them to search for a new place to live, closer to settlements on the Río Alto Madre de Dios.

## Watch Manatees Float in the Reserva Nacional Pacaya-Samiria

And not just manatees, but gray dolphins, piranhas, giant river otters and rare river turtles. That doesn't even include the prized birdlife found in the reserve (p297): macaws, tanagers, parrots and, of course, highly charming Amazon kingfishers. The best way to get there: take a meandering river cruise from nearby Iquitos, which travels along beaches and inlets, and into remote jungle settlements. Macaws

2

3

## Venture to the Remote Río Heath

If the lodges in the immediate vicinity of Iquitos and Puerto Maldonado feel a mite too urban for you, this meandering river within the confines of the Parque Nacional Bahuaja-Sonene (p303) in the southern Amazon offers extravagant wildlife-watching opportunities: from capybaras to countless avian species, to a faraway clay lick that attracts dense clusters of macaws. Capybara

DAVID TIPLING/GETTY IMAGES ©

## 4 Look for Punk Chickens

On the shores of the Río Tambopata (p305), one of the Amazon's weirdest birds can be seen. This oversized wild chicken with a blue face and a large crest on its head makes for a highly unusual sight. Known as the hoatzin, these startling-looking creatures are as big as a pheasant but have a punk look that is all their own. Only in the Amazon...

PAUL HARRIS/GETTY IMAGES ©

NATURE'S IMAGES/GETTY IMAGES ©

## 5 Embrace the Chaos of Iquitos

The largest city that can't be reached by road, the pumping Iquitos (p290) is home to half a million people, legions of growling *mototaxis* (motorcycle rickshaw taxis), floating markets and a few priceless examples of rubber-boom architecture – all on the shores of one of the world's most famous rivers, the Río Amazonas. It may not be pastoral, but it's a requisite jungle experience.

## 6 Play Golf...with Piranhas

If you were looking for a particularly surreal Amazonian sight, try this one on for size: a nine-hole golf course on the outskirts of the jungle city of Iquitos (p293). In addition to getting the highly unusual experience of playing golf in the middle of the rainforest, hole 4 provides the thrill of teeing onto an island surrounded by piranhas. Piranha

# Iquitos & the Amazon's Best...

## Waterways

- **Río Amazonas** (p291) The mack daddy of global waterways
- **Río Madre de Dios** (p303) Comfortable lodges nestled into steamy rainforest
- **Río Heath** (p303) As remote as it gets
- **Río Tambopata** (p305) Macaw-central in the southern Amazon

## Places to Eat

- **Frío y Fuego** (p295) A foodie paradise in the middle of the Río Itaya in Iquitos
- **Burgos's House** (p302) The best of Amazonian cuisine in Puerto Maldonado
- **Amazon Bistro** (p295) In Iquitos, tasty pizza and mezzanine seating
- **Belén Mercado** (p295) The Iquitos market is *the* spot for fresh-squeezed tropical fruit juices...and fried leafcutter ants!

## Places to Stay

- **Casa Morey, Iquitios** (p294) A former rubber mansion equipped with voluminous suites
- **Hacienda Concepción, Río Madre de Dios** (p305) Spacious rooms made from reclaimed timber
- **Aqua Expeditions** (p291) See the Pacaya-Samiria reserve in style on these luxurious, multi-day cruises
- **Amazon Yarapa River Lodge, Around Iquitos** (p299) A stunning jungle spot with its own laboratory

## Wildlife-Watching Spots

- **Parque Nacional Manu** (p307) One of the Amazon's most pristine parks
- **Reserva Nacional Pacaya-Samiria** (p297) A web of waterways that protects caimans and manatees
- **Río Madre de Dios** (p303) Excellent bird-watching and fishing
- **Río Tambopata** (p305) Boasting one of the most spectacular macaw clay licks in the Amazon

**Left:** Red-backed poison dart frog; **Above:** Río Madre de Dios (p303), Parque Nacional Manu



# Need to Know

### ADVANCE PLANNING

- **Five months before** Book your multiday Amazon cruise out of Iquitos – these fill up fast!
- **Three months before** Arrange a stay at a jungle lodge
- **One month before** Make sure all of your inoculations are up to date
- **One week before** Check that you have necessary gear, such as boots, a hat, repellent and any required medications

### RESOURCES

- **Tropical Nature** Authors Adrian Forsyth and Kenneth Miyata make tropical biology endlessly fascinating – a must-read book for the Amazon traveler
- **One River** By Wade Davis, author of *The Serpent and the Rainbow*. Ethnobotany in the Amazon has never been this gripping
- **Tree of Rivers** By John Hemming, this is a highly readable history of the world's most storied river
- **Mongabay** (www.mongabay.com) A website for all things rainforest

### GETTING AROUND

- **Air** There are daily flights from Lima into Iquitos and Puerto Maldonado; you can also catch flights to Puerto Maldonado from Cuzco
- **Boat** The way to get around the Amazon, whether it's a high-end river cruise or in a little *peki-peki*, the small canoes used as water taxis
- **Taxis** Available in Puerto Maldonado and Iquitos, though far more plentiful are *mototaxis*

### BE FOREWARNED

- **Illnesses** Malaria and yellow fever still make appearances in the Amazon; make sure you are vaccinated
- **Insects** They are legion, take repellent with DEET
- **Robberies** Can be an issue in crowded markets in Puerto Maldonado and Iquitos; watch your wallet

# Iquitos & the Amazon Itineraries

*You could spend weeks – or just a few days – exploring the Amazon Basin. A couple of well-situated airports and a network of comfortable jungle lodges make visiting the world's most fabled river basin relatively easy.*

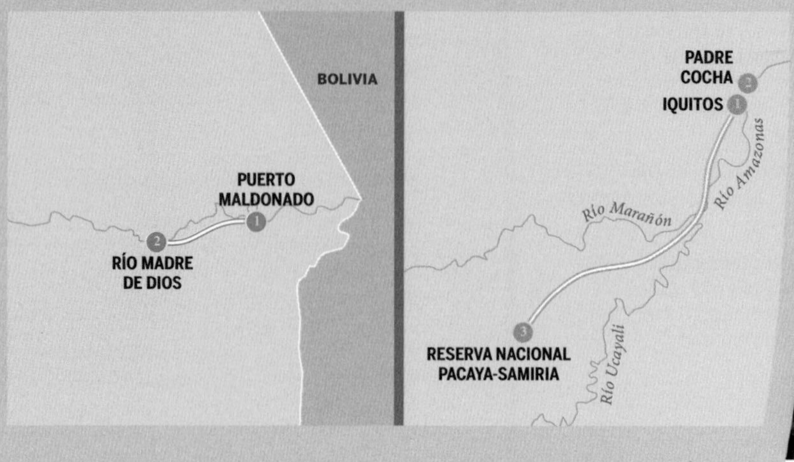


3 DAYS

**AROUND PUERTO MALDONADO**

## Quick Jungle Hop

Start by jetting into the southern jungle town of **(1) Puerto Maldonado**, which can be reached by direct flights from Lima or Cuzco. While you wait for your boat to transport you to your lodge, walk around the colorfully ramshackle town, and climb up the 30m tower known as the Obelisco, which offers terrific views of the area. Something else worth searching out while you're in town: *juanes,* tasty jungle tamales crafted with yucca and rice, with seasoned chicken, and steamed in *bijao* leaves.

From Puerto Maldonado, boat over to one of the nearby lodges on the **(2) Río Madre de Dios** – many of which are less than an hour out of town. From the comfort of your hotel, you can organize hikes through the jungle and explorations by boat. Look for the macaws, parrots and myriad monkeys that inhabit the Amazon. Likewise, you could also laze around on the deck of your lodge and wait for the wildlife to come to you!

## IQUITOS TO THE JUNGLE
# Amazon Cruise

The journey starts in **(1) Iquitos**, the largest city in the world that cannot be reached by road. Spend the first day taking in this old rubber boomtown, including the tropical architecture, such as the Casa de Fierro, and the floating shantytown of Belén where, in the mornings, you'll find a colorful market. Keep your eyes peeled for exotic fruits, such as the pineapple-shaped *aguaje,* which is made into creamy ice pops. If you've got an extra half-day, hop on a *peki-peki* taxi boat over to the village of **(2) Padre Cocha**, where you can pay a visit to the Pilpintuwasi Butterfly Farm to visit its rescue animals (such as Pedro Bello, the jaguar).

On the second day, board your river cruise. Day trips are available, but if you really want to know what the Amazon is all about, book a three-day expedition along the Río Marañón or the Río Ucayali, which will lead into the waterlogged **(3) Reserva Nacional Pacaya-Samiria**. This sprawling park is home to interesting aquatic jungle animals, including pink and gray river dolphins, caimans and South American river turtles. The further you get away from Iquitos, the more wildlife you are likely to see.

Puerto Maldonado (p300)

# Discover Iquitos & the Amazon

## At a Glance

- **Iquitos** Jungle metropolis serving as a gateway to the Amazon River.
- **Reserva Nacional Pacaya-Samiria** (p297) See giant water lilies and rare river turtles.
- **Puerto Maldonado** (p300) Boisterous settlement that lies near the wildest areas.
- **Parque Nacional Manu** (p307) Remote home to caimans, macaws, jungle chickens and jaguars.

Black huacary monkey
JUDY BELLAH/GETTY IMAGES ©

## Iquitos

☎ 065 / POP 430,000 / ELEV 130M

Linked to the outside world by air and by river, Iquitos is the world's largest city that cannot be reached by road. It's a prosperous, vibrant jungle metropolis – one in which unadulterated nature encroaches on air-conditioned bars.

You may well arrive in Iquitos for a boat trip down the Amazon or to hole up in a lodge amid extravagant jungle. But whether it's sampling rainforest cuisine, checking out the buzzing nightlife or exploring one of Peru's most fascinating markets in the floating shantytown of Belén, this thriving city may entice you to take a second look.

### Sights

**CASA DE FIERRO** Historic Building

**(cnr Putumayo & Prospero, Plaza de Armas)** Every guidebook tells of the 'majestic' Casa de Fierro (Iron House), designed by Gustave Eiffel (of Eiffel Tower fame). It was made in Paris in 1860 and imported piece by piece into Iquitos around 1890, during the opulent rubber-boom days, to beautify the city. It's the only surviving one of three different iron houses originally imported here. It may be important, but it looks like a stack of scrap-metal sheets bolted together.

While you're wandering around the central part of the city, look for the 19th-century *azulejos* – handmade ceramic tiles from Portugal – that decorate the old mansions that once belonged to rubber barons. You can find these

## Herzog's Amazon

Eccentric German director Werner Herzog shot two movies in Peru's jungle – *Aguirre, the Wrath of God* (1972) and *Fitzcarraldo* (1982) – about men facing nature in the Amazon. The movies are cult favorites among cinema fans, but the fact that Herzog even survived the shoots is what's remarkable.

For starters, there was the leading man: Klaus Kinski, a volatile actor prone to fits of rage. During the filming of *Aguirre,* he had altercations with an extra and, later, a cameraman – after which he tried to desert the shoot on a speedboat. (To make him stay, Herzog threatened him with a rifle.) Later, while filming *Fitzcarraldo,* Kinski so antagonized the Matsiguenka tribespeople working as extras that one of them offered to murder him. Then there was the weather: droughts so dire that the rivers dried, halting shooting, followed by flash floods that wrecked everything.

Herzog once said he saw filming in the Amazon as 'challenging nature itself.' The fact that he completed the films is evidence that in some ways, he did challenge nature – and triumphed.

on buildings along Raimondi and the Malecón Tarapacá.

**BELÉN** Neighborhood

At the southeast end of town is this floating shantytown, consisting of scores of huts, built on rafts, which rise and fall with the river. During the dry season, these rafts sit on the river mud and are dirty, but most of the year they float – a colorful and exotic sight. Around 7000 people live here, and canoes float from hut to hut selling and trading jungle produce. The best time to visit the shantytown is at 7am, when villagers arrive to sell their produce. To get here, take a cab to 'Los Chinos,' walk to the port and hire a canoe to take you around.

**Belén mercado** (market; at Hurtado & Jr 9 de Diciembre) is a raucous, crowded affair where all kinds of strange and exotic products are sold. Remember to watch your wallet.

**BIBLIOTECA AMAZÓNICA** Library

(cnr Malecón Maldonado & Morona; admission for both S3; Mon-Fri) An old building on the corner houses this library, which contains the largest collection of historical documents in the Amazon Basin. In the same building is the small **Museo Etnográfico**. This museum has life-sized fiberglass casts of members of various Amazon tribes.

# Activities

### River Cruises

Cruising the Amazon is a popular pastime – and one of the best ways to see the area. Cruises focus on the Río Amazonas, both downriver towards the Brazil–Colombia border and upriver to Nauta, where the Ríos Marañón and Ucayali converge. Beyond Nauta, trips continue to the Pacaya-Samiria reserve. Excursions can also be arranged on the three rivers surrounding Iquitos: the Itaya, the Amazonas and the Nanay.

Operators quote prices in US dollars and most tours include food, transfers and English-speaking guides. A useful booking website for most of the following is www.amazoncruise.net. Reserve well in advance.

## Iquitos

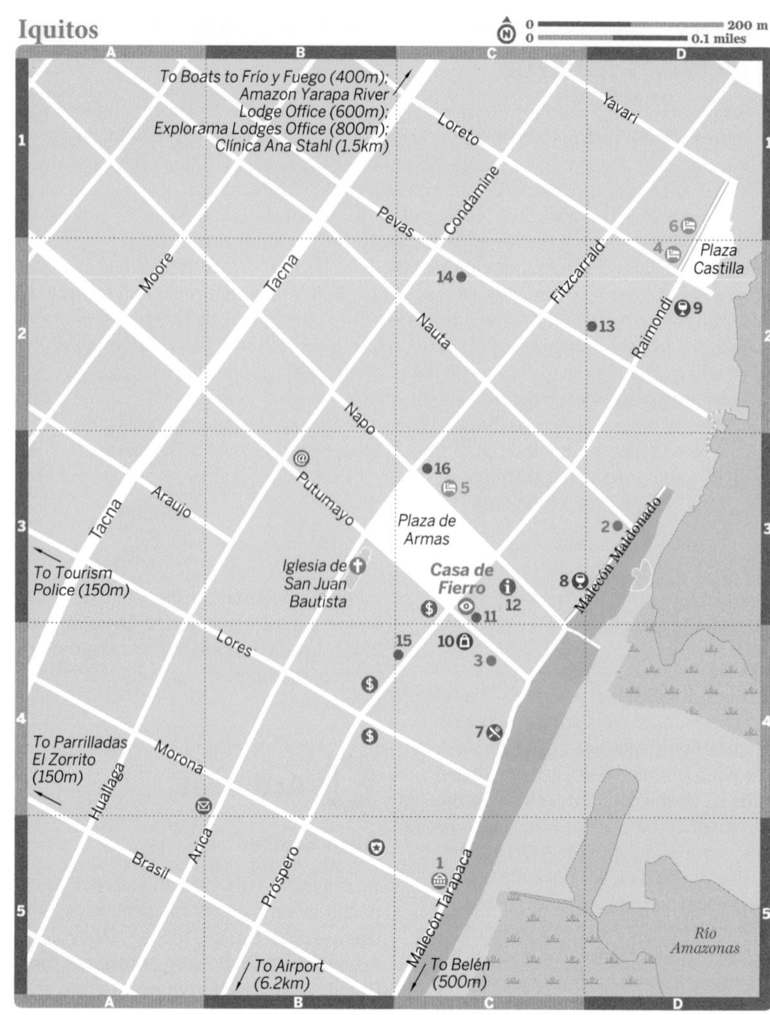


**DAWN ON THE AMAZON TOURS & CRUISES** Cruise

(☎22-3730, 965-939-190; www.dawnontheamazon.com; Malecón Maldonado 185; day trips incl lunch per person US$74.75, multiday cruises per person per day US$199) This small outfit offers the best deal for independent travelers. The *Amazon I* is a beautiful 11m wooden craft with modern furnishings, available for day trips or longer river cruises up to two weeks. You can travel with host Bill Grimes and his experienced crew along the Amazon, or along quieter tributaries. The tri-river cruise is a favorite local trip.

**AQUA EXPEDITIONS** Cruise

(☎60-1053, 965-83-2517; www.aquaexpeditions.com; Prolongación Iquitos 1187; 3-night Marañon & Ucayali cruise per person in suite US$2685) Aqua is the operator of luxury riverboats MV *Aria* and MV *Aqua* which have twice-weekly departures into the Pacaya-Samiria reserve. Expect luxury cabins on both, though the *Aria* comes with the added bonus of an on-board Jacuzzi.

## Iquitos

**Top Sights**
Casa de Fierro ... C3

**Sights**
Biblioteca Amazónica ... (see 1)
1 Museo Etnográfico ... C5

**Activities, Courses & Tours**
2 Dawn on the Amazon Tours & Cruises ... D3
3 Flycatcher Tours ... C4

**Sleeping**
4 Casa Morey ... D2
5 Hotel El Dorado Plaza ... C3
6 Posada del Cauchero ... D1

**Eating**
7 Amazon Bistro ... C4

**Drinking**
8 Arandú Bar ... C3
9 Musmuqui ... D2

**Shopping**
10 Mad Mick's Trading Post ... C4

**Information**
11 Cumaceba Lodge Office ... C3
12 iPerú ... C3
Muyuna Amazon Lodge Office ... (see 10)
Otorongo Lodge Office ... (see 10)
13 Paseos Amazonicos Offices ... D2
14 Reserva Nacional Pacaya-Samiria Office ... C2

**Transport**
15 LAN ... C4
16 Star Perú ... C3

Both boats have beautiful observation lounges to watch the waters drifting by. Meals are included and small launches are available for side trips.

**GREENTRACKS** Cruise
**(☎in the USA 970-884-6107, 800-892-1035; www.greentracks.com; 416 Country Rd 501, PMB 131 Bayfield, CO81122; 7 days & 6 nights s/d $US2750/5000)** GreenTracks offers four- to seven-day excursions on one of three luxury ships. The *Ayapua* is a 20-passenger, rubber-boom-era boat with air-conditioned rooms, a bar and even a library. The *Clavero* is a smaller boat offering the same excursion. *Delfín I* is a more modern vessel, accommodating 12 passengers for four- and five-day cruises into the reserve.

### Other Activities

**AMAZON GOLF CLUB** Golf
**(☎963-1333, 975-4976; Quistacocha; admission per day incl club rental S60; 6am-6pm)** Founded in 2004 by a bunch of nostalgic expats, the 2140m course was built on bushland just outside Iquitos and boasts (apart from its nine greens) a wooden clubhouse. Hole 4 is a beauty: you tee onto an island surrounded by piranha-infested waters. Don't go fishing for lost balls!

## Tours

Jungle 'guides' will approach you everywhere in Iquitos. Legitimate guides should have a permit or license – if they don't, check with the tourist office. Get references for any guide, and proceed carefully. Lodges have their own stable of guides (frequently the best ones).

**GERSON PIZANGO** Guided Tour
**(☎965-012-225; www.amazonjungleguide.com; daily per person US$50-70)** Gerson comes reader-recommended and is renowned as one of Iquitos' best independent guides. Tailored tours can include activities such as wildlife-spotting, boating excursions down little-plied tributaries and visits to local communities.

**FLYCATCHER TOURS** Adventure Tour
**(☎24-1228; www.flycatchertours.com; Putumayo 155; 7-day wilderness adventure per person US$999)** This outfit, formerly Amazon Adventure Expeditions, is recommended for providing lengthier excursions into the jungle. These are true adventures, where you do things like catch your own food.

## Sleeping

Jungle lodges outside of Iquitos are listed starting on p298.

**LA CASA FITZCARRALDO** Guesthouse **$$**
(**☎60-1138/39; http://lacasafitzcarraldo.com; Av La Marina 2153; r S180-350;** ) Sequestered within a serene walled garden, this is the most interesting accommodation option in Iquitos. The house takes its name from Werner Herzog's film *Fitzcarraldo*. Stay in the mahogany-floored Mick Jagger room or the luxuriantly green Klaus Kinski suite. There is a tree house (with wi-fi!), a lovely swimming pool and huge breakfasts.

**CASA MOREY** Boutique Hotel **$$$**
(**☎23-1913; Loreto 200; www.casamorey.com; s/d incl breakfast S155/260;** ) This former mansion of rubber baron Luis F Morey dates from 1910 and has been renovated to its former grandeur, with 14 sprawling suites, plenty of original *azulejos,* voluminous bathrooms, river views, a courtyard pool and a library with a stupendous collection of Amazon-related literature.

**POSADA DEL CAUCHERO** Guesthouse **$$**
(**☎22-2914; ermivaya@yahoo.es; Raimondi 449; s/d/ste S100/120/180;** ) Above the restaurant of the same name lurk 12 massive, chalet-style rooms (seven with air-con), some of which are suites. All are decorated with tribal-themed art. There is a pool and some of the best river views in Iquitos.

**HOTEL EL DORADO PLAZA** Luxury Hotel **$$$**
(**☎22-2555; www.grupo-dorado.com; Napo 258; r incl breakfast from S575;** ) With a prime plaza location, this modern hotel is the town's best, with 64 well-equipped, spacious rooms (some with plaza views; others overlooking the pool). Jacuzzi, sauna, gym, several suites, 24-hour room service, two bars and attentive staff make this a top option.

**Left:** Kapok tree roots, Parque Nacional Manu (p307); **Below:** Aracari toucan





## Eating

The local culinary repertoire includes *chupín de pollo* (a tasty soup of chicken, egg and rice) and *juanes* (tamales made with yucca, rice and chicken, and wrapped in a *bijao* leaf). Be wary of regional specialties featuring endangered animals, such as *chicharrón de lagarto* (fried alligator) and *sopa de tortuga* (turtle soup). *Paiche*, a local river fish, is now making a comeback thanks to breeding programs.

**FRÍO Y FUEGO** Fusion **$$**
(**☎965-607-474; Embarcadero Av La Marina 138; mains S15-35; ⏰noon-4pm & 7-11pm Tue-Sat, noon-5pm Sun**) This floating foodie paradise in the mouth of the Río Itaya serves up the city's best food, with an emphasis on river fish (anything with *doncella* is delectable). The *parrillas* (grills) are inviting, too – including the tender beef medallions served with a mozzarella-and-pepper-stuffed *bijao* leaf. The address given is the boat embarkation point.

**AMAZON BISTRO** International **$$**
(**Malecón Tarapaca 268; breakfasts S12, mains S15-40; ⏰6am-midnight**) Laid out with TLC by the Belgian owner, this restaurant has mezzanine seating, tasty pizzas, Argentine steaks, crepes and a range of beers (Belgian, of course). It also serves up the city's best coffee. It's a good evening drinking spot.

**PARILLADAS EL ZORRITO** Parrilla **$**
(**Fanning 355; mains S5-10**) Food is cooked outside on a grill at this ambient, immensely popular local joint. *Juanes* and river fish are the things to go for here. Portions are huge. There is great live music at weekends.

**BELÉN MERCADO** Market **$**
(**cnr Prospero & Jirón 9 de Diciembre**) There are great eats at Iquitos' markets, particularly the Belén *mercado* where a *menú* (set meal), including *jugo especial* (fresh juice), is less than S5. Look out for specialties such as meaty Amazon worms, *ishpa* (simmered *sabalo* fish intestines

and fat) and *sikisapa* (fried leafcutter ants; abdomens are supposedly tastiest). Watch your valuables.

## Drinking & Entertainment

The Malecón is the cornerstone of the lively nightlife scene.

**ARANDÚ BAR** Bar
**(Malecón Maldonado 113; late)** This is the liveliest of several thumping Malecón bars, great for people-watching.

**MUSMUQUI** Bar
**(Raimondi 382; to midnight Sun-Thu, to 3am Fri & Sat)** Locally popular bar with two floors and an extensive range of aphrodisiac cocktails concocted from Amazon plants.

## Shopping

There are a few shops on the first block of Napo selling jungle crafts, some of high quality. A good place for crafts is Mercado de Artesanía San Juan, on the road to the airport – taxi drivers know it.

Don't buy items made from animal bones and skins, as they are made from jungle wildlife. It's illegal to import many such items into the US and Europe.

You can buy, rent or trade almost anything needed for a jungle expedition at **Mad Mick's Trading Post (965-75-4976; michaelcollis@hotmail.com; Putumayo 163; 8am-8pm)**.

## Information

Internet cafes charge about S3 per hour; hotel wi-fi is usually the best option.

### Dangers & Annoyances

Street touts and self-styled jungle guides tend to be aggressive, and many are both irritatingly insistent and dishonest. There have been reports of these guides robbing tourists. It is best to make your own decisions by contacting hotels, lodges and tour companies directly. Exercise particular caution around Belén, where petty thieving is common. That said, violent crime is almost unknown in Iquitos.

### Emergency

**Clínica Ana Stahl (25-2535; www.caas-peru.org; Av La Marina 285; 24hr)** Good private clinic.

**Tourism police (Poltur; 24-2081; Lores 834)**

### Money

Several banks change traveler's checks and give advances on credit cards. **BCP (cnr Prospero & Putumayo)** has a secure ATM.

### Tourist Information

Look for free copies of the monthly *Iquitos Times* **(www.iquitostimes.com)**, which features the latest goings on about town.

**iPerú Airport** Airport **(26-0251; Main Hall, Francisco Secada Vignetta Airport; whenever flights are arriving/departing)** City Center **(23-6144; Napo 161; 9am-6pm Mon-Sat, to 1pm Sun)** English spoken at the airport branch.

**Reserva Nacional Pacaya-Samiria Office (22-3460, Pevas 339; 8am-4pm Mon-Fri)** Entry to the reserve for three days costs S60, payable at Banco de la Nación around the corner.

## Getting There & Around

### Air

Iquitos' small but busy **airport (code IQT)** lies 7km from the center. There are daily flights to and from Lima via **LAN (23-2421; Próspero 232)** and **Star Perú (23-6208; Napo 256)**.

Charter companies at the airport have five-passenger planes to almost anywhere in the Amazon.

### Boat

**Puerto Masusa (Av La Marina)** is where the city's numerous riverboats dock. It's 3km north of the town center.

### Taxis

Taxis are relatively few, but squadrons of busy *mototaxis* can oblige with lifts. Most rides around Iquitos cost about S2.

JUDY BELLAH/GETTY IMAGES ©

## Don't Miss Pilpintuwasi Butterfly Farm

A visit to the fascinating Pilpintuwasi Butterfly Farm is highly recommended. Ostensibly this is a conservatorium and breeding center for Amazonian butterflies. Butterflies aplenty there certainly are, including the striking blue morpho (*Morpho menelaus*) and the fearsome-looking owl butterfly (*Caligo eurilochus*). But it's the farm's exotic animals that steal the show. Rescued as orphans and protected within the property are several mischievous monkeys, a tapir, an anteater and Pedro Bello, a majestic jaguar.

To get there, take a boat from Bellavista-Nanay, a small port 2km north of Iquitos, to the village of Padre Cocha. The farm is signposted: a 15-minute walk through the village from the Padre Cocha boat dock.

**NEED TO KNOW**

(☎065-23-2665; www.amazonanimalorphanage.org; Padra Cocha; admission S20; ⌚9am-4pm Tue-Sun)

## Around Iquitos

Though Iquitos may be a bustling city, the countryside around it offers plenty of nature-soaked sights – from butterfly farms to untamed wilderness reserves.

### Sights & Activities

**LAGUNA QUISTACOCHA** Lagoon

**(admission S10)** This lake, just 15km south of Iquitos, has a small zoo of local fauna and an adjoining fish hatchery. The latter helps support the 2m-long *paiche* (a local river fish), which is now endangered – a situation that is being rectified with the breeding program here. A pedestrian trail circles the lake and paddleboats are available for hire. There are also several restaurants.

*Mototaxis* can bring you here (S12).

**RESERVA NACIONAL PACAYA-SAMIRIA** Reserve

**(www.pacaya-samiria.com)** Located on the Río Ucayali, west of Iquitos, the 20,800-sq-km

## If You Like… Jungle Lodges

If you like the total jungle-immersion experience, the northern Amazon area has no shortage of lodges. Find your base, then explore the jungle to your heart's delight.

**1 PASEOS AMAZONICOS**
**(☎01-241-7576; Office 4, Bajada Balta 131, Miraflores, Lima; www.paseosamazonicos.com; 3 days & 2 nights per person US$220-260)** This long-time company runs three lodges around Iquitos, including Tambo Yanacu, Tambo Amazonico and Amazonas Sinchicuy, on a small tributary 30km northeast of Iquitos.

**2 CUMACEBA LODGES**
**(☎065-22-1456; www.cumaceba.com; Putumayo 184, Iquitos; 3 days & 2 nights s US$260-370, d US$210-260)** In business since 1995, Cumaceba operates three budget lodges all aimed at providing travelers with a less-costly Amazon experience. These are: Cumaceba Lodge (known for adventurous trips), Amazonas Botanical Lodge (with a focus on plants) and Piranha Ecoexplorer (all about adventure). Guides speak English, French and even Japanese. They also organize day trips within the Iquitos area for US$65.

**3 MUYUNA AMAZON LODGE**
**(☎065-24-2858; www.muyuna.com; Putumayo 163, ground fl, Iquitos; 3 days & 2 nights s/d US$485/805)** About 140km upriver from Iquitos on the Río Yanayacu, this intimate lodge is surrounded by 10 well-conserved lakes in a remote area less colonized than the jungle downriver, which makes for a great rainforest experience.

**4 CEIBA TOPS**
**(3 days & 2 nights per person s/d US$515/910; ❄@≋)** About 40km northeast of Iquitos on the Amazon, this is Explorama's and the area's most modern lodge and resort. Landscaped grounds surround a pool complex, complete with hydro-massage, waterslide and hammock house.

Pacaya-Samiria Reserve is one of the largest parks in Peru. An estimated 40,000 people live on and around the reserve, juggling the needs of longtime human inhabitants with protecting area wildlife.

Pacaya-Samiria is home to aquatic animals such as Amazon manatees, pink and gray river dolphins, two species of caiman, giant South American river turtles and many other bird and animal species. Noteworthy points include **Quebrada Yanayacu**, where the river water is black from dissolved plants; **Lago Pantean**, where you can check out caimans and go medicinal-plant collecting; and **Tipischa de Huana**, where you can see giant *Victoria regia* waterlilies, big enough for a small child to sleep upon without sinking.

From Iquitos, the best way to get to the reserve is by boat – either on guided canoe tours or a multiday river cruise. The best time to go is during the dry season, when you are more likely to see animals along the riverbanks. Rains ease off in late May; it then takes a month for water levels to drop, making July and August the best months to visit (a good time for fishing).

## Sleeping

There are numerous lodges both upriver and downriver from Iquitos that offer a mix of relaxation and wildlife spotting (July to September is the best time). Many have offices in Iquitos.

All prices quoted here generally include meals, at least one tour and transfer from Iquitos. Lodges will provide containers of purified water for you to drink when there, but bring extra water for the journey.

The following lodges are listed in order of distance from Iquitos.

**OTORONGO LODGE** Lodge **$$**
**(☎065-22-4192, 965-75-6131; www.otorongoexpeditions.com; Departamento 203, Putumayo 163, Iquitos; 5 days & 4 nights per person d US$761)** Travelers have been giving great

feedback about this relatively new, rustic-style lodge, 100km from Iquitos. It's a down-to-earth place, with 12 rooms containing private bathrooms and a relaxing common area, as well as walkways to maximize appreciation of the surrounding wildlife. Otorongo is run by a former falconer who can imitate an incredible number of bird sounds. The five-day option can include off-the-beaten-path visits to nearby communities.

**AMAZON YARAPA RIVER LODGE** Lodge **$$$**

(**065-993-1172; www.yarapa.com; Av La Marina 124, Iquitos; 4 days & 3 nights s/d US$1020/1840, without bathroom US$940/1680; @**) Approximately 130km upriver from Iquitos on the Río Yarapa, this lodge is simply stunning. It has a huge and well-designed tropical biology laboratory, powered by an expansive solar-panel system. Facilities are beautifully maintained and rooms are connected by a series of screened walkways. Eight huge bedrooms with oversized private bathrooms are available and 16 comfortable rooms share a multitude of well-equipped bathrooms. The trip from Iquitos takes three to four hours. Recommended.

**TAHUAYO LODGE** Lodge **$$**

(**1-813-907-8475, 1-800-262-9669; www.perujungle.com; 10305 Riverburn Dr, Tampa, Florida 33647, USA; 8 days & 7 nights per person US$1295**) This lodge, 140km from Iquitos, has exclusive access to the 2500-sq-km Tamshiyacu-Tahuayo reserve, an area of pristine jungle where a record 93 species of mammal have been recorded. The 15 cabins are located 65km up an Amazon tributary, built on high stilts and connected by walkways; half have private bathrooms.

Wildlife-viewing opportunities are among the best of any lodge listed.

**HATUCHAY HOTEL PACAYA-SAMIRIA** Lodge **$$**

(**www.hatuchayhotelsperu.com; per 1/2 people 4 days & 3 nights US$640**) **Iquitos** (**065-22-5769**); **Lima** (**1-446-2739; Av José Pardo 601, Off 602-703, Miraflores**) About 190km upriver on the Marañón, this excellent lodge (the former Pacaya-Samiria Amazon Lodge) is past Nauta on the outskirts of the Pacaya-Samiria reserve. The only lodge within the reserve buffer zone, it can arrange overnight stays within the reserve. Rooms feature private showers and porches with river views, and there is electricity in the evening.

**EXPLORAMA LODGES** Lodge **$$**

(**065-25-2530; www.explorama.com; Av La Marina 340, Iquitos**) This well-established and recommended company owns and operates various lodges at different price points in the area and is an involved supporter of the Amazon Conservatory

Amazonian palm viper

PAUL BERTNER/GETTY IMAGES ©

of Tropical Studies (ACTS). It has a lab at the famed **canopy walkway**, which gives visitors a bird's-eye view of the rainforest canopy and its wildlife. You could arrange a trip to visit one or more lodges combined with a visit to the walkway. Children under 12 pay half price.

## Puerto Maldonado

☎082 / POP 57,000 / ELEV 250M

Unlike Amazon cities further north, this is a rawer, untidier jungle town with a mercilessly sweltering climate and a fair quantity of mosquitoes. But there's a payoff: the watery wildernesses in this area offer some of the most unspoiled-yet-accessible jungle locales in the country – as well as excellent accommodation options for travelers who want a dash of luxury with their rainforest. The best part: it's all situated at an easy flight's reach from Cuzco.

### Sights

**OBELISCO** Tower

**(cnr Fitzcarrald & Madre de Dios; admission S2; ⏲10am-4pm)** Although this strangely cosmic blue building was designed as a modern *mirador* (lookout), its 30m height unfortunately does not rise high enough above the city for viewers to glimpse the rivers. But the view is still fantastic: a distant glimmer of jungle and plenty of corrugated-metal roofs. Photos displayed on the way up document historic moments, like when the first *mototaxi* arrived in town.

**BUTTERFLY FARM** Farm

**(Av Aeropuerto Km 6; admission S20)** Peru boasts the greatest number of butterfly species in the world (some 3700) and you can see many of them at this well-run butterfly conservation project, initiated in 1996. There are also displays on rainforest conservation. If you're staying at one of the Inkaterra jungle lodges, admission is free.

**INFIERNO** Village

About an hour southeast of Puerto Maldonado is the village of Infierno (translation: Hell!), home of the Ese'eja tribespeople. It's a lively, spread-out settlement, which is establishing a reputation for its ayahuasca rituals. There may not be a lot on offer, but at least you can say you've been...

Arrange your own transport here via car or motorbike: *mototaxis* won't make the rough journey.

### Warning: Ayahuasca

Throughout the Peruvian Amazon, countless places offer the chance to partake of ayahuasca, a derivative of a hallucinogenic jungle vine consumed for ceremonial purposes. Traditionally, it is taken as part of a ritual ceremony that can last for hours or days under the guidance of a shaman. But as its profile has increased among travelers, many lodges and other tourist outfits have begun staging their own ceremonies.

Be wary and do your research. Not only can ayahuasca have serious medical side effects (convulsions, dramatic rises in blood pressure – even death), there are charlatans out there who have been known to rob and, on occasion, rape unsuspecting gringos under the influence. In 2012 a US traveller died during an ayahuasca ceremony. According to newspaper reports, the shaman and his accomplices, who tried to cover up the death, have been arrested for murder.

Lonely Planet does not recommend taking ayahuasca and those who do, do it at their own risk.

# Puerto Maldonado

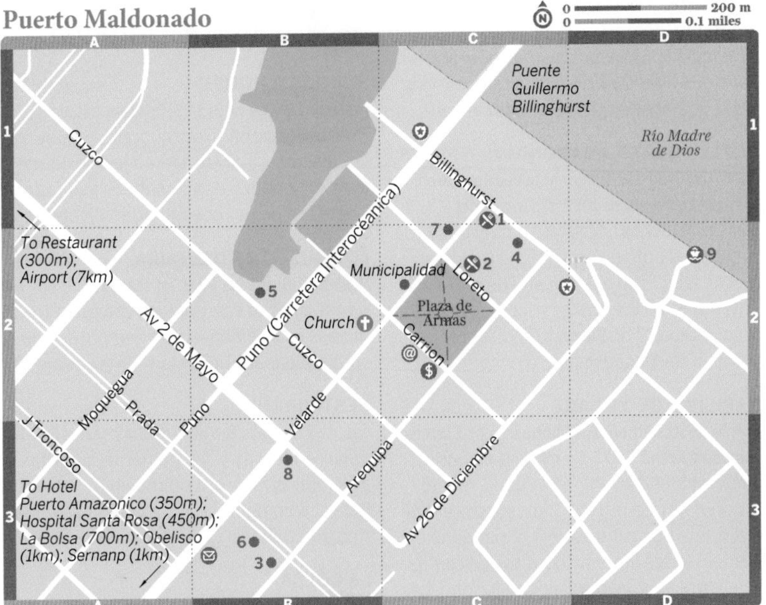


## Puerto Maldonado

**Eating**

1 Burgos's House ........ C1
2 Los Gustitos del Cura ........ C2

**Information**

3 Cayman Lodge Amazonie Office ........ B3
4 Corto Maltes Office ........ C2
Estancia Bello Horizonte Office .. (see 2)
5 Inkaterra office ........ B2
6 Libertador Tambopata Lodge Office ........ B3
7 Yakari Canopy Adventure Office ........ C2

**Transport**

8 LAN ........ B3
9 Madre de Dios Ferry Dock ........ D2

## Tours

There are about 30 guides with official licenses granted by the local Ministerio de Industria y Turismo. Many of the best ones work full time for one of the local jungle lodges. Beware of sketchy guides at the airport, who try and take you to a 'recommended' hotel. Guides charge from S75 to S175 per person per day.

The following are recommended:

**Gerson Medina Valera** (57-4201; www.tambopatahostel.com) Lots of experience in bird-watching tours and speaks fluent English.

**Jony Valles Rengifo** (982-704-736; jhovar@hotmail.com) Speaks English and French.

**Nilthon Tapia Miyashiro** (982-788-174; nisa_30@hotmail.com) A well-known, experienced guide; also reachable through **Tambopata Hostel** (57-4201).

## Sleeping

Jungle lodges outside of Puerto Maldonado are listed starting on p306.

**ANACONDA LODGE** Lodge **$$**
(79-2726; Av Aeropuerto Km 6; www.anacondajunglelodge.com; bungalow s/d/tr S100/160/220, bungalow without bathroom s/d S50/80; ) Cocooned in its own tropical garden on the edge of town, this lodge has eight

double-room bungalows with shared bathroom and four luxury bungalows with private facilities. There is a small pool and a spacious two-floor restaurant-bar serving great Thai food and pancake breakfasts.

**HOTEL PUERTO AMAZONICO** Hotel $$
**(☎57-2170, 50-2354; www.hotelpuertoamazonico.com.pe; León Velarde 1080; s/d incl buffet breakfast S180/240; )** It may be a little overpriced but you can't argue that the rooms aren't the city's best. The more you pay, the more the size of your flat-screen TV increases. The views from the roof are some of the best around.

**KAPIEIVI ECO VILLAGE** Lodge $$
**(☎79-5650; katherinapz@hotmail.com; Carretera Tambopata Km 1.5; 1/2-person bungalow incl breakfast S100/125; )** This rustic, reader-recommended retreat, 2km southwest of town, lets budget travelers experience a taste of lodge life – without the price tag. There are several bungalows (for one, two or four people) with private bathrooms, as well as a swimming pool. Food and drink is an additional S18 per person per day.

## Eating & Drinking

**BURGOS'S HOUSE** Peruvian $$
**(Velarde 127; mains S15-23; 11am-midnight)** Puerto Maldonado's standout restaurant serves beautifully rendered jungle classics in an airy, courteously-staffed restaurant. There are plenty of vegetarian dishes, too.

**LOS GUSTITOS DEL CURA** Cafe $
**(Loreto 258; snacks S3-8; 11am-10pm)** For a sweet treat or the best ice cream in town, drop in to this French-owned patisserie with a pleasant courtyard at the rear.

**RESTAURANT** Peruvian $
**(cnr Av 2 de Mayo & Madre de Dios; mains S10-15; dinner)** It may have no name, but this grill joint is far from unknown by the locals, who flock here for great fish with rice and *plátano* (plantain bananas).

**LA BOLSA** Live Music
**(to 2am Thu-Sat)** If you want a view while you drink, come to this renowned local *peña* (bar or club featuring live folkloric music).

## Information

Internet is slower here than in other Peruvian cities, costing about S2 per hour. **Locutorio** (Carrión cuadra 2) also has international call services.

### Medical Services

**Hospital Santa Rosa** (☎57-1019, 57-1046; Cajamarca 171)

### Tourist Information

**Sernanp** (☎57-3278; www.sernanp.gob.pe/sernanp; Av 28 de Julio 875) The national-park office gives information and collects admission to the Tambopata reserve zone (some guides do this for their groups). Standard entry fee is S30, but

Trekking in the Amazon
INGA SPENCE/GETTY IMAGES ©

## Detour: Parque Nacional Bahuaja-Sonene

About two hours south of the Río Madre de Dios and along the Río Heath, the **Parque Nacional Bahuaja-Sonene** (admission S30) has some of the best wildlife in Peru's Amazon region, including rarities such as the maned wolf and spider monkey, although these are not easily seen. Infrastructure in the park, one of the nation's largest, is limited – making this a spot for dedicated adventurers.

The best (read: only) place to stay in the area is the **Heath River Wildlife Center** (s/d 4 days & 3 nights US$725/1150), a 10-room lodge owned by the Ese'eja indigenous people, located five hours by boat from Puerto Maldonado. Units in the simple thatched lodge come equipped with hot water, and guiding and cultural services are available. Travelers can also take advantage of trails that lead right into the Bahuaja-Sonene. Capybaras are frequently seen and guided tours to a nearby *colpa* (clay lick), to see macaws and parrots, can be arranged.

Park entrance fees are included. The first and last nights of tours are spent at a lodge on Lago Sandoval. To arrange a stay, contact **InkaNatura** (www.inkanatura.com) Cuzco (084-23-1138; Ricardo Palma J1 Urb Santa Mónica & Plateros 361); Lima (01-440-2022; Manuel Bañón 461, San Isidro).

increases to S65 for visiting areas away from the riverside lodges.

## Getting There & Around

### Air

The airport is 7km outside town. There are daily flights from Lima, via Cuzco, with **LAN** (57-3677; www.lan.com; Velarde 503) and **Star Perú** (57-3564; www.starperu.com; Velarde 151).

### Boat

Getting around is done almost exclusively by boat. Boats for local excursions can be found at the Río Madre de Dios ferry dock. The Tambopata dock, 2km south of town, has boats to the Tambopata reserve. Boats to jungle lodges leave from both docks.

### Taxi

While the center of town is compact, you'll likely need to take a *mototaxi* to get around – since the docks and other sights are spread around. *Mototaxis* can take two or three passengers (and light luggage) to the airport for S7. Short rides around town cost S2 or less.

# Around Puerto Maldonado

## Río Madre de Dios

This important river flows eastwards past Puerto Maldonado, heading into Bolivia, Brazil and the Amazon proper. In the wet season it is brown, flows swiftly and looks very impressive, carrying huge logs and other jungle flotsam and jetsam downstream. The main reason people come here is to stay for a few days in one of several jungle lodges, all of which are found between 20 minutes and three hours downstream from Puerto Maldonado itself.

### Sights & Activities

Activities consist of hiking, canoeing, fishing, exploring local lakes and tributaries and wildlife watching. A couple of canopy walkways – **Inkaterra Reserva Amazonica** (www.inkaterra.com) and **Yakari Canopy Adventure** (www.yakaicanopyadventure.com) – provide a distraction from normal jungle activities. The latter's is approached by a 200m zipline.

# Around Puerto Maldonado

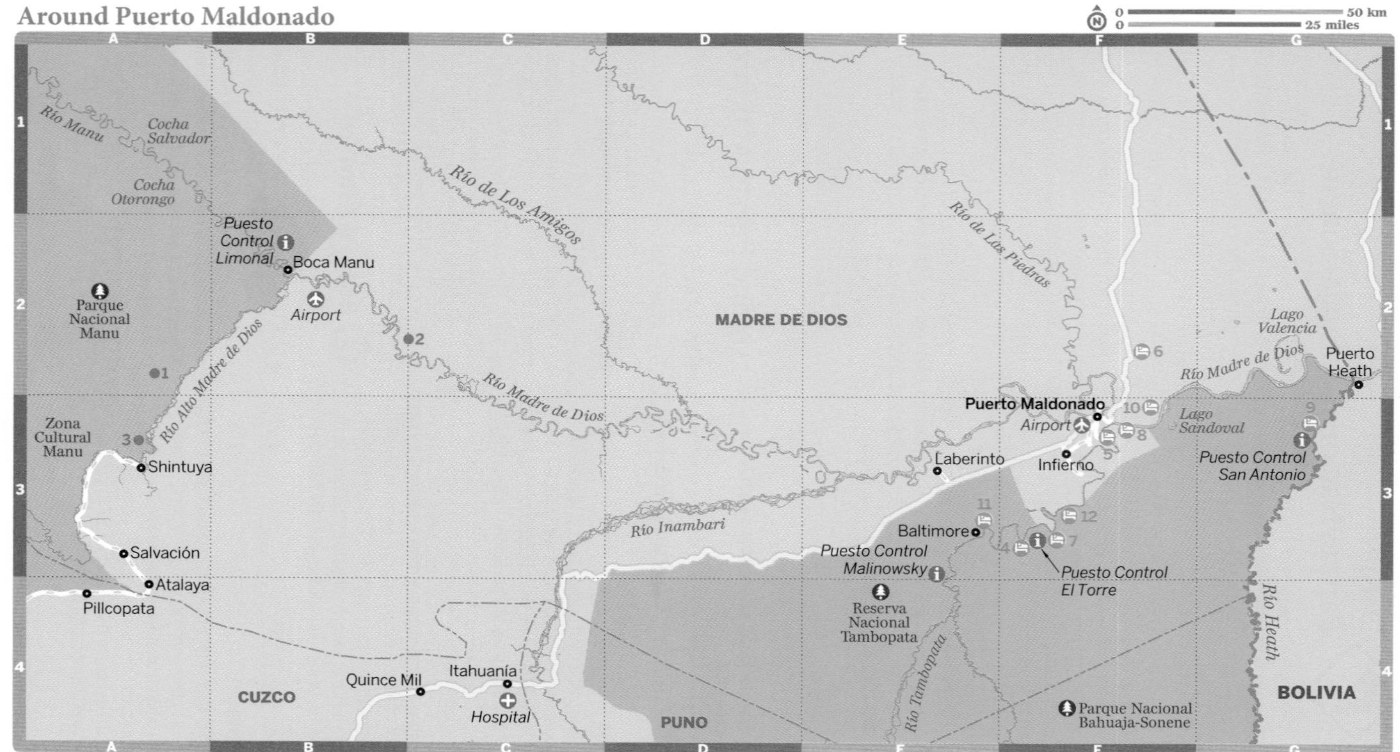

## Around Puerto Maldonado

**Activities, Courses & Tours**



**Sleeping**

## Sleeping & Eating

**CORTO MALTES** Lodge $$

(**082-57-3831; www.cortomaltes-amazonia.com; Billinghurst 229, Puerto Maldonado; s 3 days & 2 nights US$255**) The closest lodge to Puerto Maldonado offers 15 comfortable, fully screened, high-ceilinged bungalows with solid mattresses, eye-catching indigenous wall art, patios with hammocks, and cheerful decorative touches in the public areas. Electricity is available from dusk until 10:30pm.

**HACIENDA CONCEPCIÓN** Lodge $$

(**Inkaterra; www.inkaterra.com; 3 days & 2 nights s/d US$357/616, cabins s/d US$434/704**) Cuzco (**084-24-5314; Plaza Nazarenas 167**); Lima (**01-610-0400; Anda-lucía 174, Miraflores**); Puerto Maldonado (**082-57-2823; Cuzco 436;** ) This bright, enticing lodge is one of the southern Amazon's best. Its spacious rooms, fashioned out of reclaimed timber, make you feel like a well-to-do early 20th-century traveler. The serene location could hardly be better, with an on-site rainforest learning center and laboratory, its own private *cocha* (an indigenous word for lagoon) and the beautiful Lago Sandoval barely a stone's throw away. There is electricity a few hours a day.

**INKATERRA RESERVA AMAZONICA** Lodge $$$

(**www.inkaterra.com; 3 days & 2 nights cabin s/d US$673/1082**) Cuzco (**084-24-5314; Plaza Nazarenas 167**); Lima (**01-610-0400; Andalucía 174, Miraflores**) Puerto Maldonado (**082-57-2823; Cuzco 436**) Further down the Madre de Dios, almost 16km from Puerto Maldonado, this luxurious choice has 10km of private hiking trails, canopy walkways, and a bar built around a fig tree. About 40 rustic individual cabins have bathrooms and porches with two hammocks. Six suites boast huge bathrooms, writing desks and two queen beds each. There is also a library and a relaxation area and some of the southern Amazon's best meals are served here.

**ESTANCIA BELLO HORIZONTE** Lodge $$$

(**082-57-2748, 982-720-950; www.estanciabellohorizonte.com; JM Grain, Puerto Maldonado; per person 3 days & 2 nights US$240;** ) Located 20km from Puerto Maldonado on the east side of the Río Madre de Dios, this superb getaway is comprised of bungalows equipped with smallish, comfortable rooms and hammocks for lounging. The child-friendly grounds include a soccer pitch, a volleyball court, a swimming pool and signposted jungle walks.

## Río Tambopata

The Río Tambopata is a major tributary of the Río Madre de Dios, joining it at Puerto Maldonado. Boats go up the river and into the **Reserva Nacional Tambopata** (**admission up to 4 nights S100**), an important protected area which also includes the *zona de amortiguamiento* (buffer zone). A highlight of the reserve is the *Colpa de guacamayos* (Macaw Clay Lick), one of the country's largest natural clay licks. It attracts hundreds of birds and is a spectacular sight.

Travelers heading up the Río Tambopata must register their passport numbers at the *puesto control* (guard post) and show their national-park entrance permits obtained in Puerto Maldonado at the Sernanp office (p302). Guided tours will arrange this for you.

## Punk Chickens

Listen carefully as your boat passes the banks of the Río Tambopata. If you hear lots of hissing, grunting and sounds of breaking vegetation, it is likely that you have stumbled upon the elaborate mating ritual of one of the Amazon's weirdest birds, the hoatzin. This is an oversized wild chicken with a blue face and a large crest on its head (hence the nickname 'punk chicken').

Scientists have been unable to classify this bird as a member of any other avian family, mainly due to the two claws the young have on each wing. To evade predators, hoatzin chicks will fall out of the nest to the river and use their claws to help them scramble back up the muddy banks. The clawed wing is a feature no other airborne creature since the pterodactyl has possessed. The bird's appearance is outdone by its terrible smell, which may well be the first indication they are nearby. They also taste bad, so are rarely hunted. In this age of rainforest depletion, they are one of the few native birds with a flourishing population.

### Sleeping

Lodges are listed in the order in which you would arrive at them if traveling from Puerto Maldonado.

 **POSADA AMAZONAS** Lodge **$$$**
**(Rainforest Expeditions; www.perunature.com; s/d 3 days & 2 nights US$485/750)** Cuzco (**084-24-6243; cusco@rainforest.com.pe; Portal de Carnes 236**); Lima (**01-421-8347; postmaster@rainforest.com.pe; Aramburu 166, Miraflores**); Puerto Maldonado (**082-57-2575; pem@rainforest.com.pe; Av Aeropuerto Km 6, CPM La Joya**) About two hours from Puerto Maldonado along the Río Tambopata, this *posada* is on the land of the Ese'eja community of Infierno, and tribal members are among the guides. There are excellent chances of seeing macaws on a small salt lick nearby, and giant river otters are often found swimming in area lakes. There is a medicinal-plant trail and a 30m-high observation platform. The lodge has 30 large double rooms with private showers and windows overlooking the rainforest. Electricity is only available a few hours a day.

**EXPLORER'S INN** Lodge **$$**
**(www.explorersinn.com; s/d 3 days & 2 nights US$238/396)** Cuzco (**084-23-5342; Plateros 365**); Lima (**01-447-8888, 01-447-4761; sales@explorersinn.com; Alcanfores 459, Miraflores**) Puerto Maldonado (**082-57-2078**) About 58km from Puerto Maldonado (three to four hours of river travel), this pleasant lodge has 15 rustic double and 15 triple rooms, all with bathrooms and screened windows. Around since the 1970s, it is more open than many other area lodges, and has 38km of trails that can be explored.

**CAYMAN LODGE AMAZONIE** Lodge **$$$**
(**082-57-1970; www.cayman-lodge-amazonie.com; Arequipa 655, Puerto Maldonado; s/d 3 days & 2 nights US$400/560**) Some 70km from Puerto Maldonado, Cayman has an open, relaxing environment with banana, *cocona* (peach tomato) and mango trees in a lush tropical garden. The rooms are a little on the small side, but are more than comfortable. One of its more arresting features is the hammock house, from where you can watch the sun set over the river.

**LIBERTADOR TAMBOPATA LODGE** Lodge **$$$**
(**082-57-1726, 082-968-0022; www.tambopatalodge.com; Prada 269, Puerto Maldonado; s/d 3 days & 2 nights US$417/676**) Set mainly near secondary forest, this considerably more luxurious lodge is still within the Reserva Tambopata and boasts 12km of well-marked trails, spacious individual bungalows, tiled patios and well-manicured gardens. The overall effect is like a set from the TV series *Lost*.

# Manu Area

The Manu area encompasses the Parque Nacional Manu and much of the surrounding area. Covering almost 20,000 sq km, the park is divided into three zones: the largest sector is the *zona natural*, comprising 80% of the total park area and closed to unauthorized visitors. The second sector, still within the park proper, is the *zona reservada*, where controlled research and tourism activities are permitted. The third sector, covering the southeastern area, is the *zona cultural*, where most other visitor activity is concentrated.

## Parque Nacional Manu

This national park starts in the eastern slopes of the Andes and plunges down into the lowlands, playing host to a great diversity of wildlife over a wide range of cloud forest and rainforest habitats. Unesco declared it a World Natural Heritage site in 1987. During a one-week trip you can reasonably expect to see scores of different bird species, several monkey species and possibly a few other mammals, including jaguars, tapirs, giant anteaters, tamanduas, capybaras, peccaries and giant river otters. Colorful butterflies and less pleasing insects also abound.

The best time to go is during the dry season (June to November); Manu may be inaccessible or closed during the rainy months (January to April), except to visitors staying at the two lodges within the park boundaries.

It is illegal to enter the park without a guide. Travelers often report delays upon returning from Manu (of up to several days), so don't plan an international airline connection for the day after your trip.

### Tours

The number of permits to operate tours into Parque Nacional Manu is limited; only about 3000 visitors are allowed in annually. Visitors must book well in advance. All of the tours listed here are licensed to operate in the park and maintain some level of low-impact practices. Tours include transportation, food, purified drinking water, guides, permits and camping equipment or lodge rooms. Personal items such as sleeping bags (if camping), insect repellent, sunblock, flashlights, suitable clothing and bottled drinks are the traveler's responsibility. Binoculars and a camera with a zoom lens are highly recommended. English-speaking guides are available.

**BONANZA TOURS** Adventure Tour
(**084-50-7871; www.bonanzatoursperu.com; Suecia 343, Cuzco**) This local family-operated company is run by Ryse Choquepuma and his brothers, who grew up in Manu and know it better than most. Tours are arranged to the family home, which has been converted into a well-appointed lodge. There are trails, as well as a clay lick that attracts plenty of wildlife. The four day/three night option costs US$435.

**PANTIACOLLA TOURS** Adventure Tour
(**084-23-8323; www.pantiacolla.com; Garcilaso 265 interior, 2nd fl, Cuzco**) Pantiacolla own three lodges in the Manu region and is frequently recommended by a variety of travelers for its knowledgeable and responsibly executed tours. It offers a a mix of tours, starting at US$1275 per person for seven days, including a mix of camping and lodge accommodations.

**MANU EXPEDITIONS** Adventure Tour
(**084-22-5990, 084-22-4235; www.manuexpeditions.com; Clorinda Matto de Turner 330, Urb Magisterial, Cuzco**) Manu Expeditions owns the only tented camp within the national park and offer more than two decades of Manu experience. Its guides are excellent. A popular trip leaves Cuzco every Sunday (except January to March when it's the first Sunday of the month only) and lasts nine days. This costs US$2445 per person, based on double occupancy. Customized trips are also offered.

# Peru In Focus



Arequipa (p114), with El Misti in the background

# Peru Today

> *The good times have resulted in a surge of cultural productivity*

**belief systems**
(% of population)

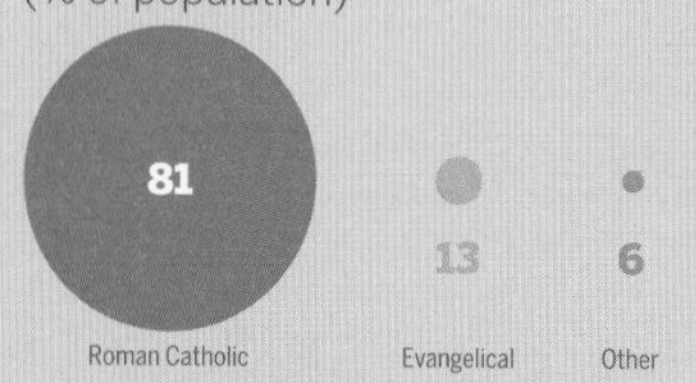


**if Peru were 100 people**

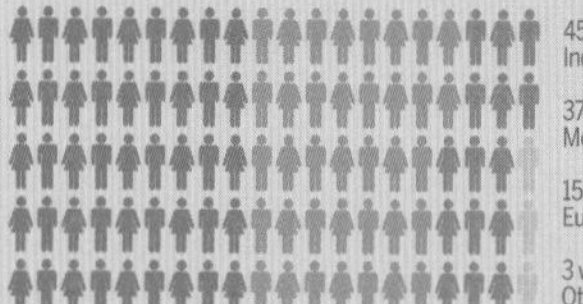


**population per sq km**

≈ 10 people

Peru USA UK

La Catedral on the Plaza de Armas (p178), Cuzco

## An Unparalleled Boom

Between the violence of the conquest, the chaos of the early republic and the succession of dictatorships that swallowed up much of the 20th century, stability has been rare in Peru. But so far, the new millennium has treated the country with uncharacteristic grace. Peru's economy has grown every year since 2003. Foreign investment is up and the country's exports – in the areas of agriculture, mining and manufacturing – have been strong. Tourism is also big: the number of foreign travelers going to Peru doubled between 2003 and 2011 from 1.3 to 2.6 million.

Since 2000 a succession of peaceful elections has also provided political stability. In 2011 former army officer Ollanta Humala was elected to the presidency. The son of a Quechua labor lawyer from Ayacucho, he has made social inclusion a theme of his presidency. One of his early acts was to make it a legal requirement for native peoples to be consulted on mining or other extractive activities in their territories.

DANITA DELIMONT /GETTY IMAGES ©

## A Cultural Renaissance

The good times have resulted in a surge of cultural productivity – much of it revolving around food. Once considered a place to avoid, Lima is now a foodie bastion, where gastronomic festivals attract visitors from all over the world. La Mistura, an annual culinary gathering organized by celebrity chef Gastón Acurio, drew more than 400,000 people in 2011.

The relentless focus on food has had a ripple effect. Young fashion designers produce avant-garde clothing lines with alpaca knits. Innovative musical groups fuse folk and electronica. And the contemporary-arts scene has been refreshed: the country's most important museum, the Museo de Arte de Lima (MALI) recently reopened after a top-to-bottom renovation, and a handful of galleries have blossomed in Lima's bohemian quarters.

## A Ways to Go

None of this means there aren't serious challenges. Though the country's poverty rate has plummeted 23% since 2002, the economic boom has not benefited everyone – rural poverty, for example, is nearly double the national average.

In addition, Sendero Luminoso (Shining Path), the Maoist guerilla group that took the country to the brink of civil war in the 1980s, has seen a comeback – occasionally launching attacks on police and industrial projects in the central Andes. While the group isn't threatening the government's hold on power (it's estimated to have only 500 members), it is funding itself with money from the cocaine trade, according to the US Drug Enforcement Agency. (Peru now rivals Colombia in terms of cocaine production.) Moreover, a botched government raid on one of Sendero's highland strongholds led to the deaths of 10 police officers in April of 2012, generating an avalanche of criticism for the Humala administration.

There are also environmental pressures to contend with. In 2012 the northern city of Cajamarca was racked by months of civil unrest over a proposed gold-mining concern in the region – with protests over the mine's possible effect on the water supply. And, of course, there is the Amazon – now bisected by the Interoceánica highway, an important overland trade route that will further connect Peru and Brazil. While it's an engineering marvel, the road has generated deep apprehension among scientists about the impact it will have on one of the world's last great wilderness areas.

# History

Inti Raymi (Festival of the Sun; p43), Cuzco

HUGHES HERVÁ/HEMIS.FR/GETTY IMAGES ©

*When the Spanish arrived in the 16th century, the Andes had already seen epic clashes among civilizations. There had been the deity-obsessed Chavín, the militaristic Wari and the artistic Moche. But the encounter that remains most embedded in the Peruvian psyche is the seismic encounter between the Incas and Spaniards. It's a tragic history, yet one that has produced a new culture, a new race and a fascinating new civilization.*

## Civilization's Early Roots

Along with Egypt, India and China, Peru is considered one of the six cradles of civilization (a site where urbanization accompanied agricultural innovation) – and the only one located in the southern hemisphere. Some of the earliest human settlements began to flourish here at about 3000 BC, with the oldest

**c 3000 BC**

Some of the first structures are built at the coastal ceremonial center of Caral.

remains discovered at Caral, a 626-hectare ruins site found about 200km north of Lima. Almost five thousand years old, the temple mounds and irrigation canals here are evidence of the oldest civilization in the Americas. In 2009 it was declared a Unesco World Heritage site.

## The Best... Ruins

1 Machu Picchu (p217)

2 Chan Chan (p261)

3 Sillustani (p154)

4 Sacsaywamán (p203)

5 Huacas del Sol y de la Luna (p262)

6 Kuélap (p272)



## The Chavín Horizon

Fast forward a couple of thousand years and you'll end up in the era known as the Chavín Horizon – named after the site of Chavín de Huántar, east of Huaraz. This was a rich period of development for Andean culture – when greater urbanization occurred and artistic and religious phenomena appeared all over the central and northern highlands, as well as the coast. Lasting roughly from 1000 BC to 300 BC, the salient feature of Chavín is the repeated representation of a stylized jaguar or puma.

## The Birth of Local Cultures

After Chavín, numerous regional cultures became important in scattered areas of the country. South of Lima, near the Península de Paracas, was a coastal community whose most significant phase is referred to as Paracas Necropolis (AD 1–400), after a large burial site. Some of the finest pre-Columbian textiles have been unearthed here: intricate fabrics that depict feline warriors and stylized anthropomorphic figures. Nearby, the Nazca culture (200 BC–AD 600) carved giant, enigmatic designs into the desert. Known as the Nazca Lines (p112), these were mapped early in the 20th century, though their ultimate purpose remains unknown.

On the north coast, it was the Moche who were influential. They settled the area around Trujillo from about AD 100 to 800 and are known for their astonishing, highly individualistic ceramic heads, no two of which are exactly alike. They also left behind temple mounds, such as the Huacas del Sol y de la Luna (Temples of the Sun and Moon), near Trujillo, and the impressive burial site of Sipán, north of Chiclayo.

**200 BC**
The Nazca culture builds giant glyphs that adorn the southern desert to this day.

**AD 500**
The Moche construct the Huacas del Sol y de la Luna, adobe temples near present-day Trujillo.

**c 800**
The fiercely independent Chachapoyas build Kuélap, a citadel in the northern highlands.

## Wari Expansion

The Wari – an ethnic group from the Ayacucho Basin – emerged as a force to be reckoned with for 500 years, beginning in AD 600. They were vigorous military conquerors that built important outposts throughout a vast territory from Chiclayo to Cuzco. As with many conquerors, the Wari attempted to subdue others by emphasizing their own traditions over local belief. Thus from about AD 700 to 1100, Wari influence is noted in the art, technology and architecture of cultures around Peru. These include finely woven textiles, some of which contain record-breaking thread counts. The Wari are most significant, however, for creating an extensive network of roadways and for expanding the terrace agriculture system, an infrastructure that the Incas would employ to their advantage centuries later.

## Regional Kingdoms

The Wari were replaced by a number of small nation-states that thrived from about AD 1000 to the early 1400s, when the Incas came into the picture. One of the biggest of these were the Chimú, of the Trujillo area, whose capital was the famed Chan Chan, the largest adobe city in the world. Nearby were the Sicán, from the Lambayeque area, renowned metallurgists who produced the *tumi* – a ceremonial knife with a rounded blade used in sacrifices. (It has since become a national symbol.)

Other coastal cultures emerged at this point, including the Ica, the Chincha and the Chancay – the latter of whom were known for their geometric lace and crudely humorous pottery, in which just about every figure seems to be drinking.

In the northern Andes, the cloud-forest-dwelling Chachapoyas culture erected the expansive mountaintop settlement of Kuélap in a remote patch of the Utcubamba Valley.

## Enter the Incas

The Inca presence dates back to the 12th century, in the area around Cuzco. For several hundred years, they remained a small regional state, until 1438, when their ninth king, Inca Yupanqui, defended Cuzco from the invading Chanka people to the north. Emboldened by his victory, he took the name Pachacutec, which means 'Transformer of the Earth,' and proceeded to bag much of the Andes. Under his reign, he grew his territory from a regional fiefdom in the Cuzco Valley into an empire of 10 million people, covering most of Peru, as well as parts of Ecuador, Bolivia and Chile.

Pachacutec's grandson, Huayna Cápac, continued this expansion. By the early 16th century, the Inca empire extended well into present-day Colombia. Unfortunately, Huayna Cápac wouldn't be around to savor his victories. He died unexpectedly in 1525. Without a clear plan for succession, two of the king's children fought for control: the Quito-born Atahualpa, who commanded the Inca armies of the north, and Huáscar, who was based in Cuzco. The ensuing struggle plunged

**c 1000**

The Chimú begin development of Chan Chan, a sprawling adobe city outside Trujillo.

**1100–1200**

The Incas emerge as a presence in the Cuzco Valley.

the empire into a bloody civil war, with Atahualpa emerging the victor in April of 1532. The vicious nature of the conflict left the Incas with enemies throughout the Andes, which is why some tribes were willing to cooperate with the Spanish when they arrived just five months later.

## The Best... Historic Churches

1 Iglesia de Santa Domingo, Lima (p68)

2 Iglesia de La Compañía de Jesús, Cuzco (p180)

3 Iglesia de San Pedro, Andahuaylillas (p184)

4 Monasterio de Santa Catalina, Arequipa (p115)

5 Basilica Menor Catedral, Trujillo (p255)



## The Spanish Invade

Francisco Pizarro landed in Tumbes, on the north coast of present-day Peru, in September of 1532 with a shipload of arms, horses and slaves and a battalion of 168 men. Atahualpa, at this time, was in the northern highland city of Cajamarca, on his way to Cuzco to claim his throne. The Spaniard quickly deduced that the empire was in a fractious state. Pizarro went to Cajamarca and approached Atahualpa with promises of brotherhood, but soon enough, he and his men had launched a surprise attack that left thousands dead and Atahualpa a prisoner of war. And thus began one of the most famous ransoms in history: in order to regain their leader's freedom, the Incas filled an entire room with silver and gold. But it was never enough. The Spanish eventually sentenced Atahualpa to death by strangulation.

The invasion would bring on a cataclysmic collapse of indigenous society. One scholar estimates that the native population – around 10 million when Pizarro arrived – was reduced to 600,000 within a century.

## The Tumultuous Colony

The Spanish established their administrative capital in Lima, on the central desert coast, on January 6, 1535. The unrest began almost immediately, with conquistadors fighting among themselves over the spoils of the new viceroyalty. Many of them met violent deaths, including Pizarro, who was stabbed to death by a rival faction in 1541. Things grew relatively more stable after the arrival in 1569 of Viceroy Francisco de Toledo, an able Spanish administrator who brought some order to the emerging colony.

In the new colonial society, Spaniards held the leadership positions, while *criollos* (Spaniards born in Peru) were confined to middle management. *Mestizos* (people who were of mixed descent), were further down the social scale. Full-blooded *indígenas* (indigenous people) resided at the bottom, exploited as *peones* (laborers).

**1438–71**
Machu Picchu is built during the reign of Inca Yupanqui.

**1532**
Atahualpa wins control over Inca territories; the Spanish land in Peru and execute him months later.

**1671**
Santa Rosa de Lima, the first saint of the Americas, is canonized.

Tensions between *indígenas* and Spaniards reached boiling point in the late 18th century, when the crown levied a series of new taxes that hit the indigenous poor the hardest. In 1780 José Gabriel Condorcanqui, a descendant of Inca king Túpac Amaru, executed a Spanish administrator on charges of cruelty. His act unleashed an indigenous rebellion that spread throughout the Andes. The Spanish reprisal was swift – and brutal. In 1781 Condorcanqui watched his followers, his wife and his sons being killed in the main plaza in Cuzco, before being drawn and quartered himself.

## Independence

For Peru, the struggle for nationhood happened on two fronts. Argentine revolutionary José de San Martín led independence campaigns in Argentina and Chile, before entering Peru at the port of Pisco in 1820. With his arrival, royalist forces retreated into the highlands, and, on July 28, 1821, independence was declared. But real independence wouldn't materialize for another three years: with Spanish forces still at large in the interior, San Martín needed more men to fully vanquish the Spanish.

Enter Simón Bolívar, the venerated Venezuelan revolutionary, who had led independence fights in Venezuela, Colombia and Ecuador. San Martín met with

Moche carving
DANITA DELIMONT/GETTY IMAGES ©

**1821**
Independence from Spain is declared on July 28, but battles continue for several years.

**1879–83**
Chile wages war against Peru over nitrate-rich lands in the Atacama Desert. Peru loses.

**1911**
US historian Hiram Bingham arrives at Machu Picchu.

Bolívar privately in 1822 to seek help on the Peruvian campaign. Within a year, Bolívar had defeated the Spanish. In early 1826 the last detachment of royal soldiers left Peru.

## The New Republic & War of the Pacific



Through much of the 19th century there was a revolving door of regime changes as regional *caudillos* (chieftains) scrambled for power. In 1845 the country would find some measure of stability under the governance of Ramón Castilla, who abolished slavery, paid off some of Peru's debt and established a public school system. But with his passing, in 1867, the country once again descended into chaos and fiscal mismanagement.

By 1874 Peru was bankrupt and in a weak position to deal with the expanding clash between Chile and Bolivia over nitrate-rich lands in the Atacama Desert. The war was a disaster for Peru. The Chileans, who had the support of the British, led a land campaign deep into the country, ransacking Lima and making off with the priceless contents of the National Library in the process. By the time it was all over, in 1884, Peru had permanently lost its southernmost region of Tarapacá and wouldn't regain the area around Tacna until 1929. The Bolivians, in the meantime, lost their entire coast.

## A New Intellectual Era

As one century gave way to the next, intellectual circles saw the rise of *indigenismo,* a continent-wide movement that advocated for a dominant role for indigenous people. In Peru, this translated into a wide-ranging (if fragmented) cultural movement. Historian Luis Valcárcel attacked his society's degradation of the indigenous class. Poet César Vallejo wrote critically acclaimed works that took on oppression. And painter José Sabogal led a generation of artists who explored indigenous themes in their paintings. In 1928 journalist José Carlos Mariátegui penned *Seven Interpretive Essays on Peruvian Reality,* in which he celebrated the communal aspects of the Inca social order. (It remains vital reading to this day.)

In this climate, in 1924 political leader Victor Raúl Haya de la Torre founded the American Popular Revolutionary Alliance (APRA) party, which espoused populist values and celebrated 'Indo-America.' It would remain illegal for long periods of the 20th century.

## Dictatorships & Revolutionaries

After the start of the Great Depression in 1929, the country's history becomes a blur of dictatorships punctuated by periods of democracy. Augusto Leguía, an autocratic sugar baron from the north coast, gained power in 1919 via a coup d'état and ruled for almost a dozen years. He was followed by Colonel Luis Sánchez Cerro, who served a couple of short terms in the 1930s. Though his time in office was turbulent, Sánchez was later

**1955**
Women are granted the right to vote.

**1969**
Quechua is made an official language.

**1980**
Sendero Luminoso burns ballot boxes in Ayacucho, marking the beginning of the Internal Conflict.

## The Best... Peruvian Writers

1 El Inca Garcilaso de la Vega, chronicler

2 Ricardo Palma, writer

3 Abraham Valdelomar, essayist

4 César Vallejo, poet

5 José Carlos Mariategui, political theorist

6 Mario Vargas Llosa, novelist

celebrated for abolishing a conscription law that required able-bodied men to serve on road-building projects. (The law affected indigenous men disproportionately.) By 1948 another dictator had taken power: former army colonel Manuel Odría, who spent his time in office cracking down on APRA and encouraging US foreign investment.

The most fascinating of Peru's 20th-century dictators, however, is Juan Velasco Alvarado, the former commander-in-chief of the army who took control in 1968. Though he was expected to lead a conservative regime, in his rhetoric Velasco celebrated the indigenous peasantry, championed agrarian reform and even made Quechua an official language. Ultimately, however, his economic policies were failures, and he was pushed out of office by fellow military commanders in 1975.

## The Internal Conflict

The country returned to civilian rule in 1980, but with the economy stalled, the inequities facing indigenous peasants fell off the radar. It was at this time that a radical Maoist guerrilla group from Ayacucho began its unprecedented rise. Sendero Luminoso (Shining Path) wanted nothing less than a complete overthrow of the social order through armed struggle. This resulted in two decades of escalating violence, with Sendero (in addition to smaller guerrilla groups) assassinating political and community leaders and carrying out bomb attacks.

In response, the government sent in the military, which knew little about how to handle a guerilla insurgency. Caught in the middle were thousands of peasants, who bore the brunt of the casualties. The conflict ultimately left an estimated 70,000 dead.

Aggravating the situation was the wheezing economy. In the late 1980s President Alan García suspended foreign debt payments and nationalized the banks – actions that eventually led to a hyperinflation rate of 7500%. There were food shortages and riots, and the government declared a state of emergency. Soon after his term was over, García fled the country after being accused of embezzling millions of dollars. (He returned in 2001, when the statute of limitations on his case ran out.)

**1985**
Alan García is elected, the first APRA candidate to reach the presidency.

**1987**
A Moche leader's tomb is discovered near Lambayeque. He is dubbed El Señor de Sipán.

**1990**
Alberto Fujimori, an agronomist of Japanese descent, is elected president.

## Fujishock

In 1990 Alberto Fujimori, an agronomist of Japanese descent, was elected president. He implemented an austerity plan that the press dubbed 'Fujishock.' It ultimately succeeded in reducing inflation and stabilizing the economy, but not without costing the average Peruvian dearly. Fujimori followed this, in 1992, with an *autogolpe* (coup from within), a move that stocked the legislature with his allies. Peruvians tolerated the move: the economy was growing and Sendero Luminoso's leadership had been apprehended. As the country faced the new millennium, the violence began to wind down.

By the end of his second term, however, Fujimori was being plagued by allegations of corruption. After running for a third term (technically unconstitutional), it was revealed that his security chief had been embezzling government funds and bribing officials. Fujimori was declared 'morally unfit' to govern by the legislature and was voted out of office. He was later convicted of ordering extrajudicial killings and misappropriating government funds, and is now serving three decades in prison.

La Catedral (p178), Cuzco
DANITA DELIMONT/GETTY IMAGES ©

**1994**
Astrid y Gastón opens in Lima; the restaurant catapults Peruvian cuisine onto the international stage.

CAROLINA MIRANDA

**2001**
Alejandro Toledo becomes president and the first indigenous governer of an Andean country.

## A Nobel for Peru

Mario Vargas Llosa (b 1936), Peru's most famous writer, was awarded the Nobel Prize in Literature in 2010 for stories that explore the vagaries of corruption and power. The honorific caps an extraordinary life: as a young man, Vargas Llosa had an affair with an aunt, whom he later married (an incident he fictionalized in *Aunt Julia and the Scriptwriter*). In the '70s, he came to blows with Colombian Nobel laureate Gabriel García Márquez. The following decade, he ran for the presidency – and lost. Upon winning the Nobel, he told a reporter: 'Death will find me with my pen in hand.'

## A Period of Renewal

Since that time, the country has enjoyed a rare period of reconciliation. In 2001 shoeshine-boy-turned-Stanford-economist Alejandro Toledo became the first person of Quechua ethnicity to be elected president. Toledo's term was followed in 2006 by the re-election of García to the presidency. Unlike the first time, the economy performed well – despite the global economic crises of 2008. But it wasn't without problems. For one, there was the issue of corruption (García's entire cabinet was forced to resign in 2008 after widespread allegations of bribery) and there has been the touchy issue of how to manage the country's mineral wealth. In 2008 García signed a law that allowed foreign companies to exploit natural resources in the Amazon. The legislation generated a backlash among various Amazon tribes and led to a fatal standoff in the northern city of Bagua in 2009.

Congress quickly revoked the law, but the issue remains a challenge for the new president, Ollanta Humala. Elected in 2011, the former army officer was initially thought to be a populist in the Hugo Chávez vein (the Lima stock exchange dropped precipitously when he was first elected). But his administration has been quite friendly to business. Though the economy has functioned well under his governance, civil unrest over a proposed gold mine in the north, as well as a botched raid on a Sendero Luminoso encampment, sent his approval rating into a tailspin by the middle of 2012.

**2003**
An independent report on the Internal Conflict released: death toll estimates reach 70,000.

**2009**
Fujimori is convicted of embezzling, in addition to previous convictions involving illegal searches and extrajudicial killings.

**2011**
Populist former army officer Ollanta Humala assumes the presidency after winning a run-off election.

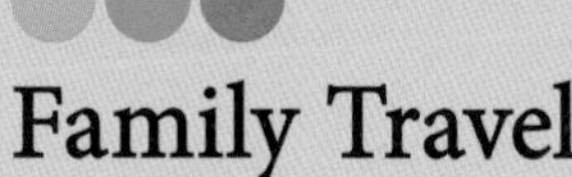

# Family Travel

Peruvian doll

NATALIE WINTER/GETTY IMAGES ©

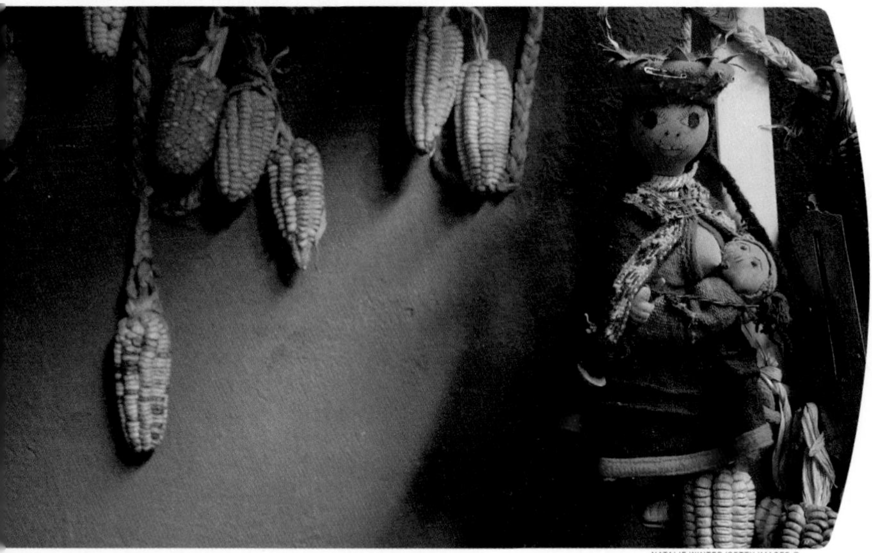

*In a country that holds family dear, children are welcome just about everywhere – so expect them to be patted on the head...a lot. Peru's vast array of archaeological sites should inspire plenty of young action heroes. If not, a few tales about pre-Columbian human sacrifice should do the trick. Though be prepared: few spots have dedicated facilities for little ones.*

## The Basics

Given the somewhat complicated nature of travel around Peru, don't try to overdo things, especially if you're traveling with small children who aren't used to being at higher elevations. Altitude sickness, which is a problem for adults in the Andes, becomes immeasurably more complicated in children (especially toddlers) who can't always articulate their symptoms. If you're going to be well above sea level, be on the lookout for signs of headache, nausea, dizziness or weakness. If you suspect that your child has altitude sickness, seek medical attention. Some pediatricians advise waiting until a child is eight years old before traveling to elevations over 3000m. Beyond that age, consult the altitude acclimatization advice on p345.

## The Best... Activities for Kids

1 River running, Cuzco (p185)

2 Beaching it, Máncora (p274)

3 Hot springs (p127), Cañón del Colca

4 Looking for wildlife (p287), Amazon Basin

5 Visiting the Choco Museo (p71), Lima

Children under the age of nine months should not be taken to jungle areas since yellow-fever vaccinations are not safe for this age group.

## Dining

'Kids' meals' (small portions at small prices) are not normally offered, but most establishments will obligingly produce simple foods on request, including *bistec a la plancha* (grilled steak) or *pollo a la plancha* (grilled chicken). Other basic items include *sándwich de queso* (cheese sandwiches), *hamburguesas* (hamburgers) and pasta. If traveling with an infant, stock up on formula and baby food before heading into rural areas.

Young children should avoid tap water and ice as they're more susceptible to stomach illnesses.

## Transportation

Children under the age of 12 receive discounts of 25% to 50% for airline travel, while infants under two pay only 10% of the fare provided they sit on their parent's lap. On buses, children pay full fare if they occupy a seat, but aren't normally charged if they sit on a parent's lap. Often, someone will give up a seat for a parent traveling with a small child, or they'll offer to put your child on their lap. (Don't be put off by this – it's normal).

## Other Practicalities

Cribs and high chairs are not usually available, except at established family hotels and restaurants, so check ahead.

Breastfeeding in public is not uncommon, but most women discreetly cover themselves. Poorly maintained public bathrooms may be a concern for parents. Always carry toilet paper and wet wipes.

For more advice, see *Lonely Planet's Travel with Children* or log on to www.travelwithyourkids.com and www.familytravelnetwork.com.

## Need to Know

- **Changing facilities** Rare beyond airports, malls and some chain restaurants.
- **Cribs** Request ahead; these may be difficult to find in remote or rural areas.
- **High chairs** Call ahead; not always available.
- **Kids' menus** Rare.
- **Nappies (diapers)** Available at supermarkets and large pharmacies in bigger cities.
- **Strollers** Bring your own.
- **Transportation** Reserve seats where possible to avoid standing.

# Ancient Peru

Inca ruins in the Sacred Valley (p205)

*Despite the best efforts of the Spanish – who ransacked temples and melted down sacred gold objects – Peru's archaeological legacy is rich. The area has been home to civilizations large and small. As a result, travelers can see sumptuous textiles, striking ceramics and monumental structures so well engineered that they have not only survived conquest, but calamitous earthquakes as well. For the Indiana Jones set, the adventure begins here.*

## Caral

Just a couple of hundred kilometers north of Lima on the Pacific coast sits one of the most exciting archaeological sites in Peru. It may not look like much – half a dozen temple mounds, a few sunken amphitheaters and remnants of structures crafted from adobe and stone – but it is. This 626-hectare spot is the oldest known city in the Americas: Caral.

Situated in the Supe Valley, this Preceramic civilization developed almost simultaneously with the ancient cultures of Mesopotamia and Egypt about 5000 years ago, and it predates the earliest civilizations in Mexico by about 1500 years. Caral was not a militaristic settlement, but a religious one that venerated its holy men and paid tribute to unknown agricultural deities (at times, with human sacrifice). They cultivated crops such as cotton, squash and beans and were knowledgeable

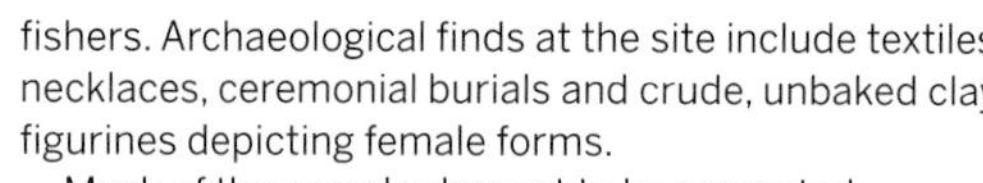

fishers. Archaeological finds at the site include textiles, necklaces, ceremonial burials and crude, unbaked clay figurines depicting female forms.

Much of the complex has yet to be excavated – expect further discoveries.

## Chavín

If Caral provides the earliest signs of functional urban settlement, then Chavín de Huántar, near Huaraz, is evidence of a unified religious and artistic iconography. In a broad swath of the northern Andes, from roughly 1000 BC to 300 BC, a common culture arose around a toothy feline deity that appears on carvings, friezes, pottery and textiles from the era. There is only patchy information available on Chavín and the structure of its societies, but its importance is without question: in Peru, this moment represents the birth of art.

It is still debated whether the temple at Chavín de Huántar was a capital or a single ceremonial site, but what is without doubt is that the setting is extraordinary. With the stunning Cordillera Blanca as a backdrop, the remnants of this elaborate ceremonial complex – built over hundreds of years – include a number of temple structures, as well as a sunken court with stone friezes of jaguars. Here, archaeologists have found pottery from all over the region filled with *ofrendas* (offerings), including shells from as far away as the Ecuadorian coast, and carved bones (some human) featuring supernatural motifs.

### The Best... Archaeology Museums

1 Museo Larco (p69), Lima

2 Museo Tumbas Reales de Sipán (p273), Lambayeque

3 Museo Inka (p180), Cuzco

4 Museo Nacional de Chavín (p253), Chavín de Huántar

5 Museo Santuarios Andinos (p114), Arequipa

## Paracas & Nazca

In the wake of Chavín, a number of smaller, regional ethnicities arose. Along the country's south coast, from about 700 BC to AD 400, the culture known as Paracas – situated around modern-day Ica – produced some of the most renowned textiles created in the Andes. The most impressive of these were woven during the period known as the Paracas Necropolis (AD 1 to 400), so named for a massive grave site on the Península de Paracas uncovered in 1927 by famed Peruvian archaeologist Julio Tello.

The magnificent textiles recovered from the graves – layer upon layer of finely woven fabrics wrapped around mummy bundles – provide important clues about day-to-day life and beliefs. Featured on these intricate cloths are depictions of flowers, fish, birds, knives and cats, with some animals represented as two-headed creatures. Also significant are the human figures, such as warriors carrying shrunken trophy heads, and supernatural anthropomorphic creatures equipped with snake tongues and feline claws.

During roughly the same period, the Nazca culture (200 BC to AD 600), to the south, was producing an array of painted pottery, as well as incredible weavings that featured geometric and other images. These works showcased everyday objects (beans, birds and fish), as well as supernatural cat- and falcon-men in an array of explosive colors. The Nazca were skilled embroiderers: some weavings feature tiny dangling figurines that must have induced blindness in their creators. But the culture is best known for producing the Nazca Lines, a series of mysterious geoglyphs of animals and abstract geometric designs carved into a 500-sq-km area in the desert.



## The Moche

Inhabiting the Peruvian north coast from about AD 100 to 800, the Moche were accomplished in many areas. Though not inherently urban, they built sophisticated ceremonial centers, such as the frieze-laden Huacas del Sol y de la Luna (Temples of the Sun and Moon), outside of modern-day Trujillo. They also created elaborate burial sites for their leaders, such as that at Sipán, near Chiclayo. They had a well-maintained network of roads and a system of relay runners that carried messages, probably in the form of symbols carved onto beans.

But it's their pottery that makes them a standout: lifelike depictions of individuals (scars and all) that are so skillfully rendered, some of them seem as if they are about to talk. In some cases, artists created many portraits of a single person over the course of their lifetime; one scholar recorded 45 different pieces depicting the same model. Many ceramics are dedicated to showcasing macho activities (hunting and human sacrifice). This doesn't mean that they didn't know a thing or two about love. The pottery artifacts of the Moche are renowned for their encyclopedic depictions of human sex.

## The Wari

From about AD 600 to 1100, the Andes saw the rise of the first truly expansive kingdom. The Wari were avid empire builders, expanding from their base around Ayacucho to a territory that occupied an area from Chiclayo to Cuzco. Expert agriculturalists, they improved production by developing the terrace system and creating a network of canals for irrigation.

In the area of weaving, the culture was highly skilled, producing elegant fabrics with elaborate stylized designs. The Wari were masters of color, using as many as 150 distinct shades, which they incorporated into woven and tie-dyed patterns. Many of these textiles feature abstract, geometric designs, as well as supernatural figures – most common is a winged deity holding a staff.

### Human Sacrifice in the Andes

Numerous pre-Columbian cultures engaged in human sacrifice, including the Incas and the Moche – the latter of whom depicted it on their ceramics. The practice was intended as a way of paying tribute to natural forces. However, details on how exactly it was carried out remain sketchy (none of the pre-Columbian cultures in the Andes left behind a written language). In recent years archaeological work has begun to shed light on the practice. The most vivid example is that of 'Juanita' – the frozen remains of a sacrificial Inca maiden – on view at the Museo Santuarios Andinos in Arequipa.

## Chimú & Chachapoyas

Following the demise of the Wari, a number of small nation-states emerged in different corners of the country. They are too numerous to detail here, but there are two that merit discussion because of the art and architecture they left behind.

The first of these is the Chimú, which were based around present-day Trujillo. Between about AD 1000 and 1400, this incredible north-coast civilization built the largest-known adobe city in the Americas. Chan Chan is a sprawling, 36-sq-km complex, which once housed an estimated 60,000 people. Within the society, there was an accomplished artisan class, which produced, among other things, some outrageous-looking textiles, some of which were covered top-to-bottom in tassels.

To the interior in the northern highlands is the abandoned cloud-forest citadel of Kuélap, built by the Chachapoyas culture in the remote Utcubamba Valley beginning around AD 800. It is an incredible series of structures, composed of more than 400 circular dwellings, in addition to some unusual, gravity-defying pieces, such as an inverted cone building known as El Tintero (The Inkpot). Unfortunately, little is known about the people who built it, who are largely remembered for having fiercely resisted the Inca conquest.

## The Incas

Peru's greatest engineers were also its greatest empire builders. Because the Incas made direct contact with the Spanish, they also happen to be the pre-Columbian Andean culture that is best documented – not only through Spanish chronicle, but also through narratives produced by some of the descendants of the Incas themselves. (The most famous of these chroniclers is El Inca Garcilaso de la Vega, who lived from 1539 to 1616.)

The Incas were a Quechua-speaking ethnicity which, from AD 1100 until the arrival of the Spanish in 1532, steadfastly grew a small territory around Cuzco into a highly

Moche mural, Huaca del Sol (p265)

organized empire that extended over more than 37° latitude from Colombia to Chile. It was an absolutist state with a strong army, where ultimate power resided with the *inca* (king). Its history is ridden with a succession of colorful royals who would make for an excellent TV movie – complete with fratricide, great battles and plenty of beautiful maidens.

The society was bound by a rigid caste system: there were nobles, an artisan and merchant class, and peasants. The latter supplied the manual labor for the Incas' many public-works projects. Citizens were expected to pay tribute to the crown in the form of labor – typically three months out of the year – enabling them to develop and maintain an extensive network of roadways and canals. The Incas also kept a highly efficient communications system: a body of *chasquis* (relay runners), who could make the 1600km trip between Quito and Cuzco in just seven days. Also notable was their social-welfare system. The Incas warehoused surplus food for distribution to areas and people in need.

## Incas versus Romans

It's not just the classical European civilizations that were expansive. At its acme, the Inca empire was larger than imperial Rome and boasted more than 40,000km of roadways. For a page-turning read about this incredible society, pick up Kim MacQuarrie's gripping 2007 book, *The Last Days of the Incas*.

On the cultural front, the Incas had a strong tradition of music, oral literature and weaving. But they are best known for their monumental architecture. The Inca capital of Cuzco, along with the constructions at Sacsaywamán, Pisac, Ollantaytambo and the fabled Machu Picchu, are all incredible examples of the imperial style of building. Carved pieces of rock, without mortar, are fitted together so tightly that it is impossible to fit a knife between the stones. Most interestingly, walls are built at an angle and windows in a trapezoidal form, so as to resist seismic activity.

Nestled into spectacular natural locales, these structures, even in a ruined state, are unforgettable. Their majesty was something the Spanish acknowledged, even as they pried them apart. 'Now that the Inca rulers have lost their power,' wrote Spanish chronicler Pedro Cieza de León in the 16th century, 'all these palaces and gardens, together with their other great works, have fallen, so that only the remains survive. Since they were built of good stone and the masonry is excellent, they will stand as memorials for centuries to come.'

León was right. The Inca civilization did not survive the Spanish, but their architecture did – a reminder of the many grand societies we are just beginning to understand.

# Outdoor Activities

The view from El Misti (p119)

DECLAN KIELTY/GETTY IMAGES ©

*Hike Inca roadways studded with ancient ruins. Raft one of the world's deepest canyons. Sandboard down oversized dunes. In Peru, this is just the beginning of a long menu of activities that can be devoured by devoted adrenaline junkies. There's also surfing, trekking, biking and paragliding. Gear up – and take the Band-Aids. You're in for one heck of a wild ride.*

## Trekking & Hiking

The variety of trails in Peru is staggering. The main trekking centers are Cuzco and Arequipa in the southern Andes, and Huaraz in the north. The country's most famous trek is the Inca Trail to Machu Picchu, but there are plenty of other less-crowded, equally magnificent routes, too.

Near Arequipa, you can trek through two world-famous canyons: the Cañón del Colca and the Cañón del Cotahuasi. The scenery is guaranteed to knock you off your feet – and, during the wet season when some routes are impassable, Colca is invitingly lush and green.

Outside Huaraz, the Cordillera Blanca can't be beat for vistas of snowcapped mountaintops. The classic trekking route is the five-day journey from Llanganuco to Santa Cruz. Shorter trips in the area go to alpine lakes and along old Inca roadways.

Certain areas of Peru, such as the Inca Trail, require guides; in other places, such as the Cordillera Huayhuash, there have been muggings, so it's best to trek with someone who knows the area. Outfitters can generally provide equipment, guides, porters and *arrieros* (mule drivers). But if you prefer to trek ultralight, bring your own gear, as rental items tend to be heavy. Whatever adventure you choose, be prepared to spend a few days acclimatizing to the dizzying altitude before you set out.

Trekking is best during the dry season (May to September) in the Andes.

**The Best... Protected Areas**

1 Cañón del Colca (p125)

2 Cordillera Blanca (p251)

3 Lake Titicaca (p146)

4 Parque Nacional Manu (p307)

5 Islas Ballestas (p106)

## Mountain, Rock & Ice Climbing

Peru has the highest tropical mountains in the world, offering some absolutely inspired climbs. The Cordillera Blanca, with its dozens of snowy mountaintops exceeding 5000m, is one of the top destinations for this in South America. Ishinca (5530m) and Pisco (5752m) provide two ascents easy enough for relatively inexperienced climbers. Nearby, the city of Huaraz is well stocked with outfitters and climbing equipment (though it's best to bring your own gear for serious ascents).

In southern Peru, Arequipa is surrounded by volcanic peaks, some of which can be scaled by beginners. The most popular climb is El Misti (5822m), which, despite its awesome height, does not involve technical climbing. (However, climbers do need to be physically fit and have wilderness experience.) Other tempting ascents can be found in the mountains that tower over the Cañón del Colca.

For beginners looking to bag their first mountain, Peru may not be the best place to start since the sport is relatively new and many guides are inexperienced.

High-elevation climbing is best done during the dry season (mid-June to mid-July). Acclimatization to altitude is essential.

## River Running

Also known as white-water rafting, river running is growing in popularity around Peru and trips can range from a few hours to several days, cruising amid Andean peaks and steamy cloud forest.

Cuzco is undoubtedly the main town for river running. The choices range from a few hours of mild rafting on the Urubamba to adrenaline-pumping rides on the Santa Teresa to several days on more remote waterways.

Arequipa is another center for the sport. Here, the Río Chili is most frequently run, with half-day beginners' trips leaving daily between March and November.

Be aware that rafting is not regulated in Peru. So book excursions only with reputable, well-recommended agencies and avoid cut-rate trips. A good operator will have insurance and guides with certified first-aid training. Choose one that provides top-notch equipment, including self-bailing rafts, US Coast Guard–approved life jackets and spare paddles.

## More Adventures

Beyond hiking, biking and trekking, Peru offers various other activities for the adventurous:

- **Sandboarding** This sport is rising in popularity at spots such as Huacachina, where boarders fly down dunes made of silky sand.
- **Paragliding** Popular paragliding sites include the coastal clifftops in Miraflores, Lima. There are few operators in Peru, so book ahead.
- **Horseback riding** Rides can be arranged in many destinations, but for a real splurge take a ride on a graceful Peruvian paso horse. Supposedly the descendants of horses with Spanish and Moorish lineage, they are reputed to have the world's smoothest gait.

# Surfing

With consistent waves and plenty of breaks, Peru attracts dedicated locals and international diehards alike.

These can be found the moment you land. Along the southern part of Lima, you'll see surfers riding curls at Miraflores (known as Waikiki), Barranquito and La Herradura. (This latter spot has an outstanding left point break, but gets busy during strong swells.) In-the-know surfers, however, prefer the less-crowded breaks to the south, near the areas of Punta Hermosa, Punta Rocas and Pico Alto, the latter of which is known as a 'kamikaze' reef break. (It boasts one of the largest waves in Peru.)

Peru's north coast is also blessed with a string of excellent breaks, including Huanchaco and Máncora. The most famous of these is at Puerto Chicama, where rides of more than 2km are possible on a wave considered to be the longest left hand in the world.

The water is cold from April to mid-December (as low as 15°C/60°F), when wet suits are generally needed. Indeed, many surfers wear wet suits year-round, even though the water is a little warmer (around 20°C/68°F, in the Lima area) from January to March. The far north coast (north of Talara) stays above 21°C (70°F) most of the year.

Note that equipment rental is limited and expensive, so it's advisable to bring your own board.

For a detailed list of just about every break in Peru, logon to www.wannasurf.com.

# Mountain Biking

In Peru mountain biking is still a fledgling sport. That said, both easy and demanding single-track trails await mountain bikers outside of Huaraz and Arequipa. If you're experienced, there are incredible possibilities around the Sacred Valley, all accessible from Cuzco.

Mountain-bike rental in Peru tends to be basic, so if you're serious, it's best to bring your own – in addition to a repair kit with extra parts.

# The Natural World

The Sacred Valley (p205)

STEVE ALLEN/GETTY IMAGES ©

*Few countries are as rugged, as forbidding and as wildly diverse as Peru. The third-largest country in South America – at 1,285,220 sq km – it is five times larger than the UK, almost twice the size of Texas and one-sixth the size of Australia. It lies in the tropics, south of the equator, straddling three strikingly different geographic zones: the arid Pacific coast, the craggy Andes mountain range and a good portion of the Amazon Basin.*

## The Land

On the coast, a narrow strip of land which lies below 1000m in elevation hugs the country's 3000km-long shoreline. Consisting primarily of scrubland and desert, it eventually merges in the south with Chile's Atacama Desert, one of the driest places on earth. The coast includes Lima, the capital, and several major agricultural centers – oases watered by dozens of rivers that cascade down from the Andes.

The Andes, the world's second-greatest mountain chain, form the spine of the country. Rising steeply from the coast, they reach spectacular heights of more than 6000m just 100km inland. Peru's highest peak, Huascarán (6768m), located northeast of Huaraz, is the world's highest tropical summit and the sixth-tallest mountain in the Americas. Though the Peruvian Andes reside in the tropics, the

mountains are laced with a web of glaciers above elevations of 5000m. Between 3000m and 4000m lie the agricultural highlands, which support more than a third of Peru's population.

The eastern Andean slopes receive much more rainfall than the dry western slopes and are draped in lush cloud forests as they descend into the lowland rainforest of the Amazon. Here, the undulating landscape rarely rises more than 500m above sea level as various tributary systems feed into the mighty Río Amazonas (Amazon River), the largest river in the world. Weather conditions are hot and humid year-round, with most precipitation falling between December and May.

## Wildlife

Peru is home to countless ecosystems and boasts a spectacular variety of plant and animal life. It is one of only a dozen or so countries in the world considered to be 'megadiverse.'

Wildlife enthusiasts come to see Peru to see a rainbow of birds, as well as camelids, freshwater dolphins, butterflies, jaguars, anacondas, macaws and spectacled bears – to name but a few.

### Birds

Peru has more than 1800 bird species – that's more than the number of species found in North America and Europe together. From the tiniest hummingbirds to the majestic Andean condor, the variety is colorful and seemingly endless; new species are discovered regularly.

Along the Pacific, marine birds of all kinds are most visible, especially in the south, where they can be found clustered along the shore. Here you'll see exuberant Chilean flamingos, oversized Peruvian pelicans, plump Inca terns sporting white-feather mustaches and bright-orange beaks, colonies of brown boobies engaged in elaborate

Llama

mating dances, cormorants, and endangered Humboldt penguins, which can be spotted waddling around the Islas Ballestas.

In the highlands, the most famous bird of all is the Andean condor. Weighing up to 10kg, with a 3m-plus wingspan, this monarch of the air (a member of the vulture family) once ranged over the entire Andean mountain chain from Venezuela to Tierra del Fuego. Considered the largest flying bird in the world, condors usually nest in impossibly high mountain cliffs that prevent predators from snatching their young. Their main food source is carrion and they're most easily spotted riding thermal air currents in the canyons around Arequipa.

Other prominent high-altitude birds include the Andean gull, which is commonly sighted along lakes and rivers as high as 4500m. The mountains are also home to several species of ibis, such as the puna ibis, which inhabits lakeside marshes. Other species include torrent ducks, which nest in small waterside caves, Andean geese, spotted Andean flickers, black-and-yellow Andean siskins and a panoply of hummingbirds.

Swoop down toward the Amazon and you'll catch sight of the world's most iconic tropical birds, including boisterous flocks of parrots and macaws festooned in brightly plumed regalia. You'll also see clusters of aracaris, toucans, parakeets, toucanets, ibises, regal gray-winged trumpeters, umbrella birds with gravity-defying feathered hairdos, crimson-colored cocks of the rock, soaring hawks and harpy eagles.

### The Best... Wildlife-Watching Spots

1 Parque Nacional Manu (p307)

2 Cañón del Colca (p125)

3 Islas Ballestas (p106)

4 Parque Nacional Huascarán (p251)



## Mammals

The Amazon is also home to a bounty of mammals. More than two dozen species of monkeys are found here, including howlers, acrobatic spider monkeys and wide-eyed marmosets. With the help of a guide, you may also see sloths, bats, piglike peccaries, anteaters, armadillos and coatis (ring-tailed members of the raccoon family). And if you're really lucky, you'll find giant river otters, capybaras (rodents of unusual size), river dolphins, tapirs and maybe one of half a dozen elusive felines, including the fabled jaguar.

Toward the west, the cloud forests straddling the Amazon and the eastern slopes of the Andean highlands are home to the endangered spectacled bear. South America's only bear is a black, shaggy mammal, known for its white, masklike face markings, that grows up to 1.8m in length.

The highlands are home to roving packs of camelids: llamas and alpacas are the most easily spotted since they are domesticated, and used as pack animals or for their wool; vicuñas and guanacos live exclusively in the wild. On highland talus slopes, watch out for the viscacha, which looks like the world's most cuddly rabbit. Foxes, deer and domesticated *cuy* (guinea pigs) are also highland dwellers, as is the puma (cougar or mountain lion).

On the coast, huge numbers of sea lions and seals are easily seen on the Islas Ballestas. Dolphins are commonly seen offshore, but whales very rarely.

## Reptiles, Amphibians, Fish & Insects

In the Amazon basin you'll find amphibians like toads, tree frogs and thumbnail-sized poison dart frogs. Rivers teem with schools of piranhas, *paiche* and *doncella*, while the

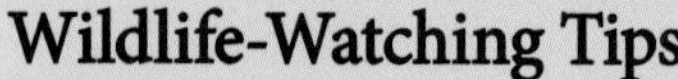

## Wildlife-Watching Tips

- Hire a knowledgeable local guide – they know what to look for and where.
- Get up *really* early – animals tend to be most active at dawn and dusk.
- Bring a pair of lightweight binoculars.
- Be quiet: animals tend to avoid loud packs of chatty humans.
- In the Amazon, opt for canoes instead of motorboats – you'll see much more.
- Have realistic expectations: vegetation can be thick and animals shy.

air buzzes with thousands of insects: armies of ants, squadrons of beetles, as well as katydids, stick insects, caterpillars, spiders, praying mantises, transparent moths, and butterflies of all shapes and sizes. A blue morpho butterfly in flight is a remarkable sight: with wingspans of up to 10cm, their iridescent-blue coloring can seem downright hallucinogenic.

Reptile species include tortoises, river turtles, lizards, caimans and, of course, that jungle-movie favorite: the anaconda. An aquatic boa snake that can measure more than 10m in length, it will often ambush its prey by the water's edge, constrict its body around it and then drown it in the river. Caimans, tapirs, deer, turtles and peccaries are all tasty meals for this killer snake; human victims are almost unheard of.

## Plants

Plant life in Peru is similarly diverse – from the cacti of the desert coast to the rugged, misty cloud forests of the Andean slopes; from alpine wildflowers to the dense, lush Amazon rainforest. Grasslands, mangrove forests and peat bogs are also in the mix.

## National Parks

Peru's vast wealth of wildlife is protected by a system of national parks and reserves with 60 areas covering almost 15% of the country. The newest is the Sierra del Divisor Reserve Zone, created in 2006 to protect 1.5 million hectares of rainforest on the Brazilian border. All of these protected areas are administered by the Instituto Nacional de Recursos Nacionales (Inrena; www.inrena.gob.pe), a division of the Ministry of Agriculture.

## Environmental Issues

Peru faces major challenges in the stewardship of its natural resources, with problems compounded by a lack of law enforcement and its impenetrable geography. Deforestation and erosion are major issues, as is industrial pollution, urban sprawl and coca eradication. In addition, the Interoceánica highway through the heart of the Amazon may imperil thousands of square kilometers of rainforest.

Some positive measures are being taken to help protect the country's environment. For example, the Peruvian government and private interests within the tourism industry have come together to develop sustainable travel projects in the Amazon. In 2005 Peru became one of 17 Latin American countries, along with Spain, to sign the Amazon River Declaration, which calls for environmental safeguards to ensure biodiversity and for the development of tourism strategies that will fight rural poverty and spur regional development in sustainable ways.

# Food & Drink

Seafood *causa*

CAROLINA MIRANDA ©

*Peru has long been a place where the concept of 'fusion' was part of everyday cooking. Here, nutty Andean stews mingle with Asian stir-fry techniques, and Spanish dishes absorb the flavors of the Amazon. Food is a religion in Peru – a place where humble street vendors are hyperattentive to preparation and high-end restaurants spotlight local flavors, serving up deft interpretations of Andean favorites. Serious foodies: consider this your paradise, found.*

## Staples & Specialties

Much of the country's cooking begins and ends with the humble potato. The tuber is from Peru, where hundreds of local varieties are transformed into a mind-boggling number of incredible dishes. Standouts include *papa a la huancaína* (potato bathed in a creamy cheese sauce) and *causa* (an architectural potato terrine layered with seafood, vegetables or chicken). Potatoes are also found in *lomo saltado,* the beef stir-fries that headline every local menus.

Peruvians typically begin their day with corn tamales or a sandwich (on the coast) or soup (in the highlands). Lunch is the main meal of the day and often includes three courses, while dinner tends to be lighter.

## The Best... Peruvian Dishes

1 Ceviche – fresh fish marinated in lime juice

2 *Ají de gallina* – shredded chicken in spicy walnut sauce

3 *Lomo saltado* – stir-fried beef with potatoes

4 *Chupe de camarones* – buttery shrimp bisque

5 *Causa* – potato terrine

### The Coast

The coast is all about seafood – and ceviche plays a starring role. A chilled concoction of fish, shrimp or other seafood marinated in lime juice, onions, cilantro and chili peppers, the fish is cooked through a process of oxidation.

Fish is prepared dozens of other ways, too: *al ajo* (in garlic), *frito* (fried) or *a la chorrillana* (in white wine, tomatoes and onions). And other seafood is employed in soups and stews such as *aguadito* (a soupy risotto) and *chupe* (bisque).

None of this means that pork, chicken or beef aren't devoured with great regularity. *Aji de gallina* (chicken-walnut stew) is a classic. On the north coast, *arroz con pato a la chiclayana* (duck and rice simmered in cilantro) and *seco de cabrito* (goat stewed in spices and beer) bear repeat sampling.

Along the coast, where the Asian presence is significant, you will also find Peruvian-Chinese restaurants known as *chifas*. The cuisine is Cantonese-inspired: simple dishes low on spice.

### The Highlands

In the chilly highlands, the focus is on soup, which tends to be a generous, gut-warming experience – stocked with squash, potatoes and locally grown herbs. *Sopa a la criolla* (a noodle soup with beef and vegetables) is a regular item on menus, as is *caldo de gallina* (chicken broth soup).

The highlands are also the source of all things *cuy* (guinea pig). It tastes similar to rabbit and is often roasted and served whole. Andean *trucha* (river trout) – prepared myriad ways – is also a staple.

Arequipa has a particularly dynamic regional cuisine. The area is renowned for its succulent *picantes* (spicy stews), *rocoto relleno* (chilis stuffed with meat) and *chupe de camarones* (river shrimp bisque).

## Practical Information

Throughout this guidebook, the order of restaurant listings follows the author's preference, and each place to eat is accompanied by one of the following pricing symbols.

- $ <S20 for a main course per person
- $$ S20 to S45 for a main course per person
- $$$ > S45 for a main course per person

Prices in major tourist centers will be more expensive. Restaurant hours are generally 10am to 10pm, though some close between 3pm and 6pm. Eateries in remote areas may only be open for lunch.

## A Pisco Primer

Pisco is the omnipresent grape brandy that is served at events from the insignificant to the momentous in Peru. The three main types are Quebranta, Italia and *acholado*. Quebranta (a pure-smelling pisco) and Italia (slightly aromatic) are named for grape varieties, while *acholado* is a blend (best for mixed drinks). There are many small-batch specialty piscos distilled from grape must (pressed juice with skins), known as *mosto verde*. These are best sipped straight.

The most common brands include Tres Generaciones, Ocucaje, Ferreyros and La Botija. Viñas de Oro, Viejo Tonel, Estirpe Peruano, LaBlanco and Gran Cruz are among the finest.



### The Amazon

Though not widely eaten throughout the country, Amazon ingredients have begun to creep into the national cuisine. This includes the increased use of river snails and fish (including *paiche* and *doncella*), as well as produce such as *aguaje* (the fruit of the moriche palm) and yucca (cassava).

*Juanes,* a tamale stuffed with rice, yucca, chicken and/or pork, is a savory area staple.

## Desserts

Desserts tend to be hypersweet concoctions. The favorites include *suspiro limeña* (a caramel mousse topped with sweet meringue), as well as *alfajores* (caramel cookie sandwiches) and *crema volteada* (flan). Lighter and fruitier is *mazamorra morada,* a purple-corn pudding that comes with chunks of fruit.

## Specialty Drinks

Herbal teas are very popular, with the most notable being *mate de coca,* coca-leaf tea. It won't get you high, but can soothe stomach ailments and help with altitude acclimatization.

In the Andes, homemade *chicha* (corn beer) can be found in traditional markets and *picanterías* (country restaurants). It is lightly sweet and has a low alcohol content. Also widely available: nonalcoholic *chicha morada,* a sweet purple-corn drink.

## Vegetarians & Vegans

It is possible to find vegetarian restaurants and dishes around Peru, especially in well-touristed areas. Common Peruvian dishes that don't contain meat are: *papas a la huancaína* (potatoes in a spiced, creamy sauce), *palta a la jardinera* (avocado stuffed with vegetables), *tortilla* (Spanish omelet) and *tacu tacu* (pan-fried beans and rice).

Vegans will have a harder time. Peruvian cuisine is based on eggs and dairy and infinite combinations thereof. Self-catering is the best option.

# Music & the Arts

Quechua weavers

FOREST WOODWARD/GETTY IMAGES ©

*The country that has been home to empires both indigenous and European has a wealth of cultural and artistic traditions. Perhaps the most outstanding achievements are in the areas of music, painting, crafts and literature – the latter of which received plenty of attention in 2010, when Peruvian novelist Mario Vargas Llosa won the Nobel Prize.*

## Music

Like its people, Peru's music is an intercontinental fusion of elements. Pre-Columbian cultures contributed bamboo flutes, the Spaniards brought stringed instruments and the Africans gave it a backbone of percussive rhythm. By and large, music tends to be a regional affair: African-influenced *landós* with their thumping bass beats are predominant on the coast, high-pitched indigenous *huaynos,* heavy on bamboo wind instruments, are heard in the Andes and *criollo* waltzes are a must at any dance party on the coast.

Over the last several decades, the *huayno* has blended with surf guitars and Colombian *cumbia* (a type of Afro-Caribbean dance music) to produce *chicha* – a danceable sound closely identified with the Amazon region. (Well-known chicha bands include Los Shapis and Los Mirlos.) *Cumbia* is also very popular. Grupo 5, which hails from Chiclayo, is currently a favorite in the genre.

On the coast, guitar-inflected *música criolla* (*criollo* music) has its roots in both Spain and Africa. The most famous *criollo* style is the *vals peruano* (Peruvian waltz), a three-quarter-time waltz that is fast moving and full of complex guitar melodies. The most legendary singers in this genre include singer and composer Chabuca Granda (1920–83) and gravel-voiced crooner Arturo 'Zambo' Cavero (1940–2009). *Landó* is closely connected to this style of music, but features the added elements of call-and-response. Standout performers include singers Susana Baca (b 1944) and Eva Ayllón (b 1956).

## The Best... Peruvian Fiction

1 *War by Candlelight*, Daniel Alarcón

2 *The War of the End of the World*, Mario Vargas Llosa

3 *Chronicle of San Gabriel*, Julio Ramón Ribeyro

## Literature

Nobel Prize–winner Mario Vargas Llosa (b 1936) is Peru's most famous writer. His novels evoke James Joyce in their complexity, meandering through time and shifting perspectives. A keen observer of Peru's social peculiarities, his more than two dozen novels are available in translation. The best place to start is *La ciudad y los perros* (The Time of the Hero), based on his experience at a Peruvian military academy. (The soldiers at his old academy responded to the novel by burning it.)

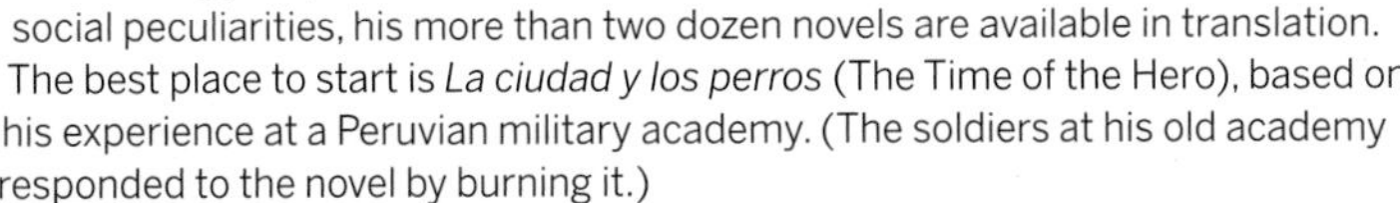

Other engaging writers include Alfredo Bryce Echenique (b 1939), who chronicles the ways of the upper class, and Julio Ramón Ribeyro (1929–94), who demonstrates a distinctly Peruvian penchant for dark humor. (His concisely written stories are an ideal place to start exploring Peruvian literature.) Also significant is rising literary star Daniel Alarcón (b 1977), a Peruvian-American writer whose debut novel, *Lost City Radio*, about a country recovering from civil war, was published to wide acclaim in 2007.

If Vargas Llosa is the country's greatest novelist, César Vallejo (1892–1938) is its greatest poet. In his short lifetime, he published only three slim books – *Los heraldos negros* (The Black Heralds), *Trilce* and *Poemas humanos* (Human Poems) – but he was one of the most innovative Latin American poets of the 20th century, known for pushing the language to its limits, inventing words when real ones no longer suited him.

## Visual Art

The country's most famous art movement dates to the 17th century, when the artists of the *escuela cuzqueña* (Cuzco School) produced thousands of religious paintings, the vast majority of which remain unattributed. Created by native and *mestizo* (person of mixed indigenous and Spanish descent) artists, the pieces frequently feature holy figures laced in gold paint and rendered in a style inspired by mannerist and late Gothic art – but bearing traces of indigenous color schemes and iconography. Today, these hang in museums and churches throughout Peru and reproductions are sold in many crafts markets.

Well-known artistic figures include 19th-century illustrator Pancho Fierro (1807–79), who created highly evocative watercolors of everyday figures, and José Sabogal (1888–1956), who influenced a whole generation of Peruvian painters by including indigenist themes in his work.

## Tips for Buying Textiles

- **Buy locally** Markets are flooded with knockoffs from Asia, so buy directly from weavers, or shops that deal directly with weavers.
- **Ask questions** Ask who made it, where it's from and what the designs represent. A good dealer will know.
- **Inspect the work** Check to see if the fibers are spun tightly and be on the lookout for synthetic materials. The best textiles are made only from alpaca or sheep's wool.
- **Be realistic** Quality textiles are expensive to produce. If the price is too good to be true, it probably isn't the real deal.

## Folk Art & Crafts

Extraordinary textiles. Stunningly crafted pottery. Brightly painted religious dioramas. Peru's folk-art traditions are among some of the best in the world.

The country is perhaps best known for its textiles. Andean indigenous cultures have long produced intricately woven rugs, ponchos and blankets decorated with elaborate geometric and anthropomorphic designs (such as felines and fish) – many of which tell stories or denote social status.

Equally worthwhile is the pottery: from the shining black ceramics of the north coast to the simple clay bulls that serve as good-luck charms on Andean homes. The most stunning designs are those made in the tradition of the pre-Columbian Moche people, known for their vivid portrait vessels.

Religious crafts come in all shapes and forms, but Peruvian artisans produce particularly striking *retablos* (three-dimensional dioramas). These elaborate box displays generally feature scenes from Christian life and include depictions of indigenous culture, such as coca leaves.

Generally, the best crafts can be found in markets in Lima and Cuzco.

# Survival Guide

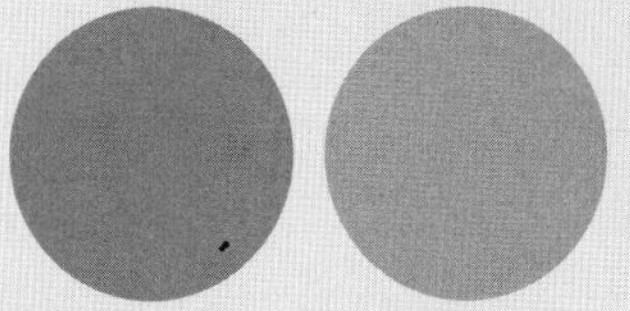



Blue-tailed emerald
GLENN BARTLEY/GETTY IMAGES ©

# Directory

## Accommodations

Accommodations in Peru range from basic crash pads to cozy Spanish-style B&Bs to luxury lodges that offer bath butlers and turndown service. Listings are organized in order of our preference, considering value for cost.

**Categories** Budget listings cover simple spots with small rooms, with a shared or private bathroom. Midrange hotels generally include private bathrooms and amenities such as air-conditioning, cable TV and in-room safes. At the top end, Peru's hotels are equipped with every amenity imaginable, from in-suite bathrooms with bathtubs to concierge services. Street noise can be an issue in any lodging, so select your room accordingly.

**Costs** Accommodation costs vary greatly, depending on the season and the region. Cities that are pricier than average include Lima, Cuzco, Iquitos, Huaraz and Trujillo. In the Amazon, and in popular beach destinations such as Máncora, all-inclusive resort-style pricing may be the norm. Foreigners do not have to pay the 18% hotel tax (sometimes included in rates quoted in soles), but may have to present their passport and tourist card for photocopying upon check-in.

**Reservations** Many flights into Lima arrive late at night, so it's best to have a room reserved. Around the country, reservations are a necessity for stays during a major festival (such as Inti Raymi in Cuzco) or a holiday such as Semana Santa (Easter Week), when all of Peru is on vacation. In the Amazon, reservations are always required at remote lodges, even in the low season.

**Room Types** Within most types of accommodations, *habitación simple* refers to a single room, *habitación doble* to a double room with two single beds, and *habitación matrimonial* to a double room with a double or queen-sized bed. It's always OK to ask to see a room before committing.

**Price Indicators** The price indicators in this book – $ (budget), $$ (midrange), $$$ (top end) – refer to the cost of a double room, including bathroom (any combination of toilet, bathtub and shower) and exclude breakfast unless otherwise noted.

| CATEGORY | COST |
|---|---|
| budget | up to S85 |
| midrange | S85–S250 |
| top end | S250 and over |

### APARTMENTS & HOUSES

A small but growing number of vacation rentals, primarily in Lima and Cuzco, attend to midrange and top-end needs. Check www.vrbo.com and www.cyberrentals.com for listings.

### B&BS

In the more well-touristed cities of Arequipa, Cuzco and Lima, bed and breakfasts offer a dollop of charm. These often inhabit vintage Spanish *casonas* (manses), some of which date back to the colony. For B&B listings throughout Peru, see www.bedandbreakfastworld.com.

### HOSTALES, HOSPEDAJES & ALBERGUES

These are Peru's cheapest accommodations and generally have a handful of small rooms, with a shared or private bathroom. In major cities, they will include hot showers; in more rural and remote areas, they likely will not. Some places will include a very simple breakfast in the rate. These are often independently or family-run.

### Book Your Stay Online

For more accommodations reviews by Lonely Planet authors, check out http://hotels.lonelyplanet.com. You'll find independent reviews, as well as recommendations on the best places to stay. Best of all, you can book online.

## A Note about Prices

Prices in this guidebook are generally listed in Peruvian nuevos soles. However, many package lodgings and higher-end hotels will only quote prices in US dollars; likewise for many travel agencies and tour operators. In these cases, we have listed prices in US dollars.

Both currencies have experienced fluctuations in recent years, so expect many figures to be different from what may be printed in the book.

### HOTELS

This category can include everything from family-owned budget spots to design-conscious boutique inns to luxury outposts housed in former monasteries. These can be independently operated or run by a regional or international chain. (Sheraton, Marriott, Libertador, Orient-Express and Casa Andina are a few of the more of the widely recognized hospitality companies operating in Peru.) Rooms, services and amenities vary widely depending on the price category. Though some hotels boast star ratings, note that Peru does not have a standardized ratings system.

### LODGES

In the Amazon, most travelers stay in lodges – usually palm-thatched bungalows set around a common outdoor area. Even at the top end, these are more rustic and offer fewer amenities than their city counterparts. Expect units to be open to the elements, with mosquito screens separating guests from the great outdoors. Meals are generally served family-style. If you have dietary issues, let the lodge know well in advance.

## Business Hours

Posted hours in Peru serve more as guideline than hard and fast rule. Be patient, and forget about getting anything done on a Sunday, when most businesses (other than restaurants) are closed.

Lima has pharmacies, bookstores and electronics supply shops that are open every day. In other major cities, taxi drivers often know where the late-night stores and pharmacies are located.

Most cities are equipped with 24-hour ATMs.

In smaller cities and towns, many shops and offices close for lunch (usually from 1pm until around 3pm). In small towns, restaurants may only be open for lunch or breakfast and lunch.

Opening hours are typically as follows:

**Banks** 9am–6pm Monday to Friday, to 1pm Saturday

**Government offices & businesses** 9am to 5pm Monday to Friday

**Restaurants** 10am to 10pm; many close between 3pm and 6pm

**Shops** 9am to 6pm, some 9am to 6pm Saturday

**Museums** Often closed on Monday

## Customs Regulations

- Peru allows duty-free importation of 3L of alcohol and 20 packs of cigarettes, 50 cigars or 250g of tobacco. You can import US$300 of gifts. Legally, you are allowed to bring in such items as a laptop, camera, portable music player, kayak, climbing gear, mountain bike or similar items for personal use.
- It is illegal to take pre-Columbian or colonial artifacts out of Peru, and it is illegal to bring them into most countries. If purchasing reproductions, buy from a reputable dealer and ask for a receipt.
- Purchasing animal products made from endangered species or even just transporting them around Peru is also illegal.
- Coca leaves are legal in Peru, but not in most other countries, even in the form of tea bags. People subject to random drug testing should be aware that coca, even in the form of tea, may leave trace amounts in urine.
- Check with your own home government about customs restrictions and duties on any expensive or rare items you intend to bring back.
- For more customs information, logon to http://peru.visahq.com/customs/.

# Climate

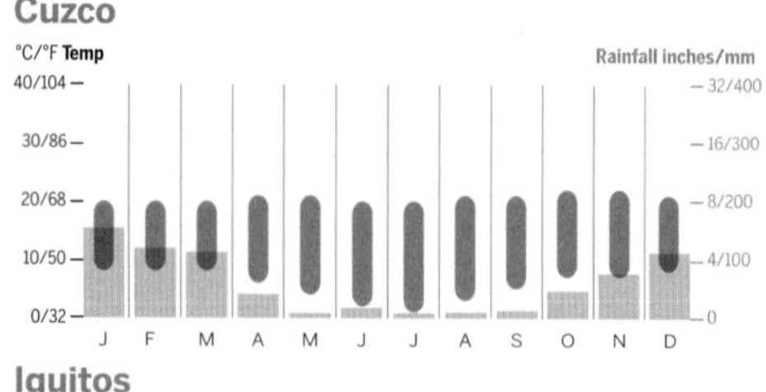


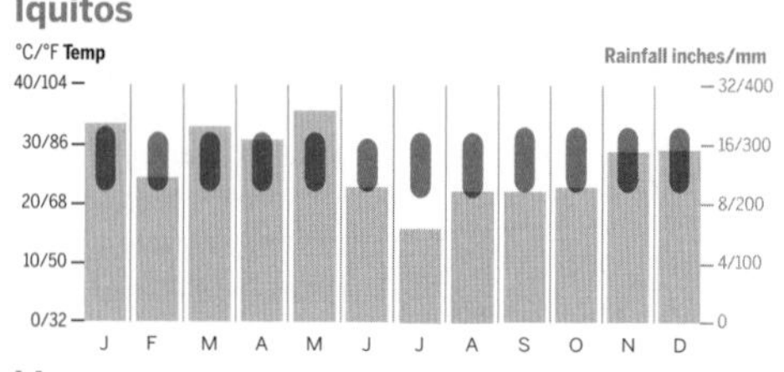


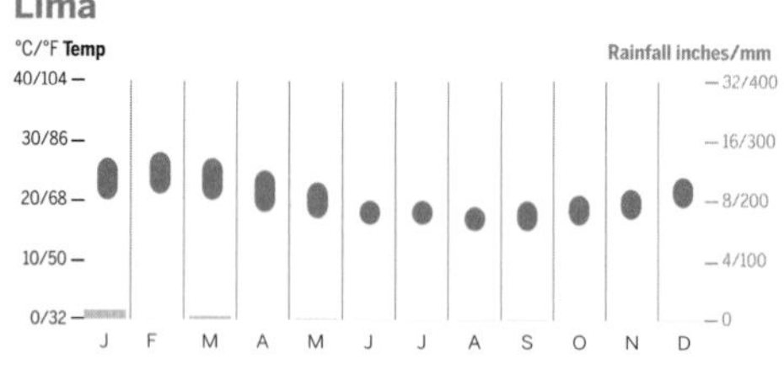


## Electricity

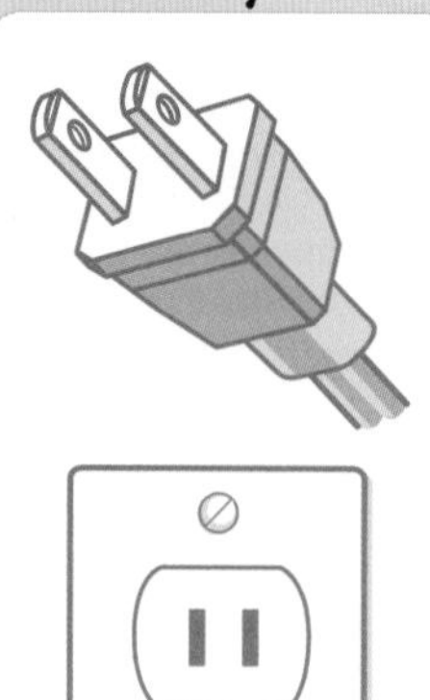

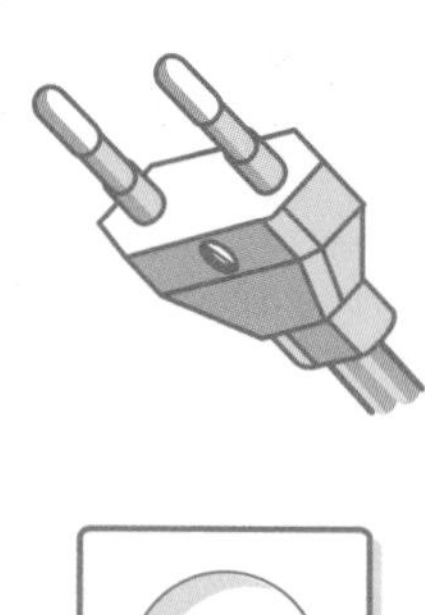

220V/60Hz

## Gay & Lesbian Travelers

Peru is an extremely conservative, Catholic country. While homosexuality is legal, many Peruvians only tolerate it on a 'don't ask; don't tell' level. Gay rights barely exist as an issue. When it does arise in public, hostility is the most common response. As a result, many gays in Peru don't publicly identify themselves as such.

- Public displays of affection among gay couples are rarely seen. Outside gay clubs, it is advisable to keep a low profile.
- HIV/AIDS transmission, both homosexual and heterosexual, is a growing problem in Peru, so use condoms.
- Lima is the city most accepting of gay people, but this is on a relative scale. Beyond that, the tourist towns of Cuzco, Arequipa and Trujillo tend to be more tolerant than the norm.
- For the record: the checkered rainbow flag seen around Cuzco and in the Andes is not a gay pride flag, it's the flag of the Quechua people.

### INTERNET RESOURCES

**Deambiente.com** (www.deambiente.com) Spanish-language online magazine about politics and pop culture, plus nightlife listings.

**Gay Lima** (http://lima.queercity.info) A guide to the latest gay and gay-friendly spots in the capital.

**Gayperu.com** (www.gayperu.com) A Spanish-language online guide that lists everything from bars to bathhouses; also runs a travel agency at www.gayperutravel.com.

**Global Gayz** (www.globalgayz.com) Excellent, country-specific information about Peru's gay scene and politics.

**Lima Tours** (Map p66; ☎ 01-619-6901; www.limatours.com.pe; Jirón Belén 1040, Central Lima) A travel agency that is not exclusively gay, but that organizes gay-friendly group trips.

**Purpleroofs.com** (www.purpleroofs.com) Massive GLBT portal with links to tour operators and gay-friendly accommodations in Peru.

**Rainbow Peruvian Tours** (Map p70; ☎ 01-215-6000; www.perurainbow.com; Río de Janeiro 216, San Isidro, Lima) Gay-owned tour agency based in Lima, with a multilingual website.

# Health

Prevention is the key to staying healthy while abroad. Travelers who follow common-sense precautions usually come down with nothing more than a little diarrhea.

## BEFORE YOU GO

- Most vaccines don't provide immunity until at least two weeks after they're given; visit a doctor four to eight weeks before departure.
- Pack medications in their original, clearly labeled containers. If carrying syringes or needles, be sure to have a physician's letter documenting their medical necessity.
- If your health insurance doesn't cover you for medical expenses abroad, get extra travel insurance. Find out if your insurer reimburses you or the provider directly.
- If you are concerned about potential life-threatening medical problems while you are on the road, be sure that your insurance covers medical evacuations. You can find a list of evacuation and insurance companies on the website of the US State Department (http://travel.state.gov/travel/tips/brochures/brochures_1215.html).

### RECOMMENDED VACCINATIONS

- The only required vaccine for Peru is yellow fever, and that's only if you are arriving from a country in Africa or the Americas where yellow fever occurs. It is strongly recommended, however, that anyone traveling to the Amazon be inoculated for the disease.
- It is strongly recommended that all travelers should also be covered and vaccinated for chicken pox, hepatitis A, hepatitis B, measles, rabies, tetanus and typhoid. Consult with your doctor and make sure children are up to date with routine vaccinations as well.
- For further information, see Lonely Planet's *Healthy Travel Central & South America*. If you're traveling with children, Lonely Planet's *Travel with Children* may also be useful.

## IN PERU

In general, regional capitals and popular tourist areas such as Lima and Cuzco have at least one good clinic or hospital that can handle emergency care and other medical problems. However, access to care becomes more problematic in remote areas. For life-threatening procedures, it is best to travel to Lima.

- There are numerous high-quality medical clinics and hospitals in Lima that are open 24 hours for all manner of emergencies. These also offer myriad subspecialty consultations – from dentistry to gynecology.
- For a list of recommended doctors and clinics in Lima, see the website for the US embassy (http://lima.usembassy.gov/acs_peru.html).
- Most doctors and hospitals in Peru expect payment in cash, regardless of whether you have insurance.
- Pharmacies in Peru are known as *farmacias* or *boticas*, and are identified by a green or red cross in the window.

## ENVIRONMENTAL HAZARDS

### ALTITUDE SICKNESS

- Those who ascend rapidly to altitudes greater than 2500m (8100ft) may develop altitude sickness. In Peru, this includes Cuzco (3326m) and Lake Titicaca (3820m). Being physically fit offers no

## Practicalities

- **Electricity** Electrical current is 220V/60Hz AC. Standard outlets accept round prongs, some have dual-voltage outlets which take flat prongs.
- **Magazines** The best-known political and cultural weekly is *Caretas* (www.caretas.com.pe), while *Etiqueta Negra* (etiquetanegra.com.pe) focuses exclusively on culture. A good bilingual travel publication is the monthly *Rumbos* (www.rumbosdelperu.com).
- **Newspapers** Peru's right-leaning *El Comercio* (www.elcomercioperu.com.pe) is the leading daily. There's also the slightly left-of-center *La República* (www.larepublica.com.pe) and *Peruvian Times* (www.peruviantimes.com) in English.
- **Online Resources** Helpful online resources in English are http://expatperu.com and www.theperuguide.com.
- **TV** Cable and satellite TV are widely available for local programming, a fix of CNN and even Japanese news.
- **Video** Videos work on the NTSC system.
- **Weights & Measures** Peru uses the metric system but gas (petrol) is measured in US gallons.

protection. The risk increases with fast ascents, higher altitudes and greater exertion.

- Symptoms of altitude sickness may include headaches, nausea, vomiting, dizziness, malaise, insomnia and loss of appetite. If these persist for more than 24 hours, see a doctor.
- When traveling to high elevations, it is important to eat light meals, abstain from alcohol and avoid overexertion.

### FOOD & WATER

Poor sanitation can lead to a variety of foodborne illnesses, so be careful where you eat and what you drink:

- Tap water in Peru is not safe to drink. Vigorous boiling of water for one minute is the most effective means of water purification. At altitudes greater than 2000m (6500ft), boil for three minutes.
- Eat vegetables and other produce that is cooked and peeled, otherwise these should be disinfected by washing with purified water.
- When consuming seafood, look for restaurants that are clean and busy.

### MOSQUITO BITES

To prevent mosquito bites, wear long sleeves and long pants and pack good insect repellent, preferably one that contains DEET. Children aged between two and 12 should use preparations containing no more than 10% DEET, applied sparingly.

### INFECTIOUS DISEASES

**Cholera** An intestinal infection acquired through ingestion of contaminated food or water. The main symptom is profuse diarrhea. While the disease occurs regularly in Peru, it's rare among travelers.

**Dengue fever** A viral infection transmitted by the aedes mosquitoes, which usually bite during the daytime and are found close to human habitations. Dengue usually causes flulike symptoms, including fever, muscle aches, joint pains, headaches, nausea and vomiting. The body aches may be uncomfortable, but most cases resolve uneventfully in a few days.

**Hepatitis A** A viral infection of the liver, usually acquired by ingestion of contaminated food or water, or via direct contact with infected persons. It is the second most common travel-related infection in Peru (after travelers' diarrhea) – and while most cases are resolved without complications, some cases do result in liver damage. The vaccine is highly effective.

**Hepatitis B** A similar type of liver infection. Unlike hepatitis A, the disease is usually acquired through sexual contact or by exposure to infected blood.

**HIV/AIDS** It has been reported in all South American countries. Exposure to blood or blood products

## Important Documents

All important documents (passport, credit cards, travel-insurance policy, drivers license etc) should be photocopied before you leave home. Leave one copy at home and keep another with you, separate from the originals.

and bodily fluids may put an individual at risk. Use condoms for all sexual encounters.

**Malaria** It is transmitted by mosquito bites. The main symptom is high spiking fevers, which may be accompanied by chills, sweats, body aches, weakness, vomiting or diarrhea. It is strongly recommended that travelers to the Amazon take malaria pills.

**Travelers' diarrhea** This comes from ingesting contaminated food or water. If it is bloody, persists for more than 72 hours or is accompanied by fever, shaking chills or severe abdominal pain, seek medical attention.

**Yellow fever** This life-threatening viral infection that begins with flulike symptoms and may include fever, chills, headache, muscle aches, backaches, loss of appetite, nausea and vomiting. A vaccine is strongly recommended for those visiting any jungle areas that lie below 2300m (7546ft).

# Insurance

- Having a travel-insurance policy to cover theft, loss, accidents and illness is recommended.

- Check the fine print to see if it excludes 'dangerous activities,' which can include scuba diving, motorcycling and even trekking.

- Also check if the policy coverage includes worst-case scenarios, such as evacuations and flights home.

- A variety of travel-insurance policies are available. Those handled by **STA Travel** (**www.statravel.com**) and other budget travel organizations can be good value.

# Internet Access

Accessing the internet is a snap in Peru. Wi-fi is increasingly common in big cities and larger towns, where internet cafes are also plentiful. Even tiny towns will usually have at least one internet cafe. In this book, @ indicates computer terminals with internet access and [wi-fi icon] indicates wi-fi access.

- Rates start at S1 per hour, with higher rates in remote areas and hotel business centers, which may charge up to US$6 per hour.

- Before plugging in your laptop, ensure that your power source adheres to Peru's 220V/60Hz AC electricity supply.

# Legal Matters

Your own embassy is of limited help if you get into trouble with the law in Peru, where you are presumed guilty until proven innocent. If you are the victim of crime, the *policía de turismo* (Poltur; tourist police) can help. Poltur stations are found in major cities.

- Be aware that some police officers (even tourist police) have a reputation for corruption, but that bribery is illegal.

- Peru has draconian penalties for possessing even small amounts of drugs; minimum sentences are several years in jail.

- Never get into a vehicle with someone claiming to be a police officer, instead insist on going to a bona fide police station on foot.

- If you are imprisoned for any reason, make sure that someone else knows about it as soon as possible. Extended pretrial detainments are not uncommon.

- If you think that you were ripped off by a hotel or tour operator, register your complaint with the **National Institute for the Defense of Competition and the Protection of Intellectual Property** (Indecopi; ☎01-224-7800; www.indecopi.gob.pe, in Spanish) in Lima.

# Money

Peru uses the nuevo sol (S), which comes in bills of S10, S20, S50, S100 and (rarely) S200. The nuevo sol (new sun) is divided into 100 céntimos, with copper- and silver-colored coins of S0.05, S0.10, S0.20 and S0.50. There are also S1, S2 and S5 coins – the latter two of which come in a combination of silver and copper.

## ATMS

- *Cajeros automáticos* (ATMs) are found almost everywhere. These are linked to the international Plus (Visa), Cirrus (Maestro/MasterCard) systems, American Express and other networks. They accept most bank cards on prominent international networks.
- Both US dollars and nuevos soles are readily available from many ATMs (especially in Lima).
- For safety reasons, use ATMs inside banks, preferably during daylight hours.

## CASH

- Peru is largely a cash economy, so make sure that you have plenty of cash on hand.
- When receiving local currency, always ask for *billetes pequeños* (small bills), as S100 bills are hard to change for small purchases. And carry as much spare change as possible, especially in small towns.
- Do not accept torn or vandalized money as it will likely not be accepted.
- It is best not to change money on the street as counterfeits can be a problem.
- Authentic bills contain watermarks, embossed printing and a metal strip running through the bill that reads 'Peru' in clear, tiny letters. In addition, tiny pieces of colored thread and holographic dots scattered on the bill should be embedded in the paper, not glued on.
- US dollars are accepted by many tourist-oriented businesses, including hotels and tour agencies.

## CHANGING MONEY

The best currency for exchange is the US dollar, although the euro is increasingly accepted – but these must be in flawless condition. In addition to *casas de cambio* (foreign-exchange bureaus), it is possible (though not necessarily recommended) to exchange cash with *cambistas* (independent money changers), who generally hang out on street corners near banks. Officially, they should wear a vest and a badge identifying themselves as legal.

## CREDIT CARDS

Credit cards are widely accepted at top-end hotels and restaurants – though some may charge a 7% (or greater) fee. The most widely accepted cards are Visa and MasterCard, although American Express and some others are valid for cash advances. Before you leave home, notify your bank that you'll be using your credit card in Peru to avoid problems.

## TAXES, TIPPING & REFUNDS

- International and domestic departure taxes are payable in US dollars or nuevos soles in cash only.
- Top-end hotels will add sales tax (18%) and service charges (around 10%); the latter is generally not included in quoted rates.
- Pricier restaurants also charge combined taxes of more than 19%, plus a service charge – *servicio* or *propina* – of 10%. At restaurants that don't do this, you can tip separately. Ten percent or more is standard for good service.
- Taxi drivers do not generally expect tips (unless they've assisted with heavy luggage), but porters and tour guides do.

# Public Holidays

On major holidays, banks, offices and other services are closed, hotel rates can triple and transportation is very crowded, so book ahead. Major holidays may be celebrated for days around the official date. Major national, regional and religious holidays include the following:

**Año Nuevo (New Year's Day)** January 1

**Good Friday** March/April

**Labor Day** May 1

**Inti Raymi** June 24

**San Pedro y San Pablo (Feasts of Sts Peter & Paul)** June 29

**Fiestas Patrias (National Independence Days)** July 28–29

**Feast of Santa Rosa de Lima** August 30

**Battle of Angamos Day** October 8

**Todos Santos (All Saints' Day)** November 1

**Fiesta de la Purísima Concepción (Feast of the Immaculate Conception)** December 8

**Christmas** December 25

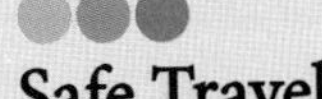

# Safe Travel

In a country where one out of every 10 people survives on less than US$1 per day, it is no surprise that petty crime is quite common and muggings aren't unusual. But a few simple, big-city precautions can prevent this from happening. The biggest annoyance most travelers will experience is a case of the runs – so don't let paranoia ruin your holiday.

## CORRUPTION & SCAMS

- The military and police (sometimes even the tourist police) have a reputation for being corrupt. While a foreigner may experience petty harassment (usually to procure a bribe), most police officers are quite courteous to tourists.
- Persistent touts at bus stations, airports and other tourist areas are perhaps the most pernicious thing travelers face. Many touts – including taxi drivers – will say just about anything to steer you to places they represent.
- It is not advisable to book hotels, travel arrangements or transportation through touts. Many demand cash up-front for services that never materialize.

## ENVIRONMENTAL HAZARDS

Some of the natural hazards you might encounter in Peru include earthquakes and avalanches. Rescues in remote regions are often done on foot because of the inability of helicopters to reach some of the country's more challenging topography.

## THEFTS, MUGGINGS & OTHER CRIME

- Street crimes such as pickpocketing, bag-snatching and muggings are all too common. Other attacks happen with less regularity. Keep your eye on your belongings, don't wear flashy jewelry and don't put passports and wallets into rear pockets.
- If you are the victim of a crime, file a report with the *policía de turismo* (Poltur). If you are unsure how to locate them, contact the main office in Lima.
- If you have taken out travel insurance and need to make a claim, Poltur will provide you with a police report. Stolen passports can be reissued at your embassy. After receiving your new passport, go to the nearest Peruvian immigration office (see www.digemin.gob.pe for listings) to get a new tourist card.
- For more on legal issues, see p347. For issues affecting female travelers, turn to p351.

## TRANSPORT ISSUES

When taking buses, choose operators carefully. The cheapest companies will be the most likely to employ reckless drivers and have roadside breakdowns. Overnight travel by bus can get brutally cold in the highlands (take a blanket or sweater). For more on transportation in Peru, see p351.

## PROTESTS & OTHER CONFLICT

During the Internal Conflict of the 1980s and '90s, civil strife meant that entire regions were off-limits. Thankfully, the situation has improved dramatically and travelers visit much of the country without ever encountering problems. Even so, Peru remains politically volatile and travel can require some care.

- Protests generally have little effects on tourists, other than contending with roadbloacks, but on some occasions they do turn violent. If a road is blocked or an area cut off, do not attempt to cross the lines – being a foreigner will not make you immune to violence.
- The resurgence of Sendero Luminoso (Shining Path) has brought isolated incidents of violence to remote areas in the provinces of Ayacucho, Cuzco, Huancavelica, Huánuco, Junín and San Martín. These are generally directed at the Peruvian military or the police. Nonetheless, exercise caution: avoid transit through isolated areas in these regions at night.

- Drug-trafficking areas can also be dangerous, especially at night. Travelers should avoid the upper Río Huallaga valley between Tingo María and Juanjui and the Río Apurímac valley near Ayacucho, where the majority of Peru's narcotics trade takes place. Exercise similar caution near the Colombian border, where trafficking also goes on.

# Telephone

Telephones – pay phones, call centers or cell phones – are widely available throughout the country.

- Pay phones operated by **Movistar** (www.movistar.com.pe) are found in public areas and work with phone cards that can be purchased at groceries and pharmacies.
- In urban areas, street vendors in fluorescent green vests rent cell phones by the minute. This is a cheap and easy way to make domestic calls.
- Many internet cafes have 'net-to-phone' and 'net-to-net' capabilities (such as Skype), to talk for pennies or even for free.
- Any telephone number beginning with a 9 is a cell-phone number. Numbers beginning with 0800 are often toll-free only when dialed from private phones.
- To make a credit-card or collect call using AT&T, dial ☎0800-50288.

## CELL PHONES

- It's possible to use a tri-band GSM world phone in Peru (GSM 1900). Other systems in use are CDMA and TDMA. Check with your cell-phone provider before you depart.
- Cell-phone rentals are often available in major cities. These generally offer cheap pay-as-you go plans that can be refilled at pharmacies and supermarkets.
- The easiest place to rent cell phones is in the baggage-claim section at the international airport in Lima.

## PHONE CARDS

Called *tarjetas telefónicas*, phone cards are widely available and are sold in various price ranges. Some are designed specifically for international calls. Movistar and Claro are the most common brands.

# Time

- Peru is five hours behind Greenwich Mean Time (GMT). It's the same as Eastern Standard Time (EST) in North America.
- Daylight Saving Time (DST) isn't used in Peru, so add an hour to all of these times between the first Sunday in April and the last Sunday in October.

# Toilets

- Peruvian plumbing, especially in remote areas, can leave something to be desired.
- Avoid putting toilet paper and other inorganic waste into the toilet. Even a small amount of paper can muck up an entire plumbing system. Instead, deposit paper and feminine hygiene items into the plastic bin that is provided.
- Public toilets are rare outside of transportation terminals, restaurants and museums, but restaurants will generally let travelers use a restroom (sometimes for a charge). Those in terminals generally charge about S0.50 per person for use.
- Public restrooms frequently run out of toilet paper, so always carry some with you.

# Travelers with Disabilities

Peru offers few conveniences for travelers with disabilities. Signs in braille or phones for the hearing-impaired are virtually nonexistent, while wheelchair ramps and lifts are few and far between. Nevertheless, it is nonetheless possible to get around. Resources for travelers with disabilities:

## Dialing Peru

When calling Peru from abroad, dial the international access code for the country you're in, then Peru's country code (51), then the area code (without the 0) and finally, the local number.

When making international calls from Peru, dial the international access code (00), then the country code of where you're calling to, then the area code and finally, the local phone number.

**Access-Able Travel Source** (www.access-able.com) Some listings of accessible transportation, tours and accommodations in Peru.

**Apumayo Expediciones** (☎/fax 084-24-6018; www.apumayo.com; Interior 3, Calle Garcilaso 265, Cuzco) An adventure-tour company that takes disabled travelers to Machu Picchu and other historic sites in the Sacred Valley.

**Emerging Horizons** (www.emerginghorizons.com) General travel magazine for the mobility-impaired.

## Visas

- With a few exceptions, visas are not required for travelers entering Peru.
- Tourists are permitted a 30- to 90-day stay, stamped into passports and onto a *Tarjeta Andina de Migración* (Andean Immigration Card). Keep it – it must be returned upon exiting the country.
- If you lose your tourist card, visit an *oficina de migraciónes* (immigration office; www.digemin.gob.pe) for a replacement.
- Extensions can be obtained at immigration offices in Lima, Arequipa, Cuzco, Iquitos, Puerto Maldonado, Puno and Trujillo. Forms and information in English can be found online – simply click on 'Extension of Stay' in the English version of the site. The cost is S12.25 for paperwork and an additional US$20 for the 30-day extension. Two extensions are allowed per year.
- Carry your passport and tourist card on your person at all times, especially in remote areas (it's required by law on the Inca Trail).

## Women Travelers

While machismo is alive and well in Peru, most female travelers won't contend with more than the occasional shouts of *mi amor* (my love). A few tips for enjoying a trip alone or with the girlfriends:

- If you are fair-skinned with blond hair, be prepared to draw more attention. Peruvian men consider foreign women to have looser morals and will often make flirtatious comments to single women.
- Whistling and catcalls are run-of-the-mill. Ignoring all provocation is generally the best response. If someone is persistent, try an ardor-smothering phrase such as *soy casada* (I'm married).
- In tourist towns such as Cuzco, it's not uncommon for fast-talking charmers – known as *bricheros* – to attach themselves to gringas. Many are looking for a meal ticket, so approach professions of undying love with skepticism.
- Outside of big cities, it is rare for a woman to belly up to a bar for a beer, and the ones that do tend to be prostitutes. If you feel the need for an evening cocktail, opt for a restaurant instead.
- As in any part of the world, use your big-city smarts: be aware of your surroundings, seek reputable tour operators and taxi companies and, if traveling alone, opt for better hotels in good neighborhoods.
- In highland towns, dress is conservative and women rarely wear shorts, opting instead for long skirts, slacks or jeans. Note that shorts, miniskirts and revealing blouses may draw unwanted attention.
- Tampons can be difficult to find in remote villages, so stock up in bigger cities and towns.

# Transport

## Getting There & Away

Arriving in Peru is typically straightforward, as long as your passport is valid for at least six months beyond your departure date. When arriving by air, US citizens must show a return ticket or an onward ticket.

### AIR

Peru (mainly Lima) has direct international flights from destinations all over the world.

An international departure tax of US$31 is now usually included in ticket costs. In some cases, however, you may need to pay this separately in cash.

## Peru Air Routes

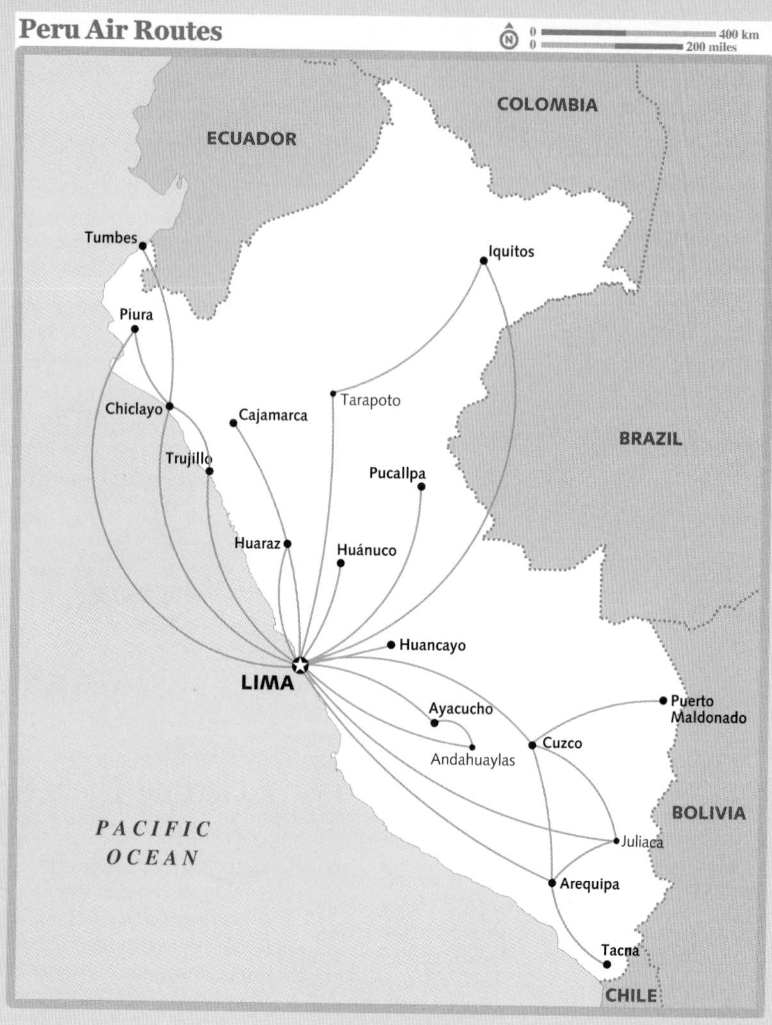


### AIRPORTS

Lima's **Aeropuerto Internacional Jorge Chávez** (01-517-3100; www.lap.com.pe; Callao) is serviced by direct flights from North, Central and South America, as well as Europe. Check the airport website or call 01-511-6055 for updated departure and arrival schedules for domestic and international flights.

Cuzco has the only other airport with international service – to La Paz, Bolivia, four times a week, on Amaszonas Airlines.

### TICKETS

From most places in the world, South America can be a relatively costly destination. The high season for air travel to and within Peru is late May to early September, as well as around major holidays. Tickets are often cheaper outside peak periods.

- Note: tickets bought in Peru are subject to a 19% tax.
- It is essential to reconfirm all flights 72 hours in advance, either by phone or online, or you may get bumped off the flight. If you are traveling in remote areas, have a travel agent do this for you.

# Getting Around

Peru has a constant procession of flights and buses connecting the country. Keep in mind, poor weather conditions can wreak havoc on schedules.

## AIR

Domestic-flight schedules and prices change frequently. Most big cities are served by modern jets, while smaller towns are served by propeller aircraft.

- Be at the airport at least 60 minutes before your flight departs (be at least 90 minutes early in Cuzco, and two hours in Lima). Check-in procedures can be chaotic, and it's not unknown for flights to leave before their official departure time because of predicted bad weather.
- The peak season for air travel within Peru is late May to early September, as well as around major holidays.

### AIRLINES IN PERU

Most airlines fly from Lima to regional capitals, but service between provincial cities is limited. The following domestic airlines are the most reliable.

**LAN** (☎01-213-8200; www.lan.com)

**LC Busre** (☎01-619-1313; www.lcbusre.com.pe)

**Peruvian Airlines** (☎01-717-2222; www.peruvianairlines.pe)

**Star Perú** (☎01-705-9000; www.starperu.com)

**TACA** (☎01-511-8222; www.taca.com)

### TICKETS

Buy tickets online or via a recommended agent and be sure to reserve well ahead for major holidays (p348), when flights sell out.

Ensure all flight reservations are *confirmed and reconfirmed* 24 and 72 hours in advance; airlines are notorious for overbooking and flights are changed or canceled with surprising frequency. Confirmation is essential during the peak months of June through August.

## BICYCLE

Reasonably priced rentals (mostly mountain bikes) are available in popular tourist destinations, including Cuzco (p174), Arequipa (p114) and Huaraz (p242). These bikes are rented for local excursions, not to make trips all over the country.

## BOAT

- There are no passenger services along the Peruvian coast.
- In the Andean highlands, there are boat services on Lake Titicaca. Small, motorized vessels take passengers from the port in Puno to the islands on the lake (p153).
- In Peru's Amazon Basin, boat travel is the principal way of getting around. Larger vessels ply the bigger rivers, while dugout canoes powered by outboard engines – known as *peki-pekis* – act as water taxis on small waterways.

## BUS

- Buses are the most common form of transportation around Peru. Fares are cheap and services are frequent, but buses are of varying quality. There are scores of companies; no single company covers the entire country.

## Climate Change & Travel

Every form of transport that relies on carbon-based fuel generates $CO_2$, the main cause of human-induced climate change. Modern travel is dependent on airplanes, which might use less fuel per kilometer per person than most cars but travel much greater distances. The altitude at which aircraft emit gases (including $CO_2$) and particles also contributes to their climate change impact. Many websites offer 'carbon calculators' that allow people to estimate the carbon emissions generated by their journey and, for those who wish to do so, to offset the impact of the greenhouse gases emitted with contributions to portfolios of climate-friendly initiatives throughout the world. Lonely Planet offsets the carbon footprint of all staff and author travel.

- The bigger companies often have luxury buses (called Imperial, Royal, Business, Executive or something similar), for which there is an extra charge. These come with express service, toilets, snacks, videos and climate control. Some offer *bus-camas* (bus beds), in which seats recline halfway or almost fully.
- *Económico* buses are cheaper and might lack heating, ventilation or bathrooms. These often make frequent stops.
- For popular destinations, reserve well in advance.
- For short trips, just go to the terminal and buy a ticket for the next bus out.
- Buses can be significantly delayed during the rainy season, from January through April, because of landslides and other conditions.
- For a rundown of recommended companies with offices in Lima, see p89.

## LUGGAGE

- In bus and train terminals, be sure to watch your luggage carefully. Some terminals have left-luggage facilities. If you use this service, don't leave any valuables in your bag.
- Never leave hand luggage with important valuables (such as passports and money) in the overhead racks of a bus since theft is common.

## CAR & MOTORCYCLE

It's a long ride from Lima to most destinations, so it's best to fly to most cities around the country and then rent a car from there. But given all the headaches and potential hazards of driving yourself around, consider hiring a taxi instead, which is often cheaper and easier.

Note: if you are driving and are involved in an accident that results in injury, know that drivers are routinely imprisoned for several days or weeks until innocence has been established. For more advice on legal matters, see p347.

### DRIVER'S LICENSE & RENTAL

- A driver's license from your own home country is sufficient for renting a car.
- Major rental companies have offices in Lima and a few other large cities. Renting a motorcycle is an option mainly in jungle towns, where you can go for short runs around town on dirt bikes, but not much further.
- Make sure you completely understand the rental agreement before you sign. A credit card is required, and renters normally need to be over 25 years of age.
- Economy car rental starts at US$25 a day – without the 19% sales tax, 'super' collision-damage waiver, personal accident insurance and so on, which together can climb to more than US$100 per day, not including excess mileage.
- Vehicles with 4WD are more expensive.

### ROAD RULES & HAZARDS

- Driving is on the right-hand side of the road.
- Conditions are challenging: rental cars often aren't well maintained, roads are potholed (even the paved Pan-American Hwy), gas is expensive and drivers are aggressive. Moreover, road signs are often small and unclear.
- Driving at night is not recommended because of poor conditions, speeding buses and slow-moving, poorly lit trucks. At night, bandits can be a problem on roadways in remote regions.
- Do not leave your vehicle parked on the street. When stopping overnight, park the car in a guarded lot (the better hotels have them).
- Gasoline or petrol stations (called *grifos*) are few and far between.

## LOCAL TRANSPORTATION

In most towns and cities, it's easy to walk or take a taxi, which are plentiful. Using local buses and *combis* (minivans) can be tricky, but it's very inexpensive.

### TAXI

- There are no meters, so negotiate a fare in advance. It's acceptable to haggle.
- Tipping is not the norm, unless you have hired a driver for a long period or your driver has helped you with luggage or other lifting.

- Private cars that have a small taxi sticker in the windshield aren't necessarily regulated.
- Safer, regulated taxis usually have a lit company number on the roof and are called for by telephone. These are more expensive than taxis flagged down on the street, but are more reliable.
- Hiring a private taxi for long-distance trips costs less than renting a car and can be safer and more convenient. Not all taxi drivers will agree to drive long distances, but if one does, check the driver's credentials and vehicle before hiring.

### TRAIN

Few areas of Peru are serviced by rail. However, in the area of Cuzco, the privatized rail system, **PeruRail** (**084-58-1414; www.perurail.com**), has daily services between Cuzco and Aguas Calientes (for Machu Picchu), and services between Cuzco and Puno on the shores of Lake Titicaca. Check the website for details.

# Language

Spanish pronunciation is not difficult as most of its sounds are also found in English. You can read our pronunciation guides below as if they were English and you'll be understood just fine.

Peruvian Spanish is considered one of the easiest varieties of Spanish, with less slang in use than in many other Latin American countries, and relatively clear enunciation.

To enhance your trip with a phrasebook, visit **lonelyplanet.com**. Lonely Planet iPhone phrasebooks are available through the Apple App store.

## BASICS

**Hello.**
*Hola.*
*o*·la

**How are you?**
*¿Qué tal?*
ke tal

**I'm fine, thanks.**
*Bien, gracias.*
byen *gra*·syas

**Excuse me. (to get attention)**
*Disculpe.*
dees·*kool*·pe

**Yes./No.**
*Sí./No.*
see/no

**Thank you.**
*Gracias.*
*gra*·syas

**You're welcome./That's fine.**
*De nada.*
de *na*·da

**Goodbye./See you later.**
*Adiós./Hasta luego.*
a·*dyos*/*as*·ta *lwe*·go

**Do you speak English?**
*¿Habla inglés?*
*a*·bla een·*gles*

**I don't understand.**
*No entiendo.*
no en·*tyen*·do

**How much is this?**
*¿Cuánto cuesta?*
*kwan*·to *kwes*·ta

**Can you reduce the price a little?**
*¿Podría bajar un poco el precio?*
po·*dree*·a ba·*khar* oon *po*·ko el *pre*·syo

## ACCOMMODATIONS

**I'd like to make a booking.**
*Quisiera reservar una habitación.*
kee·*sye*·ra re·ser·*var* *oo*·na a·bee·ta·*syon*

**How much is it per night?**
*¿Cuánto cuesta por noche?*
*kwan*·to *kwes*·ta por *no*·che

## EATING & DRINKING

**I'd like ..., please.**
*Quisiera . . . , por favor.*
kee·*sye*·ra . . . por fa·*vor*

**That was delicious!**
*¡Estaba buenísimo!*
es·*ta*·ba bwe·*nee*·see·mo

**Bring the bill/check, please.**
*La cuenta, por favor.*
la *kwen*·ta por fa·*vor*

**I'm allergic to ...**
*Soy alérgico/a al . . .* (m/f)
soy a·*ler*·khee·ko/a al . . .

**I don't eat ...**
*No como . . .*
no *ko*·mo . . .

| | | |
|---|---|---|
| **chicken** | *pollo* | *po*·yo |
| **fish** | *pescado* | pes·*ka*·do |
| **meat** | *carne* | *kar*·ne |

## EMERGENCIES

**I'm ill.**
*Estoy enfermo/a.* (m/f)
es·*toy* en·*fer*·mo/a

**Help!**
*¡Socorro!*
so·*ko*·ro

**Call a doctor!**
*¡Llame a un médico!*
*ya*·me a oon *me*·dee·ko

**Call the police!**
*¡Llame a la policía!*
*ya*·me a la po·lee·*see*·a

## DIRECTIONS

**I'm looking for (a/an/the) ...**
*Estoy buscando . . .*
es·*toy* boos·*kan*·do . . .

| | | |
|---|---|---|
| **ATM** | *un cajero automático* | oon ka·*khe*·ro ow·to·*ma*·tee·ko |
| **bank** | *el banco* | el *ban*·ko |
| **... embassy** | *la embajada de . . .* | la em·ba·*kha*·da de . . . |
| **market** | *el mercado* | el mer·*ka*·do |
| **museum** | *el museo* | el moo·*se*·o |
| **restaurant** | *un restaurante* | oon res·tow·*ran*·te |
| **toilet** | *los servicios* | los ser·*vee*·syos |
| **tourist office** | *la oficina de turismo* | la o·fee·*see*·na de too·*rees*·mo |

# Behind the Scenes

## Our Readers

Many thanks to the travelers who used the last edition and wrote to us with helpful hints, useful advice and interesting anecdotes:

Jennifer File, A Grant, Juan Camilo Gomez, Yuri Leveratto and Meredith Wehrle

## Author Thanks

### CAROLINA A MIRANDA

To my husband, who tolerates my wandering (and all of my related stomach illnesses). To Arturo Rojas, who always teaches me something new about Peruvian food. To Juan Cincunegui, the patient librarian at the Monastery of Santo Domingo in Cuzco, for turning me on to so many wonderful books. And to the people of Peru, who are always gracious and generous. Thank you!

## Acknowledgments

Climate map data adapted from Peel MC, Finlayson BL & McMahon TA (2007) 'Updated World Map of the Köppen-Geiger Climate Classification', Hydrology and Earth System Sciences, 11, 163344

Illustrations p218-19 by Michael Weldon

Cover photographs: Front: Machu Picchu, Image Source/Getty Images ©; Back: Canoeing in the Loreto region, near Iquitos, Paul Kennedy/Getty Images ©

## This Book

This guidebook was commissioned in Lonely Planet's Oakland office, and produced by the following:

**Commissioning Editor** Kathleen Munnelly
**Coordinating Editor** Kate Mathews
**Coordinating Cartographer** Andy Rojas
**Coordinating Layout Designer** Jessica Rose
**Managing Editors** Bruce Evans, Martine Power, Angela Tinson
**Managing Cartographer** Alison Lyall
**Managing Layout Designer** Chris Girdler
**Assisting Editors** Charlotte Orr, Lorna Parkes, Alison Ridgway
**Cover Research** Naomi Parker
**Internal Image Research** Kylie McLaughlin
**Illustrator** Michael Weldon
**Language Content** Branislava Vladisavljevic

**Thanks to** Ryan Evans, Larissa Frost, Genesys India, Trent Paton, Raphael Richards, Gerard Walker

### SEND US YOUR FEEDBACK

We love to hear from travelers – your comments keep us on our toes and help make our books better. Our well-traveled team reads every word on what you loved or loathed about this book. Although we cannot reply individually to postal submissions, we always guarantee that your feedback goes straight to the appropriate authors, in time for the next edition. Each person who sends us information is thanked in the next edition, the most useful submissions are rewarded with a selection of digital PDF chapters.

Visit **lonelyplanet.com/contact** to submit your updates and suggestions or to ask for help. Our award-winning website also features inspirational travel stories, news and discussions.

Note: We may edit, reproduce and incorporate your comments in Lonely Planet products such as guidebooks, websites and digital products, so let us know if you don't want your comments reproduced or your name acknowledged. For a copy of our privacy policy visit lonelyplanet.com/privacy.

# Index

## A



**000** Map pages



## B



## C

## D



## E

**000** Map pages

**000** Map pages

## T



## U



## V



## W



## Y



## Z

# How to Use This Book

**These symbols will help you find the listings you want:**

- Sights
- Beaches
- Activities
- Courses
- Tours
- Festivals & Events
- Sleeping
- Eating
- Drinking
- Entertainment
- Shopping
- Information/ Transport

**These symbols give you the vital information for each listing:**

- Telephone Numbers
- Opening Hours
- Parking
- Nonsmoking
- Air-Conditioning
- Internet Access
- Wi-Fi Access
- Swimming Pool
- Vegetarian Selection
- English-Language Menu
- Family-Friendly
- Pet-Friendly
- Bus
- Ferry
- Metro
- Subway
- London Tube
- Tram
- Train

**Reviews are organised by author preference.**

**Look out for these icons:**

- FREE No payment required
- A green or sustainable option

*Our authors have nominated these places as demonstrating a strong commitment to sustainability – for example by supporting local communities and producers, operating in an environmentally friendly way, or supporting conservation projects.*

# Map Legend

**Sights**
- Beach
- Buddhist
- Castle
- Christian
- Hindu
- Islamic
- Jewish
- Monument
- Museum/Gallery
- Ruin
- Winery/Vineyard
- Zoo
- Other Sight

**Activities, Courses & Tours**
- Diving/Snorkelling
- Canoeing/Kayaking
- Skiing
- Surfing
- Swimming/Pool
- Walking
- Windsurfing
- Other Activity/ Course/Tour

**Sleeping**
- Sleeping
- Camping

**Eating**
- Eating

**Drinking**
- Drinking
- Cafe

**Entertainment**
- Entertainment

**Shopping**
- Shopping

**Information**
- Bank
- Embassy/ Consulate
- Hospital/Medical
- Internet
- Police
- Post Office
- Telephone
- Toilet
- Tourist Information
- Other Information

**Transport**
- Airport
- Border Crossing
- Bus
- Cable Car/ Funicular
- Cycling
- Ferry
- Monorail
- Parking
- Petrol Station
- Taxi
- Train/Railway
- Tram
- Underground Train Station
- Other Transport

**Routes**
- Tollway
- Freeway
- Primary
- Secondary
- Tertiary
- Lane
- Unsealed Road
- Plaza/Mall
- Steps
- Tunnel
- Pedestrian Overpass
- Walking Tour
- Walking Tour Detour
- Path

**Geographic**
- Hut/Shelter
- Lighthouse
- Lookout
- Mountain/Volcano
- Oasis
- Park
- Pass
- Picnic Area
- Waterfall

**Population**
- Capital (National)
- Capital (State/Province)
- City/Large Town
- Town/Village

**Boundaries**
- International
- State/Province
- Disputed
- Regional/Suburb
- Marine Park
- Cliff
- Wall

**Hydrography**
- River/Creek
- Intermittent River
- Swamp/Mangrove
- Reef
- Canal
- Water
- Dry/Salt/ Intermittent Lake
- Glacier

**Areas**
- Beach/Desert
- Cemetery (Christian)
- Cemetery (Other)
- Park/Forest
- Sportsground
- Sight (Building)
- Top Sight (Building)

## Our Story

A beat-up old car, a few dollars in the pocket and a sense of adventure. In 1972 that's all Tony and Maureen Wheeler needed for the trip of a lifetime – across Europe and Asia overland to Australia. It took several months, and at the end – broke but inspired – they sat at their kitchen table writing and stapling together their first travel guide, *Across Asia on the Cheap*. Within a week they'd sold 1500 copies. Lonely Planet was born.

Today, Lonely Planet has offices in Melbourne, London, Oakland and Delhi, with more than 600 staff and writers. We share Tony's belief that 'a great guidebook should do three things: inform, educate and amuse'.

# Our Writers

### CAROLINA A MIRANDA

**Coordinating Author** The daughter of a Peruvian father, Carolina has spent her life making pilgrimages to Peru to eat ceviche and sip pisco sours. An avid student of Peruvian history (she has a degree in Latin American Studies), she has read Mario Vargas Llosa novels in Spanish, danced to Peruvian waltzes, and spent countless hours studying the arts and textiles of the Andes. She also makes a mean *aji de gallina*. Find her at *C-Monster.net*, or on Twitter at @cmonstah.

Read more about Carolina at:
lonelyplanet.com/members/carolinamiranda

### CAROLYN MCCARTHY

**Lima, Lake Titicaca, Cusco & the Sacred Valley** Author Carolyn McCarthy first discovered *cumbia* camping on the Inca Trail many years ago. For this trip, she sampled hundreds of Peruvian delicacies, climbed Wayna Picchu and visited one medical clinic. Some of her other Lonely Planet titles include *Argentina, Panama, Yellowstone & Grand Teton National Parks, USA, The Travel Book, Best in Travel* and *Trekking in the Patagonian Andes*. She has also written for *National Geographic, Outside* and *Lonely Planet Magazine*, among other publications. You can follow her Americas blog at www.carolynswildblue yonder.blogspot.com.

### KEVIN RAUB

**North Coast, Huaraz & the Cordilleras, Northern Highlands** Kevin Raub grew up in Atlanta and started his career as a music journalist in New York, working for *Men's Journal* and *Rolling Stone* magazines. He ditched the rock 'n' roll lifestyle for travel writing and moved to Brazil. Working on *Peru* he logged over 2500km in his beige Renault tank, canvassing up and down the North Coast. He even stood his ground on a shakedown from Policía Nacional on one of the nine times they stopped him. After that, he opted for buses in the Northern Highlands and Huaraz areas. You can find him at www. kevinraub.net.

Read more about Kevin at:
lonelyplanet.com/members/kraub

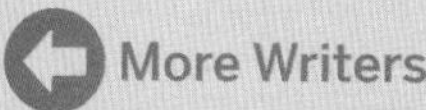

More Writers

**Published by Lonely Planet Publications Pty Ltd**
ABN 36 005 607 983
2nd edition – June 2013
ISBN 978 1 74220 569 4

10 9 8 7 6 5 4 3
Printed in China

## BRENDAN SAINSBURY

**South Coast, Arequipa & Canyon Country** An expat-Brit now living in Vancouver, Canada, Brendan first visited Peru as part of an epic South American traveling odyssey in the early 2000s; a trip that involved getting hailed on in Machu Picchu, getting lost in the middle of the Bolivian salt pans, and teaching local Uruguayans how to do the 'Madness dance' in Punta del Este. He has since covered numerous Spanish-speaking countries for Lonely Planet including Cuba, Mexico, Puerto Rico and Spain.

## LUKE WATERSON

**Amazon Basin** Two near-death experiences (including almost drowning in Río Madre de Dios) made for a poignant sixth trip to Peru for Luke. He's been traveling (hiking/hitching/boating on vessels of dubious quality) across the country since 2004. His writing about close encounters with bizarreness in Latin America, Cuba and central Europe has graced several publications, including 15 Lonely Planet guidebooks and the UK magazine, *Real Travel*, which he helped relaunch. This is the second time he's worked on *Peru*. Tweet him (@lukewaterson1) for anything South/Central America–related.